I0804712

MODERNISM, SPACE AND THE CITY

Edinburgh Critical Studies in Modernist Culture
Series Editors: Tim Armstrong and Rebecca Beasley

Available

Modernism and Magic: Experiments with Spiritualism, Theosophy and the Occult
Leigh Wilson

Sonic Modernity: Representing Sound in Literature, Culture and the Arts
Sam Halliday

Modernism and the Frankfurt School
Tyrus Miller

Lesbian Modernism: Censorship, Sexuality and Genre Fiction
Elizabeth English

Modern Print Artefacts: Textual Materiality and Literary Value in British Print Culture, 1890–1930s
Patrick Collier

Cheap Modernism: Expanding Markets, Publishers' Series and the Avant-Garde
Lise Jaillant

Portable Modernisms: The Art of Travelling Light
Emily Ridge

Hieroglyphic Modernisms: Writing and New Media in the Twentieth Century
Jesse Schotter

Modernism, Fiction and Mathematics
Nina Engelhardt

Modernist Life Histories: Biological Theory and the Experimental Bildungsroman
Daniel Aureliano Newman

Modernism, Space and the City: Outsiders and Affect in Paris, Vienna, Berlin and London
Andrew Thacker

Forthcoming

Slow Modernism
Laura Salisbury

Primordial Modernism: Animals, Ideas, Transition (1927–1938)
Cathryn Setz

Modernism and the Idea of Everyday Life
Leena Kore-Schröder

Modernism Edited: Marianne Moore and The Dial *Magazine*
Victoria Bazin

Modernism and Time Machines
Charles Tung

www.edinburghuniversitypress.com/series/ecsmc

MODERNISM, SPACE AND THE CITY

Outsiders and Affect in Paris, Vienna, Berlin and London

Andrew Thacker

EDINBURGH
University Press

Edinburgh University Press is one of the leading university presses in the UK. We publish academic books and journals in our selected subject areas across the humanities and social sciences, combining cutting-edge scholarship with high editorial and production values to produce academic works of lasting importance. For more information visit our website: edinburghuniversitypress.com

Edinburgh University Press Ltd,
The Tun – Holyrood Road,
12(2f) Jackson's Entry,
Edinburgh EH8 8PJ

First published in hardback by Edinburgh University Press 2019

Typeset in 10/12.5 Sabon by
Servis Filmsetting Ltd, Stockport, Cheshire, and

A CIP record for this book is available from the British Library

ISBN 978 0 7486 3347 0 (hardback)
ISBN 978 0 7486 3348 7 (paperback)
ISBN 978 0 7486 3349 4 (webready PDF)
ISBN 978 1 4744 4194 0 (epub)

CONTENTS

LIST OF ILLUSTRATIONS

ACKNOWLEDGEMENTS

This book has taken a very long time to complete and so my first thanks must be to the series editors, Tim Armstrong and Rebecca Beasley, for their tremendous patience. They have also proved to be exemplary editors in their supportive, helpful, yet properly critical comments upon earlier versions of the typescript of the book. Thanks are also due to Jackie Jones and Edinburgh University Press for their own patient support for the project.

I have presented numerous papers and talks based upon material in the book at many venues and occasions over the period of the writing of the book and I would like to thank the audiences at these talks for their many helpful comments, particularly those at various MSA and EAM conferences over the years. I would also like to thank the organisers of the following events for inviting me to speak and share my ideas: the 'Phobias' conference of the British Society for Literature and Science, University of Glamorgan; the 'Travelling Narratives' conference, University of Zurich; the 'Thinking Space' conference, Humboldt University, Berlin; the 'Modernist Moves' conference, Brunel University; the 'Motion and Space' conference, King's College, London; the 'Literary Dynamics of Place' Symposium, Durham University; 'The Cultural Relations of the Railway' Symposium, Pembroke College, Oxford; the Nineteenth Century Research Seminar, Institute of English Studies; and the Northern Modernism Research Seminar, Newcastle University.

Much earlier versions of certain portions of the book have been published in the following places: 'Uncompleted Life: The Modernist Underground' in *The*

Railway and Modernity: Time, Space, and the Machine Ensemble, ed. Matthew Beaumont and Michael Freeman (Bern: Peter Lang, 2007); 'Lost Cities and Found Lives: The "Geographical Emotions" of Bryher and Walter Benjamin' in *Life Writing and Space*, ed. Eveline Kilian and Hope Wolf (Farnham: Ashgate, 2016); '"Hellhole and Paradise": The Heterotopic Spaces of Berlin' in *Utopian Spaces of Modernism: British Literature and Culture, 1885–1945*, ed. Rosalyn Gregory and Benjamin Kohlmann (Basingstoke: Palgrave Macmillan, 2012); and 'London: Rhymers, Imagists, and Vorticists' in *The Oxford Handbook of Modernisms*, ed. Peter Brooker, Andrzej Gasiorek, Deborah Longworth and Andrew Thacker (Oxford: Oxford University Press, 2010). I am grateful to the editors of these volumes for allowing me to test out some of the ideas in this book in their pages.

I am also grateful for the following institutions for permissions to reproduce a number of illustrations in the book: the Advertising Archive; the British Museum; the Estate of George Grosz, Princeton, NJ/DACS; the Landesarchiv, Berlin; the London Transport Museum Collection; the Ludwig-Meidner Archive, Jüdisches Museum der Stadt Frankfurt am Main; and the Staatliche Museen zu Berlin, Nationalgalerie.

I have benefitted greatly from conversations with many people about this book and from numerous helpful comments from those who have read and commented upon parts of chapters. These include: Isobel Armstrong, James Atlee, Christina Britzolakis, Peter Brooker, Sascha Bru, Eric Bulson, Tom Conley, Melba Cuddy-Keane, Ann Marie Einhaus, Charles Forsdick, Susan Stanford Friedman, Andrzj Gasiorek, Jason Harding, Ken Hirschkop, Suzanne Hobson, Andreas Huyssens, Eveline Kilian, Benjamin Kohlmann, Scott McCracken, Jo McDonagh, Tyrus Miller, Alexandra Peat, Vike Plock, Johannes Riquet, Rod Rosenquist, Anna Snaith, Robert T. Tally, Jo Winning, Hope Wolf, Alice Wood, Tim Woods and Tim Youngs. I am also grateful to Birgit van Puyembroeck for help with translation and to Rachel Farebrother for information about Gwendolyn Bennett. Thanks are also due to my current colleagues at Nottingham Trent University for providing such a supportive and stimulating environment in which to work.

My final thanks are to Moya Lloyd for her continuing support for all that I do and, in particular, for allowing me to act as her 'research assistant' while attending a conference in Vienna. The book is dedicated to my son Daniel, who I hope enjoys cities as much as I do; and to John, my father, who many years ago travelled from the country to the city, and thus introduced me to the pleasures of urban life.

SERIES EDITORS' PREFACE

This series of monographs on selected topics in modernism is designed to reflect and extend the range of new work in modernist studies. The studies in the series aim for a breadth of scope and for an expanded sense of the canon of modernism, rather than focusing on individual authors. Literary texts will be considered in terms of contexts including recent cultural histories (modernism and magic; sonic modernity; media studies) and topics of theoretical interest (the everyday; postmodernism; the Frankfurt School); but the series will also reconsider more familiar routes into modernism (modernism and gender; sexuality; politics). The works published will be attentive to the various cultural, intellectual and historical contexts of British, American and European modernisms, and to interdisciplinary possibilities within modernism, including performance and the visual and plastic arts.

Tim Armstrong and Rebecca Beasley

For Daniel and John

INTRODUCTION: GEOGRAPHICAL EMOTIONS AND THE MODERNIST CITY

A Typical Modernist City

I have never lived for any sustained period of time in any of the cities discussed in this book, but have visited them as an outsider. However, I was brought up in a modernist city, though not one that is often thought about in these terms. I was born in Birmingham, an industrial city in the English midlands, and nominally the second city of England. In the latter half of the twentieth century Birmingham was a city long marked by the industrial revolution that had led to its growth in the nineteenth century: it was known as the 'workshop of the world' or the 'city of a thousand trades', due to the variety of industrial activities that took place there. This history of capitalist modernization was matched, in the period after World War II, by a reshaping of the very fabric of the city to fit the contours of modernity: this meant functional high-rise housing for many of the working-class inhabitants, and a streamlining of the streets to facilitate the movement of cars through the city centre, including the building of many 'expressways' and underpasses that still, to many, disfigure the city today, and which was summed up in the motorway interchange nicknamed 'Spaghetti Junction'. As a young child I was taken by my father to witness the construction of buildings that would later be seen as icons of the modernist brutalism that Birmingham, along with many other cities worldwide, would embrace in this period: New Street Station, burrowed under the centre of the city; the Rotunda, a circular office block on one of the highest points of the city; and the

Bull Ring Shopping centre, an enclosed shopping mall aping American models and illustrating post-war consumer affluence (now replaced by an even newer model). The commitment in post-war Birmingham to the materials of concrete and steel, as used in the buildings of John Madin, and to the free flow of traffic demonstrated something like a realization of the modernist city as envisaged by Le Corbusier in his *The City of Tomorrow* or the Futurist Sant'Elia in his New City project.[1] Though Birmingham, then, is never thought of as a 'modernist city' it might be said to typify many of the key features of such cities, being typical in the sense in which Georg Lukács thought that certain characters in nineteenth-century realist fiction typified class positions in society. In this sense we might think that Birmingham and Baltimore are more typical modernist cities than Paris or London.[2]

However, one major difference would be that these cities, although typifying the processes of modernity and modernization in Western capitalist countries throughout the twentieth century, have never captured the imagination of writers and artists in quite the same way that Paris or London have. A much stronger affective pull is exerted upon cultural producers by the four cities discussed in this book (Paris, Vienna, Berlin, London) than is evident in other European cities in the twentieth century. Equally, other European cities have never contained the extensive cultural infrastructure that has been essential to the production of much new or experimental art since the late nineteenth century: art galleries, publishers, bookshops, literary cafés, or other meeting places of a bohemian ilk. And although W. H. Auden would eulogize the industrial landscape between Wolverhampton and Birmingham in 1936 for its embodiment of technological modernity ('Tramlines and slagheaps, pieces of machinery, / That was, and still is, my ideal scenery'),[3] the concept of a Birmingham bohemian quarter to rival the Parisian Left Bank has, regrettably, never really materialised.[4]

Structure and Method

There is a plethora of literary and cultural products that could be placed under the rubric of 'modernism, space and the city', and in order to manage and structure this material this book focuses upon three broad features of urban modernism in four European cities: the built environment; cultural institutions; and the perceptions of the 'outsider'. It also employs two, related, theories to understand these features of urban modernism: the idea of a critical literary geography; and the notion of 'geographical emotions'.

All of the cities discussed here were subject to massive restructuring in the period under consideration (roughly the mid-nineteenth to mid-twentieth centuries). Such changes in the built environment of the city profoundly affected literary and cultural representations. This is what David Harvey calls the 'urbanisation of consciousness', and prompts us to consider how developments in the material space of the city revised how people lived, experienced and thought about the places in which they lived.[5] Many writers and artists took the city in general, and certain cities in particular, as the subject matter of their works, particularly in long novels about individual cities: James Joyce on Dublin in *Ulysses*; Alfred Döblin on Berlin in *Berlin Alexanderplatz*; or Andrei Bely on St Petersburg.[6] Such novels not only represent specific examples of city experience but also illustrate the general effects of Harvey's 'urbanisation of consciousness'. In this respect modernist experimentation in these cities coincided with attempts by psychologists and sociologists to understand the wider effects of urbanisation. The categorisation of spatial phobias, such as agoraphobia, by psychologists at the end of the nineteenth century was, for instance, closely linked to alterations in the physical fabric of cities such as Vienna and Berlin.

Much of the experimental style of modernist writing has frequently been traced to the impact of the urbanisation of consciousness, refracted through the particular qualities of the cities being considered. In a discussion of metropolitan modernism, Andreas Huyssen notes: 'Psychic experiences are more than simply internal as they are always embodied and related to the urban environment', such that there is a 'reciprocity between the external and the internal'.[7] Another way to put this point is by saying that although modernist texts often represent particular cities, we need also to pay attention to how specific social spaces within these cities shape the resulting literary forms. This book thus will often focus upon fundamental changes in the built environment of the modern city, such as the development of urban forms of transport. Underground transit became established in many cities after the first, in London in 1863, including Budapest (1896), Paris (1900), Berlin (1902), New York (1904), Philadelphia (1907), Buenos Aires (1913), Tokyo (1927) and Moscow (1935). Analysing the impact of the expansion of the London Underground, as occurs in Chapter 4, is important in a study of modernism because, as Matthew Beaumont and Michael Freeman argue, the history of such innovations as the railways represents 'a rich and contradictory cultural experience that has taken place within a complex and developing network of social relations'.[8] Analysis of how such crucial changes in the built environment affected modernist writers thus enables us to understand further Huyssen's notion of the 'reciprocity between the external and the internal'.

The second set of features discussed in the book are urban cultural institutions vital for the propagation of modernism: bookshops, independent publishers and presses, literary cafés, discussion circles or salons.[9] Such material institutions were essential for the development of key cultural features within modernism, such as 'little magazines', aesthetic manifestos, or the formation of movements and isms. Sometimes, these two aspects coincided, as in the Café des Westens in Berlin, which hosted an Expressionist circle of artists around the avant-garde magazine *Der Sturm* (see Chapter 3), or the semi-mythical founding of the Imagist poetry movement in a café (either Kensington or the British Library) in London. Due to the presence of such cultural institutions, particular spaces within cities were often seen as quarters particularly hospitable to modernists, such as the Left Bank of Paris, or the West End of Berlin. Such spaces not only provided the infrastructure necessary for the production of cultural works within these cities, but also formed nodal points in transnational networks of modernism around the globe. Thus, from a bookshop such as Harold Monro's Poetry Bookshop in London or Sylvia Beach's Shakespeare and Company in Paris one could pick up modernist magazines published from around the world. Modernism has long been understood as a phenomenon of magazines, manifestos and movements, but it is only relatively recently that more attention has been paid to the geographical and spatial locations of these cultural formations in urban centres. In order to understand *what* modernism in Europe was, we need to examine *how* it came to be published or experienced, and to understand this it is essential to consider *where* precisely in Paris, London, Vienna and Berlin it emerged.

The third aspect of urban modernism this book considers is those modernist writers and artists who were, in multiple ways, 'outsiders' to the urban centres of London, Paris, Vienna, and Berlin. The perception of the linguistic outsider to a city has long been identified by critics as an important stimulus to modernist creation, and this book will examine many figures, mainly Anglophone writers, whose innovations were stimulated by living as 'exiles and émigrés', such as Jean Rhys in Paris, Joseph Conrad in London and Bryher in Berlin.[10] One of the earliest sociologists of modernity and the city, Georg Simmel, argued that 'the stranger' has always been a key figure of human societies. The stranger within a given city or society is, argues Simmel, 'a very positive relation', as she or he can import qualities into 'a particular spatial group' which do not originate in that group. The qualities of 'nearness and remoteness' which characterise the stranger also mean that they possess a certain attitude called 'objectivity' by Simmel; that is, as the stranger comes from outside of the social group they are 'not radically committed to the unique ingredients and peculiar tendencies of the group', and this lack of prejudice means they possess a certain kind of freedom in relation to the perceptions, values and ideas of the society in which they reside. This 'objectivity', which Simmel also defines as 'freedom', is characterised by the features of 'distance and nearness, indifference and involvement'.[11]

Though Simmel's essay does not touch upon aesthetic modernism it is not hard to see how his arguments can be translated into this realm and his ideas developed, as in Raymond Williams' work in the 1980s on modernism. In *The Politics of Modernism* (1989) Williams sketched out how the experiments of Anglo-European modernism were indebted to the role played by strangers or immigrants to cities such as London, Paris, and New York. Williams argued that the character of the metropolis effected a profound transformation in the formal properties of modernist culture. These changes were prompted by the many cultural innovators who were immigrants, able to bring Simmel's qualities of 'objectivity' and 'freedom' to their view of cultural production in these cities: it 'is a very striking feature of many Modernist and avant-garde movements', writes Williams, not only that they were located within such cities, 'but that so many of their members were immigrants into these centres, where in some new ways all were strangers'.[12] The effect of this interaction between the stranger and the city focused on the available mediums of expression:

> Liberated or breaking from their national or provincial cultures, placed in quite new relations to those other native languages or native visual traditions, encountering meanwhile a novel and dynamic common environment from which many of the older forms were obviously distant, the artists and writers and thinkers of this phase found the only community available to them: a community of the medium; of their own practices.[13]

Williams asserts that although the perception of language as a medium was noticed more intensely by those for whom English, say, was a second language, even to native speakers 'the new relationships of the metropolis, and the inescapable new uses in newspapers and advertising attuned to it, forced certain productive kinds of strangeness and distance'.[14] The productivity of these perceptions emerged due to an awareness that language was not a 'customary and naturalized' phenomenon, but a set of arbitrary conventions, and thus amenable to experimentation and alteration. Thus, features of the subjective experience of the stranger, Williams' 'strangeness and distance' or Simmel's 'distance and nearness', became translated into the experimental textures of modernist practice. Novels, for example, did not have to track the spread of generations across decades, as in the novels of Charles Dickens, but could set their entire action on a single day (*Ulysses*, *Mrs Dalloway*); a poetic snapshot composed in 'free verse', such as an Imagist poem, might more accurately capture a poet's impression of a city than the ballad stanzas employed by many nineteenth-century poets writing on cities. Samuel Beckett's innovations in drama and prose writing owed much to being based in Paris for the majority of his career: the articulation of Beckett's own aesthetic of 'strangeness and distance' can also be traced to his decision to publish in the French language from *Molloy* (1951) and *En Attendant Godot* (1952) onwards.[15] Hence Beckett's 'distance' from his native tongue (English) and his native country (Ireland) proved a profound factor in the liberation of his work towards the perceived 'strangeness' of his literary productions.[16] It is worth remembering too that one of the most influential figures of the European avant-garde, F. T. Marinetti, the founder of the Italian modernist movement, Futurism, was regarded as an outsider in Milan when he founded the magazine *Poesia* there in 1905: as Eric Bulson notes, when he arrived in Milan Marinetti was a 'doubly displaced expatriate', who had arrived speaking and writing in French from an upbringing in Alexandria, in Egypt. The startling and inventive attack upon the *passéism* of Italian culture that was articulated by Futurism arguably owes much to its founder's status as another modernist outsider.[17]

The work of Simmel and Williams, of course, has its limitations, one of which is clearly that colonialism and empire do not figure highly in their explanations.[18] *Modernism, Space, and the City* engages more deeply with these issues and, implicitly, with recent work in modernist studies considering related questions of cosmopolitanism and transnationalism.[19] However, I still find compelling the notion of the outsider who interrogates 'strangeness and distance' within the textures of modernist activity, wherever and whenever it is located. This book thus operates with a very ecumenical notion of the 'outsider', extending the trope beyond that of actual exiles and immigrants by examining those writers who felt themselves – perhaps due to ethnic or sexual identity – to be outsiders in these cities, even though their nationality might have declared them to be insiders. The term 'outsider' is thus chosen for its very neutrality and capaciousness: it covers migrants, refugees, exiles, tourists and 'inner émigrés' of various sorts.[20] This, however, is not to ignore the many political and socio-economic differences that exist between, for example, intellectuals in exile and refugees forced to seek a new life in a new location.[21]

In his book on *Weimar Culture* (1968) Peter Gay noted how the image of Weimar Germany signified 'modernity in art, literature, and thought' and how the death of the Republic in 1933 produced a 'dazzling array' of exiles 'who exported Weimar culture all over the world'.[22] Listing names such as Albert Einstein, Walter Gropius, Bertolt Brecht, and Wassily Kandinsky, Gay – who also fled, with his family, from Germany to the United States in 1939 – notes the combination of 'exuberant creativity' and the 'rising sense of doom' that characterised the culture of the period and, in a phrase that gave his book its subtitle, wrote that 'Weimar culture was the creation of outsiders, propelled by history into the inside, for a short, dizzying, fragile moment'.[23] This notion of the 'inside-outsider' is a significant one, and this book often concentrates upon such figures, as in the discussion in Chapter 2 of the Jewish intellectuals who created much of Viennese modernism. It also adapts the notion in other chapters, for example, in the discussion of several male writers in Chapter 1 who visit Paris as outsiders, but who then become identified with the city and thus came to be regarded as insiders. As Gay notes, that many German 'inside-outsiders' themselves became exiles, often in the United States, is a significant feature of the story of modernism.[24] This book, then, uses a broad understanding of the notion of the 'outsider', encompassing Gay's 'inside-outsiders', as well as colonial migrants to the imperial metropolis, or self-imposed artistic exiles.

Theoretically this book is informed by two sets of ideas. First it implicitly revisits some of the questions that preoccupied me in an earlier book, exploring issues relating to space and place, heterotopias, and how social space shapes literary forms.[25] The approach outlined in that book – what I call a 'critical literary geography' – seems no longer in need of extended explanation and justification, for there has been considerable work since 2003 exploring the interface between literature and geography. There is, for instance, an online journal of 'literary geographies' and a Palgrave book series on the same topic; Franco Moretti's work on graphs, maps, trees and atlases has pioneered a method of 'distant reading' of literary texts designed to trace global patterns of publication and reading; work on globalization and world literature has also done much to introduce a keener sense of space and geography into discussions of modernism such that the appeal to 'always spatialise' is now a familiar enough strategy.[26] Therefore the analysis undertaken here presumes the legitimacy of a spatial and geographical approach to modernism, and will employ rather than pause to elucidate, for instance, the work of Henri Lefebvre on spatiality.

The second, related, set of ideas informing the book is the notion of 'geographical emotions'. This is a phrase used by the British writer and critic Bryher (discussed in Chapter 3), and is employed throughout this book to refer to a loosely articulated theory of affect and mood, that is, how particular cities are experienced, viscerally and vitally, by the writers discussed here. Exploring 'geographical emotions' in the cities and writers discussed here entails a broad understanding of affect, encompassing features such as spatial phobias, sensory responses to urban geographies, and Heidegger's conception of mood (*Stimmung*).[27]

The editors of the volume *Emotional Geographies* define their approach as a 'concern with the spatiality and temporality of emotions, with the way they coalesce around and within certain places' and state that they understand emotion 'in terms of its socio-spatial mediation and articulation' rather than as an interiorised mental state.[28] This book builds upon this understanding by focusing upon how a variety of modernist texts link geographies and emotions, analysing how particular spaces produce affective responses, often registered in discourses of bodily reactions (such as smiling with joy or sweating with nerves) and sensory perceptions (such as smells or sounds). These can be positive moods of delight at the urban sensorium, or they can result in phobic responses to what are felt as strange and alienating spaces in the city.

This idea can best be illustrated by looking briefly at an example of writing about the city by the English novelist and critic Ford Madox Ford. In his introduction to *The Soul of London* (1905) Ford claims that his book eschews the 'encyclopaedic, topographical, or archaeological' in favour of trying to capture 'the atmosphere' of modern London: rather than 'writing about' the city, the perfect book on this topic 'would throw a personal image of the place on to the paper'.[29] *The Soul of London* is thus a kind of experiential spatial history without any facts – indeed Ford says that his ideal book on the city would not contain sentences that indicate that there are '720 firms of hat manufacturers employing 19,000 operatives' in the city, but would rather 'be a picture of one, or two, or three hat factories, peopled with human beings' at work in these factories.[30] Ford's project can therefore be considered as a form of affective geography, capturing the 'feel' of a city. It is thus a more subjective sense of the metropolis, rejecting the facticity of cultural history for the affective and sensory response of the writer to their environment. To an extent it resembles Henri Lefebvre's concept of representational space, which he defines as 'space as directly *lived*', the city as *imaginative* space that is often in conflict with the more official representations of space found in city planning or architectural maps.[31] While the *representation of space* is conceptualised space (associated with town planners, urbanists, governmental bodies), *representational space* is irredeemably experiential and marked indelibly by the qualities of affect:

> Representational space is alive: it speaks. It has an affective kernel or centre: Ego, bed, bedroom, dwelling, house; or: square, church, graveyard. It embraces the loci of passion, of action and of lived situations . . . it may be qualified in various ways: it may be directional, situational or relational, because it is essentially qualitative, fluid and dynamic.[32]

It is, then, the 'loci of passion' that constitute Ford's soul of the city. Adapting an idea from Raymond Williams, we could argue that different cities have different 'structures of feeling' about them: something that is not just about their architecture, or how they have been planned (such as the grid of Manhattan versus the Haussmann boulevards of Paris), but about the typical sounds or smells or sights of these cities and how they affect the citizens or visitors to these locations.[33] Refining this concept further, many of the chapters in this book focus upon how writers register the moods and structures of feeling encountered and sustained by particular locations within individual cities: for example, a housing estate in Vienna or a particular café in Paris.

Here, for instance, is Ford writing in *The Soul of London* of how we remember places in the city as the setting for emotionally resonant experiences:

> Above all his London, his intimate London, will be the little bits of it that witnessed the great moments, the poignant moods of his life; it will be what happened to be the backgrounds of his more intense emotions.
>
> Certain corners of streets, certain angles of buildings, the spray of dishevelled plane-trees, certain cloud-forms, gusts of white smoke, odours, familiar sounds – these, in their remembrance will wring his heart. He will have noticed them, or hardly noticed them, glancing aside in his moments of terror, of perplexity, of passion, of grief.[34]

This is a piece of writing replete with the language of affect, of 'intense emotions' and 'poignant moods' such as terror or grief, and which argues that these affects derive from encountering certain spatial features of the city. Sounds, odours and sights in the city produce these affects, rather than ideas or texts. The passage recalls a later theorist of space, Gaston Bachelard, who in *The Poetics of Space* (1958) produced what he termed 'a phenomenological study of the intimate values of inside space'.[35] Bachelard's 'topoanalysis', however, focuses purely upon the house and its spaces (e.g. cellars, garrets, staircase, drawers, chests and wardrobes), producing an analysis of how our childhood develops within a definite spatial context: 'the house we were born in is physically inscribed in us', he writes and, in a nod to the embodied philosophy that is phenomenology, adds that his study will consist of 'this passionate liaison of our bodies . . . with an unforgettable house'.[36]

The differences between Ford and Bachelard are, however, instructive. First, Bachelard's focus is purely upon what he terms 'felicitous space', 'the space we love' or 'eulogized space'.[37] The affective relationship to space is purely positive, while Ford's vocabulary extends to include the more negative sensations of terror, perplexity and grief. Second, Ford's focus on 'intimate space', to use a phrase of Bachelard's, relates to the external environment: 'corners of streets, certain angles of buildings'. For Bachelard an affective relationship to space can only be conceived in terms of how the body inhabits a house: 'all really inhabited space bears the essence of the notion of home', he writes, perhaps because notions of safety and felicity are, for him, only possible within the interior.[38] For Ford, and for many modernist writers and artists, this kind of affective geography can also be discovered in the street corners or squares of the modern metropolis: intimacy here happens outdoors and, as Ford understood, evokes multiple emotions. The cultural geographer Nigel Thrift, in an article upon the spatial politics of affect, summarises how cities can be understood in terms of the kinds of affective geographies outlined by Ford:

> Cities may be seen as roiling maelstroms of affect. Particular affects such as anger, fear, happiness and joy are continually on the boil, rising here, subsiding there, and these affects continually manifest themselves in events which can take place either at a grand scale or simply as a part of continuing everyday life.[39]

Many of the texts considered in this book exhibit such 'maelstroms of affect', from Bryher's joy in the cinemas of Berlin to Jean Rhys' anger and fear in the cafés of Paris.

A comment on theorising 'affect': the term itself is somewhat difficult to define, and my use of 'geographical emotions' might be accused of conflating *emotion* with *affect* in a way that certain theorists of the 'affective turn' refuse.[40] For example, Lawrence Grossberg distinguishes them, arguing that 'emotion is the articulation of affect and ideology. Emotion is the ideological attempt to make sense of some affective productions.'[41] Affect, in this sense, writes Grossberg, comes to denote 'everything that is non-representational or non-semantic', particularly as experienced by the body during interpersonal contact. Affect can thus be seen as somewhat 'precognitive' in its disturbance of the body's physiology prior to its articulation as some recognisable emotional state.[42] Following the work of Deleuze, Brian Massumi also distinguishes affect and emotion, referring to affect as a form of vitality and 'intensity' that is 'qualified' when 'captured' as an emotion: however, Massumi also suggests that emotions can be seen as 'translations' of affect 'captured' in discourse.[43] However my work follows the approach of Sianne Ngai, in *Ugly Feelings*, who tends to use the terms 'emotion' and 'affect' interchangeably, arguing that their difference is a modal one of 'intensity or degree, rather than a formal difference of quality or kind'.[44] For Ngai affects are somewhat 'less formed and structured than emotions', but still possess structure, form and meaning, and her approach allows a focus upon what she calls the 'transitions' from affect to emotion and vice versa: 'the passages whereby affects acquire the semantic density and narrative complexity of emotions, and emotions conversely denature into affects'.[45] To these transitions between affect and emotion I would also add transitions between affect and sensation, and affect and phobia, considering how the sights, sounds and smells of certain European cities produce Ford's 'moments of terror, of perplexity, of passion, of grief'. Throughout this book we find myriad examples of modernist texts that demonstrate how urban spaces produce many of the nine basic affects noted in the pioneering work by Silvan Tomkins: shame, disgust, interest, joy, fear, anger, surprise, distress and contempt (or 'dissmell').[46]

A study of the geographical emotions of modernism, therefore, would explore, first, how particular places affect people, bodily or non-semantically, and are then translated into emotions and moods; and second, how such affects and emotions are articulated into various forms of modernist culture. Analysing the *place of affect* in modernism requires us to pay attention to the *affect of places* upon modernist writers and artists, analysing the responses of these individuals to specific locations within individual cities, along with the attendant processes of modernisation that have restructured these cities (e.g. urbanisation, commodification, industrialisation, imperialism). Indeed, Jonathan Flatley, in his book *Affective Mapping: Melancholia and the Politics of Modernism* (2008), suggests that we can only really understand the aesthetic experiments of modernism by grasping the 'affective impact of modernization' and the ways in which 'the social forces of modernity work *through* emotions, the ways we become the subjects that we are by the structuring of our affective attachments'.[47] Affect is often understood as a *relational* term, particularly between subjects, as in the work by Tomkins and others upon, for example, the sense of shame as an affective interaction between human beings.[48] Flatley thus notes that affect is 'something relational and transformative' of the person experiencing the affect; one possesses emotion, notes Flatley, but 'one is affected *by* people or things'.[49] Thus affect, for Seigworth and Gregg, is found 'in those intensities that pass from body to body'.[50] However, Eve Kosofsky Sedgwick broadens the kinds of possible relations affect can possess: 'Affects can be, and are attached to things, people, ideas, sensations, relations, activities, ambitions, institutions, and any number of other things, including other affects.'[51] This book, therefore, follows this and focuses more often upon moments when intense affects flow from cities to subjects, between subjects and spaces, and between bodies and urban environments. As Flatley notes, 'our spatial environments are inevitably imbued with the feelings we have about the places we are going, the things that happen to us along the way, and the people we meet'.[52]

The phrase 'poignant moods', noted above in the example from Ford Madox Ford's *The Soul of London*, emphasises one other element of the theory of geographical emotions articulated in this book. Flatley's work on affect draws upon the philosophy of Heidegger to theorise the significance of mood in our spatial environments. In *Being and Time* Heidegger uses the German term '*Stimmung*' to refer to a particular concept of mood, which he defines as one which 'comes neither from "outside" nor from "inside", but arises out of Being-in-the-World'.[53] Moods thus does not solely belong to an individual as an internal state, but are instead part of a person's relationship to an external environment; Heidegger thus also uses the term '*Stimmungen*' to indicate a process of the individual's *attunement* to this environment and the overall situation which they are in.[54] As Flatley puts it, moods can thus be regarded as a kind of 'affective atmosphere'; they are 'not in us; we are in them; they go through us'.[55] In this sense, mood, as Rita Felski and Susan Fraiman argue, is always with us and conveys an 'overall orientation to the world'; it thus 'muddies distinctions between the subjective and the objective' since it is a 'feeling of I-and-World together'.[56] In this book I adapt this notion of a reciprocal relationship between the mood of the individual and that of the spatial environment to explore how writers seek to capture the 'poignant moods' that are provoked and sustained by particular urban locations: being in a city is always being in a mood, experiencing geographical emotions in a process of becoming attuned to one's spatial surroundings. Throughout the book, if I am using the word 'mood' in this particular sense, derived from Heidegger but also informed by the work of Flatley, Felski and Fraiman, amongst others, I will indicate this by noting the German term afterwards, i.e. 'mood (*Stimmung*)'.

Four Cities

How modernist writers register affect in their engagements with particular locations therefore adds a new and revealing dimension to a materialist spatial history of modernism. This book could have been written about many other cities in relation to the themes of modernism and space. Remaining just within Europe it could have discussed Lisbon, Prague, or Milan, examining respectively the leading figure of Portuguese modernist poetry and the disassociated self, Fernando Pessoa (Lisbon), the archetypal alienated modernism of Franz Kafka (Prague), or the key avant-garde movement of Futurism (Milan). Perhaps most obviously the book could have discussed New York, noted by Williams as the original city of exiles and émigrés, and a metropolis in which, by 1910, over 40 per cent of the population had been born abroad.[57] Or, to break from a European and Anglo-American perspective, why not discuss modernism in Shanghai or Tokyo, the Latin American avant-garde of Rio de Janeiro, or the Indian modernist innovators of Calcutta?[58] With the ongoing expansion in modernist studies it sometimes seems as if the real challenge would be to locate a city in the world with no discernible modernist activity. My choice of London, Paris, Vienna, and Berlin was made because these four cities are still acknowledged as fundamental locations for tracing the development of modernism in Europe. I also wanted to explore what I call the affective pull of these specific cities upon outsiders, whether seen in Americans visiting Paris as cultural tourists or in colonial subjects migrating to metropolitan capitals, such as Jean Rhys and Sam Selvon in London. By studying the writings and geographical emotions of non-European outsiders drawn to these four cities this book thus hopes to break free of a purely European outlook, and offers something of a transnational perspective on modernism while retaining a materialist perspective anchored in the study of a particular urban geography.

The choice of these four European cities is, as noted above, also justifiable for their importance as sites of innovation and for their own interconnections within histories of modernism. Though they differ in many respects, Paris, Vienna, Berlin, and London are united as European capitals in which many modernist ideas and practices circulated via shared cultural networks of exchange. It might be plausible to start to think of these four cities not as the major centres of an international modernism, as tended to happen in earlier accounts of the history of modernism, but rather as nodal points in a particular *transnational region of modernism* within the wider world of modernisms.[59] Here I am drawing upon the work of Laura Doyle, who, in outlining a philosophy of transnationalism, calls for a study of 'regional transnational networks of culture and economy' that explores 'cross-border histories, conflicts, and identifications' within a particular bounded geography, and which, in turn, can 'shed light on the larger dialectical interaction of local or regional culture, and global or "external" economy'.[60] Exploring the interactions between these four cities, as revealed in the travels of writers between them, both presents a richer picture of modernism in this particular region of the world, and also begins to reveal the interactions between this transnational region and other areas of the world, as seen in the work of colonial expatriates such as Mulk Raj Anand, Jean Rhys and Sam Selvon in London, or Léopold Senghor and Aimé Césaire in Paris.[61] As Scott McCracken comments, to 'understand a city's modernism, we have to understand its networks' and thus the 'modernist city is characterized by its traffic, through and between cities'.[62] Hopefully, some of the cultural traffic between the modernism of the four cities discussed here becomes more visible, as does the way in which particular spaces and locations within these cities helped produce the specific forms of modernism that appeared in London, Paris, Berlin and Vienna.

Traffic and networking between the cities discussed in this book can be discerned in many different instances, and illuminating comparisons can be drawn between the geographical emotions of literary outsiders in these locations. For many of the Anglophone writers discussed in the book, for example, contrasts and comparisons between the four cities were significant: W. H. Auden, Bryher and Christopher Isherwood all – for differing reasons – preferred Berlin to Paris. Auden and Isherwood's friend, John Lehmann, preferred Vienna to Berlin, while another in this circle, Stephen Spender, attempted to write a modernist poem in the mode of Eliot's *The Waste Land* about Vienna, viewing the Austrian capital through Eliot's depiction of a Parisian-coloured London. Jean Rhys wrote and compared her experiences of London, Paris and Vienna throughout her fiction, even setting one novel, *After Leaving Mr Mackenzie*, as a text that shuttled between the cities of London and Paris. This book thus considers Rhys' work in several of its chapters since she is such an exemplary writer for exploring the geographical emotions of modernism, producing brilliant comparisons in her fiction between the different European cities she visited. Rhys, born on the Caribbean island of Dominica, was a white colonial outsider in Europe whose life and texts drift back and forth across three of the cities discussed in this book: rather than place her in just one city, therefore, we gain a better sense of her geographical emotions as an outsider by tracing her transnational identity across all of these locations. Focusing upon only four major European cities thus enables us to highlight more clearly the multiple comparisons and contrasts between geographical emotions as articulated by an outsider such as Rhys.

Another outsider in Europe, the American poet Ezra Pound, lived in London between 1908 and 1920 and then in Paris for the next five years. At times Pound seemed to conceive of London and Paris as part of the same transnational region of modernist ideas. He referred to the 'double city of London and Paris',[63] and in 1917 wrote that as the present 'centre of the world is somewhere on an imaginary line between London and Paris, the sooner that line is shortened, the better for all of us'.[64] In this article Pound promoted the building of a channel tunnel to facilitate the circulation of ideas between London and Paris and to produce 'a richer civilization' by the 'closer union of the two capitals': transportation 'is civilization', he notes, because a 'tunnel is worth more than a dynasty'.[65] In places modernists such as Pound or his fellow American T. S. Eliot seemed to try to create the literary equivalent of tunnels between the two cities, shortening the distance between them by an interchange and exchange between the two languages and cultures. Eliot's experience of Paris was, as Chapter 1 shows, formative in the development of his poetry, and several of his early verses were composed in French ('Le Directeur', 'Mélange Adultère de Tout', 'Lune de Miel' and 'Dans le Restaurant'), showing an identification with French modernist poets that shaped Eliot's own English-speaking modernism. Even when Eliot composed his famous lines on the 'unreal city' of London in the first section of *The Waste Land*, he framed the representation through the words of Charles Baudelaire on the 'swarming city' (*Fourmillante cité*) of Paris.[66] One of Pound's most famous poems, 'In a Station of the Metro', is an attempt to capture in English a set of impressions and sensations that the poet experienced while exiting the Paris Metro,[67] while another poem, 'Dans un Omnibus de Londres', tries to represent an experience of travelling through the English capital but is written in French.[68] In these two poems, both fascinatingly concerning modes of transport, Pound offers something like an attempt to culturally shorten the line of cultural traffic between London and Paris.

Another instance of the networks and traffic between modernist cities can be found in the work of important cultural institutions such as bookshops. Perhaps the most famous foreign-language bookshop in early twentieth-century Paris was Sylvia Beach's Shakespeare and Company, which published James Joyce's *Ulysses* in 1922. Before opening the bookshop in 1919 Beach, an American, visited two significant London bookshops, Harold Monro's Poetry Bookshop and Elkin Mathews' shop in Cork Street. Both booksellers offered advice on running a bookshop and sold her stock, such as editions of Joyce, Pound and Yeats that Mathews had published; Monro also persuaded Beach that her initial idea of opening a French bookshop in London was a mistake as there would be no market for it.[69] Modern independent bookshops thus served as crucial nodal points in the networks that distributed modernism not only between London and Paris, but across the globe, seen in the famous subscription list for the first edition of *Ulysses* which noted its circulation beyond Europe and North America (though not in large numbers) in cities such as Buenos Aires, Madras, and Peking.[70] Bookshops were thus vital institutions facilitating the exchange of modernist texts and ideas worldwide, demonstrating the dialectical interchange between the local and the global that Doyle characterises as a feature of transnationalism.

However, I want to sound a note of caution about tracing transnational networks under the rubric of a geography of modernism. My approach to the transnational is rooted in the material history of specific cities and the affective responses to the spaces encountered by writers in these spaces. This approach differs slightly from that of one proponent of a transnational modernism, Jessica Berman, who brilliantly traces the ethical and political connections between writers such as Mulk Raj Anand and James Joyce, but whose focus is upon what she calls 'the worldwide sphere of textual activity' within transnational modernisms.[71] One potential problem with such an approach is that though it brings into focus some fascinating comparative connections in modernism around the world, it does so at the risk of evacuating the geographical specificity of the writers and texts involved.[72] There is thus a tendency for the 'transnational' to operate in a kind of geographical vacuum, existing within worldwide 'textual activity', without acknowledging sufficiently how particular writers react to and engage with specific geographical locations in their texts. To avoid this geographical vacuum this book emphasises the spatial history of various locations and institutions within the four cities studied, and stresses the affective response of literary outsiders to particular spaces within these cities.

It might be objected that discussing expatriates in cities such as Paris or London is not exactly novel. As Daniel Katz notes, in a fascinating account of the role of translation in expatriate American modernism, the 'association of modernism with expatriation and exile is venerable to the point of being a cliché'.[73] However, this book hopes to avoid cliché by focusing upon material spaces and institutions in a productive fashion, and by the stress upon the affective quality of these spaces as represented in modernist texts. Equally, the wider definition of the 'outsider' utilised here avoids some of the overfamiliarity associated with expatriate writing. And while at times the book does consider certain figures who are well-known expatriate writers (Christopher Isherwood and W. H. Auden in Berlin, for instance), it hopes to shed a different light upon their literary representations by stressing their geographical emotions while abroad; equally, the book often highlights other literary outsiders who have received far less attention, such as Naomi Mitchison in Vienna or Gwendolyn Bennett in Paris. To illustrate this point we can turn to one such figure.

If American expatriates in 1920s Paris are overly familiar territory, then the view of a quite different kind of outsider in London in the 1920s is much less well known. Mulk Raj Anand's *Conversations in Bloomsbury* (1981) is a retrospective memoir of the times that the Indian novelist and critic spent in London in the 1920s. Active in Indian nationalist politics in the years after the Jallianwalla Bagh (Amritsar) Massacre of 1919, Anand travelled to London in 1924 to study philosophy, becoming acquainted with many of the key figures of literary Bloomsbury. Anand's memoir recalls meeting T. S. Eliot, the Woolfs, Aldous Huxley, and E. M. Forster, amongst others, and his conversations record discussions on literature, art, philosophy, spirituality and politics, as well as indicating the influence on Anand's career of his reading in London, such as texts by James Joyce.[74]

Two features of Anand's account, however, stand out. The first is the role of the multiple cultural institutions of London that he maps in the book: the British Museum Reading Room (where he encounters Huxley); the bookshops of Jacob Schwartz, Arthur Probsthain, and Harold Monro (in whose Poetry Bookshop at a party he meets Eliot, D. H. Lawrence and Edith Sitwell); Eliot's office at the publishers Faber & Gwyer, where he edited *The Criterion* (to which Anand contributed); and the Tavistock Square offices of the Woolfs' Hogarth Press (where Anand quarrelled with Clive Bell about Indian art). In addition the memoir also records a network of cafés, pubs, and restaurants in which the literary work of London was planned and discussed, with Anand noting the 'convention established by the whole Bloomsbury set of intellectuals, poets and artists, to interdine frequently'.[75] He thus lunches with Eliot at the Etoile and Schmidt's restaurant, and eats crumpets with Nancy Cunard at Whytelady's café in Great Russell Street. Anand's account of these spaces of cultural production (there is very little description of the rest of the city) indicates an understanding of the importance of these institutional locations in the development of modernism in London; it also indicates his awareness of himself both as a colonial outsider and as determined to carve out a cultural and political space for himself in this environment. On the way to lunch with Eliot at Schmidt's, Anand describes himself as 'itching all the time to have a confrontation with him [Eliot] about Western civilization'; during the lunch, after Eliot is coolly dismissive of Indian politics ('I wish that the Indians would tone down their politics and renew their culture'), Anand holds his tongue, but writes that though 'I had come to learn from not to teach Eliot' he also had 'the irrepressible urge . . . out of my disillusionment with Europe, to show the concave mirror to the Western intellectuals, however eminent they may be'.[76] Here we see the colonial outsider refusing the position of cultural inferiority assigned him by many of the metropolitan intellectuals he meets; as he says to Eliot at another point: 'I am going to rewrite Kipling's *Kim* . . . from the opposite point of view.'[77] Commenting on the memoir Anna Snaith notes that, through 'its topographical detail, Anand literally charts his claim over the spaces of Bloomsbury . . . His is not the observing gaze of a tourist, but through dialogue and debate, he positions himself as a producer of space, creator of an alternative map of modernist London.'[78]

However, the second distinctive feature of *Conversations in Bloomsbury* that speaks to the issues traced in this book is the affective form of Anand's responses to his engagement with modernist London. Anand offers few examples of how London affects him directly as a city (other than noting that he doesn't 'feel easy in the world of buses and trams and tubes');[79] rather his discourse of affect illustrates the difficulty he faced as a colonial outsider in becoming a 'producer of space', as Snaith terms it. Repeatedly in his encounters with Western intellectuals in the cultural spaces of bookshops, cafés and restaurants Anand feels nervous, insecure, and inferior, with many of these feelings being registered physiologically in the classic manner of precognitive affect theory, in features such as facial behaviour.[80] Thus Anand blushes when discussing Joyce and feels 'waves of warmth rise in my body and become sweat' when first talking to Eliot; his 'nerves were taut' and his face is 'hot and flushed' when meeting Forster; a negative comment from Clive Bell on Indian art produces 'an uprush of Punjabi blood'; and on his way to meet Eliot for lunch he is 'uneasy, uncertain, feeling inferior and weak'.[81] Such affects, however, represent more than mere nerves before meeting 'big names', for they also relate to Anand's political status as colonial outsider. In the discussion with Eliot and Bonamy Dobrée that leads to him announcing defiantly that he will rewrite *Kim*, Anand has just been listening to the two men smugly defend the British Empire in India for providing 'unity' and railways. Anand's response condenses his physical unease in the restaurant with an angry memory of his experience of the violence of the British Empire in India: 'I was perspiring under the collar, through the humiliation of having been flogged by the police. I had been cultivating the will to decide on the struggle against, what Gandhi called, the satanic British.'[82] The humiliation felt here, suggests Anand, is not the memory of the physical violence of the police, but the affective encounter with metropolitan imperialism that makes him 'perspire'.

Not all his affective encounters are negative, however, as he feels 'elated' when discussing art and politics with Leonard Woolf and Forster, figures whom Anand appreciated for their 'humanness, without the bluff of the white Sahib superiority'.[83] With Woolf and Forster, Anand ventures a comparison between Caliban in Shakespeare's *Tempest* and Gandhi, and is 'surprised at my eloquence' with 'my cheeks warming and my eyes burning, from the feeling that I was dramatizing my own inner hates'.[84] Here Anand's attempt to rewrite and revise imperialist discourse, to remap the space of modernist London, takes him by surprise, with the physical signs of affect on his cheeks and eyes producing 'elation' rather than the 'humiliation' of the other scene. Such positive affects are, sadly, in the minority in the book, and it is revealing that perhaps the most common affective term Anand employs is that of feeling 'gauche', as when he walks with Huxley into the galleries of the British Museum and feels 'stupid and gauche and naïve'.[85] As well as describing the social awkwardness of Anand as colonial outsider in the august spaces of metropolitan culture, 'gauche' is an interesting term for its other associations: it is a spatial term of hierarchy, from the French for 'left', and denotes how being, for example, left-handed has stereotypically been regarded as less 'normal' and more awkward than being 'right-handed'. At one level feeling gauche thus captures the spatial regime that positions Anand as an inferior in modernist London. However, being gauche also has a political resonance for Anand, with the awkward colonial outsider becoming the *gauchiste* radical unwilling to silence himself entirely at the centre of empire, instead exhibiting the 'irrepressible urge' to show 'the concave mirror to the Western intellectuals'.

The following chapters thus track a range of responses by outsiders such as Anand to the four cities being discussed. Sometimes the emphasis of the individual chapter falls more upon one theme than another, as when the built environment and cultural institutions dominate in the chapter on London; sometimes affect predominates, as with the chapters on Berlin and Vienna, which often focus upon how mood (*Stimmung*) or atmosphere are experienced in these cities. The story of modernism and space in these four cities is a capacious and fascinating one and I hope that by interweaving the themes of the outsider, the built environment and cultural institutions – guided by the concept of 'geographical emotions' and spatial theory – this book reveals new approaches and insights to some of the most familiar cities of modernism.

The book starts in Paris, a city in which the earliest manifestations of modernism in Europe were articulated, and discusses many writers, including Guillaume Apollinaire, Gwendolyn Bennett, T. S. Eliot, Hope Mirrlees, and Jean Rhys. It then discusses two cities of German modernism, Vienna and Berlin, locations in which the geographical emotions of urban life were obsessively theorised and explored: outsiders in Vienna that are discussed include Stephen Spender, John Lehmann, and Naomi Mitchison, while the Berlin chapter considers, amongst others, Christopher Isherwood, Bryher and the magazine *Broom*. The book then concludes with London, partly as an act of defamiliarisation towards the Anglophone reader who might be more acquainted with the story of modernism in this city: London, the book implies, looks different as a city of modernism once you have travelled via the other European cities. A second reason for concluding with London is that in its final discussion of the Trinidadian-born writer Sam Selvon, and his novel *The Lonely Londoners*, Chapter 4 takes us into a later spatial history of modernism than is found in the earlier chapters, one in which the affective life of the outsider as insider speaks also to our own contemporary experience of modernism and cities.

Notes

1. See Le Corbusier, *The City of Tomorrow and its Planning*, trans. Frederick Etchells (New York: Dover, 1987), and Antonio Sant'Elia, 'Futurist Architecture' (1914) in *Futurism: An Anthology*, ed. Lawrence Rainey, Christine Poggi and Laura Witman

(New Haven: Yale University Press, 2009), pp. 198–201. For the work of John Madin (many of whose buildings from the 1960s and 1970s are now demolished) see http://www.john-madin.info (last accessed 30 October 2017).

2. See Georg Lukács, *The Historical Novel*, trans. H. and S. Mitchell (London: Merlin, 1962), p. 39. This is a point made to me in conversation with Ken Hirschkop.
3. W. H. Auden, 'Letter to Lord Byron' in *Collected Poems*, ed. Edward Mendelson (London: Faber, 1991), p. 89.
4. Perhaps I am being too negative about my home town here. There was, for example, a 'Birmingham Group' of writers in the 1930s, including Walter Allen, Walter Brierley, Peter Chamberlain, Leslie Halward, and John Hampson. Hampson's novel *Saturday Night at the Greyhound* was published by the Hogarth Press in 1931. See Lara Feigel, 'Buggery and Montage: Birmingham and Bloomsbury in the 1930s' in *Woolfian Boundaries*, ed. Anna Burrells, Steve Ellis, Deborah Parsons and Kathryn Simpson (Clemson, SC: Clemson University Digital Press, 2007), pp. 51–7. There was also a Birmingham Surrealist group, including Emmy Bridgewater, Conroy Maddox and Robert Melville; see Michael Remy, *Surrealism in Britain* (Aldershot: Ashgate, 1999), pp. 220, 284–5.
5. David Harvey, *The Urban Experience* (Oxford: Blackwell, 1989), pp. 229–55.
6. Jeremy Tambling notes that long modernist novels are 'urban, but resist being mapped'. See Tambling, 'Judaism and Heterogeneity in the Modernist Long Novel', *Modernist Cultures* 10:3 (2015), pp. 357–79; p. 358.
7. Andreas Huyssen, *Miniature Metropolis: Literature in an Age of Photography and Film* (Cambridge, MA: Harvard University Press, 2015), p. 6.
8. Matthew Beaumont and Michael Freeman (eds), *Railways and Modernity: Time, Space, and the Machine Ensemble* (Bern: Peter Lang, 2007), p. 7.
9. For the broad significance of cultural institutions see Lawrence Rainey, *Institutions of Modernism: Literary Elites and Public Culture* (New Haven: Yale University Press, 1998).
10. The phrase derives from an early account of this phenomenon by Terry Eagleton, *Exiles and Émigrés: Studies in Modern Literature* (London: Chatto and Windus, 1970).
11. See Georg Simmel, 'The Stranger' (1908) in *The Sociology of Georg Simmel*, trans. Kurt Wolff (New York: Free Press, 1950), pp. 402–8; p. 404. Richard Sennett distinguishes between the stranger as an 'unknown' and the stranger as 'outsider' in *The Fall of Public Man* (London: Faber, 1986), pp. 48–9. For a psychoanalytic consideration of the idea of the outsider see Julia Kristeva, *Strangers to Ourselves*, trans. Leon S. Roudiez (London: Harvester Wheatsheaf, 1991).
12. Raymond Williams, *The Politics of Modernism: Against the New Conformists*, ed. Tony Pinkney (London: Verso, 1989), p. 77.
13. Ibid. p. 45.
14. Ibid. p. 46.
15. James Knowlson notes that Beckett began to compose in French soon after his arrival in Paris in the late 1930s; see Knowlson, *Damned to Fame: The Life of Samuel Beckett* (London: Bloomsbury, 1996), pp. 293–5.
16. Beckett's use of Anglo-Irish dialect in certain texts only adds another layer of linguistic and cultural 'distance' to his work.
17. See Eric Bulson, 'Milan, the "Rivista", and the Deprovincialization of Italy: *Le Papyrus* (1894–6); *Poesia* (1905–9); *Il Convegno* (1920–40); *Pan* (1933–5); and *Corrente di vita giornale* (1938–40)' in *The Oxford Critical and Cultural History of Modernist Magazines, vol. 3: Europe 1880–1940*, ed. Peter Brooker, Sascha Bru, Andrew Thacker and Christian Weikop (Oxford: Oxford University Press, 2013), pp. 511–35; p. 516.

18. On this point see Michael North, *Reading 1922: A Return to the Scene of the Modern* (New York: Oxford University Press, 1999), pp. 11–15.
19. See, for instance, Jessica Berman, *Modernist Commitments: Ethics, Politics, and Transnational Modernism* (New York: Columbia University Press, 2011); Susan Stanford Friedman, *Planetary Modernisms: Provocations on Modernity Across Time* (New York: Columbia University Press, 2015); and Rebecca Walkowitz, *Cosmopolitan Style: Modernism Beyond the Nation* (New York: Columbia University Press, 2006).
20. The phrase 'inner émigré' is from Seamus Heaney, *North* (London: Faber, 1975), p. 73.
21. Edward Said, however, argues that there are interesting links between these two categories; see Said, *Culture and Imperialism* (London: Vintage, 1993), pp. 402–4. For a critique of this view see Caren Kaplan, *Questions of Travel: Postmodern Discourses of Displacement* (Durham, NC: Duke University Press, 1996), pp. 117–22.
22. Peter Gay, *Weimar Culture: The Outsider as Insider* (Harmondsworth: Penguin, 1968), p. xi.
23. Ibid. p. xii.
24. Ibid. p. 152.
25. See Andrew Thacker, *Moving Through Modernity: Space and Geography in Modernism* (Manchester: Manchester University Press, 2003), especially ch. 1.
26. See *Literary Geographies*, http://www.literarygeographies.net/index.php/LitGeogs (last accessed 30 October 2017). For an overview of geographical work on literature see Sheila Hones, 'Text as It Happens: Literary Geography', *Geography Compass*, 2:5 (2008), pp. 1301–17. For general work on literature and space see Robert T. Tally Jr., *Spatiality* (London: Routledge, 2013); Tally (ed.), *Geocritical Explorations: Space, Place, and Mapping in Literary and Cultural Studies* (New York: Palgrave Macmillan, 2014); and Tally (ed.), *The Routledge Handbook of Literature and Space* (London: Routledge, 2017). See also Bertrand Westphal, *Geocriticism: Real and Fictional Spaces* (New York: Palgrave Macmillan, 2011). The two key works by Franco Moretti in this respect are Moretti, *Atlas of the European Novel, 1800–1900* (London: Verso, 1998) and *Graphs, Maps, Trees: Abstract Models for a Literary History* (London: Verso, 2005). For work on modernism and geography see Jon Hegglund, *World Views: Metageographies of Modernist Fiction* (New York: Oxford University Press, 2012); Christopher GoGwilt, *The Fiction of Geopolitics: Afterimages of Culture from Wilkie Collins to Alfred Hitchcock* (Stanford: Stanford University Press, 2000); GoGwilt, *The Passage of Literature: Genealogies of Modernism in Conrad, Rhys, and Pramoedya* (Oxford: Oxford University Press, 2010); Susan Stanford Friedman, *Mappings: Feminism and the Cultural Geographies of Encounter* (Princeton: Princeton University Press, 1998); Rebecca Walsh, *The Geopoetics of Modernism* (Gainesville: University Press of Florida, 2015); and the essays in *Geomodernisms: Race, Modernism, Modernity*, ed. Laura Doyle and Laura Winkiel (Bloomington: Indiana University Press, 2005).
27. Heidegger's discussion of *Stimmung* (which means something like 'being attuned to one's surroundings') can be found in his *Being and Time*, trans. John Macquarrie and Edward Robinson (Oxford: Blackwell, 1962), pp. 172–9, 388–96. See the account given of this notion in Jonathan Flatley, *Affective Mapping: Melancholia and the Politics of Modernism* (Cambridge, MA: Harvard University Press, 2008), pp. 19–24.
28. Liz Bondi, Joyce Davidson and Mick Smith, 'Introduction: Geography's Emotional Turn' in *Emotional Geographies*, ed. Davidson, Bondi and Smith (Farnham: Ashgate, 2005), pp. 1–18; p. 3.

29. Ford Madox Ford, *The Soul of London*, ed. Alan G. Hill (London: Everyman, 1995), p. 3.
30. Ibid.
31. Henri Lefebvre, *The Production of Space,* trans. D. Nicholson-Smith (Oxford: Blackwell, 1991), p. 39.
32. Ibid. p. 42.
33. See Raymond Williams, *Marxism and Literature* (Oxford: Oxford University Press, 1977), pp. 128–35. Another dimension would be to explore how these urban texts might affect us as readers today, taking us into the territory of reader-response theory. For discussions of affect and reading see Derek Attridge, 'Once More with Feeling: Art, Affect and Performance', *Textual Practice* 25:2 (2011), pp. 329–43, and Alex Houen, 'Introduction: Affecting Words', *Textual Practice* 25:2 (2011), pp. 215–32.
34. Ford, *Soul of London*, p. 22.
35. Gaston Bachelard, *The Poetics of Space*, trans. Maria Jolas (Boston, MA: Beacon Press, 1969), p. 3.
36. Ibid. pp. 14, 15.
37. Ibid. p. xxxi.
38. Ibid. p. 5.
39. Nigel Thrift, 'Intensities of Feeling: Towards a Spatial Politics of Affect', *Geografiska Annaler: Series B Human Geography*, 86:1 (March 2004), pp. 57–78; p. 57. And see his book, *Non-Representational Theory: Space, Politics, Affect* (London: Routledge, 2008).
40. See *The Affective Turn: Theorizing the Social*, ed. Patricia Ticineto Clough with Jean Halley (Durham, NC: Duke University Press, 2007).
41. Lawrence Grossberg, 'Affect's Future: Rediscovering the Virtual in the Actual' in *The Affect Theory Reader*, ed. Melissa Gregg and Gregory J. Seigworth (Durham, NC: Duke University Press, 2010), pp. 309–38; p. 316. It is interesting to note that in this interview Grossberg says that his first introduction to something resembling a theory of affect came when reading Raymond Williams' notion of a 'structure of feeling' (p. 310).
42. See Felicity Callard and Constantina Papoulias, 'Affect and Embodiment' in *Memory: Histories, Theories, Debates*, ed. Susannah Radstone and Bill Schwarz (New York: Fordham University Press, 2010), pp. 246–62.
43. See Brian Massumi, 'The Autonomy of Affect', *Cultural Critique* 31 (Autumn 1995), pp. 83–109; pp. 88, 103. And see Gilles Deleuze and Félix Guattari, *What is Philosophy?,* trans. Graham Burchell and Hugh Tomlinson (London: Verso, 1994), pp. 163–99.
44. Sianne Ngai, *Ugly Feelings* (Cambridge, MA: Harvard University Press, 2005), p. 27.
45. Ibid.
46. See Silvan Tomkins, *Shame and its Sisters: A Silvan Tomkins Reader*, ed. Eve Kosofsky Sedgwick and Adam Frank (Durham, NC: Duke University Press, 1995), p. 74.
47. Flatley, *Affective Mapping*, p. 4. For other work on modernism and affect see the essays in *Modernism and Affect*, ed. Julie Taylor (Edinburgh: Edinburgh University Press, 2015), and Taylor, *Djuna Barnes and Affective Modernism* (Edinburgh: Edinburgh University Press, 2012).
48. See, for instance, Tomkins, *Shame and its Sisters*, pp. 133–78, and Elspeth Probyn, *Blush: Faces of Shame* (Minneapolis: University of Minnesota Press, 2005).
49. Flatley, *Affective Mapping*, p. 12.
50. Gregory J. Seigworth and Melissa Gregg, 'An Inventory of Shimmers' in *Affect Theory Reader*, pp. 1–25; p. 1.

51. Eve Kosofsky Sedgwick, *Touching Feeling: Affect, Pedagogy, Performativity* (Durham, NC: Duke University Press, 2003), p. 19.
52. Flatley, *Affective Mapping*, pp. 77–8.
53. Heidegger, *Being and Time*, p. 176. See also pp. 172–9 and 388–96.
54. On the complexities of the translation of Heidegger's terms see Flatley, *Affective Mapping*, pp. 19–24 and 205 fn.34. For an influential discussion of Heidegger's ideas see Charles Guignon, 'Moods in Heidegger's *Being and Time*' in *What is an Emotion? Classic Readings in Philosophical Psychology*, ed. Cheshire Calhoun and Robert C. Solomon (New York: Oxford University Press, 1984), pp. 230–43. For an application of the concept of mood to the cultural field see Ben Highmore, *Cultural Feelings: Mood, Mediation and Cultural Politics* (London: Routledge, 2017).
55. Flatley, *Affective Mapping*, pp. 19, 22.
56. Rita Felski and Susan Fraiman, 'Introduction' to Special Issue of *New Literary History* on Mood, *New Literary History* 43:3 (Summer 2012), pp. v–xii; p. vii. And for the notion of a 'critical mood' see Rita Felski, *The Limits of Critique* (Chicago: Chicago University Press, 2015), pp. 18–26.
57. Williams, *Politics of Modernism*, p. 34; Cyrus Patell, 'Introduction' in *The Cambridge Companion to the Literature of New York*, ed. Cyrus Patell and Bryan Waterman (Cambridge: Cambridge University Press, 2010), p. 4. For work on New York and modernism see, inter alia, the essays in Patell and Waterman, *Literature of New York*; Peter Brooker, *New York Fictions: Modernity, Postmodernism, The New Modern* (London: Longman, 1996); Ann Douglas, *Terrible Honesty: Mongrel Manhattan in the 1920s* (New York: Farrar, Straus, and Giroux, 1995); Shaun O'Connell, *Remarkable, Unspeakable New York: A Literary History* (Boston, MA: Beacon Press, 1995); and Christine Stansell, *American Moderns: Bohemian New York and the Creation of a New Century* (New York: Henry Holt, 2000).
58. See, for example, Seiji M. Lippit, *Topographies of Japanese Modernism* (New York: Columbia University Press, 2002); Stephanie Hemelryk Donald and Yi Zheng, 'Chinese Modernisms' in *The Oxford Handbook of Modernisms*, ed. Peter Brooker, Andrzej Gasiorek, Deborah Longworth and Andrew Thacker (Oxford: Oxford University Press, 2010); Eric Hayot, 'Chinese Modernism, Mimetic Desire, and European Time' in *The Oxford Handbook of Global Modernisms*, ed. Mark Wollaeger and Matthew Eatough (New York: Oxford University Press, 2012); Sharon Lubkemann Allen, *EccentriCities: Writing in the Margins of Modernism, St. Petersburg to Rio de Janeiro* (Manchester: Manchester University Press, 2013); and Partha Mitter, *The Triumph of Modernism: India's Artists and the Avant-Garde 1922–1947* (London: Reaktion, 2007).
59. Thus Malcolm Bradbury and Alan MacFarlane, in their seminal study, tend to see these cities as the main outposts of a shared international modernism; see Bradbury and McFarlane (eds), *Modernism 1890–1930* (Harmondsworth: Penguin, 1976). For a discussion of the limitations of this view see my 'Placing Modernism' in *Moving Modernisms: Motion, Technology, and Modernity*, ed. David Bradshaw, Laura Marcus and Rebecca Roach (Oxford: Oxford University Press, 2016), pp. 11–26.
60. See Laura Doyle, 'Toward a Philosophy of Transnationalism', *Journal of Transnational American Studies* 1:1 (2009); available at http://escholarship. org/uc/item/9vr1k8hk (last accessed 30 Oct. 2017).
61. For a fascinating approach to such 'diasporic modernisms' see Susan Stanford Friedman's reading of Césaire's 1956 text, *Notebook of a Return to My Native Land* [*Cahier d'un retour au pays natal*]; see Friedman, *Planetary Modernisms*, pp. 283–309.

62. Scott McCracken, 'Imagining the Modernist City' in *Oxford Handbook of Modernisms*, pp. 637–54; pp. 638, 654. An interesting later example of this point is that of COBRA, an avant-garde network of artists after World War II whose name was taken from the three cities in which they were based: Copenhagen, Brussels and Amsterdam.
63. Ezra Pound, 'Patria Mia VIII', *The New Age* 11:26 (24 Oct. 1912), pp. 611–12; p. 611.
64. Ezra Pound, 'Provincialism the Enemy' (1917) in Pound, *Selected Prose 1909–1956*, ed. William Cookson (London: Faber, 1973), p. 170.
65. Ibid. pp. 172, 169.
66. See T. S. Eliot, *The Waste Land* (ll.60–76) in his *Collected Poems, 1909–1962* (London: Faber, 1974), p. 65. Eliot's notes (p. 81) refer to Baudelaire's poem 'Les sept vieillards' from his 1859 volume, *Les Fleurs du mal.*
67. See Pound's account of the poem's composition in 'Vorticism' (1914), reprinted in his *Gaudier-Brzeska: A Memoir* (1916; New York: New Directions, 1970), pp. 86–7.
68. See Pound, *Collected Shorter Poems* (London: Faber, 1984), pp. 109, 160.
69. See Noel Riley Fitch, *Sylvia Beach and the Lost Generation: A History of Literary Paris in the Twenties and Thirties* (London: Norton, 1985), pp. 39–40.
70. Details of the subscribers for *Ulysses* can be found in the Sylvia Beach Papers, Boxes 47 and 48, Firestone Library, Princeton University.
71. Berman, *Modernist Commitments*, p. 31.
72. I should say that Berman's *Modernist Commitments* does not really suffer from this problem, but the theoretical point is still relevant.
73. Daniel Katz, *American Modernism's Expatriate Scene: The Labour of Translation* (Edinburgh: Edinburgh University Press, 2007), p. 1.
74. On Anand and Joyce see Berman, *Modernist Commitments*, pp. 90–138.
75. Mulk Raj Anand, *Conversations in Bloomsbury* (Oxford: Oxford University Press, 1995), p. 40.
76. Ibid. p. 169.
77. Ibid. p. 50.
78. Anna Snaith, *Modernist Voyages: Colonial Woman Writers in London, 1890–1945* (Cambridge: Cambridge University Press, 2014), p. 10.
79. Anand, *Conversations*, p. 107.
80. Flatley notes how Tomkins' theory of affect is rooted in 'physiological phenomena – facial behaviour above all'; Flatley, *Affective Mapping*, p. 13; see Tomkins, *Shame and its Sisters*, p. 30.
81. Anand, *Conversations*, pp. 6, 16, 71, 72, 117, 163.
82. Ibid. p. 50.
83. Ibid. p. 77.
84. Ibid.
85. Ibid. p. 26.

1

PARIS

Introduction: A New Babel

In the context of a discussion of modernism Paris is a thoroughly overdetermined cultural space: the city of light, the capital of modernity, the home of the 'lost generation', or a magnet for avant-garde writers and artists across Europe and far beyond – these are just a few of the epithets and descriptions used to capture the cultural standing of the French capital. Given the extent of Paris' role in the history of modernism this chapter will concentrate upon a selection of texts written by outsiders to the city, including Guillaume Apollinaire, Gwendolyn Bennett, Blaise Cendrars, T. S. Eliot, Hope Mirrlees and Jean Rhys; it will follow a rough chronology from Eliot, Apollinaire, and Cendrars in the 1910s, through to Mirrlees in 1919, and Rhys and Bennett in the 1920s and 1930s. These figures have been chosen to illustrate the myriad ways in which the geographical emotions of Paris stimulated modernist creativity, and have been grouped into two sections. The first set clusters together Eliot, Apollinaire and Cendrars, three white male poets whose relationship to Paris we might define as 'outside-insiders', adapting Peter Gay's ideas as outlined in the Introduction. These are figures who come from outside of the city but who, by virtue of status, education or identity, are able to function somewhat as insiders, finding a place for themselves within the cultural geography of the city. The response of these poets to the modernist spaces of Paris focuses particularly upon the new features of technological modernity, such as the iconic

Tour Eiffel, and exemplifies what we can characterise as a quite positive set of geographical emotions overall. The second set of writers includes Mirrlees, Rhys and Bennett, three figures who remain, the chapter argues, female outsiders within Paris, unable to quite locate themselves as 'insiders': that Rhys and Bennett are marked by, respectively, colonial and racial categories only adds to their continued status as 'outsiders' within Paris. Mirrlees is closest in her representations of the city to the male poets, but with significant differences in her attitudes towards certain features of its geography. In Rhys we witness most strikingly the idea of affect as a relational term flowing between subjects and their environments in a series of novels (*Quartet*, *After Leaving Mr Mackenzie* and *Good Morning, Midnight*) which show the difficult geographical emotions experienced by the solitary woman in Paris in the 1920s and 1930s. Rhys' works deserve the extended discussion afforded them in this chapter not only because of their detailed engagement with particular locations in Paris, but also because they demonstrate a remarkable attention to an affective and emotional response to these spaces and places. As Rhys herself noted of Paris: 'I've . . . never really loved any other city.'[1] The chapter concludes by considering a short story by Gwendolyn Bennett, in whom we discern an ambivalent response to the spatial and political freedoms offered to black subjects in the city.

Paris itself has long been a city of outsiders, artistic or otherwise, for, as Colin Jones notes, the 'average Parisian' for many periods in the city's history 'was almost certainly born outside the city, or was the child of outsiders'; population growth in Paris has often relied upon immigration, meaning that frequently 'between a half and three-quarters of "Parisians" were thus non-Parisian'.[2] For example, in the early 1930s 'outsiders' from the rest of France were joined by large numbers of foreign visitors, amounting to nearly 10 per cent of the city's populace, a proportion, Jones notes, that was the highest amongst large European cities.[3] From the nineteenth century through to the 1930s many of these foreign outsiders in Paris were writers and artists. In Anglophone literary criticism there has tended to be an overemphasis upon the 'lost generation' of American writers in Paris in the 1920s, but the attraction of the city was felt by many other foreign nationals with an artistic inclination, and from much earlier on.[4] From 1830 to 1945, argues Pascale Casanova, Paris became the 'capital of the literary world, the city endowed with the greatest literary prestige on earth', attracting artistic dissidents inspired by the intellectual promise of the French Revolution, its perceived cosmopolitanism and the reputation of its avant-garde.[5] Encouraged by the many representations of the city in literature – Balzac described it as the 'city of a thousand novels'[6] – Paris attracted writers, artists and political exiles from around the world. Writers such as Adam Mickiewicz (Poland), Oswald de Andrade (Brazil), César Vallejo (Peru), Vicente Huidobro (Chile), Kafu Nagai (Japan), Rainer Maria Rilke

(Austria), and Rubén Darío (Nicaragua) were just some of the major figures of non-Anglophone world literature that made, in Casanova's words, Paris into a 'new "Babel", a "Cosmopolis", a crossroads of the artistic world'.[7] The city thus became a home to what Casanova terms a 'transnational realm' or 'universal republic of letters', where writers proudly 'proclaimed themselves to be stateless and above political laws'.[8]

Oddly, Casanova's account tends to ignore two other formations of literary outsiders that in the interwar years occupied the 'transnational realm' of Paris. These, discussed below, were the numerous Black writers and intellectuals associated with the 'New Negro' movement of the Harlem Renaissance who visited and wrote about the city, including Gwendolyn Bennett, Langston Hughes and Claude McKay; and a related group of Francophone colonial writers from the Caribbean and Africa, such as Aimé Césaire, René Maran and Léopold Sédar Senghor, connected to the development of the theory of négritude.[9] Together these groups formed what Tyler Stovall has described as 'Paris Noir', producing a unique vision of the city as a space for black transnational and international dialogue.[10]

The affective pull of Paris was also felt by those in the visual arts. The rise, for instance, of Impressionist and Post-Impressionist painting helped stimulate a market which commodified Parisian art and presented Paris as *the* modern city, attracting the aesthetic avant-garde of Europe and beyond: the number of artists living in the city, for instance, doubled between 1870 and 1914.[11] To take two examples, the Dutchman Vincent Van Gogh and the Norwegian Edvard Munch both travelled to Paris in the mid-1880s in order to learn more about Impressionism, and for both the experience proved pivotal in their artistic development.[12] In other words, Paris was the place where one *modernised* oneself as an artist, and a partial list of significant European artists in the early decades of the twentieth century who based themselves in Paris is extensive: Modigliani (Italian), Gris, Miro, Picasso (Spanish), Chagall (Russian), Soutine, Lipchitz (Lithuanian) and Brancusi (Romanian). It is not surprising, then, that F. T. Marinetti announced the founding of Futurism – that most well-travelled of modernist movements around Europe – on the front page of Paris' main newspaper, *Le Figaro*, in 1909: Marinetti clearly understood the centrality of the Paris art world to the launch of a new ism.

In the years prior to World War I Paris drew writers and artists into it primarily because of the esteem of its cultural institutions and its openness to creative experimentation. However, visitors to the city also became influenced by wider intellectual forces operative in the city, foremost of which were the philosophical ideas of Henri Bergson. For example, the important Anglophone modernist magazine *Rhythm* (1911–13) was founded by John Middleton Murry after a series of visits to Paris in 1910 provided access to a cosmopolitan 'republic of art' very different from that he found in London.[13] *Rhythm*'s close connection with Parisian art and thought is demonstrated by the fact, as Faith Binckes notes, that it was the first magazine in Britain to print an image by Picasso.[14] In addition to art, however, Paris proved formative for Murry because it was there that he encountered the philosophy of Bergson, whose ideas pervaded the early issues of *Rhythm*, and whose popularity as an intellectual in French cultural life was at its highest at this time.[15] In a 1911 piece for *The New Age*, entitled 'Bergson in Paris', Murry argued that Bergson's ideas heralded progress in 'every intellectual sphere' and that if critics in England were able to comprehend 'Bergsonian theories of time and change, creative art would receive a new lease of life', as had occurred in France with Post-Impressionism, which Murry saw (probably incorrectly) as a result of Bergsonian thought.[16] In another article, 'Art and Philosophy', Murry proclaims that Bergson's philosophy is a 'living artistic force' in France, which demonstrates 'the open avowal of the supremacy of the intuition, of the spiritual vision of the artist in form, in words and meaning'.[17] Murry concludes the article with an convoluted, yet fascinating, early definition of modernism:

> The artist attains to the pure form, refining and intensifying his vision till all that is unessential dissolves away. . . . He must return to the moment of pure perception to see the essential forms, the essential harmonies of line and colour, the essential music of the world. Modernism is not the capricious outburst of intellectual dipsomania. It penetrates beneath the outward surface of the world, and disengages the rhythms that lie at the heart of things, rhythms strange to the eye, unaccustomed to the ear, primitive harmonies of the world that is and lives.[18]

This is a heady mix of Bergson's ideas on intuition and vitalism, a late 'art for art's sake' formalism, coupled with an interest in Fauvist 'primitive' art viewed by Murry in Paris (the first issue of *Rhythm* also contained an article on Fauvism).[19] Though rather unformulated, this article testifies to the way in which Bergson's thought, and Murry's wider experience of Paris, influenced his attempt to articulate a modernism around the concept of 'rhythm'.[20]

T. S. Eliot and the Sordid City

Another foreign modernist whose visit to Paris was marked by the impact of Bergson was the American T. S. Eliot. Eliot spent a year in the city in 1910–11, attending Bergson's lectures at the Collège de France and coming 'very much under [Bergson's] influence during the year', and later giving lectures in England on Bergson's thought.[21] Nancy Duvall Hargrove has traced in detail the impact of Paris upon Eliot, from the intellectual milieu of Bergson and the right-wing thinker Charles Maurras to the cultural world of art, theatre, dance, and opera in the city. For Hargrove it was Eliot's 'exposure to Parisian avant-garde art' that was 'to a great extent responsible for his ability to write innovative poetry', beginning with 'The Love Song of J. Alfred Prufrock'.[22] Of 'Prufrock' Ezra Pound commented that the poem showed how Eliot had 'modernized himself on his own', a judgement that, if we accept Hargrove's interpretation, might be revised to read: it was the city of Paris that modernised Eliot.[23]

Before Eliot visited the material space of Paris he had encountered the city in the metaphorical space of its literature, specifically the poetry of Charles Baudelaire and Jules Laforgue.[24] Eliot stated in 1950 that his youthful reading of these poets not only encouraged him to visit the city but, more importantly, offered 'a precedent for the poetic possibilities . . . of the more sordid aspects of the modern metropolis, of the possibility of the fusion between the sordidly realistic and the phantasmagoric'.[25] Eliot explicitly looked for poetic inspiration in what he called Baudelaire's 'imagery of the sordid life of a great metropolis'.[26] The urban space of Paris, thus meditated through the poetry of Baudelaire and Laforgue, became a representational space through which Eliot could articulate his own experience of the city: in these poets

> I learned that the sort of material that I had, the sort of experience that an adolescent had had, in an industrial city in America, could be the material for poetry; and that the source of new poetry might be found in what had been regarded hitherto as the impossible, the sterile, the intractably unpoetic.[27]

Visiting Paris in 1910 enabled Eliot to add another layer to his palimpsestic understanding of poetry and the city, grafting a new familiarity with the material spaces of Paris onto his understanding of the literary space of this city and his own adolescent experience of American cities. For Eliot the 'sordid' quality he identified in Paris functions as a productive affect in his verse, one which ambivalently attracts as much as it repels, and offers an urban experience that helped modernise his verse.

One of the poems identified by Hargrove as particularly marked by Eliot's year in Paris, 'Rhapsody on a Windy Night', clearly shows this admixture of the sordid and the phantasmagoric, as this is a poetic rhapsodic with little music but much emphasis on urban grubbiness.[28] The poem depicts an unnamed narrator drifting through city streets at night, past prostitutes ('that woman / Who hesitates toward you in the light of the door', ll.16–17), a cat in the gutter that devours 'rancid butter' (l.37) and many 'old nocturnal smells' (l.60), before returning to a room at four a.m. (l.70). The setting of Paris is suggested by the reference to the quay (given as the French *quai* in an earlier version[29]), the shutters of the windows, and the half-quote from Laforgue: 'La lune ne garde aucune rancune' (l.51), although Eliot refuses to specify directly that it is Paris, perhaps indicating that his experience of American cities is also being drawn upon here. The powerful influence of Bergson on Eliot at this time is found in the juxtaposition between the external clock time that marks the start of the majority of the stanzas in the poem ('Half-past one, / The street-lamp sputtered', ll.13–14), and the internal time (Bergson's *durée*) of the protagonist's sensations of the city and, crucially, his or her memories: 'The memory throws up high and dry / A crowd of twisted things; / A twisted branch upon the beach' (ll.23–5). This opposition is further emphasised by the fact that both clock time and the term 'memory' are mentioned five times in the poem. These references to memory recall Bergson's volume on *Matter and Memory* (1896), in which he distinguished between voluntary and involuntary memories (habit memory and image memory), privileging the role of the latter in the functioning of the memory system as 'pure memory'.[30] The memories of the 'twisted branch upon the beach' (l.25) and 'a crab one afternoon in a pool' (l.43) both appear as forms of involuntary memory, moments from the narrator's past that force themselves into the present as images with intense significance to the person recalling them, although apparently disconnected from the present scene perceived before them. The image of the moon in the street, which runs through the poem, is the initial prompt for an inward turn that disrupts order and structure, as 'Whispering lunar incantations / Dissolve the floors of memory / And all its clear relations, / Its divisions and precisions' (ll.4–7). As Donald Childs argues, this line shows Eliot's borrowing from Bergson, as the moon acts to free 'pure memory' from the 'practical intellect' represented by the rigidly ordered street lamps.[31]

The conjuncture of the 'sordidly realistic and the phantasmagoric' continues in the way in which the physical signs of the street metamorphose into fantastical figures. This is most noticeable in the way in which the street lamps come alive and speak to the protagonist: 'The street-lamp sputtered, / The street-lamp muttered, / The street-lamp said, "Regard that woman"' (ll.14–16). The regular pronouncements of the lamps act as the spatial equivalent to the clock marking time, and in many ways the lamps are the most active agents in the poem, guiding what the narrator should 'regard' in the street and, in the final stanza, directing him back home and advising upon his next actions: 'The bed is open; the tooth-brush hangs on the wall, / Put your shoes at the door, sleep, prepare for life' (ll.76–7). In this way the space of the Parisian street enters and seemingly controls the protagonist's life, resulting in a loss of agency signified in the poem's final line: 'The last twist of the knife' (l.78).

In emphasising Parisian street lamps Eliot's poem echoes the long-standing image of Paris as *la ville lumière* (city of light) whose spatial modernity was exemplified by the technology of light.[32] One nineteenth-century commentator claimed that the 'glow of the gas lamps' of the city of light meant that Paris 'emerged as a brightly-lit island in the ocean of darkness', while Joachim Schlör notes that street lighting meant that the 'Parisian boulevard could be experienced as an inner space', intensifying the nocturnal pleasures of visits to restaurants, cafés, and theatres.[33] The development of electric street lighting began in 1878 and developed rapidly during the 1880s, although it was an older lighting technology, gas, that illuminated the 22,000 lights which adorned the inauguration of the Eiffel Tower in 1889. However, the Paris Exposition of the same year, along with the Exposition of 1900, both made much of Paris as the 'City of Light', with the latter Exposition boasting a Palace of Electricity with a 'galaxy of light bulbs'.[34] A description of Paris by Guy de Maupassant from 1909 highlights how the different forms of lighting affected the perception of the city:

> I reached the Champs-Elysees, where the café concerts seemed like blazing hearths among the leaves. The chestnut trees, brushed with yellow light, had the look of painted objects, the look of phosphorescent trees. And the electric globes – like shimmering, pale moons, like moon eggs fallen from the sky, monstrous, living pearls – dimmed, with their nacreous glow, mysterious and regal, the flaring jets of gas, of ugly, dirty gas, and the garlands of coloured glass.[35]

Lighting here collapses the division between the natural and the artificial, with the painted 'phosphorescent trees' and the electric lights being compared to 'pale moons'. This feature also occurs in Eliot's poem, shown in the switch between the artificial street lights and the mysterious 'lunar synthesis' and 'lunar incantations' that open the poem, as well as in the chatty street lamps.

In 'Rhapsody on a Windy Night' the dominant lighting is that of the street lamps rather than the natural moonlight and, in stanza 5, the moon becomes transformed into a complex image of femininity:

> The lamp hummed:
> 'Regard the moon,
> La lune ne garde aucune rancune,
> She winks a feeble eye,
> She smiles into corners.
> She smooths the hair of the grass.
> The moon has lost her memory.
> A washed-out smallpox cracks her face,
> Her hand twists a paper rose,
> That smells of dust and eau de Cologne,
> She is alone
> With all the old nocturnal smells
> That cross and cross her brain.' (ll.49–61)

There is a revealing shift in imagery here, from the visual to the olfactory, the vision of a feminised moon with a face that winks and smiles being displaced by a woman with a face cracked by smallpox, who exists alone with her 'nocturnal smells'. The word 'smell' is repeated five times in the stanza, shifting from the external space of the street to interior space, as when the 'reminiscence' of the smell of chestnuts in a street is followed by 'female smells in shuttered rooms' (l.66). The visual imagery of the moon and street lamps is now replaced by a more disturbing discourse of affect, of smell and disgust, recalling Eliot's notion of the more 'sordid aspects of the metropolis', but one which, as in much of the early Eliot, is associated negatively with femininity and the female body.[36] Both 'nocturnal smells' and 'female smells in shuttered rooms' suggest sexuality overlaid with disgust, and connect the pox-marked woman to the earlier woman in the light of the door who is also disfigured, with an eye which is twisted 'like a crooked pin' (l.22). Silvan Tomkins notes the link between the bodily response to an unpleasant smell – 'a literal pulling away from the object' – and the affect of 'contempt-disgust', which he describes as a self-conscious reaction, 'with the most intense consciousness of the object, which is experienced as disgusting'.[37] Disgust clearly intrigued Eliot as an affect for poetry as, in a 1920 essay on Dante, he commended the Italian poet for his ability to render the emotion of disgust: 'The contemplation of the horrid or sordid or disgusting, by an artist, is the necessary and negative aspect of the impulse toward the pursuit of beauty.'[38] Here Eliot seems to follow Kant who, in his *Critique of Judgement*, suggested that disgust is a kind of ugliness which seeks to claim our attention, but which can never be 'regarded as beautiful'.[39] However, as Sianne Ngai notes of this claim, it appears that what makes an object disgusting for Kant is 'precisely its outrageous claim for desirability . . . imposing itself on the subject as something to be mingled with and perhaps even enjoyed'.[40] This paradoxical linking of desire and disgust seems evident in Eliot's poem too: disgust with the disfigured woman both repels and attracts the poem's protagonist, as the repeated references to 'female smells' indicate an obsessive interest in the bodies of women. In another sense, however, the disgust/desire pairing represented here is the city itself, for Eliot believed it both 'necessary and negative' for the modern poet to contemplate and depict that which is 'horrid or sordid or disgusting' in the metropolis. For Eliot, we might say, Paris at night smells like a woman disfigured, an affective state both disgusting and attractive, but ultimately necessary to a poet wishing to modernise himself.

Technology, Boulevards and the *Tour Unique*: Apollinaire and Cendrars

The Parisian street lighting noted in Eliot's 'Rhapsody on a Windy Night' was part of the technological modernity that defined the city's self-presentation as modernist space par excellence. Since the late nineteenth century the commercial status of Paris as the epitome of international modernity had been linked to its engagement with technology, with exhibitions in 1889 and 1900 displaying industrial and architectural innovations pioneered in the city. The exhibitions not only promoted Paris as a key space for modernity, but also encouraged the idea the city itself was an appropriate subject matter for modernist aesthetic representation. In 1909 the politician Guillaume Chastenet stated in the Chamber of Deputies that 'A great city . . . is a work of art. It is a collective and complex art, it is true, but this makes it an even higher form of art.'[41] However, this perception of the city itself as a work of art had its genesis in the massive spatial restructuring of Paris by Baron Haussmann from the mid-nineteenth century onwards.[42] Haussmann's creation of the *grands boulevards* was infused with a vision of Paris as a modern space in which traffic flowed freely around a radial network of city streets; adding to urban aestheticisation, each *grand boulevard* was intended to contain a vista upon a major monument or building of symbolic power, such as the Arc de Triomphe or the Panthéon. Beautifying the city also entailed that industrial production was moved to the edge of the city, with the consequent displacement of some 350,000 people and the demolition of large areas of old Paris inhabited mainly by the working class.[43] 'I have been named artist-demolitionist',[44] proclaimed Haussmann, also noting that his creative destruction led to the 'evisceration of old Paris, of a neighbourhood of riots and barricades'.[45] After the 1848 revolutions across Europe, along with many other populist revolts and riots, Napoleon III supported Haussmann's spatial restructuring of the city to produce what Jones terms a 'form of social discipline' that 'broke up swarming zones of militancy into discrete and more manageable chunks'.[46] Haussmannisation was thus simultaneously a project which turned Paris into a 'work of art' and an attempt to maintain state power through spatial organisation of the city, and the influence of the Baron's vision continued to shape building works in Paris throughout the nineteenth century. This culminated in the 1889 Exposition which offered to the world Paris as the city of modernity, a city whose spatial aesthetic was that pioneered by Haussmann: as Jones notes, at the 1889 Exposition the 'prime exhibit' was the city itself, a 'Haussmannian landscape of power'.[47]

In the early decades of the twentieth century writers and painters in Paris increasingly turned to the modern spaces of the city itself for their subject matter, with the centrepiece of the 1889 Exposition, the Tour Eiffel, becoming a key motif for several of them (see Fig. 1.1).[48] Initially the Tour attracted the ire of figures such as Guy de Maupassant, Alexandre Dumas, J. K. Huysmans and Camille Pissarro: a petition to the Minister of Public Works protested at 'the erection in the heart of our capital of the useless and monstrous Eiffel Tower', arguing that when 'foreigners visit our Exposition . . . they will be right to mock us'.[49] Rather than mock the monstrous erection, however, a number of 'foreign' writers and artists perceived the Tour as a central symbol of Parisian modernity. The Chilean avant-garde poet Vicente Huidobro praised the Tour

Figure 1.1 Georges Garen, *Embrasement de la Tour Eiffel pendant l'Exposition universelle de 1889.*

as a 'guitar of the sky' ('Guitare du ciel') in 1917, while the leading figure of the Russian avant-garde, Vladimir Mayakovsky, wrote a poem in which he wooed the Tower and promised to obtain a visa for it to travel to Moscow.[50]

Some of the most remarkable depictions of the Tour come from three figures often assimilated into the 'French' avant-garde even though they were initially outsiders to it: Guillaume Apollinaire, Blaise Cendrars, and Sonia Delaunay.[51] Apollinaire (Guillaume-Albert-Wladimir-Alexandre-Apollinaire Kostrowitzky) was born in Rome to a Russo-Polish mother and Italian father and arrived in Paris in 1899; Cendrars was born in Switzerland as Frederic-Louis Sauser, assuming the name Cendrars in 1907 when he settled in Paris after spending several years in Russia, Siberia, and New York; while the painter Delaunay was born in the Ukraine to Jewish parents as Sonia Terk and was raised in St Petersburg, travelling to Paris to study art in 1905. For all three the Eiffel Tower proved inspirational and, more generally, their affective responses to Paris resulted in some of the most influential experiments in spatial form within the history of modernism. As 'outsiders' they saw Paris differently, and it was these perceptions of urban space that fed into the startling avant-garde spatial arrangements of their works, demonstrated especially by the typographical experiments of Apollinaire's *Calligrammes* (1918) or the hybrid text/image production of Cendrars and Delaunay's *La Prose du Transsibérien et de la petite Jehanne de France* (1913).

Apollinaire's first major volume of poems, *Alcools* (1913), opened with 'Zone', a poem which loudly proclaimed its embrace of modernity in its famous first line: 'A la fin tu es las de ce monde ancien' ('In the end you're weary of this ancient world').[52] The next line figures the Eiffel Tower as a paradoxical symbol of both the new and the old world of Paris, imagining the Tour as a 'shepherdess' to a 'flock of bridges' bleating in the city ('Bergère ô tour Eiffel le troupeau des ponts bêle ce matin') and bemoaning the fact that the protagonist (and the city too) have 'lived too long in ancient Rome and Greece'. Apollinaire's poem takes the form of a journey through the 'zone' of the city, taking its cue from Baudelaire's *flâneur*, and renders the experience in a disconnected set of impressions. It then shifts to other locations – the Mediterranean, Prague, Rome and Amsterdam – before returning to a Paris of emigrants at the train station, Gare St Lazare, and the Jewish quarter around the Rue des Rosiers; finally, the protagonist walks home to the western suburb of Auteuil.[53] This imagery of travel and of outsiders in the city is part of a textual voyage across space, both external and internal, but also through time, with the antiquated world of the start of the poem being displaced by modern images of aeroplanes and aircraft hangars, buses, and commuters travelling to work. In one memorable image of the old being displaced by the new, Christ's resurrection is figured as an aviator who 'holds the world high altitude record'.[54] The poem's modernity is also shown in its celebration of streets replete with 'billboards and hoardings' ('Les plaques les avis à la façon des perroquets criaillent') and in a eulogy to 'the grace' of an industrial street in the north-west suburbs of the city ('J'aime la grâce de cette rue industrielle').[55]

These fragmentary impressions brilliantly demonstrate the perception of the outsider in the city, captured in Apollinaire's experimental style which employs a variety of long and short unstructured stanzas and an absolute lack of punctuation. In particular, the absence of punctuation tends to produce blocks of text and type more akin to the visual design of painting, an art form which lacks the spatially disruptive markings of grammar for the written word. Some of the impetus for these experiments undoubtedly came from his acquaintance with the Cubists and other modernist painters in Paris,[56] but Apollinaire's interest in creating a new spatial form for his poetry was also a direct response to the spaces of the modern city. In 'Vendémiaire' he expresses a thirsty desire that the 'cities of France Europe the globe / Flow down my wide throat' ('J'ai soif villes de France et d'Europe et du monde / Venez toutes couler dans ma gorge profonde'),[57] and the poem ends with Apollinaire proclaiming himself, 'the gullet of Paris' ('je suis le gosier de Paris') about to produce songs of 'cosmic intoxication' ('mes chants d'universelle ivrognerie').[58]

This ingestion of urban experience culminated in his 1918 collection, *Calligrammes*, which contains a number of typographically experimental poems, positioning the text with an overriding concern for the visual design of the page. In 'Il pleut' ('It's Raining'), for example, the raining of women's voices and other metaphorical senses of raining are displayed vertically as five lines of type aping the fall of literal rain.[59] In such works Apollinaire demonstrates Peter Nicholls' claim that here we see a modernism which conceived of 'modernity less as a content to be represented than as an instigation to *form*'.[60] Nicholls thus argues that Apollinaire, like the Cubist painters and the poet Cendrars, refused the idea that art or language can easily represent the world in a transparent and realistic fashion; instead these poets 'block the illusion of reference by emphasising the material nature of language, the marks and spaces which make up the words on the page'.[61] The spatial forms of Apollinaire's calligrammes are thus intended to 'offer an *experience* of the modern rather than an image of it'.[62] We can usefully link this claim about the experience of modernity embodied in the spatial form of the poems to Raymond Williams' argument, discussed in the Introduction, that the artistic outsider to the metropolis, as Apollinaire was, found a home in the 'community of the medium' or the materiality of words themselves. Experiments with form and the material nature of language were thus stimulated by the very sense of being outsiders in these cities, resulting in the 'productive kinds of strangeness and distance' that Williams refers to as characteristic of metropolitan modernism.[63]

However, at times, the formal innovations stimulated by Apollinaire's metaphorical swallowing of the city of Paris produce poems whose experience of modernity has its origins in the material spaces of the city. This can be seen in the poet's use of the Eiffel Tower in one of the most famous of his 'calligramme' poems. 'Lettre-Océan' was published first in the modernist magazine edited by Apollinaire, *Les Soirées de Paris* (June 1914),[64] and takes the form of two pages dominated by a central spiralling of words, representing a postcard message to 'mon frère Albert' who worked in a bank in Mexico (Fig. 1.2).

The spiral on the left is identified as the Eiffel Tower by the phrase at its centre, which refers to its location on the left bank near the Iena bridge ('Sur la rive gauche devant le pont d'Iena'); in the centre of the image on the left the phrase refers to the height of the Tour ('Haute de 300 mètres'). The other words clustered in the two spirals represent the radio waves emanating from the transmitters of the wireless mast that had been placed on the Tour in 1908. In one sense the poem is about the centrality of the Tour Eiffel and Paris within the space of a global communication network, as the city had recently hosted the International Conference on Time in 1912, which finally provided a uniform system for 'determining and maintaining accurate time signals and transmitting them around the world'.[65] Less than a year before Apollinaire's poem was published the Tour's transmitters sent the first time signal around the world on the morning of 1 July 1913. One French journalist, L. Houllevigue, patriotically welcomed the role of the Tour in positioning Paris once again at the centre of the world after the 1884 Prime Meridian Conference had established Greenwich in London as the zero meridian: now Paris, 'supplanted by Greenwich as the origin of the meridians, was proclaimed the initial time centre, the watch of the universe'.[66] Apollinaire's poem celebrates a similar perception of Paris and the Tour as the geographical centre of temporal modernity. However, as Christopher Butler notes, the 'poem does not simply imitate an object', such as the legs of the Tour in the lines of type radiating from its central point: rather the effect of the visualisation of language here is to make the reader reflect upon how the spatial form 'of a series of messages might affect their meaning'.[67] Once again, we see, in Nicholls' term, an *experience* of the modern rather than just an image of it and an 'instigation' to modernist form: we are meant to reflect not upon the shape of the Tour as a structure, but upon the centrality of its spatial location within the world of modernity. This is perhaps the reason that the point of view upon the Tour in the poem is from a bird's-eye perspective, capturing not only the shape of the Tour but its centrality within the globe itself. Equally, the bold claim of Apollinaire's poem is also to position the formal experiments of the Parisian avant-garde as exemplified by the calligramme of 'Lettre-Océan' at the centre of international modernism.[68]

Apollinaire utilised the outline of the Tour in a second poem, '2e canon-

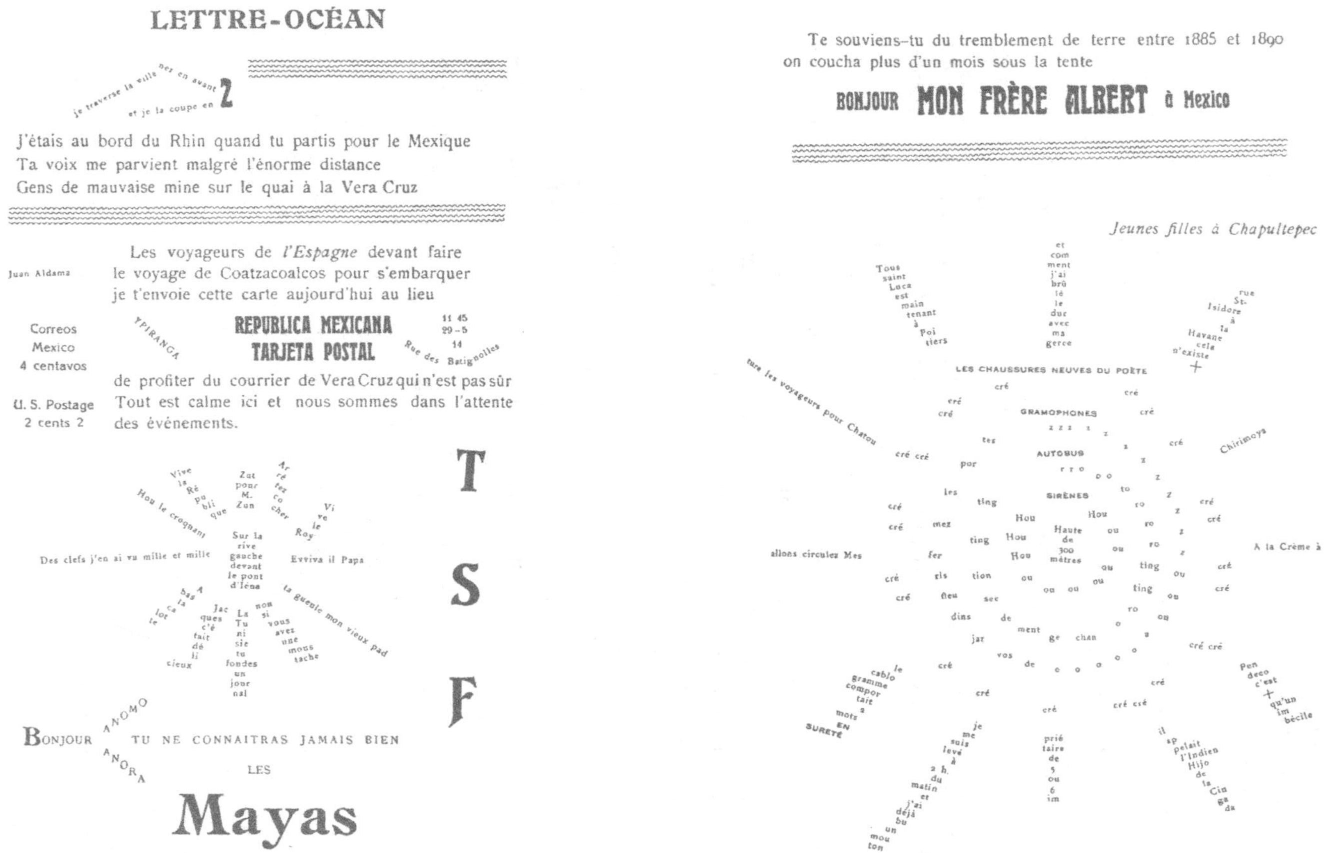

Figure 1.2 G. Apollinaire, 'Lettre-Océan', *Les Soirées de Paris* (June 1914).

nier conducteur', this time viewing it from ground level and symbolising it as an 'eloquent tongue' against the Germans during World War I. A third, conventionally laid-out, poem in *Calligrammes* is a simple paean to the geographical reach of the Tour:

> To the North to the South
> Zenith Nadir
> And the great cries of the East
> The Ocean swells to the West
> The Tower to the Ferris Wheel
> Appeals.[69]

This poem was dedicated to the painter Robert Delaunay, with whom Apollinaire had travelled to Berlin in 1913 to view an exhibition of Delaunay's work. Delaunay had, since around 1910, been engaged in a series of paintings of the Tour, drawing upon the Cubist innovations of Braque and Picasso to present Delaunay's concept of 'simultaneity' or 'simultaneous colours'.[70] However, perhaps the most remarkable illustration of the concept of 'simultaneity' was that produced by Robert's wife, Sonia Delaunay (Terk), in collaboration with Blaise Cendrars, in a text/image book, *La Prose du Transsibérien et de la petite Jehanne de France* (1913), in which the Tour was again a major presence.

La Prose du Transsibérien was composed of a single sheet of paper, divided between a left-hand side on which were found the near-abstract 'simultaneous colours' of Sonia Delaunay's painting, and upon the right-hand side was printed Cendrars' text, itself interspersed with washes of colour and experimental in its varied typography and spacing. The single sheet of paper was folded into twenty-two panels, but when unrolled reached a length of almost seven feet. The book – if it can be called that – was advertised as 'poems, simultaneous colours, in an edition attaining the height of the Eiffel Tower: 150 copies numbered and signed'.[71] By laying the 150 copies end to end the height of the Tour was achieved. The final panel also contains a bare red representation of the Tour, an image which is echoed in the final lines of Cendrars' text: 'Paris / City of the incomparable Tower of the Rack and the Wheel' ('Paris / Ville de la Tour unique du grand Gibet et de la Roue').[72]

The poem itself is, like Apollinaire's 'Zone', a text of travel but a wider geography is embraced, as the poem details the picaresque adventures of Cendrars and his companion Jeanne on the train from Moscow across Siberia and beyond, with references to Fiji, Mexico and New York. In this voyage – part imagined, part biographical as Cendrars had worked for a merchant for three years, travelling across Russia and Siberia – the panorama of world space is anchored back to Paris by the repeated cry of Jeanne: 'Tell me, Blaise, are we very far from Montmartre?'[73] Much like the way that Apollinaire centres the wireless network of 'Lettre-Océan' on the image of the Tour, here the expansive geography of Cendrars' rumbustious text is brought back to Paris in the final section of the poem, a Paris marked by two key locations: 'la Tour unique', symbol of technological modernity, and Montmartre, the key zone for artistic experimentation for writers and artists in the city in the pre-war years. Cendrars' final journey across a Paris figured as a 'Central station last stop of desire crossroads of unrest' is by bus to Montmartre, resulting in a nostalgic final drink in the Lapin Agile, a venue on the Rue des Saules much frequented by the pre-war avant-garde.[74] Although careering wildly across international space the poem finally comes to rest in the unique geography of Parisian modernism.

Marjorie Perloff has offered a brilliant reading of the spatial innovations of *La Prose du Transsibérien,* linking it to the train and the Tour Eiffel as symbols of modernity, and to the status of Cendrars and Sonia Delaunay as outsiders to France, whose work demonstrates a fundamental tension in the European avant-garde between the forces of nationalism and internationalism.[75] Perloff notes how the doctrine of 'simultaneity' in *La Prose* refers at once to the spatial act of reading whereby the reader 'is meant to take in text and image simultaneously: the eye travels back and forth between Delaunay's coloured forms and Cendrars's words', while another sense of the term refers to the 'spatial and temporal distortions' in the poem, which collapse 'past and present, the cities and steppes of the Russian orient and the City of the Tower', producing a text in which 'time is spatialized . . . history gives way to geography'.[76] Perloff also illustrates how Delaunay's images work against some of the textual meaning of the poetic lines, creating a spatial disjuncture in the experience of reading *La Prose* between an internationalist celebration of urban modernity (Delaunay's images) and a foreboding sense that technologies such as the train and the aeroplane are linked to wars between nations (Cendrars' text).[77]

Just before the publication of *La Prose* Cendrars composed another paean to the Eiffel Tower. 'Tour' is initially set in southern Italy in 1910, but then a vision of shocks and 'simultaneous horizons' uproots the poet back to the Tour Eiffel. The Tour yet again occupies a central position in world space: 'on the open sea you are a mast', at the North Pole 'You shine with all the splendour of the aurora borealis of your wireless telegraph.'[78] The Tour is also fancifully located in America, Africa and Australia before a cacophonous finale again celebrates its status:

> Gong tam-tam Zanzibar jungle beast X-rays express scalpel symphony
> You are everything
> Tower
> Ancient god

Modern beast
Solar spectrum
Subject of my poem
Tower
Globe-encircling tower
Tower in motion[79]

Once more the Tour is a symbol of the supremacy of Parisian modernity, collapsing time (both ancient and modern) and encircling the globe. After the random and meaningless signifiers of the first line here ('Gong tam-tam Zanzibar'), the dominant meaning of the Tour is stressed in the assonance of the next lines: 'Tu est tous / Tour' ('You are everything / Tower').

In a 1924 essay on the Tour and Delaunay's paintings, which also contains a brief account of visiting the elderly Gustav Eiffel, Cendrars boasts that in 1910–11 only Robert Delaunay and himself in Paris were 'talking about machines and art and with a vague awareness of the great transformation of the modern world'.[80] The essay suggests that the formal experiments of modernist painters and writers in Paris were profoundly linked to the experience of the modern metropolis and, in particular, to the significance of the Tour Eiffel:

> I talk to him [Delaunay] about New York, Berlin, Moscow, about prodigious centres of industrial activity spread out over the whole surface of the earth, about the new life being formed . . . and that tall youth, who had never left Paris and was only interested in questions of form and colour, had guessed all that while he was contemplating the Tower.[81]

For the well-travelled Cendrars the mysteries of modernity and modernism exemplified in the 'new life' of cities around the world were thus resolved in one site in Paris: 'Tu est tous / Tour'.

Hope Mirrlees on the Metro

Both Apollinaire and Cendrars were poets whose status as 'outsiders' in Paris changed over time. Writing in French they become 'consecrated', to use Bourdieu's term, as figures of high literary value (or symbolic capital) within French modernism.[82] In contrast to what Peter Gay describes as the 'inside-outsiders' of German modernism – born in the cities of Berlin and Vienna but forever marked as 'outside' by some facet of their identities, such as being Jewish (see Chapters 2 and 3) – Apollinaire and Cendrars appear in Paris as 'outsiders' who, in the international crucible of the Parisian avant-garde, became rapidly transformed into 'outside-insiders'.

Hope Mirrlees was more obviously a foreign outsider to Paris, an English writer who, until recently, appears nowhere on a modernist version of Bourdieu's field of cultural production. She does not appear, for instance, in

Shari Benstock's seminal *Women of the Left Bank* (1986).[83] In 2007 Julia Briggs, introducing an edition of Mirrlees' major poem, *Paris* (1919), described her as a 'forgotten maker' of modernism and her poem as 'modernism's lost masterpiece'.[84] Some of her disappearance was due to the fact that locating Mirrlees within existing networks of modernism has proved somewhat difficult. The poem was published by Virginia and Leonard Woolf's Hogarth Press but, unlike the relationship between Virginia Woolf and Katherine Mansfield, there is little evidence of sustained discussion between Woolf and Mirrlees.[85] Woolf's most famous comment on the poem was that it was 'a very obscure, indecent and brilliant poem'.[86] Mirrlees also knew T. S. Eliot but, again, there is little evidence of intellectual dialogue between the two.

In some ways the poem *Paris* might be said to have emerged directly from the spaces of the city. Along with her partner, the Cambridge anthropologist Jane Harrison, Mirrlees spent considerable amounts of time in Paris between 1913 and 1925. And while it is difficult, as Sandeep Parmar notes, to determine any direct evidence of Mirrlees being influenced by French avant-garde writers such as Apollinaire or Cendrars, she did acknowledge the impact of Jean Cocteau's poem *Le Cap de Bonne-Espérance*.[87] Mirrlees and Harrison were also members of Sylvia Beach's English-language bookshop on the Left Bank, Shakespeare and Company, which along with its sister-shop across the road, Adrienne Monnier's La Maison des Amis des Livres, were important cultural institutions for disseminating both French and Anglophone modernism, especially for expatriates.[88]

Clearly, as both Briggs and Parmar acknowledge, features such as its use of white space on the page, typographical experiments, the layering of temporalities, and a switching between inner and outer space all mark *Paris* as a text aware of the experiments of the French avant-garde.[89] However, in another sense, it could be said that the geography and history of the city are equally responsible for the startling originality of Mirrlees' poem. In a revealing description, Katherine Mansfield commented that she thought Mirrlees was 'a foreigner who knows her Paris – *from within*'.[90] This intriguingly positions Mirrlees as another 'outside-insider' to the city, shown in the many references in the poem to key locations, people and events in the city, such as the Tuileries and the Louvre; the houses where Molière, Voltaire, and Chateaubriand died (ll.354–65); politicians such as Gambetta (l.34) and Clemenceau; paintings by Manet and David depicting the revolutions of 1789 and 1848 (ll.290–1); and the context of two key contemporary events in the history of the city, the Paris Peace Conference of 1919 and the General Strike held in the city on 1 May (ll.235–59).[91] This latter event is represented in one of the most striking experiments with spatial form of the poem, as a line of individual letters appear vertically on the page:

The first of May
T
h
e
r
e

i
s

n
o

l
i
l
y

o
f

t
h
e

v
a
l
l
e
y (ll.235–59)

Briggs glosses how the displacement of the standard horizontal line by the vertical line can be interpreted as a symbol of how the strike disrupts the normality of Parisian life (as lilies were often given on May Day to friends) or, alternatively, as a representation of the lines of marching strikers, punningly referred to in the later line, 'silence of *la grève*' (l.263), where the French word *grève* refers both to the strike and to the location on the river bank, Place de *Grève*, where the strikers assembled.[92] The spatial form here seems indebted to Apollinaire's calligrammes but her gender, and possibily her sexuality, distinguish Mirrlees from the Apollinaire/Cendrars axis of the avant-garde: as Briggs aptly notes, Mirrlees was a 'sympathetic outsider, writing of a French city in a French style evolved by an almost exclusively masculine artistic group'.[93]

There is a sly nod to the men of the French avant-garde in the second line of the poem ('I want a holophrase / NORD-SUD'), with its reference to a journey on the Metro line Nord-Sud, which had opened in November 1910 and which ran north–south connecting the two cultural quarters of Montparnasse and Montmartre; however, *Nord-Sud* was also the name of a modernist magazine edited by Pierre Reverdy in 1917–18.[94] *Nord-Sud*'s geographical title signalled, as Simon Dell notes, 'an ambition to link various elements of the Parisian avant-garde', but the central presence was Apollinaire, who contributed a poem to almost every issue and mourned its passing in a later poem.[95] It is quite likely that Mirrlees knew of the magazine from its availability in the bookshops of Monnier and Beach.[96] In addition to Apollinaire the contributors were almost exclusively male representatives of the Parisian avant-garde, including Louis Aragon, Georges Braque, André Breton, Paul Dermée, Max Jacob, Fernand Léger, Philippe Soupault and Tristan Tzara. It is also tempting to view the initial line of the poem ('I want a holophrase') as a desire to find a voice within the masculine avant-garde of Paris as articulated in a journal such as *Nord-Sud*. 'Holophrase' was a term used by Jane Harrison to refer to a single word which stood for an entire phrase or complex of ideas, and was characteristic of language in a primitive stage of development.[97] Did Mirrlees think that her poem, with its own version of avant-garde experimentation, was at an early stage? Or did she fear it was merely a 'hollow phrase' in comparison to the more advanced words of the male poets found in *Nord-Sud*? The 'want' or need for the holophrase can thus be interpreted as an appeal for a feminine take on the avant-garde writers of *Nord-Sud*, for her phrases to be heard rather than regarded as empty or hollow.

It is interesting, too, that the poem starts with something of a rejection of the male tradition of the *flâneur*, by initially exploring the experience of the *voyageur* on the Metro, flashing through stations at the Rue du Bac and Solférino, full of advertisements for modern consumers (see the references to Dubonnet, shoe polish and drinking chocolate). According to Briggs the poem also attempts to capture the sound of the rattling Metro carriages in a line which quotes, too, from Aristophanes, combining past and present in one textual location: 'Brekekekek coax coax we are passing under the Seine' (l.10).[98] And though the poem initially tracks the Nord-Sud line between the avant-garde quartiers of Montparnasse and Montmartre, the geography that it depicts once the protagonist exits from the Metro at Place de la Concorde (l.17) is more central to the city, being located mainly on the Right Bank around the Louvre, Tuileries and Grands Boulevards (ll.198–234) and then upon the 7th arrondissement on the Left Bank around the Rue de Beaune where Mirrlees and Harrison were staying (the hotel referred to in l.319). Mirrlees' rejection of the bohemian zones at either end of the Nord-Sud metro line (though there is a brief reference to the Moulin Rouge nightclub near Montmartre) signals her detachment from male French avant-garde formations, but also fits certain of the themes of the poem itself, with its focus on the political repercussions of World War I (there is much reference to the French dead in the poem) and the subsequent Peace Conference and General Strike. Much of the geography figured in the poem is thus not the marginal bohemian zones of the avant-garde north and south, but the establishment spaces of French public life in the centre of the city, such as the Louvre museum, Haussmann's Grands Boulevards, the Place de la Concorde (site of the guillotine during the Revolution) or statues of political figures such as that of Gambetta positioned then outside the Louvre (l.34). References to French imperialism also run throughout the poem, linking Parisian sites to the spaces of empire, as in the 'ZIG-ZAG' (l.3) cigarette paper advertised in the Metro, which features a 'Zouave' or Algerian soldier in its imagery, or the mention of 'Algerian tobacco' and the blue and red uniform of the Zoaves (ll.203–4).[99] The French Empire is implicitly contrasted to the Roman Empire in several places, as when the Arc de Triomphe is described as 'Square and shadowy like Julius Caesar's dreams' (l.56); significantly, Mirrlees is unenthusiastic about this site: 'I hate the Etoile' (l.60).

The Grands Boulevards on the Right Bank, those symbols of Haussmann's modernisation of the city, also produce an ambivalent set of affects in the poem. While it is said to be 'pleasant to sit on the Grand Boulevards' the primary affect of this space is of an assault upon the senses, recalling Eliot's identification of smell with disgust in 'Rhapsody on a Windy Night':

> They smell of
>   Cloacae
> Hot indiarubber
>   Poudre de riz
> Algerian tobacco (ll.199–203)

Fragments of sounds of the speakers in the streets or cafés also appear here, from 'YANKEES' (who may be Black American servicemen, according to Briggs) to people with 'Lizard-eyes' jabbering about cheese ('Ouiouioui, c'est passionnant . . . /Le fromage n'est pas un plat logique' (l.220)). The conclusion to the section on the Boulevards seems to represent Mirrlees as being somewhat overwhelmed by the spaces of the city here, struggling to turn the vivid sensory affects of the city into poetry:

>   Cell on cell
>   Experience
>   Very slowly
>   Is forming up
> Into something beautiful – awful – huge
>
>   The coming to. . . . . .
> Thick halting speech – the curse of vastness. (ll.228–32)

The spatial form of the text here enacts the attempt of the poet to turn disconnected urban images ('cell on cell') in very short lines into longer lines of something 'beautiful'; but the speech is 'halting' and breaks down ('The coming to . . . '), recalling the poem's opening fear of merely producing a 'hollow phrase'. The 'vastness' of the spaces of the street may provoke affects of fear or the sublime ('awful – huge'), but seemingly they cannot easily be represented in the textual space of the page. Rather than being impressed by the grandeur of the Haussmann boulevards the affect of these modern spaces veers more towards the phobic.[100]

'Paris' is a complex and fascinating response to the city, and in its layering of past and present, history and mythology, as well as its explorations of sexuality, recalls Eliot's *The Waste Land*, a poem which might possibly have been influenced by Mirrlees' earlier text.[101] Regardless of any such line of influence, Mirrlees' text certainly deserves further discussion and analysis. In some ways the experiments with spatial form that she produces might be said to spring as much from her affective response to the spaces of the city as they do from her reading in the French or Russian avant-garde (Mirrlees and Harrison studied Russian in Paris, including the works of Mayakovsky).[102] Living in a foreign city and studying a language – Russian – that is also alien to the place one lives, the 'strangeness and distance' of Mirrlees' text seem to have appeared from her encounter as a resolute outsider with the sights, sounds and smells of the city streets, as much as from any reading in poets such as Apollinaire or Cendrars.

Jean Rhys: Being Faithful to Paris

The year 1919 was when Mirrlees published her poem on Paris; it was also the year in which Jean Rhys first visited the city, before she returned in 1922, to remain in the city until sometime in 1928.[103] Rhys was a supreme literary cartographer of Paris, exploring the city as a white colonial outsider from the Caribbean island of Dominica, and whose fiction, amongst other topics, explores the themes of the gendering of city spaces, commodification, and prostitution.[104] Unlike Mirrlees, Rhys did not enjoy the wealth and status that allowed her to live without financial worries in Paris. And, crucially, as a woman Rhys was an outsider to the tradition of the male *flâneur* within the streets of Paris, as theorised in writers on the city such as Walter Benjamin and André Breton.[105] In a sense Rhys' work offers something of a critique of the idea of woman as commodity, or at least a resistance to the strain of thought running through much of the theory of the *flâneur*, that the woman on the streets of Paris is a merely a commodity for male pleasure and consumption. Her depiction of women in the city is also marked by a fascinating attention to affect and geographical emotions, linking the experience of urban space to innovations in literary form and style.

Paris played a key role in Rhys' geographical imagination, and was the setting for her first volume of short stories, *The Left Bank* (1927), and for two of her novels, *Quartet* (1928) and *Good Morning, Midnight* (1939), and a key location in another novel, *After Leaving Mr Mackenzie* (1930). For Rhys as for the other writers discussed in this chapter, the city played a pivotal role in her transformation into a modernist writer. In later life she described her first visit to Paris as a trip to 'a known world – a déjà-vu world' and wrote that she had 'been very faithful and never really loved any other city'.[106] Paris produced a powerful affective relationship for Rhys, one that contrasts with her largely negative feelings for London, to which she was sent as a colonial migrant by her family in 1907.[107] The enduring strength of her attachment to the French capital is demonstrated in a comment from 1959: 'When I say I write for love I mean that there are two places for me. Paris (or what it was to me) and Dominica.'[108] The intensity of this feeling resurfaces when she later criticises the accounts of 'Americans in Paris' presented by writers like Ernest Hemingway and Henry Miller for being about the expatriates, rather than about Parisians: 'As soon as the tourists came the *real* Montparnos packed up and left. . . . And if I saw something of the other Paris – it's only left me with a great longing which I'll never satisfy again.'[109] Here love has been replaced by a kind of melancholy attachment to a lost location, a mood (*Stimmung*) that runs through much of Rhys' Paris fictions, as when the sound of a concertina playing a popular song in *Quartet* produces in the heroine, Marya Zelli, 'the same feeling of melancholy pleasure as she had when walking along the shadowed side of one of those narrow streets full of shabby perfumeries, second-hand book-stalls, cheap hat-shops, bars frequented by gaily-painted ladies and loud-voiced men, midwives' premises'.[110]

Quartet fictionalises Rhys' affair with the writer Ford Madox Ford and her failing first marriage to Jean Lenglet, with the fourth character in the 'quartet' being Ford's first wife, Stella Bowen.[111] Ford had criticised Rhys' first publication, *The Left Bank*, for its supposed lack of topographic detail, and *Quartet* appears to rebut that charge in the precision of its geographical references.[112] Almost every café, restaurant and street can be located on a map of Paris, and just as Marya's life is said to sway 'between two extremes, avoiding the soul-destroying middle',[113] so the novel oscillates between two key Parisian geographies, as connected by the Nord-Sud metro line of Mirrlees' *Paris*:[114] Montmartre, on the Right Bank, and Montparnasse, on the Left Bank. Montmartre is associated with Marya's husband, Stephan, a petty thief who has lived in the quartier for fifteen years. Initially we find Marya and Stephan in a 'cheap Montmartre hotel' that lacked 'solidity', the Hotel de l'Univers, Rue Cauchois, not far from the Moulin Rouge.[115] Marya's sensitivity to her location frequently takes the form of an affective geography of her environment. Her sense of Montmartre is of 'the dingy streets, the vegetable shops kept by sleek-haired women, the bars haunted by gaily dressed little prostitutes . . . Over the whole of the quarter the sinister and rakish atmosphere of the Faubourg Montmartre spread like some perfume.'[116] Like Eliot, Marya is very attuned to smell and other sensory impressions in the city, as with this description of the view from her Hotel de l'Univers window out onto the Place Blanche and Rue Lepic running up the hill to Montmartre:

> It was astonishing how significant, coherent and understandable it all became after a glass of wine on an empty stomach.
>
> The lights winking up at a pallid moon, the slender painted ladies, the wings of the Moulin Rouge, the smell of petrol and perfume and cooking.
>
> The Place Blanche, Paris. Life itself. One realized all sorts of things. The value of an illusion, for instance, and that the shadow can be more important than the substance.[117]

The fragmented, impressionistic prose here seems to undercut the initial claim to make the city 'coherent and understandable', as Marya realises the value of illusions and the sexual commodification of women, symbolised by the 'painted ladies' of the Moulin Rouge nightclub. Marya's own surname, Zelli, was perhaps suggested by another famous venue, Au Zelli's topless bar and club in nearby Pigalle.[118] Her sense of the 'hazards of Montmartre'[119] at the start of the novel are fulfilled when the novel ends back on the Right Bank, in an apartment in a 'dilapidated house in the Rue Bleue', in the 9th arrondissement, near to another Parisian site of illusions, the Folies Bergère.[120] The apartment, which grotesquely has enlarged photos on the walls, produces a feeling of terror in Marya, 'the terror of being left alone in that sinister, dusty-smelling room with the enlarged photographs of young men . . . smirking down at her'.[121] In the final pages of the novel Marya tells Stephan of her affair with Heidler (the Ford character in the novel), they quarrel and he hits her, leaving her unconscious on the floor of a room while he departs.

The second prominent geography in the novel is that of the Left Bank of Montparnasse, the centre of artistic and cultural Paris in the 1920s, where Ford Madox Ford, the real-life Heidler, edited the *transatlantic review*, in which magazine Rhys was first published.[122] Nicholas Hewitt has shown how it is necessary to be careful when tracing those Parisian locations that became areas of important cultural production.[123] Understanding the significance of the Parisian Left Bank for the geography of modernism requires a sensitive delimitation of how, for example, specific cafés and restaurants became important meeting points for writers, artists and intellectuals. Hewitt argues that twentieth-century Left Bank culture is divided between two significant traditions: an intellectual and academic circle linked to the institutions of higher education and publishing houses; and a second, bohemian tradition. While the first tradition remains relatively stable in its geography, the second shifts across the city, and is linked to factors such as changing patterns of migration, centres of entertainment and pleasure, areas around railway stations, the availability of cheap accommodation, and what he terms 'the indispensable frontier between the bourgeois city and the *classes dangereuses* that constitute the marginal space in which bohemian activity takes place.'[124] This bohemian tradition became established around Montmartre by 1900, continued here up till the outbreak of war, and was then re-established around Montparnasse after 1918. Montparnasse, however, was eclipsed after 1929, and the cultural centre of the 1930s shifted back to the Latin Quarter and the academic and publishing institutions of St Germain.[125] Rhys shows a keen awareness of this cultural history in her fiction, as when the narrator of her early short story 'In the Rue de l'Arrivée' notes that 'Montparnasse, that stronghold of the British and American middle classes, was a devil of a place and what Montmartre used to be.'[126]

The popularity of Montparnasse in the 1920s can thus be traced back to the spatial history of Paris as a whole. Hewitt shows how the creation in 1784 of the so-called 'tax-collectors wall' (*Mur des Fermiers Généraux*) around the entire city split Paris into two areas: one area within the wall had high taxes on such items as alcohol, while the other area, outside of the wall that ran along the outer boulevards such as the Boulevard du Montparnasse, lacked such taxes. Because of this difference the areas around the entries to the inner city, the *barrières* or customs posts, became zones of pleasure, populated by dance halls (such as the Bal Bullier) and places to drink and eat (for example, the Closerie des Lilas).[127] As Hewitt notes, the 'geography of pleasure in the nineteenth- and twentieth-century city is closely allied to the Wall'.[128]

The geography of Montparnasse is thus something of a shorthand for the cultural pleasures of Paris in the 1920s, with literary cafés such as the Dôme, the Select, the Rotonde and the Closerie de Lilas featuring as key sites frequented by American and British expatriate writers in accounts such as that of Hemingway's memoir, *A Moveable Feast*. Rhys' novel does contain some scenes set in this milieu, such as when Marya meets various artists in Lefranc's restaurant on Boulevard du Montparnasse (a venue for Ford's literary gatherings in 1925), including a bohemian woman, Lola Hewitt (possibly Nina Hamnett), and a Mr Porson who invites her to 'a literary gathering at the Café Lavenue' with the writers 'Rolls and Boyes', names which sound suspiciously like Joyce, who was also a habitué of these venues.[129] Marya, however, always seems semi-detached from this environment, as in the scene in the Bal du Printemps, where she agrees with Lois Heidler that the Café Dôme was 'a dreadful place',[130] a judgement shared by Hemingway.[131] However, while Hemingway, along with many other male writers, eulogised the habit of sitting and writing in cafés such as the Closerie de Lilas (a place Marya visits briefly), Marya's only significant writing in a café is an abject letter to Heidler asking for money – and this is composed in a café in Nice, not Paris.[132]

The opening page of *Quartet* is set in a Montparnasse café, but Rhys' treatment of this space differs from that, say, of Hemingway in *The Sun Also Rises*

(1927), where Jake Barnes appears at ease in the many cafés of the quarter. Chapter 6 of the first part of Hemingway's novel is set almost entirely within two cafés, the Select and the Dôme, situated opposite one another on the Boulevard du Montparnasse. Barnes takes a taxi to the Select and muses on the pleasures of Paris ('The river looked nice. It was always pleasant crossing bridges in Paris') and why another American character in the novel, Robert Cohn, was incapable of enjoying the city.[133] The taxi stops outside another café, the Rotonde, and Barnes wanders 'past the sad tables of the Rotonde to the Select'.[134] The rest of the chapter consists of extended conversations between the novel's central characters within the cafés: in a sense the characters occupy the space comfortably and are clearly at ease here, and their status as foreign nationals is not marked in any way. This is thus a location in which the characters feel located, a place of belonging.

Marya's experience in another café on the same road, the Lavenue, offers a quite different engagement with social space. Unlike Hemingway's characters, Marya has been sitting alone for an hour and a half, drinking coffee, smoking cigarettes and reading a magazine. Her lack of companions here already marks her as something of an outsider. After a short physical description of Marya we learn that she is often approached by 'shabby youths' on the Boulevards St Michel and Montparnasse, where they would 'glide up to her and address her hopefully in unknown and spitting tongues'. Marya replies to them in English 'I'm very sorry; I don't understand what you are saying.'[135] The incidents represent Marya's relation to Parisian space in two ways: first, she is routinely perceived as a sexual commodity, whether as a prostitute or a single woman available for being picked up; second, the 'unknown' tongues, and Marya's reply in English, mark her (and possibly the youths) as linguistic outsiders in the city, even though Marya does understand French. She then leaves the café and walks along the Rue de Rennes, which depresses her as it reminds her of Tottenham Court Road in London: here Rhys demonstrates her acute sense of geographical emotions, with certain streets or sites producing very deeply felt sensations in her heroines. To 'distract herself' Marya stops to look at a 'red felt hat in a shop window'. Fashion and its display in windows are a key trope in Rhys' writings, and situate her heroines, who are themselves often commodified by men in her novels, in a complex relationship to the commodity culture of Parisian fashion.[136] As Andrea Zemgulys notes in another context, Rhys' work shows how 'women, specifically poor women, manage the market as a system of exchange that structures the world and values them for their exchangeability as things'.[137] Thus this opening page brilliantly sets a scene for a novel exploring the multiple affects of geography, female sexuality in the city, commodification, and the experience of being a linguistic outsider in the city. Unlike the characters in *The Sun Also Rises*, Marya never quite settles in the spaces of cafés or the Montparnasse streets, and is unable to turn abstract social spaces into places of belonging because she is repeatedly identified as an outsider and commodified for her sexuality.

The most significant Montparnasse location for Marya is thus not the exterior space of a famous café, but the interior space of a hotel where she conducts her affair with Heidler. This is not, for instance, the celebrated Hotel Unic of the Rue du Montparnasse, used by Robert McAlmon, Harriet Shaw Weaver and William Carlos Williams, but the shabby and unknown Hotel du Bosphore which overlooks Montparnasse railway station, a suitable symbol of the transitory nature of Marya's belonging in the city.[138] The hotel has little charm and instead is characterised by the kind of sordid affects of smell and disgust that so appealed to Eliot: the hotel possessed an 'extraordinary mixture of smells. Drains, face powder, scent, garlic, drains. Above all, drains.'[139] Rhys frequently stresses her characters' affective and sensory response to spatiality, with much attention focused upon the interiors of rooms. In the hotel Marya is more or less a sexual commodity for Heidler, a state that the space of the room itself exudes: an 'atmosphere of departed and ephemeral loves hung about the bedroom like stale scent, for the hotel was one of unlimited hospitality', that is a place where a 'succession of petites femmes . . . had extended themselves' on the bed.[140] Even the wallpaper echoes Marya's allotted role in this space: the 'wallpaper was vaguely erotic – huge and fantastically shaped mauve, green and yellow flowers sprawling on a black ground'.[141] Later, when Marya is unable to sleep, the eroticism of the room turns more malevolent, and she imagines that the flowers 'crawled like spiders over the black walls of her bedroom'.[142] When she tries to avoid thinking about 'the utter mess of her love affair' and the 'utter mess of her existence', these ugly feelings of shame and self-loathing viscerally overwhelm her: 'her obsession gripped her, arid, torturing, gigantic, possessing her as utterly as the longing for water possesses someone who is dying of thirst'.[143] Marya's affective response merges into the space of her room and she thinks, 'A bedroom in hell might look rather like this one. Yellow-green and dullish mauve flowers crawling over black walls.'[144] The shift from 'sprawling' to 'crawling' seems significant as a comment on Marya's own emotional state, despairing at her abject relationship, wondering if love was 'this perpetual aching longing, this wound that bled persistently and very slowly'.[145] Rather than sprawling on the bed, Marya seems now to be crawling around in this 'melancholy bedroom' as the affair becomes increasingly masochistic, with Heidler calling her a 'savage', while she lies 'quivering and abject in his arms, like some unfortunate dog abashing itself before its master'.[146] The different sensitivities shown to the spatial environment of the hotel by Marya and Heidler (who after sex returns to his more comfortable apartment) is summed up when Marya tries to explain to him how miserable she feels: 'Don't you understand that I hate this *louche* hotel and the bedroom and the wallpaper and the whole situation, and my whole life?' Heidler's droll response is '"Why don't you change your hotel?"'[147] Even in Montparnasse rather than Montmartre Marya cannot find 'solidity', that is, an affective belonging in the city, a situation which no change of hotel can remedy.

Rhys' sensitivity to Parisian spaces is continued in *After Leaving Mr Mackenzie* (1930) which concerns a solitary female heroine, Julia Martin, who drifts between cheap accommodation in London and Paris, and has a number of unsuccessful relationships with men and a rather more successful relationship with alcohol. Rhys' depiction of both cities is again very precise: five of the chapter titles in *After Leaving Mr Mackenzie* are toponyms.[148] However, the representational space of Paris in the novel can be understood in two ways: first, in terms of how Rhys represents certain spaces and the meanings attached to particular locations; and second, how certain formal features of her text – such as narrative form and literary style – are influenced by a geographical encounter with these cities. Combining these two aspects helps offer an understanding of the textual space of Rhys' work.

In the past Jean Rhys has often seemed to fall off the metaphoric map of modernism, but more recent scholarship has positioned her centrally within debates on the geography of modernism, as well as other aspects of modernism.[149] Peculiarly, she also drifts away from the revisionist map of modernist women writers discussed in Shari Benstock's influential guide, *Women of the Left Bank*.[150] This is a fact that Benstock is aware of, arguing that like 'the women of her fiction, Jean Rhys did not find a place for herself on the literary Left Bank; she was an outsider among outsiders'.[151] However, the geographical marginality of Rhys' heroines is not quite as clear-cut as Benstock makes out. True, Benstock mostly discusses the novel *Good Morning, Midnight*, but it does seem that a number of the key locations for Julia Martin in *After Leaving Mr Mackenzie* offer rather more complex relations to the literary Left Bank of the 1920s. For example, the two hotels in which Julia stays, shabby as they might be, are located on the Quai des Grand Augustins overlooking the Seine, and an unnamed hotel (possibly the Hotel Henri IV in the Place Dauphine) situated on the Île de la Cité. Neither site is perhaps exactly within the Latin Quarter or St Germain; but they are certainly not in the 'mean and uninteresting streets' of the more distant 13th Arrondissement to which Benstock assigns Rhys' heroines.[152] We also learn that Julia pays 16 francs for her room in the Hotel St Raphael on the Quai: it is described as a cheap, 'lowdown sort of place', but Julia likes the room as somewhere in which to hide, locking the door to feel safe. The novel is set c. 1925,[153] and Baedeker's guide to *Paris et ses environs* of 1924 indicates that a 16–franc hotel room is certainly not at the luxury end of the market – rooms at the Ritz start at 50 francs. But neither is it the cheapest that the conservative Baedeker recommends for this area (or other quartiers). The Hotel de Quai-Voltaire, just westward along the left bank of the Seine from Julia's hotel, is said to have rooms for 10 francs; some *maisons de famille* establishments offer rooms for 6 francs.[154]

Julia Martin's marginal relationship to the pleasurable pastures of Montparnasse is, therefore, complicated. Her hotel on the Quai overlooking the Seine is certainly away from the centre of Montparnasse life, if we define it, as Hemingway did in *A Moveable Feast*, as 'the cafés at the corner of the boulevard Montparnasse and the boulevard Raspail'.[155] Again, if we look at where Julia eats and drinks we notice that she has an ambiguous relationship to certain areas. In the first section of the novel she lunches in a German restaurant in the Rue de la Huchette, centrally in the Latin Quarter. After receiving a final sum of money from her former lover Mr Mackenzie she tries to find him by walking along the Boulevard St Michel to his flat; she then spies him walking into the Restaurant Albert on Boulevard Montparnasse. Julia thus moves through the 'right' area, but has a tendency to be found, unlike the men in the novel, in unnamed streets and cafés. For example, a young Englishman, George Horsfield, notices Julia's altercation with Mackenzie in the Restaurant Albert and then decides to befriend Julia. After finishing his meal Horsfield walks past the Dôme and the Rotonde and goes into the Select Bar for a drink. As noted earlier these are all celebrated Montparnasse cultural sites: Hart Crane was famously arrested in the Dôme in 1929,[156] while another American writer, Harold Stearns, described the Select as 'a seething madhouse of drunks, semi-drunks, quarter-drunks and the sober maniacs'.[157] But Julia Martin – never one to avoid a drink or three – eschews these glittery locations and Horsfield only finds her in some nearby but anonymous bar.[158]

In *Quartet* Rhys was very particular about the names of streets, cafés and restaurants, so when Julia enters an anonymous location it is somehow all the more striking. Her preference for such places is perhaps linked to her own deracinated status: early on we learn that her life has 'rubbed most of the hallmarks off her, so that is was not easy to guess at her age, her nationality, or the social background to which she properly belonged'.[159] None of the cafés or restaurants that Julia enters alone are named in the book; this contrasts strongly with those encountered in *Quartet*. Unlike the writers and artists depicted in the earlier novel, Julia does not belong to such circles and feels less comfortable in the more famous cafés frequented by literary habitués. Julia goes for a walk every day after lunch, but 'was so anxious not to meet anybody she knew that she always kept to the back streets as much as possible' and when she 'passed the café terraces her face would assume a hard forbidding expression'.[160]

The final section of the novel finds Julia back in Paris after a sojourn in London and, again, her location is not marginal, but significant in terms of the novel's literary geography. Her hotel is on the Île de la Cité, set between the left and right banks of the Seine. This island is an in-between space, a geographical microcosm of Julia's own position in the text, shuttling between Paris and

London, and between the two male lovers, Mackenzie and Horsfield. Julia decides to go to Montparnasse after dinner, a plan that is soon abandoned (after two more brandies in an unnamed café). Now she decides that she 'only wanted to walk somewhere straight ahead'[161] and crosses from the Place St Michel on the Left Bank over the river to the Place du Châtelet. But Châtelet is a 'nightmare' and she turns left and walks 'into a part of the city which was unknown to her', somewhere near the back of the Halles market, she thinks.[162] Julia stops, thinking 'I've gone too far', and sits at another café terrace, for yet another brandy.

There is a sense in which these chapters, where Julia wanders from the island to the Left Bank and then tries to go 'straight ahead', are geographical metaphors for her own life in the novel. For she ends where she began, meeting Mackenzie in a café, asking him for money, and saying that she has now left the Île de la Cité hotel for the Quai des Grands Augustins hotel mentioned at the start of the novel. This novel, like other Rhys novels, employs a circular narrative structure; Julia is unable to go 'straight ahead' and her attempt to escape from the Left Bank into some unknown part of the city fails. As a *flâneuse*, we might say, Julia is a bit of a failure, echoing what Rachel Bowlby terms the 'negative *flâneuse*' of Sasha Jensen in Rhys' later novel, *Good Morning, Midnight*. Rhys' protagonists, notes Bowlby, tread the streets to fill in empty time rather than to take pleasurable strolls through London as exhibited in, say, Woolf's *Mrs Dalloway*.[163]

Another way to read the significance of the Île de la Cité location is in terms of Rhys' own island home in the Caribbean, Dominica.[164] Historically the island had been exchanged between the colonial powers of Britain and France, and Rhys' life after she left Dominica seemed to repeat some of this division between different nationalities. *After Leaving Mr Mackenzie* enacts this partition at the level of its narrative shape, with Julia shuffling between Paris and London, and also between the two languages, another important division replicated in Dominica's official English and the French-based Creole spoken by most islanders.

Towards the end of the novel Julia notes of her visit to London that it had been 'a disconnected episode to be placed with all the other disconnected episodes which made up her life'.[165] Her narrative life is indeed disconnected and the novel figures this geographically by switching between London and Paris, and her location (living seems somehow too strong a word here) at four addresses within a few weeks. The conclusion to the previous chapter sees Mr Horsfield return to his house in London's more affluent Holland Park, finally having decided not to help Julia again. As he shuts the door he realises that he has also 'shut out the thought of Julia', while his own home 'enveloped him' in a 'familiar world'.[166] This sense of inner domestic space as comforting and familiar is not available to Julia and she is destined never to be enveloped in such a *place*; rather she is always ready to move on to another *space*, as in the next chapter's journey to Paris. Indeed the image of a journey between different locations is perhaps the dominant one in Rhys' fiction, shown in the manner in which her protagonists shift from one grubby lodging house to the next.

The novel's title suggests a story of the *time after* leaving a man; but the action often appears to revolve around the spaces moved through; *leaving* becomes a description not just of her emotional state after the relationship with Mackenzie, but of the various journeys in the novel. As the narrator comments of Julia, 'It was always places that she thought of, not people.'[167] But just as her relationships to men are perpetually doomed, so her relationships to places are always subject to eventual disconnection. Disconnection, however, is a term that can be applied not only to Julia Martin's relationship to place, but also to the spatial style of the novel. Perhaps the most noticeable spatial feature of Rhys' texts is their peculiarly fragmented and discrete appearance on the page. Visually, the pages of Rhys' novels seem full of blank space, an effect reinforced by her tendency to use numerous single-sentence paragraphs and multiple sections to chapters. Another spatial style is her use of line spaces or gaps between passages of prose. The effect of this heterotopic writing is thus to render her texts as disconnected mosaics, containing piecemeal images of her characters' lives that parallel the disjointed experience of different material geographies. One striking instance of how geography inscribes itself within the spatiality of the text is the image on the first page of the novel, a card for the Hotel St Raphael (Fig. 1.3).

This rectangle of type represents the interior space of the hotel room Julia takes, and perhaps a sense of enclosure, and hence temporary safety, in the room; it is also another little island, adrift on a page of type.

The geography of Paris in *Good Morning, Midnight* (1939) is much more circumscribed than that found in the earlier novels. Montparnasse is only rarely visited, with the heroine, Sasha Jensen, spending much of her time

HOTEL ST RAPHAEL
QUAI DES GRANDS AUGUSTINS
PARIS, 6ME
CHAUFFAGE CENTRAL. EAU COURANTE
CHAMBRES AU MOIS ET À LA JOURNÉE

Figure 1.3 Image from Jean Rhys, *After Leaving Mr Mackenzie* (1930).

in anonymous streets and neutral cafés around her hotel, which is set in an *impasse* (dead-end street) near the Panthéon on the Left Bank, and in walks in the nearby Luxembourg Gardens.[168] In a sense Sasha is located in a liminal space between the two more famous Parisian quartiers: the cultural zones of the Latin Quarter and Montparnasse, the most well-known 'bohemian' spaces in interwar Paris according to Hewitt, and which Sasha describes as 'Side by side and oh, so different'.[169] She tries to avoid the more familiar haunts of Montparnasse, such as the 'damned Dome', and when she does visit this café she meets a gigolo, René, a meeting that ultimately results in the dismal episode of sexual violence that ends the novel.[170]

The novel is set in 1937 and Sasha spends much of her time recalling past experiences in Paris in the twenties, such as her brief employment as a tour guide on the Right Bank of the city, being disorientated in the Place de l'Opéra, 'losing my head and not knowing the way to the Rue de la Paix. North, south, east, west – they have no meaning for me.'[171] Though Sasha here rejects external markers of geography, she does display a deep attachment to place in the novel, with locations in the city being suffused with mood and affect, particularly when spaces prompt melancholy memories of her past life. Most of part three consists of fragmented reminiscences of Sasha's earlier life with Enno in Amsterdam, Brussels and Calais as well as the mood (*Stimmung*) of 'blue days' in 'the streets, the houses, the bars, the cafés, the vegetable shops and the Faubourg Montmatre'.[172] Sasha's memories of the past are profoundly disorientating – like her experience in the Place de l'Opéra – and, as Benstock notes, 'the twists and turns of the city's labyrinthine streets trace the circular and involuted path of Sasha's consciousness'.[173] However, it is not only external spaces in the city that affect Sasha, but also the inner spaces of the numerous hotels she inhabits. As in previous novels the interiors of hotel rooms are deeply affective for Sasha and, at times, take on human characteristics. The first character to speak in the novel is in fact that of a hotel room, welcoming Sasha in acerbic fashion: '"Quite like old times," the room says. "Yes? No?"'[174] Early on in the novel, after contemplating a change of room to improve how she feels, Sasha returns to the same room, which welcomes her back like an old cynical friend: '"There you are," it says. "You didn't go off, then?"';[175] later, when her attempts to pursue a quiet, ordered existence have failed, she imagines the room is 'laughing, triumphant' and 'grinning at me'.[176] It is not just her hotel room that speaks, however, as when Sasha is having a drink in the Café Deux Magots, she visits the lavatory only for the mirror there to mock her: '"Well, well," it says, "last time you looked in here you were a bit different, weren't you?"'[177] The division between character and environment breaks down in these moments, a result of the strength of Sasha's affective relationship to places rather than to people, recalling Seigworth and Gregg's definition of affect as 'the passage of forces or intensities' that 'circulate about, between, and sometimes stick to bodies and worlds'.[178] Feeling hypersensitive about her location, Sasha conceives these Parisian spaces as akin to old friends or as a projection of her fears and anxieties. Sasha's experiences in these spaces thus demonstrate affect as a relational term which flows across spaces between subjects and their environments.

The intensity of this affective relationship means that the distinction between external and internal space is in danger of collapsing for Sasha and the sense of her hotel room being a place of safety and belonging ebbs away. Early in the novel she notes that all hotel rooms represent the same thing: 'a place where you hide from the wolves outside and that's all any room is'.[179] In contrast Parisian streets represent a threatening tactile experience: they 'sweat a cold, yellow slime'[180] and the 'dark houses' appear like 'monsters' which intimidate by 'Frowning and leering and sneering . . . Tall cubes of darkness, with two lighted eyes at the top to sneer'.[181] However, after a set of encounters with some male 'wolves' and gigolos Sasha's mood (*Stimmung*) alters. Now she remembers an earlier hotel room for its 'musty smell, the bugs, the loneliness', but also the fact that 'this room . . . is a part of the street outside'.[182] And then while sitting alone drinking Pernod in an unnamed *tabac* near the Panthéon it is the street rather than the room that now speaks to Sasha: 'Then you can see outside into the street. And the street walks in. It is one of those streets – dark, powerful, magical . . . "Oh, there you are," it says, walking in at the door, "there you are. Where have you been all this long time?" Nobody else knows me but the street knows me.'[183] Sasha then visits the cinema and returns to her hotel and again the collapse between inner and outer space occurs in a room 'saturated with the past . . . It's all the rooms I've ever slept in, all the streets I've ever walked in.' The paragraph, and this section of the novel, conclude with a linguistic repetition of the spatial dissolution between inner and outer: 'Rooms, streets, streets, rooms'.[184] The inversion of the terms here makes the streets enclosed by the rooms, again disrupting the normal spatial division between inside and outside, and demonstrating the flow of affect across the two environments.[185]

The dissolution of spatial categories (inner/outer, room/street) in the course of the novel parallels the narrative arc of Sasha herself, whose initial aim is to locate herself within Paris and thus to have 'arranged my little life'.[186] Arranging here is a form of spatial orientation and dwelling, in Heidegger's sense of a primal belonging to some location; for Sasha it is 'very important' to discover particular *places* in the city: 'a place to eat in at midday, a place to eat in at night, a place to have my drink in after dinner'.[187] The location of her afternoon drink is thus a café on the Avenue de l'Observatoire, because it always seems empty. As with Julia in *After Leaving Mr Mackenzie*, Sasha's arranging is thus a strategy to locate herself amidst the spatial flux of the metropolis of Paris, and entails the 'avoidance of certain cafés, of certain streets, of certain spots',[188] places in which her past may catch up with her or in which she feels uncomfortable. Sasha describes these decisions as a 'programme' which does not 'leave anything to chance – no gaps. No trailing around aimlessly . . . no "Here this happened, here that happened." Above all no crying in public.'[189] Sasha's 'programme' aims to be the opposite of that of the Baudelairean *flâneur*, whose city wandering is precisely aimless in intent. The 'programme' wishes to eradicate negative affective states (crying or painful memories) in certain spaces, choosing a 'neutral café'[190] rather than one imbued with shame or embarrassment, or walking in the Luxembourg Gardens which, revealingly, Sasha feels to be a 'gentle place – a gentle, formal place. It isn't sad here, it isn't even melancholy.'[191] However, the events of the novel undermine Sasha's attempts to locate 'gentle places', and increasingly the rooms and streets she moves through are felt as threatening and disorientating spaces rather than places to dwell.

Sasha's attempt to follow a 'programme' – 'to have a plan and stick to it'[192] – not only shows an attempt to dwell in the city, but also presents her as kind of parody of a worker or productive citizen. Rachel Bowlby notes that Sasha's 'plan' resembles the 'prescribed timetable of the office or factory worker going through a regular standardised sequence' and that by treating her 'leisure time as time to be managed, transforms freedom into the terror of a loss of control'.[193] The loss of control is principally over her own body as a commodity in the city. Though the novel contains brief descriptions of her temporary jobs, such as that of the tourist guide, Sasha's 'programme' is mostly a strategy to fill in time during her days: she does no real work but is still somehow a part of the market economy that dominates the novel. As Zemgulys notes, *Good Morning, Midnight* 'figures a system that determines some persons as valuable and others as worthless, and . . . renders almost every interaction into an exchange'.[194] Sasha thus remembers an imaginary conversation with Mr Blank, owner of a shop in which she is working and who pays her 400 francs a month: 'That's my market value, for I am an inefficient member of Society, slow in the uptake, uncertain, slightly damaged in the fray.'[195] The random encounter between two *flâneurs* – Sasha and the gigolo – that commenced in the Dôme café culminates in a miserable scene in the bedroom at the end of the novel that is dominated by a sense of the exchange-value inherent in the relationship; Sasha and the gigolo are thus commodified sexual partners in a different kind of 'arrangement' to that imagined at the start of the novel. After René leaves, Sasha curls into a foetal position on the bed and mulls over the nature of the financial arrangement just carried out: 'You've had dinner with a beautiful young man and he kissed you and you've paid a thousand francs for it. Dirt cheap at the price, especially with the exchange the way it is. Don't forget the exchange, dearie – but of course you wouldn't would you?'[196] Rhys never forgets that in Paris the *flâneur*, or more accurately the *flâneuse*, is emphatically linked to exchange-value.

Zemgulys notes that the trope of the market economy dominates the novel not only because Sasha, as an ageing woman, is losing her value as a commodity in putative sexual exchanges, but also because it is linked to the space of Paris as a metropolis, as a financial hub of empire and exhibitions (in the novel Sasha and René visit the 1937 Paris Exposition at the Trocadero), in which everything 'costs; everyone must pay; money stands for and makes possible a system of circulating persons and things'.[197] Sasha herself is acutely aware of this fact and in one brilliant passage shows how exchange-value can be traced in the very fabric of the city itself experienced by the female *flâneuse:*

> Walking in the night with the dark houses over you, like monsters. If you have money and friends, houses are just houses with steps and a front-door – friendly houses where the door opens and somebody meets you, smiling. If you are quite secure and your roots are well struck in, they know. They stand back respectfully, waiting for the poor devil without any friends and without any money. Then they step forward, the waiting houses, to frown and crush. No hospitable doors, no lit windows, just frowning darkness. Frowning and leering and sneering, the houses, one after another.[198]

Without money or friends the bricks and mortar of Paris loom as monsters, producing a set of intensely negative affects in Sasha, who lacks both, and is not a 'secure' dweller in these places. Sasha, like all of Rhys' heroines in her Paris novels, is identified as someone whose 'roots' are not 'well struck in'. As Deborah Parsons notes, in the cosmopolitan space of Paris Rhys was a '"stranger" in the city, rather than a "cosmopolitan"'.[199] Sasha feels she has 'no pride, no name, no face, no country' and that she doesn't 'belong anywhere', identifying herself as 'the stranger, the alien', an epithet also employed by the Parisian proprietor of a hat-shop she visits: 'A strange client, l'étrangère'.[200] In Rhys' fiction the view of the alien or stranger is a revealing one, illustrating the challenging geographical emotions encountered in the spaces of Parisian modernity.

Paris Noir

Rhys was an outsider in Paris, but a white colonial one from the Caribbean. Hope Mirrlees' brief reference in *Paris* to black American musicians (ll.423–4), along with the echoes in the poem of France's colonial history, point to two other groups of black writers whose response as outsiders in the city resulted in a rich set of meditations upon the cultural politics of colonial space. One group were the many American writers of the Harlem Renaissance or 'New Negro' movement that visited the city.[201] For example, W. E. B. Du Bois was in Paris at the same time as the Peace Conference mentioned in Mirrlees' poem, but attending the inaugural meeting of the Pan-African Congress, a significant event in the transnational history of black writers across America, the Caribbean and Africa. Michel Fabre has traced in detail the varied responses of Du Bois and many other black American writers to Paris in the interwar years, including Langston Hughes, Alain Locke, Countee Cullen, Claude McKay, Jesse Fauset and Gwendolyn Bennett, as well as key post-war figures such as Richard Wright and James Baldwin.[202] Over a quarter of a million African Americans had already served in segregated units of the US army in France during World War I, and many hundreds had stayed on after the war.[203] For many black Americans Paris represented an image of freedom they found lacking at home: Cullen, for instance, viewed Paris as 'a peerless city' in which 'Liberty, equality, fraternity are not only words' but 'express the spirit of which Paris is made'.[204] In particular, Paris lacked the spatial segregation of the Jim Crow laws that operated in the southern states, so that black Americans in the city could freely mingle with whites in public spaces, such as cafés, restaurants and public transport.

The second significant group of black 'outsiders' in Paris were the writers and intellectuals from French colonies in the Caribbean and Africa, such as Louis Achille, René Maran, the sisters Paulette and Jeanne Nardal, and Aimé Césaire from Martinique, Léon-Gontram Damas from Guyana, and Lamine Senghor and Léopold Sédar Senghor from Senegal. In the interwar years this diverse group, many of whom were students, pioneered discussions of modernity, black culture and political internationalism in such publications as Maran's novel *Batouala* (1921), winner of the Prix Goncourt, Césaire's long experimental poem *Notebook of a Return to My Native Land* (*Cahier d'un retour au pays natal*, 1939), and the pages of several little magazines such as the bilingual *La Revue du Monde Noir/Review of the Black World* (1930–2), *Légitime Défense* (1932) and *L'Etudiant Noir* (1935). This group is often described as the pioneers of the concept of 'négritude', a term first used by Césaire in *Notebook of a Return*, and later theorised by Senghor as 'the sum of the cultural values of the black world; that is, a certain active presence in the world'.[205] Interestingly, some of the philosophical underpinning of the concept of négritude derived from the vitalist thinking of Henri Bergson, whose influence upon the cultural milieu of Paris was discussed earlier in this chapter.[206] While many black Americans experienced Paris as a city of spatial freedoms, this group of 'French' colonial writers and thinkers were very much aware that their journey from the imperial margins to the metropolitan centre marked them indelibly as colonial outsiders.

The space of Paris, however, functioned crucially as what Fabre calls 'a meeting point for the different groups of the black diaspora',[207] a nodal point in complex transnational networks between the 'New Negro' writers of the Harlem Renaissance and the anti-colonial intellectuals of the black

Francophone world. Developing Raymond Williams' argument about the significance of the cosmopolitan space of European cities in the interwar years, Brent Hayes Edwards comments on this black diaspora that Paris was 'crucial because it allowed boundary crossing, conversations, and collaborations that were available nowhere else to the same degree'.[208] In particular, Edwards notes the dialogic relations between the distinct cultural formations prompted by two novels: Maran's *Batouala* and McKay's *Banjo*. *Batouala*'s account of African life was praised in America by Alain Locke, and extolled many times in the important black American magazines, such as *The Crisis*, *Negro World* and *Opportunity*; as Edwards argues, taking proper account of the impact of *Batouala* upon the Harlem Renaissance 'would mean reconfiguring the accepted cartography of black literary modernism',[209] by linking New York both to the French Caribbean by means of its author and to Francophone Africa by dint of the image of that continent depicted in the novel. Similarly, *Banjo*, McKay's novel of black immigrant life in the French port of Marseilles, had a profound effect upon colonial Francophone writers once published in translation in 1931: the novel's rehabilitation of notions of the 'primitive' influenced their conceptualisation of négritude, and they also praised its depiction of the negative effects of French colonialism. The novel was read widely and excerpts from McKay's work featured prominently in the magazines *La Revue du Monde Noir* and *Légitime Défense*, with Aimé Césaire describing it as 'truly one of the first works in which one saw an author speaking of the *nègre* and giving the *nègre* a certain literary dignity'.[210] Crucially, in both cases of dialogue and debate on black cultural politics it was Paris that operated as the nodal point for the transnational exchange.

However, the Parisian location for these dialogic encounters between two groups of black intellectuals was, as critics have noted, somewhat paradoxical. As Tyler Stovall notes, while 'African Americans found that in Paris the abstract ideal of worldwide black unity and culture became a tangible reality', it was also a city which 'was the seat of one of the world's great colonial empires, a place where anonymous French officials supervised the subjugation of millions of black Africans'.[211] It was a contradiction, however, that Claude McKay, radicalised as a socialist by his earlier experiences in London, New York and post-revolutionary Russia, was well aware of:

> The good treatment of individuals by those whom they meet in France is valued so highly by Negroes that they are beginning to forget about the exploitation of Africans by the French. . . . Thus the sympathy of the Negro intelligentsia is completely on the side of France . . . but it knows nothing at all about the barbarous acts of the French in Senegal.[212]

Quoting this passage by McKay, Edwards suggests that black American blindness to French colonial barbarity, or what he terms 'the paradoxes of black

Paris', is representative of wider structural difficulties within the discourses of the diaspora and black internationalism at this time.[213] It is, then, not surprising to discern that paradox and ambivalence are crucial textual features of certain depictions by black American writers of the spaces of Paris.

One fascinating example is found in a short story by the Harlem Renaissance writer Gwendolyn Bennett, who obtained a scholarship while working at Howard University to visit and study art in Paris for a year in 1925–6. After early homesickness the young Bennett began to appreciate the city:

> There never was a more beautiful city than Paris. . . . On every hand are works of art and beautiful vistas . . . one has the impression of looking through at fairy-worlds as one sees gorgeous buildings, arches and towers rising from among mounds of trees.[214]

To Langston Hughes she wrote:

> Paris has at last 'gotten' me. . . . I never loved any city the way I love this – rain and all. It took me many a day to get at this affection but here it is at last. It's so mellow and dear![215]

Her correspondence with Hughes also indicates how she became familiar with famous expatriate modernists such as Joyce and Hemingway, principally through meetings at Sylvia Beach's Shakespeare and Company bookshop, that key cultural space for outsiders in Paris. Beach also invited Bennett to her Thanksgiving dinner, and Bennett reports to Hughes that not only could one obtain copies of Joyce's *Ulysses* in the shop but she was 'so pleased' to see a copy of Jean Toomer's *Cane* available there too.[216]

Bennett's experience in the city involved many of the key sights and sounds familiar from accounts of Black Americans in Paris: she met Paul Robeson and saw Josephine Baker perform at the famous Bal Nègre, on the Rue Blomet in the 15th Arrondisement, a venue described by one journalist as 'a miniature Harlem'.[217] She also provided a description in her diary of an exhaustive yet exhilarating night out in Montmartre with a musician, Louis Jones, that included a visit to another legendary venue, the nightclub of Le Grand Duc, known as Bricktop's (the assumed name of the black Chicago entertainer Ada Louise Smith):

> Then at 4.15am to dear old 'Bricktop's'. The Grand Duc extremely crowded this night with our folk . . . 'Brick' singing as well as ever her hits . . . Louis dances with me one very lovely dance during . . . which 'Brick' and everybody teases him about how happy he is to have his little brown skin in his arms. . . . And always the inevitable 'Hot Cakes and Sausage' at the 'Duc' – Home at 6.30 in the lovely grey morning light. I shall never quite forget the shock of beauty that I got when the door was

> opened at 'Brick's' and as we stepped out into the early morning streets . . . looking up Rue Pigalle there stood Sacred Heart . . . beautiful, pearly Sacre Coeur [*sic*] as though its silent loveliness were pointing a white finger at our night's debauchery. I wished then that so worthy an emotion as I felt might have been caught forever in a poem.[218]

Here Bennett's joyful affective response to the thrilling pleasures of the evening amongst black performers is interestingly undercut by the metaphorical colour-line of the cityscape: though the streets around Pigalle are perceived as beautiful, the sepulchre of the Sacré-Coeur poses as a 'white finger' condemning the 'debauchery' of the black crowd in the club ('our folk'). In Bennett's affective reaction to the spatial fabric of the city we can thus detect one of the 'paradoxes of Paris Noir' identified by Edwards, where beauty and freedom co-exist with the wagging white finger.

Bennett did not capture the 'emotion' of this scene in a poem, but did compose a short story, 'Wedding Day', that drew upon her experiences of black nightclubs and musicians in Montmartre and Pigalle. We first meet the protagonist of the story, Paul Watson, a black boxer and sometime musician who 'had come to Paris in the days before colored jazz bands were the style', as he 'shambled down rue Pigalle'.[219] The area is described in words that echo Bennett's journal entry: 'Rue Pigalle in the early evening has a sombre beauty – gray as are most Paris streets and otherworldish. To those who know the district it is the Harlem of Paris and rue Pigalle is its dusky Seventh Avenue.'[220] Paul, who is of 'enormous height and size', is represented as something of a mythic yet tortured individual, and is known as the 'black terror' (recalling the French revolutionary 'terror') for his physical attacks upon whites who use verbal racial abuse: 'The last syllable of the word, nigger, never passed the lips of a white man without the quick reflex action of Paul's arm and fist to the speaker's jaw.'[221] Despite these attacks Paul escapes punishment, as if 'some divine power seemed to intervene in his behalf', until he is finally imprisoned for shooting two American sailors, which incurs a prison sentence. However, the outbreak of World War I results in France pardoning prisoners to fight in the war, and Paul 'became free' as a French soldier and is decorated for his bravery.[222] Paul's ability to both avenge racial slurs and become 'free' and a 'hero' represents a wish-fulfilment element of the narrative for black American readers of the story in a country where blacks were being lynched for much less. Again it indicates something of the egalitarian image that Paris represented for many black Americans as a space of freedom and equality of citizenship, where racial difference appeared to be more accepted.

However, racial divisions reappear in 'Wedding Day' when Paul meets a white prostitute, Mary, who initially proclaims that she 'ain't prejudiced like some fool women'; their relationship becomes the 'talk of Montmartre' and in 'every café where the Negro musicians congregated Paul Watson was the topic for conversation'.[223] Bennett renders this 'talk' in a technique much favoured in urban modernist texts by white writers, such as Joyce's *Ulysses* or Eliot's *The Waste Land*, where the city itself becomes a character that speaks. In 'Wedding Day' anonymous black voices emerge from the city streets, offering a fragmented and proleptic commentary upon Paul's romance, which rapidly develops towards marriage: 'Guess he thinks that skirt's gone on him. Dumb fool!'; 'They're gettin' tied up next Sunday. So glad it's not me. Don't trust these American dames. Me for the Frenchies.'[224] The story now moves to a conclusion on the wedding day, describing Paul's preparations for the ceremony as he muses on the 'queer twists life brings about' and puts on an English suit with 'a look of triumph'; Paul now walks round to Mary's hotel to greet her. We do not see him arrive and the narrative now abruptly jumps into mainly free indirect discourse, as we realise that Mary has sent him a letter to say that she 'couldn't go through with it' as 'white women just don't marry colored men'.[225] Paul's suit now feels wrong to him: 'Damn – gray suit – what did he have a gray suit on for, anyway. Folks with black faces shouldn't wear gray suits.'[226] Paul's rejection of his suit can be interpreted as a symbol of the affect of shame, defined by Tomkins as 'the affect of indignity, of defeat, of transgression, and of alienation . . . shame is felt as an inner torment, a sickness of the soul'.[227] It is revealing, then, that Paul's external discomfort with his suit is matched by an inner sensation of unease: 'What was that thought he was trying to get ahold of – bumping around in his head – something he started to think about but couldn't remember it somehow.'[228] The final paragraph of the story emphasises Paul's disorientation, replicated in the narrative by a jump in spatial location from the interior thoughts of the previous paragraph to the external space of the Paris Metro: 'The shrill whistle that is typical of the French subway pierced its way into his thoughts. Subway – why was he in the subway – he didn't want to go any place.'[229] He boards the train and we are left with a poignant metaphor for the seemingly intractable divisions explored in the story of the failed marriage: he looks at the ticket in his hand and notices that he has a 'First class ticket in a second class coach! – that was one on him.'[230] The image suggests that Paul's attempt to transgress the colour line by marrying Mary is not really as simple as buying a first class ticket, for he remains a 'second class' citizen in the eyes of white America even if, in Paris, he is able to travel 'first class' on non-segregated transport. He is defeated and his shame overwhelms him.

Bennett's story addresses both America and France, pointing to the injustices in her home country that continued to regard black subjects as second class citizens in contrast to their social and spatial freedoms in Paris, while also raising a note of caution about viewing Paris as a 'peerless city' of freedom where racial divisions did not matter. Several features point to this ambivalence in the story, which is perhaps first signalled in the early reference to the 'sombre beauty' of the Pigalle district. 'Wedding Day' first appeared in one of the most celebrated magazines of the Harlem Renaissance, Wallace Thurman's *Fire!!* (1926). With Aaron Douglas' striking visual design, and provocative work by Langston Hughes, Richard Bruce Nugent, and Zora Neale Hurston, the magazine aimed to attack black establishment culture as well aligning itself to other radical little magazines in New York such as *The Little Review* or *The Masses*. In terms of both its contents and its visual design *Fire!!*, as Martha Nadell writes, is a magazine that 'is racially modernist, attentive to racial themes and motifs combined with formal experimentation'.[231] *Fire!!* was attacked by Du Bois in his magazine, *The Crisis*, while another established black critic, Alain Locke, criticised the magazine for exhibiting 'left-wing literary modernism with deliberate intent'.[232] As Nadell notes, the characters of 'Wedding Day', a violent boxer in a relationship with a white prostitute, were likely to cause offence to Du Bois, who wished to promote more 'respectable' images of black life.[233] Bennett's story thus operates as a critique of bourgeois black culture, while its image of Paul as a 'black terror' avenging racial slurs would also clearly have alarmed white America: for black Americans to shift from second to first class citizens, the story implies, might well involve quite radical measures. It is interesting to note that one of Zora Neale Hurston's contributions to *Fire!!*, the play *Color Struck*, is set initially inside a segregated 'Jim Crow' car of a train in the southern states of the US.[234] Readers of the magazine would thus note the contrast between Paul's experience of public transport in Paris and that of his fellow black Americans in the spatial divisions of the south.

Paul's spatial freedom in the city of light is, however, compromised and in this respect the story critiques those who believed that black subjects in Paris were automatically seen as 'first class', thus aligning Bennett with McKay's view of the myopia of certain black Americans to French colonialism. Bennett's ambivalence about putative Parisian freedoms might well have come from an awareness of French colonialism derived from her own meeting with René Maran, about whom she wrote in her regular column for the magazine *Opportunity*, 'The Ebony Flute'. Upon meeting Maran, she wrote, the Frenchman 'brought out a copy of a current French news sheet and showed an article on lynching. . . . He himself, was incensed at the idea of such barbarity', noting also the 'kindredship that existed in his heart because of the irradicable black of our skins'.[235] Though Bennett's image of 'kindredship' perhaps points to the shared ideals of the négritude movement, Maran's reference to lynching points back to the fear, anger and violence at the heart of 'Wedding Day'. This is crystallised in the overdetermined image of the 'shrill whistle' of the Paris Metro that 'pierced its way' into Paul's consciousness, pointing to the contradictions of black Americans sensing freedom, or feeling 'first class', in a city which was a centre of colonial power. If the 'shrill whistle' partly symbolises the shame of Paul's affective 'inner torment', it simultaneously points outwards towards the social space of Paris as a colonial capital. The 'piercing' is thus something like a violent disruption in Bennett's story that symbolises the 'second class' status of French colonial subjects such as Maran and others: the modernist space of the Paris Metro becomes intrinsically linked to the colonial geography of empire, as much as it recalls the violence of everyday life in black America. In this sense the 'piercing' affect of the Metro is similar to Benjamin's notion of an 'awakening' into the 'space of history', seen here as a profound recognition of what it means to cross racial and spatial boundaries: from external space to internal consciousness, from the black Paul to the white Mary, from Paris to America and back again, and from the French colonies to their Parisian capital.[236]

Swooning in Paris

One of the classic accounts of white Americans in Paris in the interwar years can be found in Malcolm Cowley's memoir, *Exile's Return* (1934), which tells of how a generation of young, educated white Americans (mainly male) sought 'salvation by exile', travelling to a Europe they perceived as rich in civilisation and learning in comparison to the mercantile and industrial culture of the United States.[237] The effect of Paris upon Cowley was striking:

> Paris was a great machine for stimulating the nerves and sharpening the senses. Paintings and music, street noises, shops, flower markets, modes, fabrics, poems, ideas, everything seemed to lead toward a half-sensual, half-intellectual swoon. Inside the cafés, color, perfume, taste and delirium could be poured together from one bottle or from many bottles.[238]

This is as succinct a statement of Paris as an exciting affective geography as we might find amongst the voluminous writings of outsiders in Paris. Many shared Cowley's view of Paris as a kaleidoscope of sensations and ideas that stimulated and 'sharpened', producing something like a 'swoon' before its spatial environment. However, for others, as this chapter has demonstrated, the affects of Paris operated quite differently. For writers such as Apollinaire, Cendrars, Eliot and Mirrlees the city stimulated their writing above all: the geography of modern Paris was what modernised them as writers, as their affective responses to the spaces of the city helped shape the formal innovations of their verse.

In Jean Rhys, however, we see a rather tougher response to Paris than that of swooning, whether intellectually or sensually. In Rhys' texts the 'machine' of Paris proves to be a difficult one for a single woman on the margins of financial security, and her nuanced mapping of different locations – streets, cafés and hotel rooms – and their affective impact upon her heroines shows the difficulties involved in being an 'alien' or 'l'étrangère' in this city. Though

Rhys was a white subject, her colonial background in the Caribbean influences her response to Paris, bringing it closer to the ambivalence found in the 'Paris Noir' writers discussed above. In contrast to Cowley's sensual swooning, Claude McKay's recollections of his time in Paris in his memoir, *A Long Way from Home* (1937), demonstrates how certain black and colonial writers experienced the city quite differently. McKay, born in Jamaica and a paradigm of the transnational writer, did not identify himself as an American overawed by the attractions of Paris. He wrote coolly that there was nothing 'worth while for me in the bohemian glamour of Montparnasse' and that the 'Montmartre of the cabarets and music halls never excited me'; and although the rest of Paris seemed 'the perfect city of civilization' McKay only 'appreciated, but was not specially enamoured of Paris', preferring the cities of Strasbourg and Marseilles.[239] Later in his memoir, McKay is a little more sympathetic in his perceptions, noting that the 'milieu' of the 'cosmopolitan expatriates' in Paris was broader and more interesting that that of the Greenwich Village radicals he had mixed with when working on *The Liberator* magazine. However, McKay always felt different from the white expatriates, describing himself as 'a kind of sympathetic fellow-traveller in the expatriate caravan'.[240] While Cowley and others were in revolt against the 'puritan conscience and the denial of artistic freedom' in America, these were 'not exactly my problems'; for McKay 'the problem of color . . . was the fundamental of my restlessness'.[241] Such a view also can also be found in Gwendolyn Bennett's representation in 'Wedding Day' of black Americans in the 'expatriate caravan': for some outsiders the main affect of Paris, then, was as much a 'piercing' as a 'swooning'.

Notes

1. Jean Rhys cited in Carole Angier, *Jean Rhys: Life and Work* (Harmondsworth: Penguin, 1992), p. 107.
2. Colin Jones, *Paris: The Biography of a City* (London: Viking Penguin, 2005), p. xviii.
3. Ibid. p. 408.
4. For biographical accounts of the 'lost generation' of American writers in Paris see Robert McAlmon and Kay Boyle, *Being Geniuses Together 1920–1930* (London: Michael Joseph, 1970); Malcolm Cowley, *Exile's Return: A Literary Odyssey of the 1920s*, ed. Donald W. Faulkner (London: Penguin, 1994); Ernest Hemingway, *A Moveable Feast* (London: Arrow Books, 2004); Matthew Josephson, *Life among the Surrealists* (New York: Holt, Rinehart, and Winston, 1962); Harold Loeb, *The Way it Was* (New York: Criterion Books, 1959); and Gertrude Stein, *The Autobiography of Alice B. Toklas* (Harmondsworth: Penguin, 1966).
5. Pascale Casanova, *The World Republic of Letters*, trans. M. B. DeBevoise (Cambridge, MA: Harvard University Press, 2004), p. 24. And see André Kaspi and Antoine Marès (eds), *Le Paris des étrangers: Depuis un siècle* (Paris: Imprimerie Nationale, 1989).
6. Quoted in Casanova, *World Republic*, p. 26.
7. Ibid. p. 30, and see pp. 23–34 for an account of the many writers who travelled to Paris.

8. Ibid. p. 29.
9. There are brief references to Senghor and Césaire in Casanova's book, but nothing about black American writers in Paris.
10. See Tyler Stovall, *Paris Noir: African Americans in the City of Light* (New York: Houghton Mifflin, 1996).
11. Jones, *Paris*, p. 369.
12. See Maite van Dijk, 'Vive la France! Munch, Van Gogh and French Modern Art' in *Munch: Van Gogh*, ed. Maite van Dijk, Magne Bruteig and Leo Jansen (Brussels: Mercatorfonds, 2015), pp. 100–23.
13. See Faith Binckes, *Modernism, Magazines, and the British Avant-Garde: Reading Rhythm* (Oxford: Oxford University Press, 2010), p. 2.
14. Ibid.
15. For an account of Murry and Bergson see Mary Ann Gillies, *British Modernism and Bergson* (Montreal and Kingston: McGill-Queen's University Press, 1996), pp. 60–1. For further discussion, see Paul Ardoin, S. E. Gontarski and Laci Mattison (eds), *Understanding Bergson, Understanding Modernism* (London: Bloomsbury, 2013).
16. John Middleton Murry, 'Bergson in Paris', *The New Age* 9:5 (1 June 1911), pp. 115–16; p. 116.
17. John Middleton Murry, 'Art and Philosophy', *Rhythm* 1:1 (Summer 1911), pp. 9–12; p. 9.
18. Ibid. p. 12.
19. Michael T. H. Sadler, 'Fauvism and a Fauve', *Rhythm* 1:1 (Summer 1911), pp. 14–18; p. 14.
20. The concept of 'rhythm' as something of a synonym for 'modernism' is discussed in Binckes, *Reading Rhythm*, pp. 61–9.
21. Eliot, letter to Shiv Kumar (21 Jan. 1953), cited in Nancy Duvall Hargrove, *T. S. Eliot's Parisian Year* (Gainesville: University Press of Florida, 2009), p. 42.
22. Hargrove, *T. S. Eliot's Parisian Year*, p. 132.
23. Pound, letter to Harriet Monroe, 30 Sept. 1914, in *The Selected Letters of Ezra Pound 1907–1941*, ed. D. D. Paige (London: Faber, 1950), p. 40.
24. For the relation between material and metaphoric space see Neil Smith, 'Contours of a Spatialized Politics: Homeless Vehicles and the Production of Geographical Scale', *Social Text* 33 (1992), pp. 54–81.
25. T. S. Eliot, 'What Dante Means to Me' in *To Criticize the Critic and Other Writings* (London: Faber, 1965), p. 126.
26. T. S. Eliot, 'Baudelaire' in *Selected Prose*, ed. Frank Kermode (London: Faber, 1975), p. 234.
27. Ibid.
28. Hargrove, *Eliot's Parisian Year*, pp. 77–8, 271–2. Hargrove also suggests that the title of the poem might be indebted to Debussy and his composition 'Rhapsodie'; see p. 50. All references to Eliot's poem are from T. S. Eliot, *Collected Poems 1909–1962* (London: Faber, 1974), pp. 26–8, with line numbers given in the text.
29. See the version published in *Blast* 2 (1915), with the title 'Rhapsody *of* a Windy Night', p. 51.
30. See Mary Ann Gillies, 'Bergsonism' in *A Concise Companion to Modernism*, ed. David Bradshaw (Oxford: Blackwell, 2003), pp. 95–115; p. 104.
31. See Donald J. Childs, *From Philosophy to Poetry: T. S. Eliot's Study of Knowledge and Experience* (London: Athlone Press, 2001), pp. 55–6. The whole of his chapter (pp. 49–64) offers a detailed discussion of Eliot and Bergson. And see Rebecca Beasley, *Theorists of Modernist Poetry: T. S. Eliot, T. E. Hulme, Ezra Pound* (London: Routledge, 2007), pp. 41–6.

32. For the history of Paris as the 'city of light' see David Downie, *Paris, Paris: Journey into the City of Light* (New York: Broadway, 2011), p. 213.
33. Joachim Schlör, *Nights in the Big City: Paris, Berlin, London 1840–1930* (London: Reaktion, 1998), p. 63.
34. See Jones, *Paris*, pp. 335, 344; Hargrove, *Eliot's Parisian Year*, pp. 71–2.
35. Guy de Maupassant, *Claire de lune* (1909), cited in Walter Benjamin, *The Arcades Project*, trans. Howard Eiland and Kevin McLaughlin (Cambridge, MA: Belknap/Harvard University Press, 1999), p. 570.
36. See Lyndall Gordon, 'Eliot and Women' in *T. S. Eliot: The Modernist in History*, ed. Ron Bush (Cambridge: Cambridge University Press, 1991), pp. 9–22.
37. Silvan Tomkins, *Shame and its Sisters: A Silvan Tomkins Reader*, ed. Eve Kosofsky Sedgwick and Adam Frank (Durham, NC: Duke University Press, 1995), p. 135.
38. T. S. Eliot, *The Sacred Woòd: Essays on Poetry and Criticism* (London: Methuen, 1960), p. 169.
39. Immanuel Kant, *The Critique of Judgement*, trans. James Creed Meredith (Oxford: Clarendon Press, 1952), pp. 173–4.
40. Sianne Ngai, *Ugly Feelings* (Cambridge, MA: Harvard University Press, 2005), p. 335. It is interesting to note that Tomkins revised his theory to distinguish contempt from disgust, calling the former 'dissmell'; see Tomkins, *Shame and its Sisters*, p. 135.
41. Cited in Hargrove, *Eliot's Parisian Year*, p. 64
42. Discussions of Haussmannisation are legion: I have drawn upon David Harvey, *Paris, Capital of Modernity* (London: Routledge, 2003); Benjamin, *Arcades*, Convolute E, pp. 120–49; Jones, *Paris*, pp. 299–343; and Donald J. Olsen, *The City as a Work of Art: London, Paris, Vienna* (New Haven: Yale University Press, 1986).
43. Jones, *Paris*, p. 318.
44. Haussmann cited in Benjamin, *Arcades*, p. 128.
45. Haussmann cited in Jones, *Paris*, p. 318.
46. Jones, *Paris*, p. 319.
47. Ibid. p. 335.
48. Jones notes that the Impressionists and Post-Impressionists were the first groups to make Paris the subject matter of their art; see Jones, *Paris*, p. 368.
49. *Protestation des artistes* (1887) cited in Marjorie Perloff, *The Futurist Moment: Avant-Garde, Avant Guerre, and the Language of Rupture* (Chicago: University of Chicago Press, 2003), p. 201. For an overview of artistic responses to the Tour see Peter Conrad, *Modern Times, Modern Places: Life and Art in the 20th Century* (London: Thames and Hudson, 1998), pp. 280–5.
50. Vicente Huidobro, 'Tour Eiffel', *Nord-Sud* 6–7 (Aug.-Sep. 1917), pp. 24–5; Vladimir Mayakovsky, 'Paris' in *Mayakovsky: Poems*, trans. Herbert Marshall (New York: Hill and Wang, 1965), p. 150.
51. My account of these three draws upon Perloff's brilliant discussion of them in *Futurist Moment*.
52. Guillaume Apollinaire, 'Zone' in *Selected Poems*, trans. Martin Sorrell (Oxford: Oxford University Press, 2015), p. 6. Translation my own.
53. Ibid. pp. 14–15.
54. Ibid. p. 9.
55. Ibid. p. 14.
56. See Apollinaire, *Apollinaire on Art: Essays and Reviews, 1902–1918*, ed. Leroy C. Brenig, trans. Susan Suleiman (New York: Viking Press, 1972).
57. Apollinaire, 'Vendémiaire' in *Selected Poems*, p. 89.
58. Ibid. p. 99.

59. Guillaume Apollinaire, *Calligrammes* (Paris: Gallimard, 1966), p. 64. The volume also contains several conventionally laid-out poems.
60. Peter Nicholls, *Modernisms: A Literary Guide* (Basingstoke: Macmillan, 1995), p. 112. Nicholls is here contrasting this form of French modernism with the Italian Futurist desire to make modern life the subject matter of its aesthetic.
61. Ibid. p. 117.
62. Ibid. p. 123.
63. Raymond Williams, *The Politics of Modernism: Against the New Conformists*, ed. Tony Pinkney (London: Verso, 1989), p. 46.
64. 'Zone' had appeared in an issue of the same magazine in 1912. For discussion of this and other magazines connected to Apollinaire see Wilfred Bohn, 'Apollinaire and "the New Spirit"; *Le festin d'Esope* (1903); *Les Soirées de Paris* (1912–14); and *L'élan* (1915–16)' in *The Oxford Critical and Cultural History of Modernist Magazines, vol. 3: Europe 1880–1940*, ed. Peter Brooker, Sascha Bru, Andrew Thacker and Christian Weikop (Oxford: Oxford University Press, 2013), pp. 120–42.
65. Stephen Kern, *The Culture of Time and Space: 1880–1918* (Cambridge, MA: Harvard University Press, 1983), p. 13.
66. Quoted in ibid. p. 14.
67. Christopher Butler, *Early Modernism: Literature, Music, and Painting in Europe 1900–1916* (Oxford: Oxford University Press, 1994), p. 171.
68. See Willard Bohn, *Apollinaire and the International Avant-Garde* (Albany, NY: SUNY Press, 1997).
69. Apollinaire, 'Tour' in *Calligrammes*, p. 61.
70. On the wider context of this idea see Kern, *Culture of Time and Space*, pp. 67–81; Butler, *Early Modernism*, pp. 158–67; and Perloff, *Futurist Moment*, pp. 3–43.
71. Cited in Perloff, *Futurist Moment*, p. 3. A colour reproduction of *La Prose* can be found following p. 54 in Perloff.
72. Blaise Cendrars, *Selected Writings*, ed. Walter Albert (New York: New Directions, 1966), p. 99. Perloff notes that the wheel refers to the Ferris wheel placed alongside the Tower for the 1900 Exposition; see *Futurist Moment*, p. 24.
73. Cendrars, *Selected Writings*, pp. 79, 81, 83, 85.
74. Ibid. p. 99; Arlen J. Hansen, *Expatriate Paris: A Cultural and Literary Guide to Paris of the 1920s* (New York: Arcade, 1990), p. 265.
75. Perloff, *Futurist Moment*, pp. 3–43.
76. Ibid. pp. 8–9, 35.
77. Ibid. p. 29. Delaunay was later to use an image of the Tour incorporating her name as part of an advertisement for her textile and fashion designs in her Boutique Simultanée; see Tag Gronberg, *Designs on Modernity: Exhibiting the City in 1920s Paris* (Manchester: Manchester University Press, 1998), p. 46.
78. Cendrars, *Selected Writings*, p. 143.
79. Ibid. p. 145.
80. Cendrars, 'The Eiffel Tower' in ibid. p. 234.
81. Ibid. p. 238.
82. See Pierre Bourdieu, *The Field of Cultural Production: Essays on Art and Literature*, ed. Randal Johnson (Cambridge: Polity, 1993), pp. 120–5.
83. Shari Benstock, *Women of the Left Bank: Paris, 1900–1940* (London: Virago, 1987).
84. Julia Briggs, 'Hope Mirrlees and Continental Modernism' in *Gender in Modernism: New Geographies, Complex Intersections*, ed. Bonnie Kime Scott (Urbana and Chicago: University of Illinois Press, 2007), pp. 261–303; p. 261.
85. On Woolf and Mirrlees see Julia Briggs, '"Modernism's Lost Hope": Virginia

Woolf, Hope Mirrlees and the Printing of Paris' in her *Reading Virginia Woolf* (Edinburgh: Edinburgh University Press, 2006), pp. 80–95.

86. Woolf cited in Briggs, '"Modernism's Lost Hope"', p. 81.
87. Sandeep Parmar, 'Introduction' to Hope Mirrlees, *Collected Poems* (Manchester: Carcanet Press, 2011), pp. ix–xlviii; pp. xxxiii, xxxvii. I will refer by line number to the version of the poem published here between p. 3 and p. 17 in the main body of the text. See also Briggs, '"Modernism's Lost Hope"', p. 84.
88. Harrison and Mirrlees are listed as members of the lending library of Shakespeare and Company in the subscribers' book held in the Maurice Saillet archive, Harry Ransom Center, Austin, Texas. For a discussion of these two bookshops as a 'shared space' see Joanne Winning, '"Ezra through the Open Door": The Parties of Natalie Barney, Adrienne Monnier and Sylvia Beach as Lesbian Modernist Cultural Production' in *The Modernist Party*, ed. Kate McLoughlin (Edinburgh: Edinburgh University Press, 2013), pp. 127–46, and Andrew Thacker, '"A True Magic Chamber": The Public Face of the Modernist Bookshop', *Modernist Cultures* 11:3 (Autumn 2016), pp. 429–51.
89. Parmar, 'Introduction', p. xxv; Briggs, '"Modernism's Lost Hope"', p. 84.
90. Mansfield, letter to John Middleton Murry, 18 October 1919, cited in Parmar, 'Introduction', p. xxv.
91. See Briggs' superb annotations to the poem in her 'Commentary on *Paris*' in *Gender in Modernism*, pp. 287–303.
92. Ibid. p. 296.
93. Briggs, 'Hope Mirrlees', p. 267. Woolf visited what she called the 'sapphic flat' of Mirrlees and Harrison in Paris; see Parmar, 'Introduction', p. xix.
94. It could also echo the Futurist painting *The Nord-Sud (Speed and Sound)* of 1912 by Gino Severini. See David L. Pike, *Subterranean Cities: The World Beneath Paris and London, 1800–1945* (Ithaca: Cornell University Press, 2005), p. 54.
95. Simon Dell, 'After Apollinaire: *SIC* (1916–19); *Nord-Sud* (1917–18); and *L'Esprit Nouveau* (1920–5)' in *Modernist Magazines, vol. 3*, p. 147.
96. For Monnier on Reverdy, see *The Very Rich Hours of Adrienne Monnier*, trans. Richard McDougall (Lincoln: University of Nebraska Press, 1996), pp. 83–6.
97. See Briggs, 'Commentary', p. 287.
98. Ibid. p. 288.
99. Ibid.
100. For more on phobic responses to modern spaces see Chapters 2 and 4.
101. On Eliot and Mirrlees see Briggs, '"Modernism's Lost Hope"', p. 83, and Parmar, 'Introduction', p. xxxvii.
102. Parmar, 'Introduction', p. xxxiii. The poem also refers in several places to works of Russian literature.
103. Angier, *Jean Rhys*, p. 107.
104. Terri Mulholland makes the point that Rhys and Walter Benjamin share an interest in threshold spaces in the city; see her essay 'Between Illusion and Reality, "Who's to Know": Threshold Spaces in the Interwar Novels of Jean Rhys', *Women: A Cultural Review* 23:4 (2012), pp. 445–462. See also Terri Mulholland, *British Boarding Houses in Interwar Women's Literature: Alternative Domestic Spaces* (Abingdon: Routledge, 2017).
105. See Deborah L. Parsons, *Streetwalking the City: Women, the City and Modernity (Oxford: Oxford University Press, 2000)*, pp. 132–48. For more on the *flâneur* see Benjamin, *Arcades*; André Breton, *Nadja*, trans. Richard Howard (London: Penguin, 1999); and Keith Tester (ed.), *The Flâneur* (London: Routledge, 1994). For the female *flâneuse* see Lauren Elkin, *Flâneuse: Women Walk the City in Paris, New York, Tokyo, Venice and London* (London: Vintage, 2017).

106. Jean Rhys, *Letters 1931–1966*, ed. Francis Wyndham and Diana Melly (London: Penguin, 1985), p. 284; Angier, *Jean Rhys*, p. 108.
107. See the fictionalised account of this in Jean Rhys, *Voyage in the Dark* (1934; Harmondsworth: Penguin, 1969).
108. Rhys, *Letters*, p. 171.
109. Ibid. p. 280.
110. Jean Rhys, *Quartet* (Harmondsworth: Penguin, 1973), p. 9. See the Introduction for a discussion of the Heideggerean conception of mood (*Stimmung*).
111. For accounts of the background to the novel see Angier, *Jean Rhys*, and Max Saunders, *Ford Madox Ford: A Dual Life, vol. 2* (Oxford: Oxford University Press, 2012), pp. 281–99.
112. On the limitations of Ford's criticism see Andrew Thacker, *Moving Through Modernity: Space and Geography in Modernism* (Manchester: Manchester University Press, 2003), pp. 209–10; Parsons, *Streetwalking the Metropolis*, pp. 137–9; and David Armstrong, 'Reclaiming the Left Bank: Jean Rhys's "Topography" in *The Left Bank* and *Quartet*' in *Rhys Matters: New Critical Perspectives*, ed. Mary Wilson and Kerry L. Johnson (New York: Palgrave Macmillan, 2013), pp. 169–85.
113. Rhys, *Quartet*, p. 20.
114. Very few other locations appear: there is a brief interlude in Cannes, when Marya is sent away by Heidler to recover; and she travels to the Quai des Orfèvres and the Palais de Justice to visit Stephan after he is arrested, then visiting him in prison at Fresnes.
115. Rhys, *Quartet*, p. 10.
116. Ibid. p. 129.
117. Ibid. pp. 20–1.
118. See Hansen, *Expatriate Paris*, p. 268.
119. Rhys, *Quartet*, p. 14.
120. Ibid. p. 132.
121. Ibid. p. 143.
122. On Ford and the magazine see Bernard J. Poli, *Ford Madox Ford and the Transatlantic Review* (Syracuse, NY: Syracuse University Press, 1967). For an analysis of the story Rhys published in *transatlantic review*, 'Vienne', see Chapter 2 below.
123. Nicholas Hewitt, 'Shifting Cultural Centres in Twentieth-century Paris' in *Parisian Fields*, ed. Michael Sheringham (London: Reaktion, 1996), pp. 30–45.
124. Ibid. p. 31.
125. Here I am paraphrasing Hewitt, ibid. pp. 31–43.
126. Jean Rhys, *Collected Short Stories* (New York: Norton, 1987), p. 51.
127. Hewitt, 'Shifting Cultural Centres', p. 31.
128. Ibid.
129. Rhys, *Quartet*, p. 34.
130. Ibid. pp. 54–5, 13.
131. Hansen, *Expatriate Paris*, p. 124. On the significance of the Dôme in Rhys see Armstrong, 'Reclaiming the Left Bank', pp. 179–80.
132. Rhys, *Quartet*, pp. 72, 121.
133. Ernest Hemingway, *Fiesta: The Sun Also Rises* (London: Arrow Books, 2004), p. 36.
134. Ibid. p. 37.
135. Rhys, *Quartet*, p. 7.
136. See Maroula Joannou, '"All Right, I'll Do Anything for Good Clothes": Jean Rhys and Fashion', *Women: A Cultural Review* 23:4 (2012), pp. 463–89.

137. Andrea Zemgulys, 'Menu, Memento, Souvenir: Suffering and the Social Imagination in *Good Morning, Midnight*' in *Rhys Matters*, p. 22.
138. On the Hotel Unic see Hansen, *Expatriate Paris*, pp. 154–5.
139. Rhys, *Quartet*, p. 99.
140. Ibid. p. 87.
141. Ibid.
142. Ibid. p. 91.
143. Ibid.
144. Ibid. p. 93.
145. Ibid. pp. 95–6
146. Ibid. pp. 88, 102. The theme of masochism in Rhys is well discussed; see, for example, Jennifer Mitchell, 'The Trouble with "Victim": Triangulated Masochism in Jean Rhys's *Quartet*' in *Rhys Matters*, pp. 189–212.
147. Rhys, *Quartet*, p. 100.
148. Jean Rhys, *After Leaving Mr Mackenzie* (Harmondsworth: Penguin, 1971).
149. For some recent work on Rhys see Wilson and Johnson, *Rhys Matters*; the special issue of *Women: A Cultural Review* 23:4 (2012); and Erica L. Johnson and Patricia Moran (eds), *Jean Rhys: Twenty-First-Century Approaches* (Edinburgh: Edinburgh University Press, 2015).
150. For example, Rhys does not appear on the map of 'Expatriate Paris' in the frontispiece of Benstock's *Women of the Left Bank*, although Benstock does offer an extended discussion of Rhys' *Good Morning, Midnight*; see *Women of the Left Bank*, pp. 437–41.
151. Ibid. p. 448.
152. Ibid. p. 449.
153. I base this on the fact that the Café le Select is mentioned, an establishment only opened in 1925; see Hansen, *Expatriate Paris*, p. 121.
154. Karl Baedeker, *Paris et ses environs: Manuel du voyageur* (Leipzig: Baedeker, 1924), pp. 9–10.
155. Hemingway, *Moveable Feast*, p. 72.
156. See Hansen, *Expatriate Paris*, pp. 121–4 for details.
157. Cited in William Wiser, *The Crazy Years: Paris in the Twenties* (London: Thames and Hudson, 1983), p. 207.
158. Rhys, *After Leaving*, pp. 28–9.
159. Ibid. p. 11.
160. Ibid. p. 13.
161. Ibid. p. 135.
162. Ibid. p. 136.
163. Rachel Bowlby, '"The Impasse": Jean Rhys's *Good Morning, Midnight*' in *Still Crazy After All These Years: Women, Writing and Psychoanalysis* (London: Routledge, 1992), pp. 34–58; p. 53.
164. See Peter Hulme, *Remnants of Conquest: The Island Caribs and their Visitors, 1877–1998* (Oxford: Oxford University Press, 2000), particularly ch. 5 'The Return of the Native: Jean Rhys and the Caribs (1936)'.
165. Rhys, *After Leaving*, p. 129.
166. Ibid. p. 127.
167. Ibid. p. 9.
168. Jean Rhys, *Good Morning, Midnight* (Harmondsworth: Penguin, 1969). From the reference to the *impasse* being near the Rue Victor-Cousin (p. 11) we can perhaps identify the street as either Impasse Chartière, near Lycée Louis-le-Grand, close to the Panthéon, or Impasse Royer-Collard, nearer to the Luxembourg Gardens in which Sasha spends some time. On the symbolism of the *impasse*

see Bowlby, '"Impasse"', and Christopher GoGwilt, 'The Interior: Benjaminian Arcades, Conradian Passages, and the "Impasse" of Jean Rhys' in *Geographies of Modernism: Literatures, Cultures, Spaces*, ed. Peter Brooker and Andrew Thacker (London: Routledge, 2005), pp. 65–75.

169. Rhys, *Good Morning, Midnight*, p. 56.
170. Ibid. p. 60. Sasha does also visit the Closerie des Lilas briefly on two occasions.
171. Ibid. p. 26.
172. Ibid. p. 107.
173. Benstock, *Women of the Left Bank*, p. 438.
174. Rhys, *Good Morning, Midnight*, p. 9.
175. Ibid. p. 34.
176. Ibid. pp. 149, 150.
177. Ibid. p. 142. Elaine Savory notes the attention given to the space of the lavatory in this novel; see *The Cambridge Introduction to Jean Rhys* (Cambridge: Cambridge University Press, 2009), pp. 71–2.
178. See Gregory J. Seigworth and Melissa Gregg, 'An Inventory of Shimmers' in *The Affect Theory Reader*, ed. Gregg and Seigworth (Durham, NC, and London: Duke University Press, 2010), pp. 1–25; p. 1.
179. Rhys, *Good Morning, Midnight*, p. 33.
180. Ibid. p. 37.
181. Ibid. p. 28.
182. Ibid. p. 109.
183. Ibid. p. 89.
184. Ibid. p. 91.
185. It also recalls a comment by Benjamin on the bourgeois domestic interior: 'The street becomes room and the room becomes street'; see Benjamin, *Arcades*, p. 406. However, Rhys' experience is a kind of failed attempt to produce the space of a bourgeois interior.
186. Rhys, *Good Morning, Midnight*, p. 9.
187. See Martin Heidegger, 'Building, Dwelling, Thinking' (1951) in *Poetry, Language, Thought*, trans. Albert Hofstadter (New York: New Directions, 1971), pp. 143–62, and Edward S. Casey, *The Fate of Place: A Philosophical History* (Berkeley: University of California Press, 1997), pp. 243–84.
188. Rhys, *Good Morning, Midnight*, p. 14.
189. Ibid.
190. Ibid. p. 56.
191. Ibid. p. 46. For an excellent discussion of the theme of shame and affect in the novel see Erica L. Johnson, 'Haunted: Affective Memory in Jean Rhys's *Good Morning, Midnight*', *Affirmations: of the Modern* 1:2 (Spring 2014), pp. 15–38; available at http://tinyurl.com/gpyoky6 (last accessed 30 Oct. 2017). For other discussions of affect in Rhys see the essays by John J. Su, Patricia Moran, and another by Johnson in *Jean Rhys: Twenty-First-Century Approaches*.
192. Rhys, *Good Morning, Midnight*, p. 45.
193. Bowlby, '"Impasse"', pp. 40–1.
194. Andrea Zemgulys, 'Menu, Memento, Souvenir: Suffering and Social Imagination in *Good Morning, Midnight*' in *Rhys Matters: New Critical Perspectives*, ed. Mary Wilson and Kerry L. Johnson, pp. 21–40; p. 29.
195. Rhys, *Good Morning, Midnight*, p. 25.
196. Ibid. p. 154.
197. Zemgulys, 'Menu, Memento, Souvenir ', p. 30. Christina Britzolakis elegantly demonstrates the significance of the 1937 Paris Exposition in the novel, relating it to the wider global politics of the period and to Parisian surrealism, in her essay,

'"This Way to the Exhibition": Genealogies of Urban Spectacle in Jean Rhys's Interwar Fiction', *Textual Practice* 21:3 (2007), pp. 457–82.

198. Rhys, *Good Morning, Midnight*, p. 28.
199. Parsons, *Streetwalking the Metropolis*, p. 136. Many of the other characters in the novel are also outsiders, such as the Russian Jewish painter Serge Rubin, based on the painter Simon Segal that Rhys knew while in Paris; see Angier, *Jean Rhys*, pp. 365–6.
200. Rhys, *Good Morning, Midnight*, pp. 38, 46, 59.
201. For an overview see the essays in Fionnghuala Sweeney and Kate Marsh (eds), *Afromodernisms: Paris, Harlem and the Avant-Garde* (Edinburgh: Edinburgh University Press, 2013).
202. Michel Fabre, *Black American Writers in France, 1840–1980* (Urbana: University of Illinois Press, 1991). McKay, of course, is not easily assimilated as 'American' as he was born in Jamaica.
203. Brent Hayes Edwards, *The Practice of Diaspora: Literature, Translation, and the Rise of Black Internationalism* (Cambridge, MA: Harvard University Press, 2003), p. 3; and see Stovall, *Paris Noir*, pp. 1–24.
204. Cullen cited in Fabre, *Black American Writers*, p. 81.
205. Léopold Sédar Senghor, 'Negritude: A Humanism of the Twentieth Century' in *Colonial Discourse and Post-Colonial Theory: A Reader*, ed. Patrick Williams and Laura Chrisman (New York: Harvester Wheatsheaf, 1993), pp. 27–35; p. 28. And see Gary Wilder, *The French Imperial Nation-State: Négritude and Colonial Humanism between the Two World Wars* (Chicago: Chicago University Press, 2005).
206. See Donna V. Jones, *The Racial Discourses of Life Philosophy: Négritude, Vitalism, and Modernity* (New York: Columbia University Press, 2010).
207. Fabre, *Black American Writers*, p. 8.
208. Edwards, *Practice of Diaspora*, p. 5.
209. Ibid. p. 70; and see pp. 69–118.
210. Césaire cited in Edwards, ibid. p. 187; and see pp. 187–240 and Fabre, *Black American Writers*, pp. 146–59.
211. Stovall, *Paris Noir*, p. 90.
212. McKay cited in Fabre, *Black American Writers*, pp. 93–4.
213. Edwards, *Practice of Diaspora*, p. 6.
214. Bennett, diary entry, 26 June 1925; cited in Stovall, *Paris Noir*, p. 60.
215. Bennett to Langston Hughes, 1926, Langston Hughes Papers, Beinecke Library, JWJ mss 26, Box 14, folder 317.
216. Bennett to Hughes, 28 August 1925, Langston Hughes Papers, Beinecke Library, JWJ mss 26, Box 14, folder 317.
217. J. A. Rogers cited in Edwards, *Practice of Diaspora*, p. 173; and see pp. 173–7 on the Bal Nègre.
218. Cited in Stovall, *Paris Noir*, p. 62. For a more weary view of Montmartre nightlife, including Bricktop's, see F. Scott Fitzgerald, 'Babylon Revisited' in *The Collected Short Stories* (London: Penguin, 1986), pp. 208–9. For further discussion of Bricktop's see T. Denean Sharpley-Whiting, *Bricktop's Paris: African American Women in Paris between the Two World Wars* (Albany, NY: SUNY Press, 2015).
219. Gwendolyn Bennett, 'Wedding Day, A Story', *Fire!!* 1 (1926), pp. 25–8; p. 25. A second story by Bennett inspired by Paris is 'Tokens' in *Ebony and Topaz: A Collectanea*, ed. Charles S. Johnson (Manchester, NH: Ayer, 1927), pp. 149–50.
220. Bennett, 'Wedding Day', p. 26.
221. Ibid. p. 25.
222. Ibid. p. 26.

223. Ibid. p. 27.
224. Ibid.
225. Ibid. p. 28.
226. Ibid.
227. Tomkins, *Shame and its Sisters*, p. 133.
228. Ibid.
229. Ibid.
230. Ibid.
231. Martha Nadell, '"Devoted to Younger Negro Artists": *Fire!!* (1926) and *Harlem* (1928)' in *The Oxford Critical and Cultural History of Modernist Magazines, vol. 2: North America, 1894–1960*, ed. Peter Brooker and Andrew Thacker (Oxford: Oxford University Press, 2012), pp. 801–24; p. 808.
232. Alain Locke, 'Fire: A Negro Magazine', cited in Nadell, ibid. p. 815.
233. Nadell, 'Devoted to Younger Negro Artists', p. 812.
234. Zora Neale Hurston, *Color Struck*, *Fire!!* (1926), pp. 7–14; p. 7.
235. Bennett, 'The Ebony Flute', *Opportunity* (5 August 1927), cited in Edwards, *Practice of Diaspora*, p. 133.
236. Benjamin, *Arcades*, p. 458.
237. Cowley, *Exile's Return*, p. 74.
238. Ibid. p. 135.
239. Claude McKay, *A Long Way from Home* (London: Pluto Press, 1985), p. 230.
240. Ibid. p. 243.
241. Ibid. pp. 243, 245.

2

VIENNA

Introduction

One story of modernism in the German-speaking world goes as follows: it emerges in Vienna, the capital of Austria, at the end of the nineteenth century, and then develops in Berlin, the German capital in the north, only in the early twentieth century. In this narrative the experiments of modernism in Berlin, dominated by the Expressionist movement in the arts, are then brought to a calamitous halt when the Nazis take power in 1933. Although this narrative has the merit of simplicity it does not quite capture the full complexities of how 'German' cities became spaces where some of the essential forms of European modernism were established. Though the next two chapters do concentrate upon the two capitals, Vienna and Berlin, it is worth beginning by noting some of the other cities in which forms of 'German modernism' emerged. Doing so emphasises once again the idea of the outsider as a significant presence in modernist cities and stresses the contribution of writers and artists who can be viewed as internal émigrés or inside-outsiders. In German writers and thinkers we thus find some of the most significant theorisations of affect and geographical emotions as articulated in the urban experience, seen for example in the development of theories of spatial phobias by German psychologists.

After this short survey of the regional transnationalism of German modernisms, the chapter then considers two key instances of modernist space in Vienna: the construction of the Ringstrasse, and the role of the coffee house.

Here we see how the reshaping of the urban environment is connected to the particular forms of modern expression in the city, shown most noticeably in the 'inward turn' of Viennese modernism. The chapter then shifts to a less discussed period in the modernism of the city, the years of 'Red Vienna' after World War I when major building of social housing occurred: here British outsiders such as Stephen Spender, John Lehmann and Naomi Mitchison tried to marry the radical politics of these new spatial environments to styles of modernist experimentation. The chapter concludes with a final moment in the history of Viennese modernism, exploring the city in ruins after World War II in Carol Reed's film of 1949, *The Third Man*. The chapter thus follows the modulations of the 'outsider' in Vienna by considering two, related, themes. The first is that of the spatial dialectic between notions of the 'inner' and the 'outer' that dominate modernism in Vienna, seen for example in the link between the built environment and the theory of agoraphobia. The second is the articulation of a particular set of geographical emotions that can be best be described as the 'mood' of modernism in Vienna, a notion that also partakes of a spatial dialectic between inner and outer. Mood, or what Heidegger calls *Stimmung*, is defined by Jonathan Flatley as 'a kind of affective atmosphere . . . in which particular affects can attach to particular objects' and which as a concept 'provides a way to articulate the shaping and structuring effect of historical context on our affective attachments'.[1] Moods in this sense operate between inner and outer realms, argues Flatley, as an 'atmosphere, a kind of weather', and are thus not 'located in some interior space we can reach by introspection'; rather moods 'are not in us; we are in them; they go through us' and are part of the public, collective environment in which we live.[2] Mood (*Stimmung*) is thus a way in which we can understand how the geographical emotions of modernism are intrinsically linked to particular places within the city, exploring how the atmosphere of a place affects and shapes creativity.

German Modernism and Regional Transnationalism

By contrast with the development of modernism in the French-speaking world, dominated by Paris, attracting writers from the rest of the country as well as from its colonies, German modernism takes root in a number of diverse locations in Europe in addition to its major manifestations in Vienna and Berlin. Modernism in Germany and Austria, unlike in Britain or France, thus displays what Laura Doyle, in theorising transnationalism, describes as 'regional transnational networks of culture and economy' with 'cross-border histories, conflicts, and identifications' within a particular bounded geography.[3] Modernism in France and Britain is thus more strongly marked by the contributions of outsiders from overseas territories than is the case in Germany or Austria; the expansion of empire in the case of Austria, for instance, spread across regions of Central Europe rather than overseas.[4] For example, one of the major modernist writers to use the German language as his medium was Franz Kafka. Kafka lived in Prague, which, until the end of World War I, was a key city in the sprawling Austro-Hungarian Empire, the last iteration of the Habsburg Empire that had dominated much of Europe for centuries, and of which Vienna was the capital. In reference to its position as a second city of a larger imperial power, Prague was known as the 'Dublin of the East'.[5] As with many Habsburg cities, Prague was divided between diverse cultural and political factions: the majority of the populace were Czech-speaking, but there were also Slovak, German, Austrian, and Jewish traditions as important influences in the city. Comprising around half a million inhabitants in 1910, Prague had a sizeable minority of German speakers (around 20,000), about half of whom, like Kafka, were Jewish. While other German writers born in Prague, such as the poet Rainer Maria Rilke and the Expressionist dramatist Franz Werfel, left the city, Kafka remained until his death in 1924. Geographically situated midway between Vienna and Berlin, Prague was much influenced by the modernist arts in both of these imperial capitals.[6] For instance, modernist magazines that appeared from the 1890s onwards demonstrated an indigenous Czech modernism, filtered through German and other influences from the European avant-garde: in the period before World War I these included *Moderní revue* (begun 1894), *Volné směry* ('Free Directions'; 1896–1949) and *Umělecký měsičník* ('Art Monthly'; 1911–14).[7]

The intricate geography of the Habsburg Empire thus contained many culturally diverse cities across Central Europe in which various styles of 'German modernism' flourished, including the Hungarian capital, Budapest, the Ukrainian city of Lviv, and the ancient capital of Poland, Krakow. In many of these cities, as Scott Spector notes, the German-language writers who most embraced modernist trends were often Jewish, some of whom – as in the Galician city of Lemberg (Ukraine's Lviv) – also produced work in the Yiddish language that was 'self-consciously modernist'.[8] On the southern edge of this large empire, Trieste, the major port of Austria-Hungary, was another mongrel city where German influences mingled closely with Slavic and Italian culture. Trieste was to produce a key modernist in the Italian language, Italo Svevo, and in *Zeno's Conscience* (1923) we find a novel concerning the psychoanalysis of its hero for nicotine addiction which displays many of the self-absorbed anxieties and neuroses often associated with other tendencies within Austrian and German modernism.[9] Though he wrote in Italian, Svevo and his family were strongly influenced by German traditions: his father was a German Jew who had insisted that his son be educated in Germany.[10] Born Aron Ettore Schmitz, Svevo chose his pen name to reflect these German influences, as 'Italo Svevo' means 'Italian Swabian', in reference to the particular cultural and linguistic region of south-west Germany.

Sketching something of the complex regional transnationalism of this modernism across Central Europe thus indicates how a fuller picture of 'German' urban modernism should also include these many other diverse cities, languages and traditions. And this is even before we consider other cities in Germany itself in which varieties of modernist practice emerged, such as Munich, the Bavarian home of important periodicals such as *Simplicissimus* (1896), *Jugend* (1896) and Wassily Kandinsky's, *Der Blaue Reiter* (1912).[11] Special mention should also be made of Zurich in neutral Switzerland, which, during the years of World War I, saw an influx of artists and writers fleeing the war. Zurich witnessed the birth of one of the most significant avant-garde movements, Dada, at the Cabaret Voltaire club opened by Hugo Ball in 1916, and in keeping with the expatriate community that Zurich attracted in these years, almost all the Dadaists were non-Swiss, with a dominant faction (Hugo Ball, Emmy Hennings, Richard Huelsenbeck and Hans Richter) being German. The linguistic provocations of 'Dada' – a word with multiple meanings in different languages – were clearly in keeping with a geography of avant-garde exile aptly located in Zurich.[12]

Across the regional transnationalism of German modernism, however, the power and prestige of the two imperial cities, Vienna and Berlin, dominated the landscape. This chapter will thus concentrate upon Vienna, with the following chapter focusing upon Berlin, tracing the role of urban space, cultural institutions and the outsider in the modernisms that emerged in these two locations. In these imperial cities we encounter an emerging modernism informed strongly by the view of the outsider, whether understood as an actual migrant or as an internal émigré or minority. In Vienna, for example, the Jewish influence noted across other Central European cities of the Habsburg Empire was very pronounced: the census indicates that in 1857 about 2 per cent of the city's population were Jewish, a figure that rose to 10 percent in 1880 with migration from other parts of Europe.[13] By 1900 Vienna had the third-largest Jewish populace in Europe (after Warsaw and Budapest), with many assimilated or secular Jews having a profound influence upon the intellectual and cultural life of the city.[14] Although anti-Semitism flourished in 1890s Vienna (fuelled in part by its mayor, Karl Lueger), figures such as Arthur Schnitzler, Karl Kraus, Gustav Mahler and Sigmund Freud indicate the importance of the Jewish contribution to modernism in the city. As Peter Hall argues, the 'golden age' of the Viennese fin-de-siècle was 'peculiarly a creation of that Jewish society', characterising them as 'a society of outsiders who, for all too brief a time, had become insiders'.[15]

Vienna and *Die Moderne*

The cultural history of Vienna since the mid-nineteenth century is a fascinating story of modernity, space and power. This is first discerned in the construction of the Ringstrasse in Vienna from 1859 onwards, a project which paralleled the spatial restructuring of Paris carried out by Baron Haussmann's boulevards at roughly the same time (see Chapter 1). In both projects the military authorities of the two countries favoured broad streets to help prevent radicals from erecting barricades, as had occurred in the 1848 revolutions across Europe. However, the construction of the Ring in Vienna was more than merely an enterprise designed to quell civil unrest. The Ringstrasse stratified the city not only spatially, but also socially, enclosing a liberal bourgeois and upper class within the centre of Vienna, alongside major cultural institutions such as the opera and sites of administration and finance, while simultaneously pushing the lower middle class and proletariat to the periphery of the city, beyond the Ring. As Andreas Huyssen comments, while similar 'divisions existed in other nineteenth-century cities as well, the situation in Vienna is unique since the sociological separation was given direct architectural expression in the layout of the Ringstrasse'.[16] The Ringstrasse thus produced a far more powerful concentration of wealth and social space than was found in any other European city, including the Paris rebuilt by Haussmann.[17] This spatial restructuring was a major factor behind the particular mood (*Stimmung*) of Vienna as a city beset with 'inward' geographical emotions.

The classic account of the social implications of the Ringstrasse for the mood of urban modernism in the city is found in Carl Schorske's *Fin-de-Siècle Vienna* (1961). For Schorske, the building of the circular street, and its attendant official buildings and bourgeois apartments, is best comprehended as part of the rise of Austrian liberalism after 1860, a spatial restructuring that was a crucial factor in the 'inward turn' of Viennese culture at the fin-de-siècle, with its psychological obsession with the affective self and an enthusiastic embrace of an autotelic aesthetic life. In this interpretation Viennese modernism, seen in a panoply of artistic productions from the sensuous paintings of Gustav Klimt to the melancholic compositions of Gustav Mahler, is typified by a heady combination of aestheticism and morbid psychology or, as Schorske puts it, 'the slipping away of the world increased' as bourgeois aesthetic culture turned inwards towards 'the cultivation of the self', resulting in a 'preoccupation with one's own psychic life'.[18] For Schorske, Viennese life in this period was characterised by a particular spatial dialectic of inner and outer, as the enclosed external spaces of Vienna after the construction of the Ringstrasse produced the inward turn of its cultural productions, developing an affective atmosphere that characterised modernism in the city. It also helped produced what Schorske argues was the 'socially circumscribed character of the Viennese cultural elite', where intellectuals and artists mingled closely in the cafés, salons and other cultural institutions crowded within the Ringstrasse.[19] This was a coterie spatial environment in which the architect Otto Wagner looked to the painter Klimt for inspiration, and where Sigmund Freud could refer to the writer Arthur

Schnitzler both as his 'colleague' in the investigation of the importance of Eros in life and as his 'double'.[20]

Perhaps the most famous instance of the 'inward turn' of Viennese modernism and its focus on new affective experiences in the city was indeed that of Freud's invention of psychoanalysis. However, even in Freud's interrogations of the psychic life of bourgeois Vienna the external environment of the city plays an interesting role, emphasising the spatial dialectic of inner and outer. In *Repressed Spaces*, Paul Carter explores Freud's own admission of suffering from agoraphobia, as revealed to a former pupil, Theodor Reik, during a walk in Vienna in the 1920s:

> When we crossed a street that had heavy traffic, Freud hesitated as if he did not want to cross. I attributed the hesitancy to the caution of the old man, but to my astonishment he took my arm and said, 'You see, there is a survival of my old agoraphobia, which troubled me much in younger years.'[21]

Carter first considers how far Freud's fear of crossing open spaces stemmed from 'the immensely increased volume and accelerated pace of traffic in Vienna's new enlarged roads' as a result of the Ringstrasse;[22] but he also ponders, following Reik's suggestion, whether Freud repressed the spatial environment as a cause of this affect of fear, substituting a purely psychological neurosis as the root of his unease. For Freud, a phobia was not really a fear of some external object but a response to a threat from within the mind, or, as Freud puts it, when an 'internal danger is transformed into an external one',[23] often related to anxieties over sexuality. Hence, early in his career in 1896, Freud wrote to Wilhelm Fliess suggesting that the many cases of agoraphobia in young women that he was treating could be traced to a repressed inner desire to walk the streets, that is, to become a prostitute: 'agoraphobia', noted Freud in a stark and rather reductive fashion, 'seems to depend on a romance of prostitution'.[24]

One of Freud's most famous discussions of phobia is the case of 'Little Hans' (1909), the young boy whose agoraphobia and fear of horses Freud interpreted as an acting out of the Oedipal drama and as an illustration of children's early sexual development. What is interesting from the point of view of spatial phobias is the way that Freud rejects or, we might say, represses the role played by the spatial environment of Vienna in Little Hans' fears. As Anthony Vidler points out, Freud goes to great lengths 'to draw the "scene" of the phobia, marking all the sites of every physical clue of psychic life, in order to dismiss their relevance to the investigation and reveal them as hiding something more important'.[25] Freud offered not one, but two maps of Hans' immediate location (for one example, see Fig. 2.1), in order to consider why he feared large horses falling down (interpreted by Freud as a phantasy of his pregnant mother giving birth and as a sadistic desire to kill his father).[26]

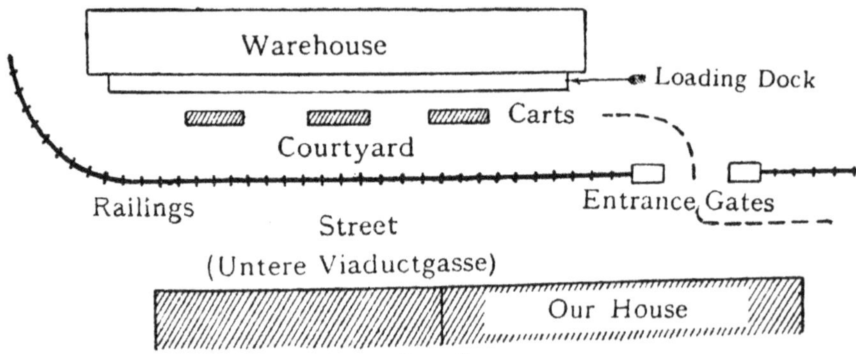

Fig. 2.

2.1 Map from Sigmund Freud, 'Analysis of a Phobia in a Five-Year-Old Boy' (1909).

Freud noted at one point that Hans' 'imagination was being coloured by images derived from traffic, and was advancing systematically from horses, which draw vehicles, to railways. In the same way railway anxiety eventually becomes associated with every street-phobia.'[27] But Freud notes such factors only to reject their causal power, as the 'relation between the anxiety and its objects' is only secondary to the true origin of Hans' fears, which relate to his Oedipal crisis. For Freud the horse-drawn carts delivering to the house opposite, along with the 'horse-bus' and the nearby railway carriages, all symbolise Hans' mother, pregnant with his baby sister, who constitutes a rival to his mother's love, as well as his father – a much bigger horse that Hans unconsciously wishes to kill off (hence his guilty fear of the falling horse).

That Freud took such care in mapping Hans' environment points to his awareness that spatiality played some role in his troubled life. But why reject an environmental interpretation of Hans' fears of urban traffic, accidents or crashes? Fear of death by traffic in a large busy city is an entirely feasible anxiety, a view confirmed by the German sociologist Georg Simmel, who, in his classic diagnosis of how the metropolis affected modern psychological life in the early twentieth century, stressed the 'unexpectedness of violent stimuli' such as happened in the city 'with every crossing of the street'.[28] Likewise Marshall Berman, in his later study of urban modernism, described the 'primal scene' for the modern subject as being 'a pedestrian thrown into the maelstrom of modern city traffic, a man alone contending against an agglomeration of mass and energy that is heavy, fast and lethal'.[29]

Freud's rejection of agoraphobia's link to modern urban traffic was, we might surmise, prompted by personal circumstances, that of his own spatial phobias, as reported by Reik, whereas for Carter and Vidler the spatial phobias of the early twentieth century cannot solely be traced back to an internal psychic economy merely *triggered* by external circumstance. Rather, the strange new environments of a modernist city such as Vienna produced a range of phobias associated with urban space, or what James Donald terms the 'psychic and spatial diseases of modernity'.[30] Such spatial phobias were thus powerful affective responses to the redesigned city streets. Doctors in the cities of Berlin and Vienna first noted this new phobia of open spaces in the 1860s and 1870s, including the Berlin psychologist Carl Otto Westphal, who popularised the term 'agoraphobia' to describe the feelings of anxiety experienced by his patients when crossing large open spaces.[31] We can, therefore, understand these phobias as exaggerated forms of affective response to the novel urban environs of a city such as Vienna.

The Viennese architect Camillo Sitte thus directly linked agoraphobia to the new urban spaces resulting from urban restructuring projects such as that of the Ringstrasse, as he argued in his major work, *Der Städtebau* (*City Building*) (1889):

> Recently a unique nervous disorder has been diagnosed – 'agoraphobia' [*Platzscheu*]. Numerous people are said to suffer from it, always experiencing a certain anxiety or discomfort, whenever they have to walk across a vast empty place. . . . Agoraphobia is a very new and modern ailment. One naturally feels very cozy in small, old plazas. . . . On our modern gigantic plazas, with their yawning emptiness and oppressive ennui, the inhabitants of snug old towns suffer attacks of this fashionable agoraphobia.[32]

For Sitte, the Ringstrasse embodied a rationalised modernity that rejected the artistic side of city building (the full title of Sitte's book translates as 'City Building According to Its Artistic Principles'), and hence produced a phobic response from its citizens. Against 'the rage for open space' Sitte called for smaller public squares, producing a sense of human community and interaction that was opposed to the ceaseless flow of traffic in the Ringstrasse, precisely the phenomenon that had prompted Freud's own agoraphobia.[33]

This uneasy combination of yawning spaces and the incessant traffic that fills them appears frequently in German modernist texts, such as in the genre of 'street' films set in Berlin in the 1920s that were noted by film critic Siegfried Kracauer (see Chapter 3).[34] However, in the brilliant opening of Robert Musil's *The Man Without Qualities* (*Der Mann ohne Eigenschaften*), first published in 1930 but set in 1913, it is a traffic accident in the streets of Vienna that is utilised as a key motif to understand the affective experiences of modernity:

> Motor-cars came shooting out of deep, narrow streets into the shallows of bright squares. Dark patches of pedestrian bustle formed into cloudy

> streams. Where stronger lines of speed transacted their loose-woven hurrying, they clotted up – only to trickle on all the faster then and after a few ripples regain their regular pulse-beat. Hundreds of sounds were intertwined into a coil of wiry noise, with single barbs projecting, sharp edges running along it and submerging again, and clear notes splintering off – flying and scattering. Even though the peculiar nature of this noise could not be defined, a man returning after years of absence would have known, with his eyes shut, that he was in that ancient capital and imperial city, Vienna. Cities can be recognised by their pace just as people can by their walk.[35]

What defines the 'pace' of the city here is not just the dense presence of traffic but also the resonance of its vehicles, 'a coil of wiry noise' referring both to the mechanical combustion engine with its coils and wires and to the 'splintering' sounds it produces. Pedestrians are reduced to 'dark patches' in 'cloudy streams' as the cars occupy the available space of the city. In a similar fashion to Ford Madox Ford's attempt in *The Soul of London* to capture the 'feel' of London (see Introduction), Musil's unseeing protagonist is able to recognise Vienna by its noise and pace, rather than by specific visual landmarks.[36] Musil's description in these opening pages thus characterises a unique mood (*Stimmung*) in Vienna, identifiable to citizens attuned to it even with their eyes closed.[37]

The city is also viewed as an aleatory phenomenon in juxtaposition to the rational planning of the Ringstrasse:

> Like all big cities, it consisted of irregularity, change, sliding forward, not keeping in step, collisions of things and affairs, and fathomless points of silence in between, of paved ways and wilderness, of one great rhythmic throb and the perpetual discord and dislocation of all opposing rhythms, and as a whole resembled a seething, bubbling fluid in a vessel consisting of the solid material of buildings, laws, regulations, and historical traditions.[38]

Musil's image of the city as a 'bubbling fluid' contained within the 'vessel' of the physical fabric is a brilliant example of what Henri Lefebvre describes as 'representational space', that is, 'space as directly lived' by the urban dweller.[39] This lived experience of the city contrasts with the rational aspect of urban modernity (Lefebvre's 'representation of space'), a contradistinction seen in the fatal lorry accident that now follows in the novel. A woman approaching the crowd that gathers around the accident has 'a disagreeable sensation in the pit of her stomach, which she felt entitled to take for compassion; it was an irresolute, paralysing sensation'.[40] However, her companion claims that the accident occurred due to the long braking-distance required by the lorry, an explanation that makes the woman feel relieved since 'the horrible happening could be fitted into some kind of pattern, so becoming a technical problem that no longer directly concerned her'.[41] In such a fashion the woman's affective response to urban space, with its potential to turn phobic, is contained by the masculine discourse of the rational and the technical. This is also seen in our first image of Ulrich, the novel's Man Without Qualities, who while the accident happened has been staring out of the house for ten minutes counting the traffic and pedestrians in the streets, with his watch in his hand, 'estimating the speed, the angle, the dynamic forces of masses being propelled past'.[42] In response to the fearfully random encounter of human and machinery – perhaps a defining image of all modernist space – Ulrich attempts to impose a Fordist regime of measurement as a strategy to dissolve its terrors.

Musil's novel thus satirises the decline of the Habsburg Empire by vacillating between the inward turn of Viennese society diagnosed by Schorske, with its mood of phobic and anxious emotions, and a more rationalised modernity operative in the metropolitan environment, as exemplified by motor cars, motion and urban planning. His satiric description of the empire as 'Kakania' depicts a Vienna where 'there was speed too, of course; but not too much speed' and cars 'but not too many cars!'; while this was an imperial power at the centre of Europe there was 'no ambition to have world markets and world power'.[43] Vienna is thus not like the 'super-American city where everyone rushes about, or stands still, with a stop-watch in his hand' and where there are 'Overhead-trains, overground-trains, underground-trains, pneumatic express-mails carrying consignments of human beings, chains of motor-vehicles all racing along horizontally, express lifts vertically pumping crowds from one traffic-level to another'.[44] Viennese modernity is thus somewhat trapped: partially attracted by the forward motion of Fordism and technology, but caught up in 'a nostalgic yearning to be brought to a standstill, to cease evolving'.[45] Hence, the mood of Vienna's geography, in Musil's eyes, is that of a stalled modernity, which is also replicated in the novel's own narrative form. As Marjorie Perloff notes, essentially *The Man Without Qualities* has no plot and is less a novel 'than a sequence of intricately related essayistic meditations and speculations'.[46]

For Edward Timms, too, Musil's novel eschews much of what we might expect in a fiction based in a specific geographical location. Timms notes that Musil does not really aim to depict the city as such, but rather explores 'states of consciousness, dissolving and reforming amid the urban turmoil', resulting in a text where 'the contours of the city streets dissolve'.[47] Timms associates this dialectic of inner and outer, and its 'loss of reality', with another innovative feature of Viennese modernism that was picked up and developed by numerous other modernist figures across Europe: the loss of faith in language as an instrument of representation.[48] Numerous writers and intellectuals in early twentieth-century Vienna shared this scepticism over language, from the satirical journalism of Karl Kraus and his magazine *Die Fackel* (1899–1936) to Fritz Mauthner's *Contributions to a Critique of Language* (1901–3) and, most famously in the field of philosophy, Ludwig Wittgenstein's *Tractatus Logico-Philosophicus* (1922). The *Tractatus* concludes by suggesting that most traditional philosophical problems are caused by a misunderstanding of the 'logic of our language' and that 'what can be said at all can be said clearly, and what we cannot talk about we must pass over in silence'.[49] Such linguistic scepticism is also evident in the famous 'Lord Chandos Letter' (1902) by the Viennese writer Hugo von Hofmannsthal, in which the protagonist states baldly: 'I have completely lost the ability to think or speak coherently about anything at all.'[50] In a striking image Hofmannsthal attacks general terms such as 'spirit' or 'soul', writing that 'the abstract words which the tongue must enlist as a matter of course in order to bring out an opinion disintegrated in my mouth like rotten mushrooms'.[51] Summing up the importance of Hofmannsthal's statement, Janik and Toulmin note that it epitomises a central feature of fin-de-siècle Viennese culture faced by all artists and intellectuals at the time: 'one had to face the problem of the nature and limits of language, expression and communication'.[52]

It may appear that this crisis of language in Viennese writers and thinkers presents a version of modernism and modernity quite distinct from that outlined by Schorske in his analysis of urban restructuring and the 'inward turn'. However, in a subtle and convincing analysis of Hofmannsthal, Musil and Arthur Schnitzler, Andreas Huyssen demonstrates how the spatial politics of the city can be linked to the modernist crisis of language outlined by Hofmannsthal and others. Huyssen argues that in the writing of Viennese modernists we can detect a 'disturbance of vision [which] flows from the experiences of urban life' and 'a rapidly modernizing urban culture at and after the turn of the century'.[53] In particular Huyssen points to the socio-spatial divisions brought about by the Ringstrasse, which 'enclosed the upper-class areas of the city, separating them from the rapidly expanding lower-middle class, proletarian, and subproletarian [*Vorstädte*]'.[54] The structures of the Ringstrasse were 'visually oriented towards the center', to the Imperial Palace and the aristocracy, meaning that the liberal bourgeois writers and artists of Vienna looked forwards at an aristocracy 'that it tried to imitate but that mostly despised it', while it literally turned its back upon the working class of the *Vorstädte*, pathologising those areas beyond the cultural pale of the Ringstrasse. As Huyssen notes, inside 'the circular and constricted space of the Ring, seeing and being seen exhibited an inevitable social pathology'.[55] The working-class geography of the *Vorstädte* became, therefore, perceived as a threat to Vienna's *literary* culture and increasingly identified – via the mass popular forms of cinema, cabaret and entertainment parks that took hold in these areas – with *visuality* as well as with pre-existing modes of oral culture. Huyssen quotes a Hofmannsthal essay of 1921 where he refers to the *Vorstädte* as 'dark nether regions into which no written word ever penetrates'.[56] Thus, concludes Huyssen, the crisis of language became central to German-language authors in Vienna in a way not experienced by writers in a city such as Berlin. The built environment of the city thus produced another example of a spatial phobia of modernity – not of open spaces but of those who lived in certain spaces of the city – while it also encouraged a modernist anxiety over the status of language as medium itself.

Within the enclave offered by the Ringstrasse one of the key cultural spaces which enabled literary artists to group together, safe from the spatial threats of the *Vorstädte*, were the famed Viennese coffee houses, institutions whose role in the development of modernism in the city has long been acknowledged. By 1900 Vienna had around 600 coffee houses, and their status as important cultural institutions in Vienna is indicated in a letter written by Stefan Zweig to Herman Hesse in 1903: 'I believe – at least this is what I observed in Berlin – that people in other countries imagine Viennese literature as a big table in a coffeehouse where we all sit around day after day.'[57] Moriz Jung's 1911 image of a typical Viennese 'man of letters' (see Fig. 2.2) only appears to confirm this perception of the centrality of the coffee house.

This humorous image, however, has more than a grain of truth about it, with venues such as the Café Griensteidl, Café Central and Café Museum gathering writers, artists and intellectuals together to debate the key social, cultural and political ideas of the day. Hofmannsthal was one of the Jung-Wien (Young Vienna) literary circle that grouped around Hermann Bahr at the Café Griendsteidl, and which included Schnitzler, Peter Altenberg, and Richard von Beer-Hofmann. The satirist and editor of *Die Fackel*, Karl Kraus, was also initially a member of this group but then rejected the circle, celebrating the closure of what he labelled 'Café Grössenwahn' ('delusions of grandeur café') in 1897. Kraus, however, soon established his own circle at the Café Central, an important venue which was itself the subject of a satiric yet illuminating analysis in Alfred Polgar's feuilleton of 1926, 'Theory of the Café Central': 'The Café Central is indeed a coffeehouse unlike any other coffeehouse. It is instead a worldview [*Weltanschauung*] and one, to be sure, whose innermost essence is not to observe the world at all.'[58] For Polgar the Café Central represented a bohemian cultural formation characterised by a complex dialectic between inner and outer spaces:

> [i]ts inhabitants are, for the most part, people whose hatred of their fellow human beings is as fierce as their longing for people, who want to be alone but need companionship for it. Their inner world requires a layer of the outer world as delimiting material.[59]

Figure 2.2 Moriz Jung, *Viennese Café: The Man of Letters* (1911).

In this description of the café as 'an organization of the disorganized' we uncover yet another image of Viennese modernism turning inwards, but in a way that is once again connected to the external social spaces, demonstrating the ubiquitous spatial dialectic of inner and outer in the city. The café thus operated as an in-between space, where artists and intellectuals created an 'inner world' that only existed in relation to the external bourgeois space of the Ringstrasse streets. Hence a quite complex set of spatialities is at work here: the cultural formations at the Central or Griensteidl dwell within the prestigious space of the Ringstrasse, clearly away from the corruptions of the suburbs, but are not part of the Viennese political elite, showing a disdain for money, as Polgar puts it, that granted 'an anti-bourgeois crown'.[60] They were *outsiders* too by means of cultural attitudes and political opinions (Leon Trotsky met the theorists of Austro-Marxism on Saturdays at the Café Central).[61] Yet members of a particular café circle could also feel like *insiders*, as Polgar's theory suggests, producing a cosy environment within the clique of the literary circle, feeding off the cultural capital accrued by membership of this cultural elite and possessing a worldview which studiously shunned the world outside the space of the café.

One of the most fascinating of the complex spatialities at work in the Viennese coffee house concerns the many habitués who were Jewish – an ambivalent Viennese saying from this period has it that 'The Jew belongs in the coffeehouse.'[62] The main theorist of political Zionism, Theodor Herzl (who frequented the Café Landtmann am Ring, also visited by Freud), thus made the hero of his utopian novel, *Altneuland* (1902), a 'coffeehouse Jew' in Vienna.[63] As Shachar Pinsker has shown, the café in Central Europe was fundamental to the development of Hebrew and Yiddish modernism, and in Vienna the existing acculturated Jewish populace was joined from the early 1910s onwards by many immigrants fleeing persecution and poverty in Eastern Europe, including writers in Hebrew and Yiddish. For these newly arrived Viennese Jews, writes Pinsker, the 'kaffeehaus proved to be the place that brought these immigrant writers together and opened new paths for them'.[64] Jewish writers such as Schnitzler, Hofmannsthal and Musil who already circulated through the Vienna coffee houses were thus joined by Hebrew and Yiddish writers such as Gershon Shofman, David Fogel, and Meir Wiener. These new immigrants often lived outside of the Ringstrasse, in Vienna's second district, Leopoldstadt, which had a long-established Jewish presence. Pinsker argues that cafés within the Ringstrasse, such as the Herrenhof and the Arkaden (which stocked Hebrew and Yiddish newspapers and was also frequented by Wittgenstein), offered locations in which the spatially and linguistically marginalised Hebrew and Yiddish writer could interact with established cultural and intellectual figures from Jewish Vienna.[65] For Pinsker the café in Central Europe was thus a form of 'thirdspace', in Edward Soja's terms, a location which operates on the borders between multiple spatial categories such as 'public' and 'private', 'inside' and 'outside', 'real' and 'imagined' space, the 'immigrant' and the 'native', as well as acting as a mediating place between Jews and non-Jews.[66] Pinsker illustrates this argument in a reading of two texts. In a story by Gershon Shofman, 'In Siege and Distress' (1922), the café is initially a space where East European Jews seek a sense of belonging, before they realise that the protective 'inside' environment of the coffee house is 'permeated by the "outside"' space of Viennese society.[67] And in what Pinsker calls 'the urban Hebrew modernist novel par excellence', *Married Life* (1929–30) by David Fogel, the Café Herrenhof, along with local Jewish cafés in Leopoldstadt, forms the location for key events in the development of the plot of the novel, which centres on Rudolf Gurdweill, a Jewish *flâneur* in Vienna who again is represented as both an insider and outsider there. This ambivalent status is typified, argues Pinsker, by the Café Herrenhof itself, which functions as a 'space that interfuses the public and the private . . . the culture of bohemia and the bourgeiosie' and which 'brings the city inside, but . . . also shields its regulars from the "crowd" and the "masses"'.[68]

After the War: Red Vienna

The Café Herrenhof rose to prominence in the years after World War I, a period which witnessed the decline of the Habsburg Empire. As Perloff notes, from being the capital of a geopolitical body which covered some 240,000 square miles, ruling over a population of some 50 million citizens in 1914, Vienna now became the capital of a 'small and fragile republic' with only 6 million inhabitants and covering a much smaller land mass of only 32,000 miles. The Republic of Austria, as French prime minister Georges Clemenceau noted, was now merely the 'remains' of the former empire.[69]

In this period after World War I we also discover some of the first depictions of Vienna by modern Anglophone writers, some of which explore the mood of a diminishing imperial capital. One curious early example of an American writer in Vienna is found in the story of Gorham Munson's modernist magazine *Secession*. Munson was one of the expatriate 'lost generation' of Americans exploring Europe after the war and had drifted on from Paris to Vienna in 1922.[70] His magazine took its name from the Secessionist artistic movement founded in fin-de-siècle Vienna[71] and led by Gustav Klimt (a key influence on Otto Wagner's architecture), but that was about all it took from its Viennese location: the first two issues were published in the city in 1922 because, as Munson unashamedly pointed out in the first issue, 'Secession is taking advantage of low printing costs in the Central Powers.'[72] A 'temporary editorial office' is listed as Hotel Zenit, Vienna, and although *Secession* contained work by some European writers (Tristan Tzara and Louis Aragon), only the cover image of the second issue, by Kassák, the Hungarian editor of *Ma*, showed any meaningful link to the cultural life of Vienna. The fact, however, that *Secession* was based in the city due to the cheap printing costs indicates the decline in the city's economic status in this period.

Another overlooked visitor to the city was Jean Rhys, discussed in the previous chapter for her depictions, as a female outsider, of Paris. Rhys also lived in Vienna for about fifteen months from April 1920, enjoying a wealthy lifestyle with her first husband, Jean Lenglet. Lenglet was working as a translator for a Japanese member of the Interallied Commission, a body which was overseeing the process of disarmament in the former Austrian republic after its defeat in World War I. Rhys and her husband were found a large flat in Favoritenstrasse, in the Fourth District, obtained the services of a maid and chauffeur, and enjoyed dining out in luxury hotels within the Ring such as the Sacher and the Imperial. Rhys, her husband and the staff of the Commission were all outsiders in a city undergoing profound political change and economic hardship, and this experience provided her with the material for her first published story, 'Vienne', which appeared in Ford Madox Ford's modernist magazine, *The Transatlantic Review*, in 1924, and then in a revised and expanded version in her first book of stories, *The Left Bank* (1927). Much of the content of the story draws upon autobiographical elements, a style repeated in much of Rhys' later fiction: thus she describes the Japanese officers her husband worked for; the luxury life they led in a section titled 'The Spending Phase' ('Good to have a car, a big chauffeur, rings and a string of pearls and as many frocks as I liked');[73] and a trip to Budapest. Finally, the story ends disastrously as Pierre (the character based on Lenglet in the story) is discovered to have been engaged in illegal money trading and the couple have to flee to Prague and then to Belgium.

Elements of Rhys' story also capture the political upheavals of Vienna at the time, and the end of the Habsburg Empire is noted obliquely, as when Rhys writes, 'Gone the "Aristokraten". They sat at home rather hungry, while their women did the washing.'[74] In a brief reference to Vienna in her later short story 'Temps Perdi', Rhys emphasises how the sensory affect of the city signified the decline of the Habsburgs: 'There was a smell of lilac when you got out into the street, of lilac, of drains and the past. Yes, that's what Vienna smelt of then.'[75] This recalls the way in which Rhys' depiction of Paris often focused upon the smells of the city and the affects they produced in her (see Chapter 1). In 'Vienne' the opening of the story – 'Funny how it's slipped away, Vienna. Nothing left but a few snapshots'[76] – ambiguously refers both to the narrator's personal memories of the city and to the luxurious Vienna of the Habsburg Empire, which has 'slipped away', and recalls Musil's post-war reflections on this decline in his *Man Without Qualities*. However, perhaps the most striking features of the story are formal and stylistic, with Rhys' characteristic impressionistic and disconnected prose being marked by multiple sections and very short, single-sentence, paragraphs that frequently end with a dash, as well as a macaronic use of French and German, denoting a sense of shifting national identities and the presence of numerous outsiders in the city in this period. These experimental qualities are even more pronounced in the version published in *The Transatlantic Review*, which, as Coral Ann Howells argues, 'lacks the embellishment that transformed it into a continuous narrative' in *The Left Bank* version, and can be described as 'quintessential modernist writing with a feminized perspective'.[77] The following section demonstrates some of these features in a paean to the power of money:

> Oh great god money – you make possible all that's nice in life – Youth and beauty, the envy of women, and the love of men –
>
> Even the luxury of a soul, a character and thoughts of one's own you give, and only you! – To look in the glass and think I've got what I wanted!
>
> I gambled when I married and I've won –
>
> As a matter of fact I wasn't exalted really, but it was exceedingly pleasant.
>
> Spending and spending And there was always more – [78]

However, such joy in the financial power Rhys enjoyed at this moment is rapidly replaced by a sense of the fragility of her position:

> We dined in a little corner of the restaurant.
>
> At the same table a few days before a Russian girl 24 years of age had shot herself.
>
> With her last money she had a decent meal and then bang. Out –
>
> And I made up my mind that if ever it came to it I should do it too.
>
> Not to be poor again.
>
> No and No and No –
>
> So darned easy to plan that – and always at the last moment – one is afraid. Or cheats oneself with hope.
>
> I can still do this and this. I can still clutch at that or that.
>
> So and so will help me.[79]

This retrospective narrative by Ella, the central character, is a fragmentary stream of consciousness that replicates Rhys' own feeling that her position in Vienna, like that of the Russian girl mentioned here, was that of an outsider whose temporary financial wealth created the impression – the 'snapshots' of the opening line – that she might have obtained what she desired. 'Vienne' thus offers not only a snapshot of an aristocratic Vienna that, like the Russian girl in the story, was on the way 'out', but also the first of many visions in Rhys' fiction of a heroine who almost obtains happiness in a European capital, only for her status as an outsider to be brutally expressed by what she calls in 'Vienne', 'the huge machine of law, order, respectability'.[80] 'Vienne' marks the first appearance of Rhys' perennial theme, honed to perfection in her later writings on Paris, of being an outsider; but the story also speaks to a Vienna itself full of outsiders, many of whom were refugees displaced after World War I.

The geography of the Habsburg Empire, whose power was symbolically concentrated within the buildings of the Ringstrasse enjoyed by Rhys and her husband, thus contracted after the war. However, a quite different geopolitical project that started in this period witnessed a considerable spatial restructuring of the city and expansion outside of the Ringstrasse. This was part of the unique socialist experiment known as 'Red Vienna' (*Rotes Wien*), begun after the Social Democrats won the 1919 election with the promise of 'a utopia of equality'.[81] Red Vienna, however, still exhibited a version of the inner/outer spatial dialectic that characterised the earlier history of the city: its project of rebuilding external social space was not only intended to provide better living conditions for workers, but was also meant to help reshape the inner life of working-class inhabitants of the city. The specific formation of Austro-Marxism in Vienna thus aimed at creating a 'revolution of souls' and a *neue Menschen* ('New Man'), a complex mixture of culture and politics that sought a transformation in the everyday lives of the working classes without the necessity for violent revolution, as in Russia.[82] As a slogan of Austro-Marxism put it: 'Against the ideas of force, the force of ideas.'[83] The key socio-spatial project informed by these ideas was the *Wiener Gemeindebauten*, which reshaped the urban fabric of the city by constructing some 400 communal housing blocks built in various locations around Vienna outside of the Ringstrasse. This new social housing for some 200,000 people (a tenth of Vienna's population) was built in the period between 1919 and 1934, including the famous red-painted facade of the Karl Marx Hof completed in 1930 (see Fig. 2.3).

The new housing was accompanied by libraries, medical facilities, schools, gardens, recreational facilities, and cultural institutions, embodying a unique social vision that, in Edward Timms' words, 'reshaped the intellectual life of the metropolis'.[84] Here was a project aimed explicitly at another group of Viennese outsiders: those working-class inhabitants displaced from the inner space of the Ringstrasse. Interestingly, many of the architects commissioned to build the *Gemeindebauten* were trained by Otto Wagner, the leading pioneer of modernist architecture in the city in the 1890s, who had rejected the historicism of the Ringstrasse in favour of buildings rooted in contemporary life, uniting materials and principles derived from urban engineering along with a functional and rational design aesthetic.[85] Thus the architectural vision of the *Gemeindebauten* in the post-war period was a unique combination of socialist ideals and modernist aesthetics, embodying what Eve Blau describes as a 'heterodox modernism'.[86]

Figure 2.3 Karl Marx Hof, Vienna.

For certain commentators the image of fin-de-siècle Viennese modernism has tended to overshadow the cultural politics of the Red Vienna period, one in which the city exhibited what Timms calls, 'a matrix for innovation',[87] and in which the inward turn of early Viennese modernism was replaced by a more outward social vision of the role of the arts and intellectual life: hence Musil advised on reform of the army; architect Alfred Loos wrote a pamphlet on arts engagement outside the middle classes; and psychoanalyst Alfred Adler helped set up counselling centres in proletarian areas of the city.[88] Even members of the Vienna Circle of Logical Positivist philosophers, such as Otto Neurath, became linked to worker education projects.[89] As in the fin-de-siècle period, secular Jews in the city played a leading role in many of the cultural and political innovations of Red Vienna. The rebuilding came at a significant moment in the city's history, as it again experienced another influx of outsiders. Some 200,000 refugees from the east, often Jews escaping pogroms in Russia, Poland and Ukraine, joined the pre-existing Jewish populace in Vienna after World War I.[90] In addition to these poorer refugees the city also became home to many intellectual exiles, such as those from counter-revolutionary Hungary after 1919, which included Marxist theorist Georg Lukács (who wrote *History and Class Consciousness* in

Vienna) and the circle around the avant-garde magazine *Ma*, edited by Lajos Kassák.[91]

For three British visitors in the early 1930s the stimulus to their forms of modernism lay beyond the Ringstrasse of fin-de-siècle Vienna. For Stephen Spender, John Lehmann, and Naomi Mitchison it was the 'matrix of innovation' represented by the Red Vienna project that inspired their imaginations. This is perhaps most starkly seen in John Lehmann's poem 'Though Time May Loiter (Karl Marx Hof, 1932)', taken from his 1934 collection, *The Noise of History:*

> But here is promise, too, among the wreck,
> New thoughts expand eclipsing forms that waste,
> The green of a new world, as the young trees
> In woods grow under withered boughs, and rock
> Supple in storms achieving fall of old.
> The future opens leaves to all the West
> Here in wide courtyards where the concrete throws
> Never full shadow, but the children play
> In sand or pool till sun has burned and filled
> Their bodies like dark honey in the comb,
> Where life is light and space and home for rest,
> With faith to hope, though factories employ
> Fewer each week at gear and plant that rust,
> Though Time may loiter and the decades tire
> Patience of millions, yet this tree shall climb,
> This thought triumphant recreate a star.[92]

The poem is a meditation upon the benefits of the social housing projects of Austro-Marxism in Vienna, exemplified in the vast structure of the Karl Marx Hof, which contained schools, baths, a library and health centre. Soon after arriving in Vienna in 1932 Lehmann became friends with a family living in the Karl Marx Hof, and the young son Karl, a member of the Schutzbund Socialist organisation, showed Lehmann around 'the beautiful tenement, the only one I had ever seen that did not remind me in any sense of a barracks'.[93] Formally the poem struggles somewhat to marry the rust of factories and the concrete of the courtyards to the pastoral imagery of trees, woods and sunshine, but the thrust of the verse celebrates these buildings as symbols for modernity or 'new thoughts . . . eclipsing forms that waste'. Fin-de-siècle Vienna has 'slipped away', in Rhys' words, and this vision of the city is now a wasteful form. Thus, in contrast to the previous era, with its 'wreck' and 'withered boughs', the poem looks to a better future ('the green of a new world') for the workers in the new housing, where 'life is light and space and home for rest'. The closing lines, however, signal a note of caution ('Time may loiter and the decades tire'), which perhaps mutes the way in which the 'promise' of the opening line returns at the end as the 'thought triumphant'.

Lehmann had arrived in Vienna after having worked at the Woolfs' Hogarth Press from 1930 to 1932.[94] From a conventional upper-class background (Eton and Cambridge) Lehmann, like many others, turned sharply leftwards, and became part of the famous radical circle of 1930s British writers that were inspired by an earlier modernism, but who sought to utilise the formal strategies of modernist experimentation for what they felt to be a more politically engaged writing, a group that included W. H. Auden and Christopher Isherwood.[95] But while these two wrote more about Berlin (see Chapter 3), Lehmann was more fascinated by Austria and based himself in Vienna for six years, until the Nazi *Anschluss* of 1938, also writing a fictionalised novel about his experiences in the city, *Evil Was Abroad* (1938).[96] He was partly attracted to Austria by a love of the poetry of Rainer Maria Rilke and, in an autobiography, *The Whispering Gallery* (1955), approvingly quotes Rilke's words: 'In order to write a single verse, one must see many cities, and men and things.'[97] Lehmann found that his own poetry was inspired by his travels through Europe to Austria, finding 'more fluid rhythms of thought' in 'the tunes that travelling, that watching and brooding on the lives of strange people in new countries started up in my mind'.[98] Lehmann felt that his travels produced 'a mingling of outer and inner, of the beleaguered past and the dissolving present, of the conscious mind with the irruptions of . . . the deeper intuitive mind', a set of feelings that found a home in Red Vienna, in which the socialist 'experiment' to provide the working classes with 'welfare and civilized conditions of life without a Communist revolution' acted as a 'magnet pulling me into the heart of Europe'.[99]

Red Vienna thus provided a deeply affective location for the young Lehmann, in which outer material space and inner experience coalesced, connecting together a modernist heritage (he mentions reading Yeats and Rimbaud in Vienna as well as Rilke) with a political climate of radical change in an innovative urban environment. Vienna in 1932 was like a 'new life' to Lehmann and he often uses a vocabulary of affect and emotion to describe the city: 'I made my first steps into intimacy with the city'; 'Vienna was the centre of my life'; the 'emotional texture of that time'; 'the wonderful panorama of the city I had become so infatuated with'.[100] Lehmann notes how he wrote many poems about the city, because the 'living truth of Vienna haunted me, like the reality of one's beloved: I was always trying to enlarge my knowledge, to define it, to encompass it in all the changing facets it presented me with, forever perplexed and fascinated by it'.[101] That Lehmann's writing was greatly inspired by the city is shown particularly in the experimental prose poems he wrote at this time, as in the following attempt to capture a kaleidoscopic vision its urban life:

> Seen from under the trees of the mountain slope, lying densely in the deep cleft of the hills, the myriad buildings of Vienna might be those of a dead city, with no single breathing inhabitant. At five o'clock in the afternoon, there is neither visible nor audible sign of the many hundred thousand human beings, whose activity can never for a moment cease.
>
> Deliberately, the mind assembles pictures to counter this deception: innumerable feet, at five o'clock hurrying from work along the pavements, some with narrow high heels, some with heels broad and low, mixing with feet that move with slower, more uncertain impulse, and heels long worn away and broken; detachments of auxiliary police, in their drab uniforms, tramping with music over the street-crossing, while the crowded trams wait; the chatter and rattle in and around shops at closing-time; taxis hooting and an ambulance ringing its bell; the noise of printing machines and radio concerts heard suddenly from open windows; weeping, laughter, voices raised in anger.[102]

Although this reads more as a piece of descriptive prose, the untitled poem does capture some of the energy and affect of the city, particularly in the emphasis on sounds ('taxis hooting') and emotions ('weeping, laughter') rising from the streets. Another, non-prose, poem, 'As the Day Burns On', attempted to catch what it called the 'splendid' 'texture' of the city:

> The bright mocking glance of eyes, and laughter in trams,
> And friends that hail across the streaming road
> Are walking fires, are signals of this joy.
> How splendid a texture they form, as the day burns on,
> How splendid the thunder of trains emerging from stations,
> And the tumbled freight of trains that take their ease
> After the rolling nights and five nations,
> The wakeful shunting at dawn.[103]

Lehmann here displays an intense delight in the 'splendid' qualities of Viennese city life, focusing upon the technology of transport ('laughter in trams'; 'thunder of trains') and the affect of 'joy' produced in him by these 'walking fires'. However, these feelings soon became tempered by the political events that occurred in February 1934, with the attempted Austro-Fascist putsch that resulted in Socialist-supporting areas of the city, including many of the Gemeinde Hauser, being shelled by the troops of the Heimwehr fascist party. As Lehmann writes, 'the guns were bombarding . . . the Karl Marx Hof, and Schutzbundler Karl's dream was smashed for ever into the rubble'.[104] Another prose poem in *The Noise of History*, 'Waiting', renders a different set of affects from those of joy that now pervaded the fabric of the city. The poem veers between a documentary-style depiction of the actions of the police and army in the city and attempts to capture the mood (*Stimmung*) of the city overall, as in the following section:

> They are waiting for the terror in this city. They feel it in their bodies, a sense of increasing pressure, as if a blood-vessel were about to burst. . . . In the central square of the workers' quarter after sunset, there is an atmosphere of suppression, a stillness that is like a feeling of sickness.[105]

The brooding atmosphere of the city is thus one that is physically felt by its citizens, the 'terror' and 'suppression' being brilliantly captured in the image of the blood-vessel about to burst from the pressure. This is a pre-cognitive set of affects experienced bodily by the citizens, demonstrating the flow of affect from the spaces of the city across to its inhabitants.

The turbulent events in Vienna, including the assassination of the right-wing dictator of Austria Engelbert Dollfuss, also form the backdrop to a long poem by Stephen Spender, who had arrived in Vienna in May 1934, partly staying in Lehmann's flat. *Vienna* (1934) is, as John Sutherland describes it, a 'filial homage' to Eliot's *The Waste Land*, with its distinct sections and a focus upon urban life.[106] Indeed, Vienna was listed in Part V of Eliot's poem as one of the 'Unreal Cities' with 'falling towers' and 'Cracks and reforms', an image of what Eliot's notes indicate to be the 'chaos' of Eastern Europe in the post-war years.[107] However, Spender's later image of the 'chaos' of Vienna presents a quite different political stance to that of Eliot.

The first section of Spender's poem is titled 'Arrival at the City' and concerns an unnamed stranger visiting Vienna, who overhears anonymous Eliotic voices of people staying at the Pension Beaurepas. These characters and the city itself are perceived as a confused amalgam of life and death, echoing the opening lines of *The Waste Land*, where lilacs are living in a 'dead land', or the start of the 'What the Thunder Said' section of the poem: 'He who was living is now dead / We who were living are now dying.'[108] In Spender's hands this trope becomes rather mangled in the condensed syntax of the opening lines:

> Whether the man living or the man dying
> Whether this man's dead life, or that man's life dying
> His real life a fading light his real death a light growing.
> Whether the live dead I live with.[109]

The question posed about 'whether' the city inhabitants are alive or dead is repeated, perhaps rather too much, throughout the section, and the lack of a resolution to the question is surely the key idea the poem is here expressing. It does, however, fit the post-war mood of a Vienna attempting to come to terms with the death of the Habsburg Empire and struggling to create a 'new life', symbolised for some in the promise of Red Vienna. Spender then tries to move the imagery forwards to describe the city itself, with a focus mainly upon the central areas with its 'statues' and 'palaces':

> Whether the man alive, or the man dying
> If the live man is dead, if the dying man
> Has life, though dying. And if this city
> With statues of desirable angels
> Whose tears are solid worlds; with palaces;
> With songs buried beneath the ground like rotted leaves
> To spring as cucumbers; has also its
> Obscene electric gestures, its glance like rape
> Hanging at doorways, I choose the wholly dead.[110]

Like the earlier ambivalence over the question 'whether', here it is not quite clear what it means to choose the 'wholly dead' – is Vienna wholly dead or only half-dead, masquerading as half-alive? Many of the more detached images of the city are confused by the use of the life/death trope:

> The Time is
> Dawn in the city with light dripping
> On speechless pavement, on mirroring parallels
> Of a surviving and dead wish, the defeated
> Staring, white canal.[111]

The 'white canal' and the 'speechless pavements' thus attempt to 'mirror' the 'defeated' inhabitants of the city, but again the juxtaposition does not quite succeed.

The second section, 'Parade of the Executive', employs the verse drama format that many other 1930s writers experimented with and is a more successful discussion of the political situation in Vienna, contrasting the words of the right-wing Executive of Dollfuss, Fey and Starhemberg with the voices of The Unemployed.[112] For the Executive, 'modern Vienna / Is not incorruptible Athens' but has to be 'controlled' and thus 'Murder is necessary. / A scalpel excellently reduces / Warts, rebels.'[113] Part Three shifts to the assaults by the Austro-Fascists upon the uprising by the Social Democrats in February 1934, action that centred upon the housing projects of Red Vienna. The story of the violence is thus told by anonymous voices, such as that of an old man who 'lived with my son and wife / In the Goethe Hof' and who witnessed 'the roaring shadow of a police aeroplane', soldiers firing in the courtyard and then Fey's howitzers thudding into the building, killing his son and 'four more whose dying choked the stairs'.[114] In a short section of prose poetry another recalls a 'mother and baby murdered in the Karl Marx Hof, which held out longest' and Schlinger Hof where 'the police drove out all the women and children in front of the building, and threatened to fire on them. The workers surrendered.'[115] Interestingly, the deaths of the inhabitants of the Hofs are symbolically outweighed by the attack upon the communal bricks and mortar here:

> There were some suffered from the destruction of houses
> More than from death of men: they weep for their houses
> That endured enormous wounds, a man's abyss.
> So the once sun-flaked walls, our elaborated pride,
> Were more our life than any man's one life, though proud.
> Heroes are instantly replaced: civilization
> Wears concrete sides: destroy these walls
> With shell-holes, and our children wear their weals.[116]

While the loss of the individual heroes of the section's title ('The Death of Heroes') can be made good, Spender suggests, the attack upon what the buildings represent is larger and represents an 'abyss', as the 'civilization' of Red Vienna has 'concrete sides'. As Spender later wrote, in the buildings of the Goethe Hof and Karl Marx Hof 'one glimpsed a new Vienna, a people's city'.[117] In the weeping at the destruction of the Red Vienna houses we see the political affect of the attack upon this new modernist Vienna, with the bombing of the external space of the buildings thus producing an inner anguish and despair.[118]

The final section of the poem, 'Analysis and Statement', reverts to the stylised multiple voices employed in *The Waste Land* once more and uses a collective chorus of five anonymous Viennese voices to try to articulate the 'fading' significance of 'what was said / by so many voices / Between the sunset and the coffee',[119] that is, the events of the previous months in the city. This initial 'Analysis' is then followed by the five anonymous voices (listed as 'A' to 'E'), representing the experiences of ordinary Viennese citizens. 'D', for instance, struggles to sum up the emotions they feel after the socialist experiment has been 'spoiled':

> 'There is no question more of not forgiving
> 'Forgiveness become my only feeling
> 'To understand their lack of understanding
> 'Has absorbed my entire loving,
> 'Yet sometimes I wish that I were loud and angry
> 'Without this human mind like a doomed sky
> 'That loves, as it must enclose, all.[120]

Spender here tries, not entirely successfully, to articulate the complex feelings of the ordinary citizens of Red Vienna whose love, forgiveness and understanding have been 'absorbed' by the political situation like a 'doomed sky' enclosing the city.

The poem then shifts to a 'Statement' by the protagonist of the first section of the poem, returning to a more personal and lyrical register:

> I, I, I.
> I think often of a woman
> With dark eyes neglected, a demanding turn of the head
> And hair of black silky beasts.
> How admirable it is
> They offer a surface bright as fruit in rain
> That feeds on kissing.[121]

From this description of Muriel Gardiner (Spender's first female lover) the poem attempts to link together Spender's various experiences of Vienna, both personal and public, and reintroduces the living/dead trope only to reject it for an image of the stranger: 'Not love, not death, not the dead living; / Supposing a stranger.'[122] The stranger 'travels through an unknown, mental country' while also being anchored in the traffic of the city, and the poem desperately tries to unite the internal states of mind and experiences of the stranger with external urban imagery and an understanding of the significance of the present:

> I reached the ambition to despair.
> Ignorant of history, all the day
> Traffic shivered my bones like a malaria.
> Time seemed foreshortened and confused with change[123]

The final lines of the poem strive for a wider understanding of the events witnessed here, situating Vienna – echoing Eliot's list of 'unreal cities' in *The Waste Land* but with a shift to purely European cities – within both a broader geography of Europe and an extended history:

> Witnessing whole Europe as large as Greece to Athens,
> Outside their stalking inner worlds, the dead man's life,
> The real life a fading light the real death a light growing;
> Berlin, Paris, London, this Vienna, emerging upon
> Further terrible ghosts from dreams. He greets the
> Historians of the future, the allies of no city.[124]

The cryptic and perhaps confused message in these final lines (it is unclear, for example, why 'real life' is 'a fading light') suggest that the poem is ultimately unable to combine 'inner worlds' with an understanding of external political events in Vienna in 1934.

This was an assessment of the poem that Spender himself reached in his later autobiography, *World Within World* (1951).[125] Here he described his poem as an example of a dilemma common to many 1930s poets, where 'public events had swamped our personal lives and usurped our personal experience', although the 'public emotions' of events like the Fascism witnessed in Vienna 'never became completely my own inner experience because . . . it invaded my personality rather than sprang out of it'.[126] The emotion that did spring out of his inner experience in the poem derived from Spender's sexual relationships with Tony Hyndman and Muriel Gardiner during his time in Vienna.[127] Spender felt that modern poetry must try to 'express the complexity of an ambivalent situation', that is, try to 'relate public passion to my private life'.[128] Thus he described *Vienna* as expressing his political indignation at the 'suppression of the Viennese Socialists by Dollfuss, Fey and Starhemberg' alongside his personal relationships: 'I meant to show that the two experiences were different, yet related. For both were intense, emotional and personal, although the one was public, the other private.'[129] Spender, quite accurately, described the attempt in *Vienna* as a failure, 'because it does not fuse the two halves of a split situation, and attain a unity where the inner passion becomes inseparable from the outer one'; perceptively he adds that the reason was because 'the world in which I was living was too terrible for this fusion to take place'.[130] Another interpretation is that the poem fails because Spender remains a more detached outsider in the city, unlike Lehmann, whose identification with Vienna and its contemporary politics is less filtered through the matrix of personal relationships and who becomes more of an 'inside-outsider'. The affects that stir Spender most intensely are complex personal ones, such as the shift from a male lover (Hyndman) to his first female lover (Gardiner), and appear quite unlike Lehmann's 'infatuation' with the 'emotional texture' of Vienna as a city. Spender's depictions of the city mostly seem infused with his 'public passion' and indignation at its politics: it is a city of 'Unhomely windows, floors scrubbed clean of love', 'oil-tarred pissoirs' and 'streets washed of their dung':[131] there is none of the 'joy' in the 'splendid' texture of the city that Lehmann finds here, even though he, like Spender, also felt the affective anguish of the Socialist defeat in the city. Lehmann's overall attitude to Vienna is one summed up in his poem 'In the Dying City': 'in this dying city, and epoch, we are happy'.[132] The mood of Old Vienna, and the imperial politics represented by the Habsburgs and the Ringstrasse, seemed for Lehmann to be eclipsed by a new *Stimmung*, where the 'green of a new world' was glimpsed all too briefly in the buildings of the Karl Marx Hof and other such spaces. Spender, in contrast, appears to try too hard to ape the universalising qualities of Eliot's *Waste Land*, signalled in the final lines of *Vienna*, where he 'greets' the 'Historians of the future', rather than addressing the affective city of the present as does Lehmann.

Vienna Diary: Naomi Mitchison

A similar tempered optimism to that of Lehmann pervades the pages of a prose account of Vienna by another Anglophone outsider. Naomi Mitchison, the

Scottish socialist novelist, visited Vienna just after the Heimwehr bombings of the Socialists in the Gemeinde Hauser dwellings, and her account of this visit was published by Victor Gollancz as *Vienna Diary 1934*. Mitchison's use of the diary format is in keeping with a tendency amongst much writing of the 1930s to document or report in a semi-factual fashion upon the pressing political events of the day. In the opening pages Mitchison emphasises her commitment to being as 'truthful' as possible and notes that as an 'observer I shall be some use', although 'I don't think I'm a good analyser.'[133] However, as Chris Hopkins acutely notes, this style of writing, found also in Lehmann, in Spender and in Christopher Isherwood's accounts of Berlin (see Chapter 3), establishes 'a middle position' between documentary journalism and 'highbrow' modernist fiction; these texts resemble journalism but 'retain a sense that they are more "literary" and structured'.[134] An example of this structuring is found in self-reflexive comments upon the process of composition throughout the book, as in the opening to the entry for 26 February: 'I want to try and get my impressions into order.'[135]

Mitchison's text is especially fascinating for its detailed descriptions of the Red Vienna housing projects and her meetings with the inhabitants of Karl Marx Hof, Schlinger Hof, Linden Hof and other residences, which demonstrate her own affective responses to the city. Like Spender and Lehmann, Mitchison is very attentive to the atmosphere or mood of Vienna, and her own emotional reactions to the modernism of Red Vienna display a strong politics of affect which also complicates the neutral documentary style of the diary format. Much of her diary is structured around visits which take Mitchison from the centre of the city to the working-class housing on the periphery:

> We got a bus at the Stephans-Platz, the middle of tourist Vienna, with its two-star cathedral and a restaurant where I remember having a very good dinner that last time I was in Vienna. . . . It bumped us mercilessly over cobbles, over the Donau Canal, and into a definitely non-tourist district – little shops, tenements, waste ground, factories, one fine-looking Gemeinde Haus.[136]

Mitchison thus rejects the two-star 'sights' in the city, and only uses her Baedeker guide when she later pretends to be a tourist to avoid the suspicions of the police.[137] Though the Baedeker map is useful she emphasises how the geography of the city in which she is interested cannot be found within its pages: 'it is funny to read about the things one ought to see, which don't seem to include the Gemeinde Hauser'.[138] Her interest is thus in a quite different spatiality from that visited by tourists to the city, one which has 'changed the face of the city' and transformed whole districts.[139] When she exits from the bus at the terminus she starts to note signs of the recent fighting, with plaster that is chipped with bullet marks and blocks with shell holes: now, the 'people's faces looked different from in the centre' and Mitchison notes that though rubble and broken glass can be tidied up easily, 'people's feelings cannot be cleared up or mended as quickly'.[140] As she approaches Schlinger Hof, 'one of the older Gemeinder Hauser, built in 1925', Mitchison again shifts her focus from the external social spaces of the houses, 'small-poxed with bullet marks', to the inhabitants who seem physically marked in similar fashion to their residences: 'But it was the faces which were worst. Everyone looked as sick as muck. All the mouths were turned down; all complexions pale as though from surgical shock; no one spoke loud or laughed.'[141]

Throughout the course of her diary Mitchison is introduced to many of these 'sick' residents and a quite different set of responses emerges in her text. Most noticeable is the way in which the social spaces of the Gemeinder Hauser are represented, with Mitchison repeatedly praising their beauty: Gartendstadt is 'most beautiful . . . high and airy and generous, with balconies and great courtyards'; Florisdorf (which reminds her of another worker housing project in England, Bourneville in Birmingham), contains a clock tower which in the moonlight appears 'more beautiful than I can say' and whose 'towers and square cliffs' are 'still beautiful' despite the 'black and ragged' shell holes in the building; while Karl Marx Hof is a 'superb building' and was 'extraordinarily beautiful', even despite its 'spatterings of bullet-marks'.[142] A woman in a shop tells her that now 'people say it is wrong to be Red, but Red Vienna was so beautiful to live in!'[143] The beauty of the buildings is also associated with the feelings provoked in her by these spaces and their inhabitants, which Mitchison contrasts with central Vienna:

> these are people who really do care for beauty, for all the things that story-book Vienna cares for. It was *they* who had the *Gemütlichkeit*, they in the light, friendly Gemeinde Hauser, and not the shop-keepers and civil servants of the centre. It is because of . . . this feeling for beauty . . . partly inborn, and partly through living with it in the beautiful houses, for I know that the way one lives alters one's thought and standards – that it was a crime against civilization to shell them.[144]

Though Mitchison might be accused of over-romanticising life in Red Vienna it is interesting to note her use of the untranslatable German term *Gemütlichkeit* (the nearest English equivalent is 'cosy') to describe a complex set of emotions including being at home, as well as warmth and friendliness, a term which vacillates between inner feelings and external belonging.

There are also a number of fascinating moments when Mitchison's affective response to the buildings is situated within the context of modernism and its politics. On 3 March she visits Sandleiten, 'a great big place, like a model town, housing perhaps 5,000 families', and describes in detail not only the particular houses and flats ('built with a pleasant irregularity'), but also the social and cultural facilities, including shops, baths, a kindergarten, playgrounds and a theatre.[145] The layout of the flats amidst trees and paths first reminds her a little of Clough Williams-Ellis' Italianate model village, Portmeirion, in north Wales,[146] but she then locates the buildings much more firmly within architectural modernism: a school employs 'very modern lines, with flat roofs and wide stretches of window' and other blocks of flats have nothing 'elaborate or affected' about the architecture and use material such as concrete and tiles. Everything, Mitchison decides, 'was done in the interests of the inhabitants; it is modernism, thoroughly domesticated for living-places'.[147] She then walks through a number of other Gemeinde Hauser, noting that architects of all schools have been used, 'so that sometimes one sees stark modernism, with the pleasing and exciting vertical line of staircase windows'. Mitchison notes that she would be 'glad and proud' to live here, and that it is the quality of the buildings that 'really annoys the middle classes', as it means that 'people who are poor, and should therefore live in humility, have been given something to be proud of'.[148] As she leaves, Mitchison notes that someone has chalked the Three Arrows, the symbol of the Schutzbund and the Socialist International on the walls, and this image – linking modernist buildings to socialist ideals – suddenly produces a powerful affect upon her: 'It is amazing how a thing like that has the power suddenly to get at whatever part of one is the romantic centre.'[149]

A similar affective reaction to the politics of space in Red Vienna also occurs after Mitchison's earlier visit to Florisdorf, where she is regaled with stories of residents being imprisoned and beaten for their socialist sympathies. As she leaves, Mitchison is addressed by a man who bemoans how the Heimwehr 'smashed our beautiful houses that we workers had built' and whispers a comradely '*Freundschaft!*' to her, before she travels back to central Vienna 'footsore, but nearly crying with joy' at what she has witnessed:

> It was one of the moments when one knows for certain that everything is worth while; that events are not unconnected; that there is a music and reason and kindness in history; that this is the thing one has waited for – this, at last, is living. I have had much love in my life . . . and I have had fame and praise and a lot of fun, but I don't think I have ever been happier that I was then.[150]

It is a potent emotional response to the combination of beautiful modernist buildings physically embodying socialist ideals and the stories she has learnt of the resilience of the inhabitants of the Gemeinde Hauser. The form of the first sentence above, with its clauses separated by semi-colons and use of anaphora ('that'), also indicates how Mitchison's style shifts into the more literary and less journalistic here, with the affect of the 'moment' demanding a more striking use of language in order to capture the feelings of 'joy' and 'happiness' that define 'living' at this moment in history, in this particular location.

Throughout the text are moments which demonstrate how Mitchison's emotions are thus attuned to the specific *Stimmung* of the social spaces of Red Vienna. For example, after hearing multiple stories of beatings and imprisonments from the inhabitants of Goethe Hof she feels she must not 'write with my body still flooded with anger'.[151] At another point she attempts to define the overall mood (*Stimmung*) of the city as a 'treble atmosphere of conspiracy': there is the 'atmosphere of Florisdorf' where people are on edge from the 'smashing up and in constant fear of betrayal and re-arrest'; the atmosphere of those still on the run from the right-wing authorities, but who are also 'full of hope and excitement'; and finally, the 'atmosphere of the other kind of conspirators who meet in the largest and most expensive cafés . . . not to speak of police spies'.[152] In a long section towards the end of the book devoted to the imprisonment and execution of the socialist leader, Wallisch, including a visit to his grave, Mitchison feels as though 'our deepest and fiercest emotions were at bursting point' and she finds herself 'crying over my typewriter'.[153]

Vienna Diary concludes with Mitchison returning home and, though she had earlier wondered whether there 'will certainly be a Nazi-German Nazi-State here within a few months', her final pages espouse the optimistic view that the 'new ideas' of socialism, with its 'new morality and the new idea of brotherhood and equality', will be the future for Austria.[154] Only a few years later, however, Mitchison's more pessimistic prediction came true, and the *Anschluss* of Austria by Nazi Germany in 1938 finally ended the 'new ideas' of interwar Red Vienna.

City of Ruins

Stephen Spender revisited Vienna after World War II and produced a further meditation upon the city and its geographical emotions in another long poem, *Returning to Vienna* (1947). The poem mulls over Spender's relationship with Gardiner again, referring to 'Vienna of my loving my first woman / She and I had senses canopied'. However, the pre-war city had now disappeared and the theme of sexuality associated with 'Feminine Vienna' is transformed into an image of sexual violence: 'Vienna Vienna raped within Vienna – / Within one single instant of one night / One flash which made streets one white'.[155] Much of Vienna was now in ruins due to wartime bombardment, a fate shared by two of the other cities discussed in this book (London and Berlin). The spaces of its previous versions of modernism were now replaced by what Spender described as 'ruined cadaverous Vienna'.[156] Over a quarter of the city's housing stock was destroyed or damaged, and some 270,000 people were homeless: city-centre bombsites included many of the venerable buildings of old Vienna such as the Opera, the Burgtheater and St Stephen's Cathedral.[157] By the end of the war the 200,000 Jews of pre-*Anschluss* Vienna had all but disappeared, initially as a result of emigration, then by deportation to the death camps.[158] The city was not only physically in rubble but also now politically and geographically divided between the four occupying Allied powers of Britain, America, Russia, and France, with the inner area within the Ringstrasse under joint control. The nervous beginnings of the Cold War division of the geography of Europe, seen in the Soviet blockade of Berlin in 1948 and the subsequent Allied airlift, were also felt in Vienna, where the Allied Commission in the city centre became one of the only meeting places between East and West: many in the city might reasonably have expected that the Soviet presence in the city would become permanent and that Vienna would disappear behind the Iron Curtain.[159] Several of the remaining great buildings on the Ringstrasse were taken over by the occupying powers, with the Americans in the Hotel Bristol, the Russians in the Hotel Imperial, and the British in the Sacher Hotel. The old Vienna, with its 'statues of desirable angels', as Spender put it, was now a set of ghostly ruins.[160]

This ruined and broken city was the backdrop for *The Third Man* (1949), a film by the English director Carol Reed, based upon a short story written specifically as a film treatment by Graham Greene. The film concerns an American, Holly Martins, who has been summoned by his fellow American friend, Harry Lime, to meet him in the city. When Martins arrives he is told that Lime is dead and he learns from a British military policeman, Calloway, that Lime has been involved in the black-market selling of adulterated penicillin in the city, resulting in many deaths. The film presents the spatial destruction of the city as paralleled in the corrupt morality of Vienna's black market and, as Martins becomes aware of the sordid nature of his friend's racket, he discovers that Lime is actually alive and has faked his own death to escape the authorities. The film's narrative is situated superbly within the geographical emotions produced by Vienna itself. This is mainly achieved by the cinematic creation of a powerful mood (*Stimmung*) which, as Flatley reminds us, works as a concept 'to articulate the shaping and structuring effect of historical context on our affective attachments'.[161] The mood of *The Third Man* is one of melancholy and loss, as noted at the start of Greene's story for the film: 'I never knew Vienna between the wars, and I am too young to remember the old Vienna with its Strauss music and its bogus easy charm; to me it is simply a city of undignified ruins.'[162] The fin-de-siècle modernism and the Red Vienna experiments in socialist culture are now long gone and the film's overwhelming 'affective atmosphere' is of a city physically ruined and made 'undignified' by black-market trading, ambiguous morality, and political uncertainty. This powerful mood is rendered in the film by an Expressionist *mise en scène* of tilted camera angles, deep focus shots, and use of heavy chiaroscuro, along with a famed soundtrack of zither music and, in the climactic scene in the Vienna sewers, a dialogue-less cacophony of sounds and images as Lime is finally tracked down.[163] There are many images of people scrabbling over the

Figure 2.4 Still of rubble from Carol Reed, *The Third Man* (1949).

rubble heaped in the streets of Vienna, adding to the mood of a city destroyed and lost both to its inhabitants and to outside visitors (see Fig. 2.4).

Rob Kitchen notes that Carol Reed was 'one of the great directors of city-experience, and what he emphasised was disorientation and alarm'.[164] One example in *The Third Man* is the many passages of spoken but untranslated German in the film, also without subtitles, replicating for the Anglophone viewer a sense of disorientation in the city. Further disorientation is found in the fact that many of the central characters in the film, almost all of whom are outsiders to Vienna, are also misidentified in various ways. Thus Lime's 'dead' body is actually that of a medical orderly, Joseph Harbin, while Lime himself impersonates the mysterious 'third man'; Lime's lover, Anna Schmidt, is actually a Czech refugee with false papers who is pretending to be Austrian so as to avoid deportation to the Russian sector; Martins is briefly and erroneously identified as a murderer, but he is also an author of pulp westerns who is mistaken for a 'serious' modern writer and asked to address a cultural meeting in the city where, embarrassed and out of place, he is quite unable to answer questions on the 'the stream of consciousness technique' in fiction; even the British officer, Calloway, is repeatedly called 'Callaghan' by Martins, much to his annoyance. Everyone in this city seems an outsider, disorientated from their 'real' selves, demonstrating that the 'affective atmosphere' we can discern in the film's overall mood (*Stimmung*) draws upon the spatial history of Vienna after World War II. Anna Schmidt, the Czech refugee, was thus one of around 600,000 displaced persons in Austria in 1948, nearly 10 per cent of the population of the country.[165] In February 1948 a communist coup in Czechoslovakia led to some 60,000 Czech refugees fleeing the country to the western areas of Germany and Austria. In Greene's original film treatment, Lime is said to have a distinguished role in the International Refugee Office in Vienna, an organisation set up by the Allies to administer the refugee crisis.[166]

The famous final scene of the film is shot in Vienna's cemetery after Lime's real funeral, and captures once again the mood of loss linked to the spatial history of a city of outsiders. Martins is being taken to the airport by Calloway and as they drive past Anna Schmidt, Martins asks whether Calloway can do anything to help Anna, who is at risk of being extradited to the Russian zone; Calloway says he will try, but there is little he can do. It is clear by now that Martins is in love with Schmidt, and the narrative seems to suggest that Schmidt might, now that Lime is dead, be reconciled to a relationship with his friend. Martins then asks to get out of the car and stands and waits for Schmidt, while Calloway drives away. In a long single take lasting about a minute, accompanied by the despondent tones of Anton Karas' zither music for the final time, Anna Schmidt walks slowly but deliberately towards the camera: she does not pause to acknowledge Holly Martins in any way, and instead walks past the camera and the viewer off-screen to the right (see Fig. 2.5).

Figure 2.5 Still of the final scene from Carol Reed, *The Third Man* (1949).

In this way the film refuses any simple narrative closure, a feature familiar from many other modernist narratives: in Greene's original story the couple end arm in arm, a finale that Greene himself admitted was bettered by that proposed by Reed for the film.[167] More than being merely a typically open modernist ending, however, Anna Schmidt's walk off-screen into an unknown future symbolises the ongoing journey of the many refugees in Vienna and across post-war Europe at this time. Schmidt seems to belong nowhere, certainly not in the arms of Martins, who, after all, was responsible for the death of Lime, her true love. Now, in her long, melancholy walk out of the picture, she sums up the 'affective atmosphere' of the ruined city depicted in the film, and also the fate of this particular kind of outsider, the refugee, determined but struggling to belong 'inside', to find a place to dwell in a world of rubble and displacement. The long history of Vienna's modernism, with its particular mood (*Stimmung*) of loss and its spatial dialectic of inner and outer, can now only be located beyond the frame of cinematic space.

Notes

1. Jonathan Flatley, *Affective Mapping: Melancholia and the Politics of Modernism* (Cambridge, MA: Harvard University Press, 2008), p. 19. See also the Introduction for further discussion of mood and *Stimmung*.
2. Flatley, *Affective Mapping*, p. 22.
3. See Laura Doyle, 'Toward a Philosophy of Transnationalism', *Journal of Transnational American Studies*, 1:1 (2009); available at http://escholarship.org/uc/item/9vr1k8hk (last accessed 30 Oct. 2017). An insightful discussion of 'Austro-Modernism' across the 'polyglot empire' of the countries of the former Habsburg Empire can be found in Marjorie Perloff, *Edge of Irony: Modernism in the Shadow of the Habsburg Empire* (Chicago: University of Chicago Press, 2016).
4. A key difference between Germany and Austria in comparison with Britain and France was that of imperialism: though Germany did colonize areas of Africa and New Guinea as part of the 'scramble for Africa' after the 1884 Berlin Conference, Austria never formally colonised any overseas territories. Germany was forced to relinquish its colonies after defeat in World War I as part of the Versailles settlement, while British and French colonies continued for decades thereafter. For a consideration of the 'colonial' dimension in Austria see Walter Sauer, 'Habsburg Colonial: Austria-Hungary's Role in European Overseas Expansion Reconsidered', *Austrian Studies* 20 (2012), pp. 5–23.
5. Malcolm Bradbury (ed.), *The Atlas of Literature* (London: De Agostini, 1996), p. 163. The status within the imperial imaginary of Dublin as the 'second city' of empire was a feature that James Joyce understood all too well.
6. See Scott Spector, 'The Habsburg Empire' in *The Cambridge Companion to European Modernism*, ed. Pericles Lewis (Cambridge: Cambridge University Press, 2011), pp. 52–74; p. 67; and Katherine David-Fox, 'Prague-Vienna, Prague-Berlin: the Hidden Geography of Czech Modernism', *Slavic Review* 59 (2000), pp. 735–60.
7. See Nicholas Sawicki, 'The View from Prague: *Moderní revue* (1894–1925); *Volné směry* (1896–1949); *Umělecký měsíčník* (1911–14); *Revoluční sborník Devětsil* (1922); *Život* (1922); *Disk* (1923–5); *Pásmo* (1924–6); and *ReD* (1927–31)' in

The Oxford Critical and Cultural History of Modernist Magazines, vol. 3: Europe 1880–1940, ed. Peter Brooker, Sascha Bru, Andrew Thacker and Christian Weikop (Oxford: Oxford University Press, 2013), pp. 1074–98. After the war the avant-garde movement known as Devětsil, led by Karel Teige, produced important magazines such as *Život*, *Disk*, *Pasmo*, and *ReD*.

8. Spector, 'The Habsburg Empire', p. 70.
9. See Saskia Elizabeth Ziolkowski, 'Svevo's *Uomo Senza Qualità*: Musil and Modernism in Italy' in *Gender and Modernity in Central Europe: The Austro-Hungarian Monarchy and its Legacy*, ed. Agatha Schwartz (Ottawa: University of Ottawa Press, 2010), pp. 83–102.
10. In the English-speaking world Trieste is perhaps best known as the place in which Svevo's good friend James Joyce began to establish his career as a writer. When Joyce escaped the constrictions of Irish life to live in Trieste from 1904 to 1920 the city, according to John McCourt, was a major influence upon the composition of *Ulysses*, with its own deracinated Jewish hero, Leopold Bloom; see John McCourt, *The Years of Bloom: James Joyce in Trieste 1904–20* (Madison: University of Wisconsin Press, 2000).
11. See Timothy Hiles, 'Reality and Utopia in Munich's Premier Magazines: *Simplicissimus* (1896–1944) and *Jugend* (1896–1940)', and Jessica Horsley, '"There You Have Munich": *Der Blaue Reiter* (1912); *Revolution* (1913); and *Der Weg* (1919)' in *Modernist Magazines, vol. 3*, pp. 709–26, 727–49.
12. See Birgitte Pichon and Karl Riha (eds), *Dada Zurich: A Clown's Game from Nothing* (New York: G. K. Hall, 1996).
13. See Peter Gay, *Freud: A Life for Our Time* (London: Papermac, 1995), pp. 19–21.
14. See Wolfgang Maderthaner and Lisa Silverman, '"Wiener Kreise": Jewishness, Politics, and Culture in Interwar Vienna' in *Interwar Vienna: Culture between Tradition and Modernity*, ed. Deborah Holmes and Lisa Silverman (New York: Camden House, 2009), pp. 59–80; p. 67.
15. Peter Hall, *Cities in Civilization: Culture, Innovation, and Urban Order* (London: Weidenfeld and Nicolson, 1998), p. 5. For an account of Jewish cultural dominance in the city see Steven Beller, *Vienna and the Jews 1867–1938: A Cultural History* (Cambridge: Cambridge University Press, 1989), and Lisa Silverman, *Becoming Austrian: Jews and Culture between the World Wars* (Oxford: Oxford University Press, 2012). For a critical interrogation of the concept of a 'Jewish modernism' see Scott Spector, 'Modernism Without Jews: A Counter-Historical Argument', *Modernism/Modernity* 134 (Nov. 2006), pp. 615–33.
16. Andreas Huyssen, 'The Disturbance of Vision in Vienna Modernism', *Modernism/Modernity* 5:3 (Sep.1998), pp. 33–47; p. 40.
17. Donald J. Olsen, *The City as a Work of Art: London, Paris, Vienna* (New Haven: Yale University Press, 1986), pp. 72–3.
18. Carl Schorske, *Fin-de-Siècle Vienna: Politics and Culture* (Cambridge: Cambridge University Press, 1981), p. 9.
19. Ibid. p. xxvii.
20. Ibid. p. 11.
21. Theodor Reik, *The Search Within* (1956), cited in Paul Carter, *Repressed Spaces: The Poetics of Agoraphobia* (London: Reaktion, 2002), p. 7.
22. Carter, *Repressed Spaces*, p. 8.
23. Ivan Ward, *Phobia* (London: Icon Books, 2001), p. 63. Freud, *New Introductory Lectures* (1932), cited in Anthony Vidler, *Warped Space: Art, Architecture, and Anxiety in Modern Culture* (Boston, MA: MIT Press, 2000), p. 40.
24. Freud to Fliess, cited in Vidler, *Warped Space*, p. 38.
25. Vidler, *Warped Space*, pp. 41–2.

26. Sigmund Freud, 'Analysis of a Phobia in a Five-Year-Old Boy ("Little Hans")' in *Case Histories I*, Penguin Freud Library, vol. 8 (Harmondsworth: Penguin, 1990), pp. 167–305; pp. 208–9. When Lacan revisited this case in 1957 he also felt the need to produce several maps to trace the spatial locus of the case, enlarging the geography from the immediate setting to include other features such as the many railway lines that ran near to Hans' house; see Vidler, *Warped Space*, pp. 42–3.
27. Freud, 'Little Hans', p. 244.
28. Georg Simmel, 'The Metropolis and Mental Life' (1903), in *The Blackwell City Reader*, ed. Gary Bridge and Sophie Watson (Oxford: Blackwell, 2002), pp.11–19; p. 11.
29. Marshall Berman, *All that Is Solid Melts into Air: The Experience of Modernity* (London: Verso, 1982), p. 159.
30. James Donald, 'This, Here, Now: Imagining the Modern City' in *Imagining Cities: Scripts, Signs, Memories*, ed. Sallie Westwood and John Williams (London: Routledge, 1997), pp. 181–201; pp. 193–4.
31. See Vidler, *Warped Space*, pp. 29–30.
32. Sitte cited in ibid. pp. 27, 28.
33. For an account of Sitte's ideas see Schorske, *Fin-de-Siècle Vienna*, pp. 62–72.
34. These included *Die Strasse* (1923), *Joyless Street* (1928), *Tragedy of the Street* (1927) and *Asphalt* (1929). See Siegfried Kracauer, *From Caligari to Hitler: A Psychological History of German Film* (1947; Princeton: Princeton University Press, 1970).
35. Robert Musil, *The Man Without Qualities*, 3 vols, trans. Eithne Wilkins and Ernst Kaiser (London: Picador, 1979), vol. 1, p. 3. For a discussion of the ironic 'double vision' of the opening to Musil's novel, see Perloff, *Edge of Irony*, pp. 71–7.
36. For a discussion of Ford's text see the Introduction and Chapter 4.
37. Heidegger's notion of mood (*Stimmung*) is closely linked to the idea of subjects being *attuned* to the surrounding atmosphere; see Flatley, *Affective Mapping*, pp. 21–2.
38. Musil, *Man*, p. 4.
39. Henri Lefebvre, *The Production of Space*, trans. D. Nicholson-Smith (Oxford: Blackwell, 1991), p. 42.
40. Musil, *Man*, p. 5.
41. Ibid.
42. Ibid. p. 7. Musil seems indebted here to the ideas of the philosopher Ernest Mach, whose positivist vision of 'psychophysics' influenced many other Viennese figures. For an account of Mach's ideas see Allan Janik and Stephen Toulmin, *Wittgenstein's Vienna* (New York: Simon and Schuster, 1973), pp. 132–45.
43. Musil, *Man*, pp. 31, 32. 'Kakania' refers both to the imperial and royal initials 'K.K.', widely used in Vienna, and to a German colloquialism for shit.
44. Ibid. p. 30.
45. Ibid. p. 31. This is in striking contrast to the image of Berlin, a city often represented as unafraid to embrace ceaseless evolution; see Chapter 3. For an elegant discussion of the relation between speed and modernity see Enda Duffy, *The Speed Handbook: Velocity, Pleasure, Modernism* (Durham, NC: Duke University Press, 2009).
46. Perloff, *Edge of Irony*, p. 77. Interestingly, Perloff also links the non-linear spatial form of Musil's 'novel', with its structure of criss-crossing remarks, to the work of another Viennese modernist, Ludwig Wittgenstein (pp. 78–9).
47. Edward Timms, 'Musil's Vienna and Kafka's Prague: The Quest for a Spiritual City' in *Unreal City: Urban Experience in Modern European Literature and Art*,

ed. Edward Timms and David Kelley (Manchester: Manchester University Press, 1985), pp. 247–63; p. 258.

48. This interpretation of Viennese modernism is most clearly propounded in Janik's and Toulmin's *Wittgenstein's Vienna*.
49. Ludwig Wittgenstein, *Tractatus Logico-Philosophicus* (1922), trans. D. F. Pears and B. F. McGuinness (London: Routledge and Kegan Paul, 1961), p. 3. For the fullest account of Wittgenstein's relation to other currents in Viennese intellectual life, including Mauthner, see Janik and Toulmin, *Wittgenstein's Vienna*. On Kraus see Edward Timms, *Karl Kraus, Apocalyptic Satirist: The Post-War Crisis and the Rise of the Swastika* (New Haven: Yale University Press, 2005).
50. Hugo von Hofmannsthal, 'A Letter' in *The Lord Chandos Letter, and Other Writings*, trans. Joel Rotenberg (New York: New York Review Book, 2005), pp. 117–28; p. 121.
51. Ibid.
52. Janik and Toulmin, *Wittgenstein's Vienna*, p. 117.
53. Huyssen, 'Disturbance of Vision', p. 35.
54. Ibid. p. 40.
55. Ibid.
56. Ibid.
57. Christian Brandstätter (ed.), *Vienna 1900 and the Heroes of Modernism* (London: Thames and Hudson, 2005), p. 336. On the coffee house in Vienna see Harold B. Segal, *The Vienna Coffeehouse Wits 1890–1938* (West Lafayette: Purdue University Press, 1993), and for the wider history see Markman Ellis, *The Coffee House: A Cultural History* (London: Weidenfeld and Nicolson, 2004).
58. Alfred Polgar, 'Theorie des "Café Central"' in *And den Rand geschrieben* (Berlin: Ernst Rowohlt, 1926), pp. 85–91; p. 85.
59. Ibid.
60. Ibid. p. 86.
61. See Helmut Gruber, *Red Vienna: Experiments in Working-Class Culture 1919–1934* (New York: Oxford University Press, 1991), p. 33.
62. Cited in Beller, *Vienna and the Jews*, pp. 40–1; Spector, 'Habsburg Empire', p. 57.
63. Brandstätter, *Vienna 1900 and the Heroes of Modernism*, p. 340; Shachar Pinsker, 'The Urban Literary Café and the Geography of Hebrew and Jewish Modernism in Europe' in *The Oxford Handbook of Global Modernisms*, ed. Mark Wolleger with Matt Eatough (New York: Oxford University Press, 2012), pp. 433–60; p. 445. Herzl had been born in Budapest, but arrived in Vienna in 1878.
64. Pinsker, 'Urban Literary Café', p. 445.
65. Ibid. pp. 444–8.
66. Ibid. p. 434; Edward W. Soja, *Thirdspace: Journeys to Los Angeles and Other Real-and-Imagined Places* (Oxford: Blackwell, 1996).
67. Pinsker, 'Urban Literary Café', p. 447.
68. Ibid. pp. 448–9.
69. See Perloff, *Edge of Irony*, p. 1.
70. For discussion of the related American magazine *Broom*, published briefly in Berlin, see Chapter 3.
71. See Gorham Munson, *The Awakening Twenties: A Memoir-History of a Literary Period* (Baton Rouge: Louisiana State University Press, 1985), p. 163.
72. Gorham Munson, 'An Old Song to New Music', *Secession* 1 (Spring 1922), p. 25. It cost only $20 to print, claimed Munson later (*Awakening Twenties*, p. 163). A later American magazine, *Story*, devoted to the short story was also begun in Vienna in 1931 by Whit Burnett and Martha Foley. For a discussion of *Secession* see Peter Nicholls, 'Destinations: *Broom* (1921–4) and *Secession* (1922–4)' in

The Oxford Critical and Cultural History of Modernist Magazines, vol. 2: North America, 1894–1960, ed. Peter Brooker and Andrew Thacker (Oxford: Oxford University Press, 2012), pp. 636–54.

73. Jean Rhys, 'Vienne', original version, reprinted in *Modernism: An Anthology*, ed. Lawrence Rainey (Oxford: Blackwell, 2005), pp. 946–9; p. 948.
74. Rhys, 'Vienne', as printed in *The Left Bank* and reprinted in Jean Rhys, *The Collected Short Stories* (New York: Norton, 1987), pp. 94–124; p. 101.
75. Rhys, 'Temps Perdi' in *Collected Short Stories*, pp. 256–74; p. 261.
76. Rhys, 'Vienne' in *Collected Short Stories*, p. 94.
77. Coral Ann Howells, 'Introduction: Jean Rhys' in *The Gender of Modernism: A Critical Anthology*, ed. Bonnie Kime Scott (Bloomington: Indiana University Press, 1990), pp. 372–77; p. 373.
78. Rhys, 'Vienne' in *Modernism: An Anthology*, p. 948.
79. Ibid. p. 949.
80. Rhys, 'Vienne' in *Collected Short Stories*, p. 115.
81. Wolfgang Maderthaner and Lisa Silverman, '"Wiener Kreise": Jewishness, Politics, and Culture in Interwar Vienna' in *Interwar Vienna: Culture between Tradition and Modernity*, ed. Deborah Holmes and Lisa Silverman (New York: Camden House, 2009), pp. 59–80; p. 72.
82. For a critical overview of the achievements of Austro-Marxism in Red Vienna see Helmut Gruber, *Red Vienna: Experiments in Working-Class Culture 1919–1934* (New York: Oxford University Press, 1991).
83. Gruber, *Red Vienna*, p. 180.
84. Timms, *Karl Kraus*, p. 106. For further discussion of Red Vienna see Eve Blau, *The Architecture of Red Vienna 1919–1934* (Cambridge, MA: MIT Press, 1999), and Gruber, *Red Vienna*.
85. On the importance of Wagner see Schorske, *Fin-de-Siècle Vienna*, pp. 72–110.
86. Blau, *Architecture of Red Vienna*, p. 7. Blau offers a careful reassessment of the achievements of the Red Vienna project, rejecting critics of it such as Manfredo Tafuri in his *Vienna Rossa* (1980).
87. See Edward Timms, 'Cultural Parameters between the Wars: A Reassessment of the Vienna Circles' in *Interwar Vienna*, pp. 21–31; p. 24.
88. See Timms, *Karl Kraus*, p. 106.
89. See Maderthaner and Silverman, ' "Wiener Kreise" ', p. 60.
90. Timms, *Karl Kraus*, pp. 28–9.
91. See Eva Forgacs and Tyrus Miller, 'The Avant-Garde in Budapest and in Exile in Vienna' in *Modernist Magazines, vol. 3*, pp. 1136–41.
92. John Lehmann, *The Noise of History* (London: Hogarth Press, 1934), p. 27.
93. John Lehmann, *The Whispering Gallery: Autobiography I* (London: Longmans, 1955), p. 208.
94. On this see J. K. Johnstone, 'John Lehmann and Bloomsbury' in *John Lehmann: A Tribute*, ed. A. T. Tolley (Ottawa: Carleton University Press, 1987), pp. 78–98, as well as Lehmann's own account in *Whispering Gallery*, pp. 164–94.
95. For the classic account of this group see Samuel Hynes, *The Auden Generation: Literature and Politics in England in the 1930s* (London: Bodley Head, 1976).
96. For discussion of this see Chris Hopkins, *English Fiction in the 1930s: Language, Genre, History* (London: Continuum, 2006), pp. 77–94.
97. Lehmann, *Whispering Gallery*, p. 198.
98. Ibid. p. 198.
99. Ibid. p. 199.
100. Ibid. pp. 208, 216, 216, 225.
101. Ibid. p. 226.

102. Ibid.
103. Lehmann, *Noise of History*, p. 32.
104. Lehmann, *Whispering Gallery*, p. 214.
105. Lehmann, *Noise of History*, p. 39.
106. John Sutherland, *Stephen Spender: The Authorized Biography* (London: Penguin, 2004), p. 172. Eliot was, of course, the editor at Faber who published Spender's poem, despite misgivings about it (see Sutherland, *Spender*, p. 173). For a short analysis of the poem's modernism see David Leeming, *Stephen Spender: A Life in Modernism* (New York: Henry Holt, 1999).
107. T. S. Eliot, *The Waste Land* in *Collected Poems 1909–1962* (London: Faber, 1974), pp. 61–86; p. 77. Eliot's notes (p. 85) indicate that this image came from his reading of Herman Hesse.
108. Eliot, *Collected Poems*, p. 64.
109. Stephen Spender, *Vienna* (London: Faber and Faber, 1934), p. 13.
110. Ibid. pp. 14–15.
111. Ibid. pp. 16–17.
112. For instance, see W. H. Auden and Christopher Isherwood, *The Ascent of F6: A Tragedy in Two Acts* (London: Faber, 1936).
113. Spender, *Vienna*, p. 22.
114. Ibid. p. 29.
115. Ibid.
116. Ibid. p. 30.
117. Stephen Spender, *World Within World* (London: Readers Union, 1953), p. 171.
118. The remainder of this section of the poem then tells the story of Koloman Wallisch, national secretary of the Socialist party, who fled the city and waged a guerrilla war on the authorities until he was captured, tried and executed, a story which also features in Naomi Mitchison's *Vienna Diary 1934* (Glasgow: Kennedy and Boyd, 2009).
119. Spender, *Vienna*, p. 37.
120. Ibid. p. 38.
121. Ibid. p. 39.
122. Ibid. p. 40. For the relationship between Gardiner and Spender see Sutherland, *Spender*, pp. 163–78.
123. Ibid. p. 41.
124. Ibid. p. 42.
125. And one shared by, for example, Hynes, *Auden Generation*, pp. 148–9.
126. Spender, *World*, p. 164.
127. See Sutherland, *Spender*, pp. 163–78.
128. Spender, *World*, pp. 164–5.
129. Ibid. p. 165.
130. Ibid. p. 165
131. Spender, *Vienna*, pp. 16, 23, 17.
132. Lehmann, *Noise of History*, p. 31.
133. Mitchison, *Vienna Diary*, p. 10.
134. Hopkins, *English Fiction in the 1930s*, pp. 78–9. The features that Hopkins notes have also led other critics to describe Mitchison as part of a group of writers described as 'Intermodernists'; see the essays in *Intermodernism: Literary Culture in Mid-Twentieth Century Britain*, ed. Kristin Bluemel (Edinburgh: Edinburgh University Press, 2009).
135. Mitchison, *Vienna Diary*, p. 26.
136. Ibid. p. 39.
137. Ibid. p. 113.

138. Ibid. p. 83.
139. Ibid. p. 135.
140. Ibid. p. 39.
141. Ibid. p. 40.
142. Ibid. pp. 42, 60, 128. On the creation of Bourneville by the Cadbury brothers see Elizabeth Outka, *Consuming Traditions: Modernity, Modernism, and the Commodified Authentic* (Oxford: Oxford University Press, 2009), pp. 32–46.
143. Mitchison, *Vienna Diary*, p. 142.
144. Ibid. p. 162.
145. Ibid. pp. 85–6.
146. See http://www.portmeirion-village.com/visit/clough-williams-ellis/ (last accessed 30 Oct. 2017).
147. Mitchison, *Vienna Diary*, p. 87. She is, however, rather less keen on the communal bathhouses.
148. Ibid. pp. 88–9.
149. Ibid. p. 89.
150. Ibid. pp. 61–2.
151. Ibid. p. 146.
152. Ibid. pp. 73–4.
153. Ibid. pp. 244, 257.
154. Ibid. pp. 133, 282.
155. Stephen Spender, *Returning to Vienna* (New York: Banyan Press, 1947), unpaginated.
156. Ibid. For more on literary visitors to post-war Vienna see Lara Feigel, *The Love-Charm of Bombs: Restless Lives in the Second World War* (London: Bloomsbury, 2013), pp. 367–96.
157. Charles Drazin, *In Search of The Third Man* (London: Methuen, 2000), p. 14.
158. George E. Berkley, *Vienna and Its Jews: The Tragedy of Success 1880s–1980s* (Cambridge, MA: Madison Books, 1988), p. 24.
159. Drazin, *In Search of The Third Man*, pp. 15–16. For more on the political context see Ralph W. Brown III, 'Making the Third Man Look Pale: American-Soviet Conflict in Vienna during the Early Cold War in Austria, 1945–1950', *The Journal of Slavic Military Studies* 14:4 (2001), pp. 81–109.
160. Spender, *Vienna*, p. 114.
161. Flatley, *Affective Mapping*, p. 19.
162. Graham Greene, *The Third Man and The Fallen Idol* (1950; London: Vintage, 2001), p. 14. For more on the background to the film see Drazin, *In Search of The Third Man*.
163. On the cinematic features employed in the film see Rob Kitchen, *The Third Man* (London: BFI, 2003).
164. Ibid. p. 46.
165. Drazin, *In Search of The Third Man*, p. 19.
166. Greene, *Third Man*, p. 16.
167. Greene, *Third Man*, pp. 119, 11.

3

BERLIN

Introduction: Hellhole and Paradise

Stephen Spender first visited Berlin in 1931, before his time in Vienna, staying initially with Christopher Isherwood. Spender's perceptions of the city epitomised one popular image of Berlin in the Weimar years of the 1920s and 1930s: it was, he wrote, 'a paradise where there was no censorship and young Germans enjoyed extraordinary freedom in their lives'.[1] After a while, however, the well-documented economic and political crises that eventually crushed the Weimar Republic in 1933 began to impinge upon the young English writer, as 'the background of our lives in Germany was falling to pieces. There was a sensation of doom to be felt in the Berlin streets.'[2] Depictions of Berlin by insiders and outsiders have often displayed this vacillation of mood between the utopian and the dystopian, shown, for instance, when the German Expressionist writer Hans Flesch-Brunningen commented: 'Berlin for us was despicable, corrupt, metropolitan, anonymous, gigantic, seminal, literary, political, painterly . . . in short, a hellhole and paradise all in one.'[3] Peter Conrad in *Modern Times, Modern Places* has suggested that it was 'Berlin's fate to be the twentieth century's dystopia: a city of expressionist anguish, just as Paris was the capital of erotic licence for the surrealists.'[4] This view somewhat polarises the two cities, for the focus upon 'erotic licence' was also a significant feature in the representation of Berlin, as discussed below.[5] The Austrian writer Stefan Zweig thus depicted Berlin as a city whose dystopian character was typified by its sexual morality:

> All values were changed, and . . . Berlin transformed into the Babylon of the world. . . . Even the Rome of Suetonius had never known such orgies as the pervert balls of Berlin, where hundreds of men costumed as women and hundreds of women as men danced under the benevolent eyes of the police.[6]

For others, however, the liberated sexuality of Berlin represented, as Spender puts it, a 'paradise', attracting several English homosexual writers of the 1930s, such as Spender, Isherwood and W. H. Auden, who experienced a utopian sense of sexual freedom allied to a cosmopolitan and experimental cultural life that seemed unavailable to them in Britain. Though their sexuality marked them as 'outsiders' in British society, as strangers in Berlin they felt somehow more at 'home'. Thus, when Isherwood arrived in Berlin in 1929, to stay for four years, he claims he contemplated informing the passport official that he was 'looking for my homeland and I've come to find out if this is it'.[7]

This chapter explores these vacillating representations of Berlin and its spaces in a rough chronology from the end of the nineteenth century to the conclusion of the Weimar years in 1933. It sketches the development of the city as one dominated by a technological modernity, in which the twin features of *spaciousness* and *restlessness* are repeatedly emphasised. It first discusses the most famous aesthetic movement in German modernism, Expressionism, which has its origins in literature and the visual arts prior to World War I but which also influenced many of the important productions of the burgeoning German film industry after the war. One such film is Walter Ruttmann's *Berlin, Die Symphonie der Großstadt* (*Berlin: Symphony of a Great City*) (1927), which combines Expressionism with the image of the city as dominated by technology. The chapter then shifts to consider the cultural visions of outsiders in the city, commencing with the large Russian expatriate community of the 1920s, as represented in Victor Shklovsky's novel, *Zoo, or Letters Not about Love* (1923), before turning to American visitors associated with the expatriate magazine *Broom* (1921–4), which for a while was based in Berlin. It then moves on to consider Anglophone visitors, such as Auden and Isherwood, in the context of a discussion of the spatiality of various cultural institutions in the city, such as cafés and bars, drawing upon Michel Foucault's concept of heterotopia. The chapter closes by analysing two retrospective accounts of living in Berlin in the late 1920s that experiment with factual genres of writing such as the memoir or the diary: Isherwood's *Goodbye to Berlin* (1939) and Bryher's *Heart to Artemis* (1962).

Two forms of affect thus dominate the various representations examined in this chapter. The first is the way in which broad forms of affect are central to the aesthetic innovations of Expressionism, which viewed art as a vision of inner energy or 'vital intensity' and which one critic described as the expression of 'violent emotions welling up from the innermost recesses of the subconscious'.[8] The oscillation between viewing Berlin as a 'paradise' or a 'hellhole', a space of utopia or dystopia, is an illustrative instance of this kind of intensified emotional vocabulary. Interestingly, many of the affects and startling emotions articulated in German Expressionist works are direct responses to the material spaces of modern Berlin. The second sense of affect explored here is that of the atmosphere of Berlin itself, how the mood (*Stimmung*) of the city is felt in terms of spatiality and constant motion, features intrinsically linked to the city's technological modernity.[9] While Vienna, as discussed in the previous chapter, was dominated by a mood of loss or melancholy, associated with the decline of the centuries-old Habsburg Empire, Berlin was a relatively 'new' city unburdened by the weight of cultural traditions. Its new spaces were defined in terms of a restiveness, summed up in the final phrase of Karl Scheffler's 1910 book *Berlin: Ein Stadtschicksal*, that Berlin was a city 'forever to become and never to be'.[10] While some found this mood (*Stimmung*) something to be lamented, as in some Expressionist works, for others, particularly Anglophone visitors in the 1920s and 1930s, the 'geographical emotions', in Bryher's phrase, of restless Berlin represented an exciting space of possibility and innovation.

Restless and Spacious

Berlin had only become the capital of the German Empire in 1871 and over the next forty years it expanded rapidly to become a *Weltstadt* ('World City'), the fourth-largest city in the world, with a population in 1910 of over three million.[11] The 1896 Berlin Trade Exhibition marked the moment when, as Dorothy Rowe asserts, Berlin 'had transformed itself from an ordinary *Großstadt* (big city) to a thriving new *Weltstadt*'.[12] Berlin was resolutely new in its architectural space and retained relatively little of the medieval city, unlike, for instance, Paris or London.[13] Berlin's embrace of modernity was also seen in its widespread deployment of new technologies such as that of electricity, readily available from the end of the nineteenth century. As Andreas Killen argues, Berlin pioneered the development of electric trams in its streets, and the siting of factories housing the large electrical companies of Siemens and AEG in the city only confirmed that industrial Berlin had shifted from a city of hand manufacturing to an *Elektropolis*.[14]

One early twentieth-century visitor, the Swiss writer Robert Walser, arrived in the city in 1905 and wrote a series of short pieces, metropolitan miniatures, on Berlin *Elektropolis*, exploring features such as its department stores, the new electric trams, and the lights of the advertisements cluttering the city streets.[15] In a piece entitled 'Friedrichstrasse' Walser emphasised the idea of restlessness in this central Berlin street:

> Up above is a narrow strip of sky. . . . The buildings to either side rise boldly, daintily, and fantastically into architectural heights. The air quivers and startles with worldy life. All the way up to the rooftops, and even above, advertisements float and hang. The large lettering is conspicuous. . . . Never in all this time this street has existed has life stopped circulating here. This is the very heart, the ceaselessly respiring breast of metropolitan life. . . . Never do the movement and commotion here fully die out, and just as life is about to cease at the upper end of the street, it starts up again at the bottom.[16]

For Walser such ceaseless motion typified the modernity of the city; Berlin, he noted, in another essay, 'will soon burst at the seams with newness' as 'everything historically notable here will vanish; no one knows the old Berlin anymore'. For the artist visiting Berlin, he wrote, 'Berlin never rests, and this is glorious . . . there is an incessant blurring together of various things, and this is good, this is Berlin, and Berlin is outstanding'.[17] A later visitor, Vita Sackville West's husband, Harold Nicholson, who worked at the British Embassy, agreed with Walser's perceptions when he noted that 'There is no city in the world so restless as Berlin.'[18]

Another early literary visitor was the American Mark Twain, who, in 1892, celebrated the modernity of Berlin, comparing it to a 'new' city in America, Chicago, and focused upon another feature that contributed to Berlin's overall *Stimmung*, its use of space:

> [Berlin] is a new city; the newest I have ever seen. Chicago would seem venerable beside it. The next feature that strikes one is the spaciousness, the roominess of the city. There is no other city, in any country, whose streets are so generally wide. Berlin is not merely a city of wide streets, it is the city of wide streets. As a wide-street city it has never had its equal, in any age of the world. 'Unter den Linden' is three streets in one; the Potsdamerstrasse is bordered on both sides by sidewalks which are themselves wider than some of the historic thoroughfares of the old European capitals; there seem to be no lanes or alleys; there are no short cuts; here and there, where several important streets empty into a common center, that center's circumference is of a magnitude calculated to bring that word spaciousness into your mind again. The park in the middle of the city is so huge that it calls up that expression once more.[19]

For Twain, Berlin equalled spaciousness itself, his repetition of the point indicating the affective and somewhat inarticulate response that places such as Unter den Linden, Potsdamerstrasse and the Tiergarten park produced in him. Twain's emphasis upon the 'spaciousness' of the city recalls the way in which many German thinkers linked urban modernity to forms of spatial phobia and nervous disorders. Killen thus argues that Berlin became both 'a site of anxiety and shock and incubator of discourses and practices that were organized around the topos of nervousness and were themselves constitutive of modernity'; thus in Berlin technological modernity 'both produced and was in turn produced by "sick nerves"'.[20] One important example was the diagnosis by a Berlin psychologist, Carl Otto Westphal, of *Platzangst*, more commonly known now as agoraphobia. Westphal coined the term in 1871 but, as Anthony Vidler has shown, the discourse of spatial phobias spread across German cities in the late nineteenth century.[21] For these early theorists *Platzangst* was essentially an urban disease generated by new spatial formations in the city and was frequently linked to the more widespread notion of a neurasthenia or nervous exhaustion caused by modernity, as popularised by George Beard.[22] Agoraphobia and claustrophobia – the latter coined by Benjamin Ball in 1879 – are, of course, deeply intertwined reactions to spatiality, rather than opposed states of mind. As Paul Carter notes, both were understood as 'characteristically urban neurasthenias, symptoms of the anxieties produced by life in the modern city'.[23] Interestingly, Ford Madox Ford suffered from agoraphobia around the time that he was writing *The Soul of London*.[24] While living in Germany in 1904 he noted in a letter: 'There's such a lot of nervous breakdown in the land. They've a regular name for lack of walking power here: Platz Angst.'[25] This modern spatial phobia was thus defined precisely by a somatic affect, that of being unable to move; to suffer from it was, strangely, to be moved (affectively) in such a way that one did not move (physically) at all. Spaciousness was thus seen here as a quality which acted against Berlin's other key feature, its restlessness, quelling the ability to move at all.

The restructuring of Berlin in the late nineteenth and early twentieth centuries thus produced a series of affective responses to the city, focusing in particular upon the spacious quality of its streets, and the ceaseless hubbub of activity found there. In Henri Lefebvre's terms, these were lived *representational spaces* whose affects veered between the phobic, the utopian, and the ecstatic as depicted in a range of diverse thinkers, writers, and artists.[26] Berlin, not surprisingly, thus became the place in which some of the most fascinating and durable theorisations of the urban experience first emerged, in the work of figures such as Walter Benjamin, Siegfried Kracauer, Georg Simmel and Max Weber.[27] Simmel, for example, in his classic essay of 1903, 'The Metropolis and Mental Life', diagnosed the emergence of a 'metropolitan type' who responds psychologically to the rapid stimuli of urban modernity by reacting intellectually rather than emotionally: 'instead of reacting emotionally, the metropolitan type reacts primarily in a rational manner'.[28] For Simmel, then, it was specifically the non-affective character of urban life that dominates. For Benjamin, in contradistinction, it was precisely the affective which defines certain aspects of the urban experience, such as that of the crowd: 'Fear, revulsion, and horror were the emotions which the big city crowd aroused in those who first observed it.'[29] Given the interest of such thinkers in how the new spaces of Berlin's modernity altered subjective experience in the city it is hardly surprising to find that the first major movement in German modernism, Expressionism, which emerged in the years prior to World War I, should also share an interest in the 'geographical emotions' provoked by the city, such as fear, revulsion and horror.

Expressionist Voices and Cries

Like many of the other modernist movements discussed in this book Expressionism was linked to the new cultural institutions of the modern city, such as little magazines, radical cafés and alternative gallery spaces. Expressionism emerged in two modernist magazines, *Die Aktion* (1911–32), edited by Franz Pfemfert, and *Der Sturm* (1910–32), edited by Herwarth Walden. Their location in Berlin, rather than in other more established cities associated with cultural production in Germany, was because, as Douglas Brent McBride notes, Berlin was 'a gravitational centre for the high-tech innovations that were the hallmark of the second industrial revolution: telephone, motion pictures, and magazines'; thus the rise of Expressionism was closely associated with the commercial culture and mass market modernity of the city.[30] The magazines were also linked to many other cultural institutions on the west side of the city. *Die Aktion* emerged from *Der Neue Club*, led by Kurt Hiller, a sort of cabaret club which became a venue for literary discussion and politics that met weekly in a room above the Nollendorf-Kasino. *Der Sturm*, after taking up new premises in Potsdamerstrasse, held many avant-garde exhibitions, such as work by the Blaue Reiter ('Blue Rider') group and the Italian Futurists in 1912, opened a bookshop, and staged travelling exhibitions of modernist art around Germany and other countries.[31] Perhaps the most striking feature of the geography of modernism here was the fact that the two magazines shared an 'ersatz editorial office' in the same café on Kurfürstendamm, the famous Café des Westens.[32] Alfred Richard Meyer thus described 'the excitement with which we sat of an evening in the Café des Westens . . . quietly sipping our drinks and waiting for the appearance of the *Sturm* or *Aktion*'.[33] One modern English writer who briefly visited the city in the pre-war years, Rupert Brooke, seems to have composed his famous paean to the English meadows around Cambridge, 'The Old Vicarage, Grantchester', while sitting in the Café des Westens. While he dreams of an England of 'water sweet and cool' and 'honey still for tea', his experience of the café is rather less charming: 'Here I am, sweating, sick and hot / . . . / *Temperamentvoll* German Jews / Drink beer around.'[34]

While spaces such as the Café des Westens fulfilled an important function in the cultural infrastructure enabling Expressionism to flourish, many of its pre-war members seemed to share something of Brooke's negative reaction to the affects produced by the city. One initial response of the Expressionists to the new spaces and restlessness of urban life had been a utopian one. Christina Lodder argues that in the years before World War I artists associated with Die Brücke ('The Bridge') and Der Blaue Reiter groups conceived of art as a form of 'spiritual utopia' that would counteract the harmful effects of modernity, such as the industrialisation and mechanisation taking place in Berlin and throughout the rest of the country.[35] Interestingly, both groups had their origins outside of Berlin, with the Blaue Reiter artists coming from Bavaria, and the Brücke group originating in Dresden (though they moved to Berlin around 1910).[36] However, as it developed, the Expressionist reaction to Berlin switched around to become dominated by a dystopian depiction of the city, illustrating Benjamin's notion of the preponderance of emotions such as fear and horror in the metropolis. Expressionists thus represented urban affects in terms, as Richard Murphy argues, of a 'cognitive overload', where 'the sheer mass of data pouring in upon the individual from all sides in the city overwhelmed the subject's ability to make sense of it'.[37] This 'cognitive overload' was due primarily to an increased burst of urban restructuring, or what David Harvey terms a period of intensified 'time-space compression', for in these years Berlin became the fastest-growing city in Europe.[38] This feeling of 'overload' was summarised by Kurt Pinthus, looking back from 1923:

> What a barrage of previously unimagined monstrosities has been clattering down upon our nerves for the last decade . . . and what a volume of noise, excitations, and stimuli the average person now had to fight through on a daily basis, with the commute to and from work, with the hazardous tumult on streets crowded with vehicles, with telephones, illuminated advertisements, and thousands of noises and distractions.[39]

An example of an Expressionist who tried to capture the affect of these 'monstrosities' in the city can be found in the works of the Jewish painter Ludwig Meidner. Another outsider, Meidner was born in Silesia, in the far east of Germany, and only settled in Berlin in 1907. His paintings of this period (his so-called 'apocalyptic landscapes') provide perfect examples of Pinthus' sensory overload, often rendered in images in which modern traffic and the angular buildings of the city crush anonymous figures in the human crowd. Meidner's *The City and I* (1913), for instance, graphically captures Nigel Thrift's idea of the city as a 'roiling maelstrom of affect' (see Fig. 3.1).[40]

Christopher Butler usefully distinguishes between the urban imagery of Meidner and the many depictions of the city in Italian Futurist painting, such as Umberto Boccioni's *The Street Enters the House* (1911), which was exhibited in Berlin in 1912 and probably seen by Meidner. While the Futurists, writes Butler, 'suggest an excited interpenetration of the observer and the

Figure 3.1 Ludwig Meidner, *The City and I* (1913).
© Private Collection, courtesy of Neue Galerie New York.

dynamism of modern city life and work, Meidner expresses discord and alienation by turning his central figure away from a disintegrating chaos'.[41] Butler also quotes from a text by Meidner which crystallises his view of the sensory overload of the city:

> The City nears. My body
> crackles. The giggles of the city
> ignite against my skin. I hear
> eruptions at the base of my skull. The
> houses near. The catastrophes explode
> their windows, stairways silently collapse.
> People laugh beneath the ruins.[42]

The city here becomes a menacing entity, whose approach appears to physically assault Meidner's body in dramatic fashion ('crackles' and 'eruptions'): urban space here becomes a set of restless monsters encroaching upon human forms. This, like *The City and I*, is an intensely somatic representation of urban affects impinging upon the human subject.

For certain writers and artists, particular places within Berlin often seemed to act as a synecdoche for the sensory overload of urban experience depicted by Meidner, and also exemplified Berlin's 'restlessness'. One location just west of the Mitte ('Centre') typified this sense of perpetual becoming: Potsdamer Platz (see Fig. 3.2).[43] The 'yawning emptiness' of the new urban spaces noted by the early theorists of *Platzangst* now metamorphosed, in places such as Potsdamer Platz, into sites jammed full with the technology of modernity, primarily that of various forms of transport. Potsdamer Platz had been the site of the earliest train station in the city, Potsdam station, opened in 1838, and was later joined by nearby Anhalt station. Then the Platz saw the appearance of the S-Bahn and U-Bahn subway and rail lines, which by 1908 were joined by some thirty-five tram lines. The growth after World War I of the ownership of motor cars only

Figure 3.2 Potsdamer Platz, c. 1930.
© Landesarchiv Berlin/Fotograf: N.N., F Rep. 290 Nr. 97007.

Figure 3.3 Traffic light on Potsdamer Platz, c. 1932.
© Landesarchiv Berlin/Fotograf: Ewald Gnilka, F Rep. 290 Nr. 172401

added to the melee of vehicles crammed into this space, and in order to exert some sort of control over the increase in traffic, Potsdamer Platz became the site of Europe's first traffic light in 1925 (see Fig. 3.3). The Platz also attracted luxury hotels, the famous department store Wertheim's, and numerous other cafés and restaurants.[44] One travel guide to the city from 1912 recommended standing on the platform of a number 5 bus as it entered Potsdamer Platz: 'The picture of unbelievable movement of people, lights, and vehicles that now presents itself to the eye – that is Berlin!'[45] In such spaces Berlin's restless modernity thus became an experience to be savoured by the tourist and local alike. Franz Hessel, in his work of urban *flânerie*, *Walking in Berlin* (1929), noted that the Platz was not really a 'plaza' at all, but rather a crossroads or intersection for the flow of vehicles into the city. Hessel commented that the 'traffic here is so heavy in such a tight space that I'm often impressed at how smoothly it flows' and pointed to the 'famed traffic-light tower, watching over the action like a referee's chair in tennis'.[46]

In Potsdamer Platz, therefore, the metaphorical sense of moving, and of *becoming* not being, space rather than place, according to certain theorists of spatiality,[47] was grounded in a material location dominated by machines that moved. The affective geography of movement typified by Potsdamer Platz also captured the imaginations of some Expressionist artists. Meidner drew the Platz in 1913 (see Fig. 3.4), showing a teeming space congested with people and vehicles, while a year later Ernst Kirchner painted a more famous image of two prostitutes in the same location (see Fig. 3.5).[48]

Another Expressionist, the writer Kurt Hiller, in a manifesto called 'The New Berliners' (1911), also stressed the affective possibilities of the Platz: 'Our conscious goal in literature is the characterization of the intellectual city dweller's experiences. We maintain, for example, that the Potsdamerplatz

Figure 3.4 Ludwig Meidner, *Potsdamer Platz* (1913).
© Ludwig Meidner Archive, Judisches Museum Frankfurt.

Figure 3.5 Ernst Kirchner, *Potsdamer Platz* (1914).

has just as much power to fill us with strong inner sensations as the smallest village.'[49] As Richard Murphy describes it, Expressionists rejected the 'coolness' and restraint demonstrated by an earlier generation of German writers, in favour of 'open passion and partiality, or what they frequently referred to as "Ekstase"', an affective language of modernist aesthetics conditioned above all by the sights and sounds of metropolitan Berlin.[50] These ecstatic urban sensations produced what Murphy interestingly terms an 'aesthetics of the ugly', something clearly noticeable in a poem by the Expressionist writer Paul Boldt, 'On the Terrace of the Café Josty' (1912), first published in the magazine, *Die Aktion*. The Café Josty was situated on the corner of Potsdamer Platz (with a fine view of the first traffic light) and Boldt's poem offers an intensely affective response to the incessant motion witnessed from its terrace:

Potsdamer Platz in an endless roar
Glaciates all resounding avalanches
The street complex: trams on rails,
Automobiles and the refuse of mankind.

People trickle over the asphalt,
Ant-like in their diligence, nimble as lizards.
Foreheads and hands, flashing with thoughts,
Swim like sunlight through the dark forest.

Night rain wraps the square in a cavern,
Where bats, white, with beating wings
And lavender jellyfish lie – colourful oils;

They multiply, dissected by the cars. –
Berlin squirts up, glistening nest of the day,
From the smoke of the night like the pus of a pestilence.[51]

Human beings here are reduced to 'ants' or 'lizards' that 'trickle over the asphalt', out-of-place figures in an urban environment devoted to the movement of trams and automobiles. By the end of the poem humans disappear entirely and the city takes on an alarming life of its own. Exemplifying again the 'aesthetics of the ugly' and the ability of a site such as Potsdamer Platz to stimulate 'strong inner sensations', this rather unpleasant image of the 'street complex' of Berlin as a pustulent entity recalls a comment by Peter Nicholls on how early Expressionist poetry stressed 'the need for a return to that which is primal in humanity, a shedding of cultural inhibition in the name of the naked "cry" (*Schrei*) rather than the "intellectual" world'.[52] Nicholls also notes – in an illuminating term that again points to the sensory overload of urban affect – the 'loudness of such writing – both literal and figurative'.[53] Faced with the 'endless roar' of the traffic around the Platz it is revealing that Expressionists responded with their own 'loudness': however, rather than a mere mimetic image of Berlin streets this was more of an affective cry of protest to be raised against the restless hubbub of the city.

After the cataclysm of World War I the ecstatic cries of Expressionism took on a different tone. By the 1920s the earlier impulses towards 'spiritual utopia' within Expressionism had been deeply questioned by the bloodshed of the war and the failed Spartacist revolution of 1919, which had been bloodily crushed on the streets of the city. As Murphy comments: 'In this context the utopian politics . . . of Expressionism and proclamations by certain of its figures may indeed have sounded somewhat hollow, such as . . . the . . . abstract faith in the development of a "neuer Mensch" (or "New Man").'[54] The anti-art of Dada which emerged in the post-war years, led by Richard Huelsenbeck, along with figures such as George Grosz, Hans Richter, John Heartfield and Hannah

Hoch, and publications such as the Berlin magazine *Der Dada* (1919–20), was much more sceptical about the pretensions of art to prefigure a utopian future, and sided more with socialist critiques of the Weimar government. Dada, in its employment of artistic strategies of fragmentation and photomontage (particularly in the work of Heartfield and Hoch), brought a new spatial form to the way in which the city was represented.[55] Another challenge to Expressionism after the war was the so-called Neue Sachlichkeit movement ('New Objectivity') which, in Murphy's words, developed a more documentary format for depicting technological modernity in the metropolis, along with a 'new sobriety, a "cool" and detached attitude' that rejected the 'ecstasies' of the Expressionists.[56] In both tendencies, however, the mood (*Stimmung*) of Berlin as a city of movements and new spaces, whether cultural, technological or political, was still a major feature to be explored and represented.

The classic novel of this restless Berlin modernism is Alfred Döblin's *Berlin Alexanderplatz* (1929) which, arguably, develops the Expressionist representation of the city by incorporating elements of both Dada and the New Objectivity. In an indication of the changed political environment of the 1920s, the geographical focus of Döblin's novel was not the affluent Potsdamer Platz in the west, but more working-class areas of the city in the east and north-east around Alexanderplatz and Rosenthalerplatz. *Berlin Alexanderplatz* is the story of how one man, Franz Biberkopf, struggles to integrate himself back into the working-class areas of north-east Berlin after being released from prison. The modernism of the text is perceived mostly strikingly in the way in which it juxtaposes episodes detailing the psychological experiences of Biberkopf with what appear as objective depictions of technological modernity in Berlin.

Thus, at one point Döblin notes Berlin's latitude and longitude only to follow it with information about the transport infrastructure of the city with its '20 main-line stations, 121 suburban lines, 27 belt lines, 14 city lines, 7 shunting stations, street-car, elevated railroad, autobus service'.[57] As Eric Bulson notes, Döblin revised the early parts of his novel after reading Joyce's *Ulysses*, adapting features of Joyce's depiction of the city such as the Dublin trams listed at the start of the 'Aeolus' episode.[58] In a description of the 'busily active' Rosenthaler Platz at the start of book 2 of *Berlin Alexanderplatz*, Döblin first notes the weather in the city, then follows it with a description of the route of the number 68 tram from Rosenthaler Platz in an attempt to 'Get to know about the lines':

> Car No. 68 runs across Rosenthaler Platz, Wittenau, Nordbanhof, Heilanstalt, Weddingplatz, Stettiner Sations, Rosenthaler Platz, Alexanderplatz, Strassberger Platz, Frankfurter Allee Station, Lichtenberg, Herzberge Insane Asylum. The three Berlin transport companies – street-car, elevated and underground, omnibus – form a tariff union. Fares

> for adults are 20 pfennigs, for schoolchildren 10 pfennigs. . . . During the winter months the front entrance shall not be opened for passengers entering or leaving, 39 seating capacity.[59]

There is a brute facticity about the writing here demonstrating a rejection of the ecstatic inner sensations utilised by the pre-war Expressionists to represent the technology of the metropolis. Another paragraph soon after elaborates the various plants of the nearby AEG factory, taking its information from the 1928 telephone directory: 'Electric Light and Power Works, Central Administration, NW 40, Friedrich-Karl-Ufer 2–4, Local Call and Long Distance Call Office, North 4488.'[60] Döblin intersperses this information with detached stories about some of the people travelling upon the trams, such as the four people who board the No. 4 at Lothringer Strasse. Here we learn of their jobs, their illnesses and, in the case of a 14-year-old boy, Max Rüst, the entire course of his later life, from work to death, ending with a lengthy obituary. In the avalanche of detail and lack of narrative progression the effect, at times, is to render the city as a massive material entity amongst whose spaces the individual citizen is dwarfed.

Such facticity is, however, more than simply a documentary representation of the city, as favoured by the New Objectivity, but illustrates Döblin's modernist technique of making the city narrate itself, a feature seemingly influenced by the Dada techniques of photomontage. As Huyssen argues, Döblin's novel rejects the temporal focus of the nineteenth-century city novel for an approach that juxtaposes Franz Biberkopf's story with features of urban montage, such as the information about Berlin's transport system and its electrical factories discussed above. This technique ensures that in the novel the 'political and economic affairs of the city became abstract and increasingly spatialized in their representation'.[61] The overall effect, suggest Huyssen, is that,

> The text of the city as a network of traffic, commerce, information, political slogans, and flows of commodities created the sense in the reader that the city narrated itself in these montages. . . . The city itself became the narrator in the chapter 'Rosenthaler Square Is Talking'.[62]

In such moments the city thus appears as a detached objective entity rather than a space represented by an author. However, Döblin, whose medical expertise was in the treatment of nervous diseases, was deeply interested in the subjective experience of the city and in how affects flowed between the city and its citizens, and in this sense the novel harks back to the Expressionist encounter with the metropolis. One marker of this is the frequent references in the novel to the physical and psychological ailments suffered by Berlin's inhabitants. Thus, in the condensed life story of the young boy, Max Rüst, we learn that he is on tram No. 4 because he is on the way to the 'clinic for the defective in speech, the hard of hearing, the weak-visioned, the weak-minded, the incorrigible, he has been there at frequent intervals, because he stutters, but he is getting better now'.[63] Döblin's satirical shift from the physical symptom to the more intangible ('weak-minded', 'the incorrigible') is an acknowledgement that urban life deeply affects the lives of Berliners, in body and in mind.

If affect is, in one definition, synonymous with 'forces of encounter' and the 'passage . . . of forces or intensities' between bodies and their environments, Döblin's novel explicitly links the body of Berlin citizens to their encounters with the mechanised forces of urban transport.[64] *Berlin Alexanderplatz* thus opens with a representation of how the city and its traffic affects Biberkopf: released from Tegel Prison, he now has to board a tramcar into the city, but is at first overwhelmed by feelings of 'terror' and 'disgust', and his first experience of 'freedom' is described as 'punishment':

> He shook himself and gulped. He stepped on his own foot. Then, with a run, took a seat in the car. Right among people. Go ahead. At first it was like being at the dentist's, when he has grabbed a root with a pair of forceps, and pulls; the pain grows, your head threatens to burst. . . . Busy streets emerged, Seestrasse, people got on and off. Something inside him screamed in terror: Look out, look out, it's going to start now. The tip of his nose turned to ice; something was whirring over his cheek.[65]

The intensity of the affects flowing between the tramcar and Biberkopf is striking in the way in which it manifests itself upon his body, with the 'terror' grossly affecting his facial sensations. He exits from the tramcar and now experiences the 'swarm' and 'hustle and bustle' of crowds in the street, making him feel that 'My brain needs oiling, it's probably dried up.'[66] As Biberkopf walks along Rosenthaler Platz 'terror' strikes him again: 'Oh, how cramped his body felt, I can't get rid of it, where shall I go?'[67] Here the novel draws more explicitly upon Expressionist ideas, as Döblin depicts how the cognitive overload of the city and its attendant affects produce various physical symptoms in Biberkopf's body: he feels 'cramped' for space in the incessant streets of Berlin, in which the very fabric of the city seems to be in motion like its traffic as 'cars roared and jangled on, house-fronts were rolling along one after the other without stopping'.[68]

Another key modernist work of the 1920s which demonstrates a reworking of Expressionist themes, along with elements of the New Objectivity, is Walter Ruttmann's 1927 film, *Berlin: Symphony of a Great City*. The infrastructure for film in Germany, centred on the UFA studios in Berlin, was another example of how the city had embraced technological modernity. The industry had grown since the 1910s to rival that of Hollywood, and by the 1920s had established an 'Expressionist' style in film associated with directors such as F. W. Murnau and Fritz Lang. German film production, for example, reached a high point in 1922 when 474 full-length feature-films were made.[69]

In Ruttmann's film, the mood (*Stimmung*) of Berlin as a city of restless spaces is paramount. The film is particularly remarkable for the way in which the formal properties of the film's editing – montage and swift cutting – register the many images depicted of urban movement, especially by train and car.[70] The film thus captures an 'urban rhythm', identifying with the energies of the city in such a way as to suggest that Berlin, rather than its inhabitants, is the real protagonist of the film: the city pulses with life, like a mechanised double of the human body, recalling Döblin's notion of the city narrating itself.[71] As if to stress the fact that the city itself seems to have a life over and above that of its inhabitants, Ruttmann repeatedly shows images of shop-window mannequins, dummies and other inert representations of human beings.

The film is set on a single day and follows the life of Berlin from dawn to evening, employing a 'symphonic' structure divided into five acts. The opening scene depicts a journey by train through the countryside to the city, echoing the journey of thousands who had migrated to Berlin over the previous decades. This image of the train is just the first example of many forms of transport repeatedly dwelt upon in the film: from the trains of the U-Bahn and S-Bahn to the electric trams, taxis, cars and bikes on the streets, and then to the barges and boats on Berlin's rivers, the film exhaustively depicts the restless quality of city life. Even the images of Berliners after work show their leisure time to be dominated by further movements, as we witness racing cars, speeding cyclists, and people skating on an ice-rink. The image of a hearse being drawn through the streets poignantly indicates that even in death Berliners seem to keep moving. Humanity thus appears to be a mere punctuation mark in the textual technologies of transport dominating the city, and the scenes of a traffic warden and policemen directing cars and buses in the street show an almost forlorn attempt to impose order upon ceaseless motion. Towards the end of act 3 the film illustrates Marshall Berman's 'primal scene' for the modern urban subject, that of 'a pedestrian thrown into the maelstrom of modern city traffic',[72] as a series of swiftly cut shots of various forms of street traffic is followed by a scene where figures try to dart across the busy street, dodging the vehicles that threaten their safety. As with Freud's fear of crossing streets in Vienna (discussed in Chapter 2), we see how Berlin's restless spaces produce affects of fear and danger.

The restless mood (*Stimmung*) of Berlin is also captured in the repeated attention to the legs and feet of commuters boarding trams or mounting stairs into railway stations, with these human rhythms echoing those of the many mechanical motions depicted in the film, such as the wheels and pistons of factory production seen at the end of act 1. In keeping with Berlin's status as an *Elektropolis* at the forefront of technological modernity, one of the factories portrayed manufactures electric light bulbs. The city in Ruttmann's film is thus a 'roiling maelstrom of affect' and at various instances the director attempts to capture the sensations of a disorientating modernity for the viewer. Thus there are scenes where the camera is positioned on a car travelling quickly through a crowded street or aboard an aircraft taking off and circling the city. The use of modernist techniques such as montage, where Ruttmann juxtaposes two seemingly unrelated images to produce a 'third meaning', in Sergei Eisenstein's terms, only intensifies this sense of disorientation and movement.[73] One recurrent motif used in montage in the film juxtaposes human subjects with animals. A stunning example of this occurs in act 3 when, after a relative pause in the city's busy pace of life for lunch, we see an image of a polar bear slowly getting to its feet, followed by a depiction of newspapers being printed, packaged and sent out for delivery. We then view a kaleidoscopic whirl of images of pages from the newspaper, with single words jumping out to the front of the screen, before the film cuts to other scenes of frantic movement: we see train tracks, then revolving doors, before the camera positions the viewer directly within a carriage upon a rollercoaster journey to experience a series of violent motions up and down. In such instances we see how the film's depiction of Berlin's restless spaces mixes the New Objectivity desire for a documentary approach to technological modernity with the Expressionist focus upon the disorientating affects of urban life.[74]

Post-War Visitors

After the close of World War I Berlin's restless modernity began to attract foreign visitors in increasing numbers. Before American and British writers appeared, however, the first outsiders to make Berlin their home came from Russia. Russian outsiders helped other Berlin writers and artists recover the spirit of utopia that the war, and the crushing of the Spartacist revolution of 1919, had diminished. For example, German Dada was to re-engage with utopian thought once again when it encountered the Constructivist group of artists that gathered in Berlin after the war, many of them émigrés from Russia, such as El Lissitzky, Kazimir Malevich, Naum Gabo, and the Hungarian László Moholy-Nagy. As Lodder argues, 'Dadaists now embraced the socialist utopian vision of emerging International Constructivism.'[75] These Russian artists brought with them not only a modernist commitment to abstraction in the visual arts but also the utopian energy of the 1917 Bolshevik Revolution: El Lissitzky, for example, talked of 'the brave new world we were building' several years before Aldous Huxley was to use the same phrase to depict a dystopian future.[76]

For diverse reasons, many Russians had left the country in the years after the Bolshevik Revolution of 1917, some as supporters of the ousted monarchy, others dismayed by the course of Soviet cultural politics. Berlin became the destination for some 360,000 Russian exiles and émigrés, and by the early 1920s a thriving cultural infrastructure for Russian literature sprang up in the city, including publishing houses, daily newspapers, magazines and bookshops. As Tobias Boes notes, between 1918 and 1924 Berlin's eighty-six Russian publishers issued more books than those in Moscow and Petrograd combined.[77] For some, Berlin functioned as a stopping point in what became a kind of regional transnational network for the avant-garde travelling between Central Europe and Paris: as Eberhard Roters puts it, Berlin was 'the cross-roads of a two-way traffic of interest for Russian artists – for those coming West from the East and for those who had already been in Paris for years (for instance Archipenko)'.[78] Or as one Russian writer, Nicolas Nabokov, put it in his memoirs: 'After the war, Berlin had become a sort of caravansary, where everybody met on their way to Moscow or to the Occident.'[79]

Affluent Russians mainly lived in the west and south-west of the city, occupying areas such as Wilmersdorf, Charlottenburg and Schöneberg: it is said that Germans would refer to Kurfürstendamm, Berlin's major road in the west, as Nepsky Prospekt, a mocking amalgam of the main street of St Petersburg (Petrograd then) and Lenin's NEP (New Economic Policy).[80] Certain cafés and clubs near the Kurfürstendamm became venues for Russian intellectuals and writers, and adopted Russian names, such as the Berlin House of the Arts (Dom Iskusstv), which met at the Café Landgraf or the Café Leon, and later the Writers' Club (Klub Pistatelej).[81] While living in west Berlin between 1922 and 1937 Vladimir Nabokov composed nine novels in Russian under the pseudonym Vladimir Sirin, including important early works such as *The Eye* (1930) and *An Invitation to a Beheading* (composed 1934, published 1938).[82] Nabokov joined many other leading figures of Russian cultural life based in Berlin, such as Andrei Bely, Marc Chagall, Ilya Ehrenburg, El Lissitzky and Boris Pasternak; Vladimir Mayakovsky also stayed briefly, while Maxim Gorky lived just outside Berlin and published a magazine, *Beseda* (*Colloquy*, 1923–5), aimed at Russian expatriate writers in Germany. One of the most interesting productions from these exiles was the trilingual magazine edited by Ehrenburg and El Lissitzky, *Veshch. Gegenstand. Objet: Revue international de l'art modern*, which published three issues in 1922. This transnational magazine attempted to cover a range of European avant-garde movements, such as Dada, Constructivism and Purism, and contained articles on Picasso, Mayakovsky, Jules Romains and Vladimir Tatlin's Tower. However, as Stephen Bury notes, the magazine's fortunes were hampered by an ambivalence over whether it was directed primarily at Russian exiles or those Germans interested in Russian art and culture, particularly as the majority of articles were written in Russian.[83]

Viktor Shklovsky, the leading theorist of Russian Formalism, arrived in Berlin in 1922, escaping the growing political persecution of liberal intellectuals in the Soviet Union. While in Berlin Shklovsky composed an experimental epistolary novel, *Zoo, or Letters Not about Love* (1923), which offers a fascinating account of Berlin from the point of view of a Russian 'outsider'. In keeping with Russian Formalism's aim of defamiliarising literary forms, Shklovsky's is a novel of love-letters to a woman, Elsa Triolet, in which the author prohibits himself from writing about love. Instead, the novel puzzles over the status of being Russian in an alien environment; Shklovsky's text thus presents 'Alya' (Elsa Triolet) as 'a person from an alien culture, because there's no point in writing descriptive letters to a person of your own culture', adding that 'I built the book on a dispute between people of two cultures.'[84] At times Shklovsky identifies Alya with the alien city of Berlin, writing 'You are the city I live in' and 'Berlin is encircled by your name', noting also that he is writing about 'an alien culture and an alien woman'.[85] The novel also offers portraits of the Russian exiles amidst this alien culture: Shklovsky devotes one letter to Zinovy Grzhebin, a Russian publisher, as 'here in the middle of nowhere, in Berlin, this Soviet bourgeois raves on an international scale and continues to publish new books';[86] other letters describe the character of Andrei Bely, author of the classic Russian city novel *Petersburg* (1916), and Ilya Ehrenburg, co-editor of *Veshch*. Boris Pasternak is said to be 'uneasy in Berlin' and is one of the many Russian outsiders that Shklovsky struggles to find the correct term to describe: 'We are refugees. No, not refugees but fugitives – and now squatters.'[87]

Pasternak's mood of unease becomes the dominant tone of Shklovsky's novel as it progresses: his failure to express his love for Alya parallels his failure to feel at home in the alien city of Berlin. Russian Berlin, he proclaims, 'is going nowhere. It has no destiny. No propulsion.'[88] In a fascinating image Shklovsky here distinguishes between a purely mechanical propulsion linked to modernity, such as the 'mechanical moan' of Berlin's trains and motor cars,[89] and the idea of the Russian Revolution as representing utopian political change, albeit one that has stalled in its utopian promise: 'The revolution has lost its propulsion.'[90] Prefiguring the later works of Ruttmann and Döblin, in Shklovky's novel Berlin's status as a pre-eminent city of technological modernity is demonstrated through frequent images of its advanced public transport system: 'From the Bahnhof on Wittenbergplatz, which looks like a mole's burrow, the train runs, shrieking like a heavy shell on the rise, to the platform on Nollendorfplatz'; or, again: 'All around, along the roofs of the long yellow buildings, run tracks; tracks run along the ground and along high iron platforms, where they intersect other iron platforms as they rise to platforms still higher.'[91] Amidst this bustle, however, the Russian community are seen as 'fugitives' and 'squatters' and in a wonderful geographical image of an immobile space 'We are going nowhere: we huddle among the Germans like a lake between its shores.'[92] It is hardly surprising, therefore, that one of Shklovsky's final letters is a plea to return to Russia from someone who remained an outsider in the city: 'I cannot live in Berlin ... Bitter is the anguish of being in Berlin, as bitter as carbide dust.'[93] In *Zoo* Berlin becomes more 'hellhole' than 'paradise', a city whose modern spaces produce an affect of anguish for those outsiders unable to find a place to dwell in its environs, other than as mere 'squatters'.

A different constituency of outsiders visiting Berlin after World War I came from the United States, writers and artists on a journey that started in Paris but then extended to other parts of Europe. These visitors were part of the 'lost generation' of young American intellectuals discussed in Chapter 1 and who were disillusioned with the technological modernity that their own country spearheaded in the first quarter of the century. Many came to Europe in search of an 'older' culture and civilization that they believed (often mistakenly) rejected the American conjunction of capitalism and culture. While this group is forever associated with the idea of 'Americans in Paris', several key figures visited and spent time in Berlin in the early 1920s, such as Berenice Abbott, Djuna Barnes, Malcolm Cowley, Marsden Hartley, Matthew Josephson, Harold Loeb, Mina Loy and Robert McAlmon. One compelling reason for the influx of Americans to Berlin in the early 1920s was the inflation that was crippling the German mark against the American dollar. Between 1918 and 1921 the value of the mark fell from 4.20 to 75 for one dollar; this monetary collapse was, however, minor compared to what followed in the next two years. In 1922 one dollar would buy 400 marks;[94] the mark then slumped to reach 130 billion to the dollar in November 1923, and then 1.3 trillion to the dollar soon after, before the currency was revalued and the German economic collapse partly halted.[95] Matthew Josephson writes drolly that his earnings of thirty dollars a week placed him in the millionaire class, and that he and his wife occupied a 'sumptuous' apartment in the upmarket Tiergarten area that possessed seven rooms and servants. The exchange rate was also one of the reasons that a key American modernist magazine, *Broom*, came briefly to be published in Berlin.[96]

Broom was one of the many North American 'expatriate' magazines of the 1920s and 1930s, such as *Gargoyle*, *This Quarter*, *Tambour* and *transition*, but it differed from those in never being published in Paris. *Broom* was first conceived by Harold Loeb while he was experiencing New York's bohemian Greenwich Village in the late 1910s. Loeb deliberately decided to publish *Broom* abroad in order to cash in on the favourable exchange rate of the dollar against European currencies, and first published the magazine monthly in Rome from November 1921, before moving to Berlin in October of the following year to take advantage of the slide in the value of the German mark: Loeb reported that in Berlin 'a suit of clothes ordered for the equivalent of thirty dollars might cost two by the time it was delivered' and that in the city 'we could live for next to nothing'.[97] Six issues of the magazine appeared from

Berlin, before Loeb brought the publication back to New York for its remaining life, the final issue appearing in January 1924.

The editorial aims of the magazine indicate a fascinating tension facilitated by its status as an outsider publication in Europe. One aim was to produce a magazine that promoted new American art and letters in Europe, while another was to bring to the attention of its mainly Anglophone readership (all articles were published in English) the exciting work of the European avant-garde. These two aims are first articulated in an article in the first issue by Emmy Veronica Sanders, 'America Invades Europe', in which she argues that both continents will profit from 'closer, more regular and organized cultural contact'.[98] America is not, asserts Sanders, a 'materialistic monster' from which Europeans need to recoil in horror, since there are currents in American cultural and intellectual life – she mentions the Young America critics Randolph Bourne and Waldo Frank – that aim to transform the country from a land 'made of the Puritan, by the Puritan, for the Puritan, remade of the Machine, by the Machine, for the Machine'.[99] *Broom* will also attempt to discover a European avant-garde beyond that of Paris, notes Sanders, and 'will sweep into the circle of its vision aspects of Europe wider than those of Parisian boulevards', while simultaneously Europe will perceive 'aspects of modern America wider than those of one or two coteries'.[100] One might envisage that the magazine's location in Rome and then Berlin would produce a deep encounter with the avant-garde of these countries, producing a transnational exchange of modernist ideas and practices conditioned by the experience of the 'outsider'. However, of the twenty-seven articles and illustrations in the first issue, only eight were by European contributors, all of which were visual material, including work by Picasso, André Derain and Juan Gris. Perhaps the only nod to the magazine's location in Rome was the cover image, by the Futurist artist Enrico Prampolini.

Certain critics thus characterise the magazine as one that displayed little awareness of its surrounding cultural environment. Peter Nicholls, for example, comments that *Broom*'s

> shift from one country to another was registered more clearly in the masthead information than in the contents of the issue. The cultural materials it presented thus seemed to exist in a peculiar transatlantic vacuum, uprooted from their social and political context.[101]

However, the magazine's Berlin-based issues do indicate something of a closer engagement with the art and culture of the city. Josephson, who replaced Alfred Kreymborg as associate editor in 1922, had suggested to Loeb that German modernism was thriving and that 'exciting material from Soviet Russia and Czechoslovakia was coming to Berlin'.[102] Though Loeb disliked the Expressionist work he found in Berlin after moving there in 1922, he was keener on the work of the Russian and Central European exiles in the city. Ilya Ehrenburg offered to collect the best work by the Russian expatriates for the magazine: thus, Berlin residents El Lissitzky and Natalie Goncharova provided several covers for the magazine, as did Ladislas Medgyes, a Hungarian artist also based in the city. The first Berlin issue of October 1922 contained a translation of an unpublished novel by Dostoevsky, while the Ukraine-born artist Louis Lozowick provided an enthusiastic article upon Vladimir Tatlin's Constructivist design for a Tower to commemorate the Third Communist International. Lozowick had already provided a piece to the August 1922 *Broom* on 'Russian Berlin', and a piece of experimental prose by Ehrenburg, 'Vitrion', representing an artist in Soviet Russia, was published in the next issue.[103]

The issue for February 1923 perhaps marked the strongest engagement of the magazine with its Berlin environment: El Lissitzky provided the cover, the German Dadaist Huelsenbeck had a prose story in translation, and Lozowick provided a critical piece on modern Russian art and a translation of a story by Vsevolod Ivanov. Most striking, however, is the prevalence of several drawings by the satirist George Grosz, famed for his politically engaged work combining elements of Dada and the New Objectivity, and which depicted the worsening social and economic conditions in Weimar Germany.[104] There is a glaring juxtaposition between an American magazine being published in Berlin due to the strength of the dollar against the feeble Deutsche Mark, and Grosz's images of what that same raging inflation was doing to the lives of working-class Berliners. Grosz's *Saturday Night* (see Fig. 3.6) thus depicts a harsh contrast between the comfortable bourgeois interior and the poverty and destitution of those on the city streets, with the cracks in the buildings symbolising the divisions affecting the body politic overall.[105]

What, then, did the American editors of *Broom* learn from their experience of Berlin? There is little indication that Grosz's cultural politics seem to have made any impression upon Loeb, or upon the aims of the magazines overall. To this extent Nicholls is right in his assessment that the magazine failed to engage with its social and political context. However, it is debatable whether the feature noted by many visitors to Berlin, the machinery of its modernity, did have an impact upon *Broom*. Many of these young intellectuals had travelled to Europe to escape American philistinism: Loeb, for example, had initially deplored America for 'the ugliness of our cities and suburbs based largely on modern industry'.[106] Paradoxically, as Michael North notes, 'the European intellectuals they contacted were full of enthusiasm for the very culture the Americans had just escaped'.[107] North reports an anecdote from Loeb to illustrate this point: when the American met F. T. Marinetti, Loeb told him

> how much Americans looked up to Europe, to England, Russia, and France for literature, to Germany for music and to France and Italy for

Figure 3.6 George Grosz, *Saturday Night*, printed in *Broom* (February 1923). © Estate of George Grosz, Princeton, NJ/DACS 2018.

> the plastic arts. In return, he burst into rhetoric extolling America. To his mind, nearly everything important in our day came out of the United States. He cited our skyscrapers, movies, jazz, even machinery and the comics.[108]

And, while in Rome, Loeb listened to Blaise Cendrars praising all things American, 'machines and jazz, comics and the cinema. It was odd sitting on a terrace in the ancient city hearing praise of a land so disparaged by its intellectuals.'[109]

Such perceptions appear to change the focus of *Broom* over its time in Berlin, and the contents of its October 1922 issue demonstrate this clearly. In this issue American voices are fewer in number, as the magazine commences with Prampolini's 'machine age' cover, an emphasis continued in a manifesto by Prampolini on 'The Aesthetic of the Machine and Mechanical Introspection in Art' and into Lozowick's article on Vladimir Tatlin's Tower. From the machinery celebrated by the European avant-garde and experienced all around in the Berlin streets, *Broom* redirected its interests to consider the technology of American modernity: thus the magazine published Fernand Léger's prints of Charlie Chaplin and, later, an article by Philippe Soupault praising American cinema.

The experience of exile in Berlin had thus prompted the editors of *Broom* to consider more closely and favourably the despised mechanical culture they had left back home. *Broom*'s co-editor, Matthew Josephson, summed up what they had learnt from their travels:

> Living in Europe for some length of time did provide one with a new perspective on America and its evolving machine-age culture, which underwent revaluation in our minds. . . . Instead of condemning the onset of mechanization and mass entertainment, we would accept it and give it welcome. Were not the new machine-objects, created by industry, things of beauty in themselves, whether sculptures in steel or images made by a camera?[110]

An advertisement in one of the final issues, now published in New York, indicates how *Broom*'s 'invasion' of a European city such as Berlin had caused it to reconsider the 'materialistic monster' of its home culture: 'The Age of the Machine in America is an age of spiritual change and growth as well as one of economic ascendancy. A new art and new literature spring sturdily from the machine civilization.'[111]

Heterotopias: Cafés and Queer Spaces

Broom was thus only a temporary visitor to Berlin, dipping its feet into the restless spaces of the city's modernity before heading for home. Though the magazine was influenced by its time in Berlin neither Loeb nor Josephson in their retrospective autobiographies express much initial enthusiasm for the city: for Loeb it lacked the '*gemütlichkeit* . . . the atmosphere of song and beer' that he had enjoyed in Munich, while Josephson's first impression was that it was 'stridently and offensively "modern", with big electric signs . . . and dreary slums . . . in short Everyman's City of modern times'.[112] Josephson's autobiography, however, indicates that he somewhat revised his feelings for what he also called 'this angry city', particularly after meeting the German Dadaists, Grosz and Richard Huelsenbeck, and encountering its nightlife. At one point Josephson gives a fascinating account of one key socio-spatial location for German modernism, the literary meeting place of the Romanisches Café:

> The Romanisches Kaffeehaus on the Kurfuerstendamm [*sic*], the focus of Bohemian life in the West End, was as good a center as any in which to meet friends and set off for an evening's entertainment. . . . It was a huge, imitation-Gothic structure like many of the city's beer-halls, accommodating fully a thousand clients or more. . . . A most curious international

> mob of people – with long hair, short hair, or shaven skulls, in rags or in furs – filled the place to bursting. George Grosz, who was then both a Dadaist and a Marxist, often appeared there dressed as an American cowboy, booted and spurred. In one part of the Kaffeehaus one heard nothing but Russian spoken – these were the White émigrés – and in another only Hungarian – by the 'Red' exiles from Budapest. The distinguished Russian sculptor, Alexander Archipenko, sometimes came here; as did his young compatriot, Ilya Ehrenburg.[113]

Josephson's description of the Romanisches thus highlights the café as an important space in which the international avant-garde, both outsiders and Berliners, could mingle. Stephen Spender too recalled the Romanisches as the centre of 'a very active intellectual life'.[114] After the war, the Romanisches Café had displaced the Café des Westens as the central venue for modernism in the city, and became a meeting place where figures such as Bertolt Brecht, Gottfried Benn, and Alfred Döblin, as well as the outsiders mentioned by Josephson, debated politics and aesthetics.

Walter Benjamin, writing while in exile from his native city in the 1930s, also noted how the Bohemians that inhabited the Café des Westens shifted after the war to the Romanisches. Benjamin dreamed of writing a 'Physiology of the Coffeehouse', which would explore the nature of the Berlin café as social space, divided into professional and recreational establishments which fulfilled different functions for different visitors.[115] Benjamin's subtle discussion thus emphasises the idea of the café as a kind of heterotopic space, in Michel Foucault's terms, a real space in which modernity is 'alternately ordered':[116]

> When the German economy began to recover, the bohemian contingent visibly lost the threatening nimbus that had surrounded them in the era of the Expressionist revolutionary manifestoes. The bourgeois revised his relationship to the inmates of the Café Megalomania (as the Romanische [*sic*] Café soon came to be called) and found that everything was back to normal. At this moment the physiognomy of the Romanische Café began to change. The 'artists' withdrew into the background, to become more and more a part of the furniture, while the bourgeois, represented by stock-exchange speculators, managers, film and theater agents, literary-minded clerks, began to occupy the place – as a place of relaxation. For one of the most elementary and indispensable diversions of the citizen of a great metropolis, wedged, day in, day out, in the structure of his office and family amid an infinitely variegated social environment, is to plunge into another world, the more exotic the better. Hence the bars haunted by artists and criminals. The distinction between the two, from this point of view, is slight.[117]

For Benjamin, therefore, cafés functioned as heterotopic spaces, places that materially exist in real locations but which feel somehow 'exotic' and otherworldly, and where the visitor can 'plunge into another world': a place where, as in Josephson's image, a German artist (Grosz) could dress up as an American cowboy. Although such loci are habitually labelled as haunts of the literati, Benjamin indicates how their 'otherness' is a feature that can be accessed by all.

As already noted above in the discussion of Expressionism, literary and artistic cafés such as the Romanisches or Westens were important venues for the emergence of modernism in Berlin. However, for many visitors (and natives) in the 1920s the 'plunge into another world' that Benjamin describes was found elsewhere, in establishments where the pleasurable affects of sexual experience were the primary mode of 'otherness'. For this was the period mythologised as the Berlin of 'decadence' and 'cabaret', where the debauchery of its nightlife transformed the reputation of the city into Zweig's 'Babylon of the world'. Since its emergence as a metropolis in the late nineteenth century, Berlin nightlife had become synonymous with moral turpitude.[118] The American writer Robert McAlmon, who lived in Berlin in 1922–3 and described the city as 'made for wildness',[119] offered a representative view of this vision of Weimar decadence in his story 'Distinguished Air', which concerns a lengthy night out with a group of fellow Americans. As the narrator drifts from café to bar to club, alcohol is replaced by cocaine, and he encounters prostitutes of both sexes before arriving home at noon the next day.[120] The description of one gay venue illustrates the open sexuality for which Berlin became famous in this period:

> While we were there an elderly fairy, well known to various psychoanalysts in Germany, came into the place. This night he was dressed as a blond-haired doll, and his fat old body looked in its doll's dress much like that of a barnstorming burlesque soubrette grown a generation or so too old for the part she played. All about the room at various tables were scattered the queer types of Berlin, many of them painted up, two or three in women's clothes, and a great number of types who were not obvious.[121]

Venues such as the famous transvestite club the Eldorado Lounge had, by the end of the 1920s, established Berlin's reputation as a city of 'queer spaces'.[122] One contemporary author, Curt Moreck, published a *Guide to Depraved Berlin* in 1931,[123] while Isherwood later suggested, with not a little irony, that Berlin's famous 'decadence' might have been mainly 'a commercial "line" which the Berliners had instinctively developed in their competition with Paris', since the French city 'had long since cornered the straight girl-market . . . what was left for Berlin to offer its visitors but a masquerade of perversions?'[124]

For many male British writers in the late 1920s and early 1930s Berlin represented a place of exciting and positive affects, ranging across the spectrum identified by Tomkins (Interest-Excitement to Enjoyment-Joy), rather than the phobias and angst found in the earlier Expressionists.[125] The heterotopic quality of 'queer spaces' in the city was thus the focus for some fascinating representations by British visitors such as W. H. Auden, Christopher Isherwood, John Lehmann and Stephen Spender, demonstrating how Berlin affected them as outsiders. When Auden, in 1928, wrote to a friend that he was off to Berlin for a year he inquired knowingly: 'Is Berlin very wicked?'[126] For these young homosexual writers Berlin represented more 'erotic licence' than they imagined could be found in supposedly heterosexual Paris, or what they had experienced in the repressed spaces of British culture. When Auden's father offered to pay for him to spend a year abroad, he rejected Paris: 'Everybody else was going to Paris, and one thing I knew was that I didn't want that. So I went to Berlin. As a matter of fact, I arrived just in time to go to the opening night of *The Threepenny Opera*. Even though I knew no German.'[127] By December 1928, two months after his arrival, Auden was to describe the city as a 'buggers daydream' in which he claimed there were '170 male brothels under police control'.[128] For Isherwood too the tales of the moral dystopia of Berlin were something that intrigued and attracted him: in his novel, *Down There on a Visit*, he fictionalises being warned off Berlin by a relative, a Hamburg shipping executive:

> I know Satanists when I see them ... in the vilest perversions of the Oriental mind, you couldn't find anything more nauseating than what goes on there, quite openly, every day. That city is doomed, more surely than Sodom ever was. These people don't even realize how low they have sunk.[129]

Such a warning, however, only attracted Isherwood further, as he noted in his later autobiographical text, *Christopher and His Kind*: 'It was Berlin itself he was hungry to meet. . . . To Christopher, Berlin meant Boys.'[130]

Auden's and Isherwood's experience of sexual transgression was often associated in their writings with the crossing of spatial or geographical frontiers, another of the key features of a heterotopia according to Foucault.[131] At the opening of *Mr Norris Changes Trains*, the highly charged affective encounter of the narrator, William, with Mr Norris takes place on a train crossing Europe towards Germany. The stranger's eyes, notes William, 'met mine for several blank seconds, vacant, unmistakeably scared' and are 'startled and innocently naughty', reminding the narrator of 'the eyes of a schoolboy surprised in the act of breaking one of the rules'.[132] Tomkins notes that the affect of surprise, which in a more intense form is the affect of being startled, is a 'general interrupter to ongoing activity' that is then followed by other affects (joy, fear, distress and so on), according to the nature of the interruption and the interpretation given to it. Tomkins' description of its general pattern accurately captures the scene between the two men here: 'We have denoted this affect surprise-startle: eyebrows up, eye blink.'[133] Affect continues to flow between the two men as William asks innocuously for a light for a cigarette, and Norris' surprise-startle is replaced by an affect of fear: 'he [Norris] started violently at the sound of my voice; so violently, indeed, that his nervous recoil hit me like repercussion . . . as though we had collided with each other bodily in the street'.[134] Finally William's message that he merely asking for a light is understood by Norris and his 'moment of agitation passed', but only after 'his fingers, nervously active, sketched a number of flurried gestures round his waistcoat'.[135]

William and Norris now strike up a friendship, of sorts, and the remainder of the chapter plays heavily upon the links between rule-breaking and crossing borders, as Mr Norris states that 'All these frontiers . . . such a horrible nuisance',[136] and that 'They ought to be done away with.'[137] William thinks that Mr Norris' anxiety about the border controls probably relates to some illegal activity such as smuggling, and asks: 'You haven't crossed this frontier before, then?'[138] When their passports are checked Norris again reacts with the affect of fear: 'his fingers twitched and his voice was scarcely under control. There were actually beads of sweat on his alabaster forehead.'[139] The border control that Norris and William then pass through thus fulfils Foucault's idea that a heterotopia requires certain entry criteria, while the stress upon breaking the rules associates transgression (not yet articulated in terms of sexuality) with the geographical space crossed at the border, experienced in terms of the negative affects outlined here. The two front doors that Mr Norris' flat possesses again emphasises the concept of points of entry and borders. That one of the nameplates on Norris' door is engraved 'Arthur Norris. Export and Import' only confirms this impression of moving across liminal spaces.

The sexual frontiers crossed by Auden and Isherwood when in Berlin produced more positive sets of affects and were experienced mainly in certain cafés and bars, such as the Cosy Corner and the Kleist Casino. The alterity of these sites as heterotopias, however, not only was sexual but also had a class dimension. For unlike the bohemian clubs and cafés of Berlin's West End, the locations these English writers frequented were in other, poorer areas of the city: one set of homosexual bars was located in the south of the city, along Bülowstrasse, and yet another in the strongly working-class area of Hallesches Tor.[140] In January 1929 Auden moved to Fürbringerstrasse 8, in the Hallesches Tor district. One advantage, he wrote to a friend, was that the new address was '50 yrds from my brothel', the Cosy Corner bar on Zossenerstrasse 7. It was to this bar that Auden took Isherwood, when the latter came to visit in March 1929. Having sex with foreign working-class youths was another way of crossing frontiers and borders for the two middle-class Oxbridge Englishmen.[141] Isherwood's description in his later memoir, *Christopher and His Kind*, indicates the impression that this particular socio-sexual space made upon the young writer, representing it as a form of heterotopia replete with affective excitement:

> I now recognise it as one of the decisive events of my life. I can still make myself faintly feel the delicious nausea of initiation terror which Christopher felt as Wystan pushed back the heavy leather door-curtain of a boy bar called The Cosy Corner and led the way inside. In the autumn of 1928, Christopher had felt a different kind of nauseated excitement, equally strong and memorable, when, as a medical student, he had entered an operating theatre in St Thomas's Hospital to watch his first surgical operation.[142]

An ambivalent set of affects are registered here, as 'delicious nausea' and 'nauseated excitement' capture fear being transformed into pleasure. The seemingly odd comparison between a gay bar and an operating theatre can be understood heterotopically, as the young Isherwood crosses a threshold, and is 'initiated' into a world where reality is ordered differently. The curtain of the Cosy Corner makes it appear as a theatrical space, where external reality is suspended momentarily. Later Isherwood describes how his perception of the bar changed, from that of a space of illusion to that of reality:

> the Cosy Corner was now no longer the mysterious temple of initiation . . . Berlin was no longer the fantasy city. . . . Berlin had become a real city and Cosy Corner a real bar . . . For now his adventures here were real, too; less magical but far more interesting.[143]

As Foucault comments, heterotopias can function not only as *fantasy* spaces, but also as *compensation* for reality, becoming a 'space that is other, another real space, as perfect . . . as well arranged as ours is messy'.[144]

On his first visit to the Cosy Corner Isherwood met and became infatuated with 'Bubi', an event described in Auden's poem, 'This Loved One'. Here Auden takes a typically detached and questioning view of the relationship, recalling that before 'this loved one / Was that one and that one', but uses again the trope of the border to represent the encounter: 'Before this last one / Was much to be done, / Frontiers to cross / As clothes grew worse.'[145] Two of the lovers Auden met in the bar, Kurt Groote and Gerhart Meyer, are commemorated rather more favourably in his important early poem, '1929', composed during his stay in Berlin. The poem does not describe any visits to bars but the sense of how these experiences transformed Auden is strongly marked throughout; it is a poem in which, as Patrick Deer notes, 'Berlin provides the stage both for a modernist redescription of the world and a liberating reinvention of the self.'[146] The poem starts in a 'Season when lovers and writers find / An altering speech for altering things, / An emphasis on new names, on the arm / A fresh hand with fresh power'.[147] The poem emphasises the 'new conditions' that Auden has felt in the city:

> Moving along the track which is himself,
> He loves what he hopes will last, which gone,
> Begins the difficult work of mourning,
> And as foreign settlers to strange country come,
> By mispronunciation of native words
> And intermarriage create a new race,
> A new language, so may the soul
> Be weaned at last to independent delight.[148]

Auden here brilliantly links the material space of Berlin – the 'track' referring to the city's traffic mentioned earlier in the poem – to the metaphoric space of his own identity and its development, through encounters, now over, with lovers such as Groote and Meyer. The path of the self to 'independent delight' is via such encounters, perceived as akin to an outsider settling in a 'strange country' and creating a 'new language' by intermarriage and linguistic hybridity. The imagery once again recalls Raymond Williams' notion of the formation of metropolitan modernism through the encounter of the outsider with linguistic strangeness. However, as Deer points out, this third section of the poem mainly concerns Auden's return from Germany to rural England ('In month of August to a cottage coming').[149] Hence, the 'new language' that Auden hopes to create as part of his new identity is a consequence of his transformation in Berlin: the 'strange country' is now revealed as an England perceived through the heterotopic spaces of the German modernist city.

Auden sums up how Berlin affected his development in a syntactically compacted set of images:

> Coming out of me living is always thinking,
> Thinking changing and changing living,
> Am feeling as it was seeing –
> In city leaning on harbour parapet[150]

This is a brilliant description of how the geographical emotions of Berlin prompted a change in both ideas ('thinking changing') and sensations ('feeling as it was seeing') for the young poet, demonstrating again how the encounter with affective spaces such as that of the Cosy Corner acted heterotopically upon Auden. Arguably, these spaces profoundly changed his life and his thinking. Auden said that it was in Berlin that 'he ceased to see the world in terms of verse' and instead encountered the world of experience.[151] Deer argues persuasively that Auden's experience of Berlin was formative for his understanding of the space and geography of England, as the 'city offered a prism through which to defamiliarize the English landscape and body politic' and which 'revealed the foreignness of home'.[152] Just as *Broom* magazine had learnt to see America afresh after its time in Berlin, so was Auden's sense of home revised by the affects he experienced while an outsider in the city. Berlin's general mood (*Stimmung*) of *restlessness* thus appears in Auden and Isherwood as an impulse to self-transformation, to ceaselessly making oneself anew in a foreign place.

It is worth noting one final location visited by Isherwood and Auden that can be viewed as a heterotopic space: Dr Magnus Hirschfeld's Institute for Sexology (*Institut Für Sexual-Wissenschaft*). Tim Armstrong describes Hirschfield's Institute as 'an important site for Modernism' in the 1920s, noting the presence in the immediate neighbourhood of Djuna Barnes and Robert McAlmon.[153] When Isherwood arrived in Berlin in November 1929 he stayed in a house in the leafy Tiergarten area, in the street In Den Zelten.[154] The house adjoined Hirschfeld's Institute, which had been founded in 1919, and in which numerous gay, transvestite and transgendered people lived in what Page calls 'a remarkable community'.[155] The large building contained teaching rooms, an extensive library and museum, and a consulting clinic. Hirschfeld, who was gay, Jewish and with socialist sympathies, had long campaigned for homosexual rights and recognition, founding the first journal of sexology in 1907 and issued many publications on homosexual life in Berlin, such as *Berlin's Third Sex* (1904). He also instigated the first Congress for Sexual Reform in 1921, which had several international successors and gained support from British intellectuals such as Arnold Bennett, J. M. Keynes, Bertrand Russell, H. G. Wells, and Virginia and Leonard Woolf.[156] Although Hirschfeld's approach arguably pathologised homosexuality as having an hereditary origin, he had long campaigned for repeal of Germany's harsh penal code against homosexuality.

Isherwood refers to visiting the Institute for lunch and feeling somewhat unsettled by the bourgeois air of the house, with its classical furniture and marble pillars. Lunch, he writes, 'was a meal of decorum and gracious smiles . . . a living guarantee that Sex, in this sanctuary, was being treated with seriousness'.[157] Isherwood admits that he was disturbed by the way in which the inhabitants of the Institute were regarded as 'naturally' as the respectable furniture:

> Christopher had been telling himself that he had rejected respectability and that he now regarded it with amused contempt. But the Hirschfeld kind of respectability disturbed his latent Puritanism. During those early days, he found lunch as the Institute rather uncanny.[158]

Curiously for Isherwood, and seemingly for Auden too, the Institute confounded their newly discovered sexual freedom precisely because here homosexuality was not associated with the cross-class transgressions of the Cosy Corner, but appeared to be inserted directly into bourgeois 'respectability'. Its 'uncanniness' can thus be interpreted as another heterotopic quality: a real place that attempted to represent sexual 'deviance' and 'perversion' in an ordered and 'normal' fashion.

GEOGRAPHICAL EMOTIONS: *GOODBYE TO BERLIN* AND *THE HEART TO ARTEMIS*

Isherwood's final representation of Berlin occurs in what he called 'a loosely connected sequence of diaries and sketches', *Goodbye to Berlin* (1939), covering the years from 1930 to early 1933.[159] In what he intended as a larger novel, Isherwood's aim was to concentrate upon outsiders in the city: 'I wanted to call it *The Lost.* About people whom society regarded with horror. I also thought of calling it *The Rejected.*'[160] The central episodes of the book thus concern outsider characters such as Sally Bowles, an American actress promised work in the UFA studios, various young homosexual men such as the working-class Otto Nowak, and the wealthy Jewish family the Landauers, based upon the owners of a large Berlin department store, Israel's (Kaufhaus N. Israel), near to Alexanderplatz. The status of the narrator, 'Christopher Isherwood', as an outsider is also stressed from the beginning, as he listens in his room at night to young men whistling to their girlfriends in the streets below: 'Because of the whistling, I do not care to stay here in the evenings. It reminds me that I am in a foreign city, alone, far from home.'[161] However, by the end of the book, roles are somewhat reversed, as Bernhard Landauer suggests to Christopher that he will always return to Berlin because, 'You seem to belong here' and that it 'is strange how people seem to belong to places – especially to places where they were not born'.[162] This emphasizes how Isherwood, like Auden, found Berlin to be a 'strange country' to which they might become affectively attached, outsiders that felt like insiders. This is in marked contrast to the Landauer family represented in the penultimate chapter of the book. Now, as Germany moved towards Fascism, it is Bernhard, as a Jew, that becomes marked as an outsider in the country of his birth, and the chapter concludes with a reference to the Nazi boycott of Jewish shops such as the Landauers' in 1933 and, finally, an overheard conversation between two anti-Semites about the Nazi plan to 'clear the Jews right out of Germany'.[163]

In places Isherwood's book suggests a complex attempt to neutralize his emotional response to the city and its politics, including the fates of the Jews and communists with whom he becomes friendly. This is achieved mainly by employing a detached documentary style, with the first and last episodes of the book being marked as 'A Berlin Diary'. However, like Naomi Mitchison's *Vienna Diary* (see Chapter 2), *Goodbye to Berlin* mixes a tone of dispassionate reportage with a more modernist set of narrative devices.[164] The famous trope of the narrator as a camera on the first page thus encourages the impression that the book will present an objective portrait of the city: 'I am a camera with its shutter open, quite passive, recording, not thinking. . . . Some day, all this will have to be developed, carefully printed, fixed.'[165] However, much of the language of this page subsequently reveals a narrator who projects his own affects and emotions onto the material spaces of the city: he views a 'solemn massive street' from his window, a street which is 'dirty', 'shabby' and 'tarnished', and is the location of a 'bankrupt middle class'; the street sounds he hears 'echo down the deep hollow street, lascivious and private and sad'.[166] Indeed, Isherwood later rejected the idea that he was a narrator who records but did not interpret, saying that he was 'in the strangest mood at this particular moment . . . a mood where I just sit and register impressions through the window'.[167] Here Isherwood demonstrates Heidegger's notion of attunement (*Stimmungen*), where the interior mood of a person is attuned to the external mood of the environment: in Flatley's words, at such moments moods 'are not in us; we are in them; they go through us'.[168] Isherwood thus records the geographical emotions of the city itself – sad, lascivious, shabby and so on – as they pass through him.

The final section of the book, 'A Berlin Diary (Winter 1932–33)', shows another such attunement, whereby the documentary format is punctuated by bursts of affect generated from the city itself. Both styles of writing now seem intensified in this chapter: there are, for example, more uses of the immediacy of the diary format, in paragraphs that start 'This evening', 'This morning' and 'tomorrow I am going to England'.[169] But there are also more extended moments of a modernist style driven by geographical emotions. The chapter thus commences with an image of the 'dead cold' of winter gripping the city, at once an accurate marker of the time of the year in a northern European city, and also a deeply symbolic winter with Hitler's ascendance to power imminent. The cold shrinks Berlin to 'a small black dot' on 'the enormous European map' and Isherwood's imaginative geography now perceives the city to be surrounded by the Prussian plains, which are described as 'an immense waste of unhomely ocean', projecting the city as an island home under threat from watery waste. This symbolic geography is then brilliantly attuned to the affective mood of the narrator:

> Berlin is a skeleton which aches in the cold: it is my own skeleton aching. I feel in my bones the sharp ache of the frost in the girders of the overhead railway, in the iron-work of balconies, in bridges, tramlines, lamp-standards, latrines. The iron throbs and shrinks, the stone and the bricks ache dully, the plaster is numb.[170]

Here Christopher merges into the material spaces of Berlin's technological modernity, experiencing its aches (a word repeated several times here) and pains as if the city where he began as an outsider is now physically inside him, like a shared skeleton. Rather than a detached camera snapping scenes of the metropolis, this demonstrates a narrator closely attuned to his environment, the wintry affects of the city running directly through him.

As the chapter progresses it becomes more fragmented in style, with shorter episodes charting how the mood (*Stimmung*) of Berlin becomes progressively more wintry with Nazi rallies at the Sportspalast and Bülowplatz, raids and arrests, before the final paragraph when we learn that 'Hitler is master of this city.'[171] Interestingly, in a book which Isherwood later criticised for its many evasions and self-deceptions, it is only in this final chapter that the character Christopher employs the term 'queer' to describe himself.[172] On a final 'farewell' tour of various Berlin bars with a friend, Fritz Wendel, Christopher visits a transvestite bar, the Salomé, and as he leaves they are confronted by several drunken American youths who seem perplexed at the idea of men dressed as women. One of the Americans asks 'As *women*, hey? Do you mean they're *queer*?', to which Fritz replies 'Eventually we're all queer.' This answer seems to floor the Americans, who are described as standing 'awkwardly' and with 'open-mouthed faces' that look a bit 'scared'. One of them then turns to Christopher: 'You *queer*, too, hey?' Yes, replies Christopher, 'very queer indeed', an answer which makes the interlocutor 'uncertain' before, finally, he and his friends rush drunkenly into the club.[173] Though Isherwood's tone here is somewhat comic and knowing, and the self-identification as queer is detached and ironised, it is significant that it occurs at this moment in the text. In the city whose queer spaces enabled his own sexual identity to flourish he is finally able to state his queerness, but only at a moment of intense political danger and with an awareness that he is about to leave Berlin. His attunement to the city is now about to be broken as the heterotopic queer spaces of the city are about to be closed.

This uneven tone and a sort of disjuncture of affects continue in the final paragraphs of the book. With the Nazis in power Christopher imagines that many of his pupils at the Workers' school, where he taught English, are now either imprisoned or dead. Of his communist friend Rudi he ponders whether he is currently being 'tortured to death'. These thoughts are then interrupted by a final image that attempts to recall the documentary impulse of the photograph:

> I catch sight of my face in the mirror of a shop, and am horrified to see that I am smiling. You can't help smiling, in such beautiful weather. The trams are going up and down the Kleiststrasse, just as usual. They, and the people on the pavement, and the tea-cosy dome of the Nollendorfplatz station have an air of curious familiarity, of striking resemblance to something one remembers as normal and pleasant in the past – like a very good photograph.[174]

Isherwood then concludes the book with the observation that he now 'can't altogether believe that any of this has really happened'.[175] The images of the trams and the station gesture towards the spatial fabric of Berlin's modernity, but the 'normality' of this photograph is broken by the irruption of contradictory affects in the opening lines: smiling is juxtaposed with horror. Tomkins notes the complexity of the smiling response as linked to the affect of enjoyment, listing at least seven different functions that it has in the psychology of the individual and society, one of which is a 'sudden relief' from a 'negative simulation' and 'negative affects' such as 'fear or distress'.[176] Isherwood's smile here might be interpreted as a momentary relief from his thoughts of torture and incarceration, prompted by the sun and the normality of Berlin's traffic and commuters. Rapidly, however, this affect swivels around as Christopher becomes horrified that he is still able to experience positive affects in the city whose overall atmosphere and mood are so bleak. Rather than a denial of affect here, as perhaps the photographic trope might imply, what we witness instead is one final moment when Isherwood's geographical emotions burst through the patina of documentary distance, where the affects of joy and horror mingle and produce perhaps a third, unstated, affect, that of shame or self-contempt at still being able to smile amidst the horror of Nazi rule.[177]

Berlin as a city whose mood (*Stimmung*) provoked a fascinating set of positive affects is also captured in another piece of life-writing by an English outsider, the lesbian writer and critic Bryher. In contrast to the representations by Auden and Isherwood, however, the sexual spaces of Berlin are never explicitly discussed by Bryher. Instead it is other modernist spaces in Berlin that she focuses upon in her memoir, *The Heart to Artemis* (1962). Like Auden and Isherwood, Bryher preferred Berlin to Paris, and she writes passionately about the time she spent in Berlin in the late 1920s and early 1930s, a time of artistic experimentation that coincided with her own self-exploration from being in analysis with Hanns Sachs (one of Freud's inner circle). 'I love Berlin so much, like a person I think',[178] she wrote to her long-term partner, H.D., in May 1931, while early in *The Heart to Artemis* Bryher notes: 'All my life I have suffered from "geographical emotions". Places are almost as real to me as people.'[179] Bryher's affective attachment to place had been demonstrated earlier in her life when Annie Winifred Ellerman adopted the name 'Bryher' for her first novel, *Development* (1920), the name deriving from one of the Scilly Isles, off the coast of Cornwall, that she had frequently visited as a child. Later she changed her name legally to Bryher, indicating a clean break from her heritage: to rename oneself in such a way as to mark a distance from one's parents is one thing, but to identify one's new name with a place rather than a person indicates the strength of Bryher's attachment to geography as a category for understanding and organising one's life.[180]

Like *Goodbye to Berlin*, *The Heart to Artemis* is a book that straddles different styles of writing, one form of which is that of travel writing, although it starts out as a fairly conventional autobiography tracing how the English-born Annie Winifred Ellerman, daughter of the one-time richest man in Britain, John Ellerman, escaped from the Victorian conventions of her upbringing to find her identity amidst the avant-garde artists of modernist Europe in the 1920s and 1930s.[181] However, as the book progresses its more experimental qualities begin to emerge. Tellingly, at one point Bryher writes: 'I should like this book to be read neither as mere autobiography nor period piece but as an attempt to show how external events and unconscious drives help or hinder development.'[182] The book is thus shaped by two major features: first, Bryher reads her own past, particularly that of her 'repressed' childhood, through the lens of psychoanalysis; second, subtitled 'A Writer's Memoirs', the book presents her engagement with literary modernism as a parallel route into a sense of self – it is dedicated to Stéphane Mallarmé, for instance, and the opening sentence situates her own birth through the device of another modernist literary frame: 'When I was born in September, 1894, Dorothy Richardson's Miriam was a secretary.'[183]

Much of the earlier part of the book charts Bryher's extensive travels as a child, exploring a different set of geographical emotions. Bryher visits France, Switzerland and Italy, in a kind of late Victorian 'Grand Tour', but then also visits Egypt and Algeria (chapter 3 memorably starts: 'Nobody ever gets over their first camel').[184] It is these happy travels that form the backdrop to her novel, *Development*, a thinly disguised autobiography of a young girl named Nancy, whose psychic development is delineated by means of her external journeys:

> Travelling has much in common with adventure, and all these days of surely an epic childhood seemed immortal to Nancy, even the hours spent moving from place to place. Her imagination, sensitive to all impressions of the loveliness and the legends ready to her hand, found time to ponder as the train jerked on, to assimilate what crowded street and ruined building had heaped there in profusion, effacing all that had held no importance from her memory, in preparation for the new atmosphere of another city.[185]

Bryher viewed her travels when young as a key factor in her embrace of modernist experimentation and in her rejection of conventional femininity and sexuality, although she never discusses these topics in the memoir. Travel, therefore, and the attendant sense of being an outsider were a liberating experience for Bryher, as they were for many other modernists.[186] She thus noted of the international cast of modernist expatriates of the Parisian Left Bank in the 1920s: 'We were all exiles. We remain so to-day. It is our destiny.'[187]

However, unlike so many of these other Left Bank writers and artists, she was not really moved or liberated by Paris. She describes herself as an 'observer' of the Left Bank coteries and writes that although 'I was utterly in sympathy with the rebellion of the group . . . their solutions did not solve my particular problem.'[188] She does not drink (which perhaps didn't help when crawling around cafés with the likes of Hemingway and Joyce) and although she recognises the 'exhilaration' of Paris at this time, she cannot identify with the 'enchantment' experienced by other expatriate modernists. Bryher, rather sadly, considers herself a 'Puritan in Montparnasse', while the Paris streets, familiar from many childhood visits, start to make her feel uneasy, reminding her 'of the restrictions of childhood'.[189] For Bryher, therefore, the geographical emotions roused by Paris are resoundingly negative.

Berlin, however, evoked a quite different response:

> I fell in love with Berlin at once to my own amazement. There is a time when if development is to continue, childhood associations must be put temporarily aside and I had known France too long and too well. In the sharp bite of the air of the North I could watch the first patterns evolve of the post-war decade. Russian and Polish refugees sat on benches in the station, clasping bundles done up in old, faded blankets, too weary at first either to look for work or beg for food. We were conscious that we were standing near the centre of a volcano, it was raw, dangerous, explosive but I have never encountered before or since so vital a response to experimental art.[190]

For Bryher, Berlin thus represents a 'development' from childhood to adulthood, figured in the geographical shift from France to Germany, and intrinsically linked to the politics of the Weimar period, replete with refugees from Central Europe, as well as avant-garde aesthetics. The restless spaces of the city thus fuel Bryher's own development, replicating her own set of travels across Europe in search of an identity. The imagery of the volcano is, partly, conditioned by the retrospective narrative of the memoir, pointing forwards to the Nazi rise to power, but also captures again her positive affective response to the city: 'raw, dangerous, explosive' and 'vital'. 'Berlin', she wrote in notes at the time of living there, 'was dangerous.'[191] The mood (*Stimmung*) of the city was thus one that Bryher, like Isherwood, responded to immediately and attempted to capture in the retrospective narrative of her memoir.

While Isherwood imagined himself as a camera taking still photographs, for Bryher it was the new modernist art of cinema that she discovered in Berlin, after travelling to the city on the advice of Robert Herring, film correspondent of the *Manchester Guardian*.[192] Living in Switzerland, Bryher began to visit Berlin for long periods of time from 1927 onwards, primarily to help gather material for the little magazine devoted to cinema, *Close-Up*, which she edited along with her then husband of convenience, Kenneth Macpherson.[193] In Berlin she travelled to the suburb of Babelsberg, site of the UFA film studios, and soon met the important director G. W. Pabst. 'I came late to the cinema and I came because of [Pabst's] *Joyless Street*', she wrote in *Close-Up* in 1927.[194]

For Bryher the emotional geography of Berlin thus comprised a number of interconnected strands: urban modernity, cinematic modernism, and her involvement with psychoanalysis. Bryher's first analyst was Hanns Sachs, whom she met at a party held by Pabst, and she later underwent initial training to become an analyst.[195] Sachs had been an adviser to the first attempt to make a psychoanalytic film, *Secrets of a Soul*, also directed by Pabst and released in 1926, demonstrating the intellectual affinities between film and psychoanalysis as modernist phenomena. Sachs also contributed some articles to *Close-Up*, whose project as a film magazine, argues Laura Marcus, 'was substantially informed by psychoanalytic thought'.[196]

For Bryher the experience of German film coalesced with the investigation into the secrets of her own soul via her analysis with Sachs. Her descriptions of Berlin are thus dominated by a discourse in which the passions of the city are identified with the release of her own unconscious, while also being influenced by the aesthetics of cinema:

> At first, however, Berlin was all excitement and promise. It was a place of violent contrasts, a baby elephant at the Zoo tossed the fallen yellow leaves about its enclosure with the petulant trunk movements of an awkward child. We went to see *Hoppla, wir leben* where shots taken on an actual battlefield were suddenly flashed on to an immense screen behind the actors' heads. The impact of the scene brought many of the audience out of their seats. We sheltered from the cold November winds inside small cafés whose red plush seats and marble-topped tables must have been a legacy of the nineties. . . . There was desperate poverty, life and death seemed to hang upon trifles, a missed bus, an unexpected meeting. I sometimes felt that a collective but unconscious mind had broken through its controls. We went to obscure cinemas to see experimental films.[197]

From the cinema and theatre to the city cafés, the restless spaces of Berlin render it an Expressionist place of 'violent contrasts', enacted in the way in which this paragraph abruptly switches topic, echoing the famous cinematic theory of montage developed by Sergei Eisenstein and discussed extensively in *Close-Up*.[198] The description of the audience leaping out of their seats during Erwin Piscator's staging of Ernst Toller's famous work of 'New Objectivity', *Hoppla, wir leben*, also points to the bodily affect of much early cinema.[199] The extremes of the psychoanalytic experience, where a 'trifle' can become vitally important, are here mapped onto the city itself, as Bryher perceives in the spaces of the city her own unconscious release writ large. Berlin, she writes, employing a fascinating set of spatialised terms, was 'easier and *nearer to me* than any city where I had lived' (emphasis added) and, again: 'I never had to translate my feelings in Berlin; in Latin countries I was a wild plant escaped into a formal garden.'[200] Berlin is thus experienced as a kind of affective home, not one where Bryher's feelings are like a 'foreign' language in need of translation. Her 'wildness' is thus at home in Berlin, much as Isherwood's queerness also found a place of belonging in the city. In Berlin, then, Bryher finds herself, and when she leaves amidst the rising terror of the Nazi rise to power, she mourns the loss of the city whose uncontrolled passions enabled her own psychic development. Bryher thus points to a quite primal relationship to place, with Berlin being the site where her 'feelings' did not need translating, echoing those theorists that define affect as a category prior to translation into a formal discourse.[201]

Another instance that demonstrates the affect of the city upon Bryher occurs immediately after she has discussed why Freudian analysis helps her illuminate the 'dark pit' of the brain:

> And outside was Berlin. It was the time of the Bauhaus and experiments in modern architecture. The schools were locked in a struggle between light and darkness. I loved the new functional furniture, the horizontal windows and the abolition of what I thought of as messy decoration. I saw the documentary film of a rocket; people laughed, I was interested. I understood very little of what was happening politically in Germany. Berlin was an international city but as in any period of great artistic expression, and we had one in the twenties, there are always centres that draw people to them to form a kingdom of their own. 'It's got to be new,' we chanted because old forms were saturated with the war memories that both former soldiers and civilians wanted to forget. We were too savage, too contemptuous, but would you have had us be prudent? We did not realise at the time that it was not the concepts themselves that were at fault but the way that they had been used. Perhaps because my own unconscious was in the process of release, the unconscious passions of the city struck me with the more force. The war losses had been the same in all countries but there had not been the total upset of all values as in Germany and Austria. I saw hunger, brutality and greed but there was also the sudden compassionate gesture, a will to help or the pre-battle awareness of the single rose, the transient beauty of some girl's face.[202]

This is a fascinating paragraph, in all sorts of ways, and one dominated by a language of affect, with Bryher being 'struck' with 'force' by the 'passions' of the city. This is then articulated into a discourse of emotions, such as savagery, contempt, brutality, greed and compassion. It is fascinating too as a form of cultural history containing a fine overview of how modernism was experienced as an exciting commitment to the new ('It's got to be new') and of being part of an international avant-garde movement prompted by the changes wrought by World War I; tellingly, this expatriate coterie understands Berlin primarily in aesthetic rather than political terms – the sentence about understanding very little of the politics of Germany is clearly the result of retrospective distance. However, what is also interesting is the way in which the structural form of this paragraph replicates another spatial move: 'And outside was Berlin.' The paragraph seems to shift from the interior psychic life of Bryher, as experienced through analytic practice, and into the external space of the city. But by the end of the paragraph the 'outside' has become cathected onto the 'inside', such that the 'unconscious passions of the city' are linked to those of Bryher's inner 'release'. 'Cathected' seems correct here because it is somewhat ambiguous which comes first: is the release of psychic inhibitions prompted by the modernist passions she experiences in the city? Or is she only able to see the city in this way because her unconscious is being released?

The first interpretation is, arguably, the more persuasive, partly because it emphasises those moments when external space intrudes upon, and actively shapes, Bryher's own psychic space. At the end of the chapter Bryher tries to sum up what Berlin meant to her. Returning to Switzerland via Vienna she visits Freud for the last time. For Bryher, 'in spite of being the birthplace of analysis and of many of my friends', Vienna was 'too southern for me in atmosphere', a statement again combining geography with emotional attachment: in other places she alludes to how her 'northernness' was more suited to cities such as Berlin.[203] Bryher concludes the chapter in the following way:

> I could not help thinking sometimes of my lost city. A moment, a memory, would come back and I could not help murmuring, it was childish but I meant it, 'Why, Berlin, must I love you so?' It had gone, I thought, for ever.[204]

There is an interesting temporal confusion here since Bryher shifts her narrative from a retrospective account of visiting Freud in Vienna in 1933 to her memories of Berlin in the years after she left the city (she last visited the city in 1932 and did not return to Germany until 1960). Berlin becomes here a lost object, functioning in her psychic life somewhat like the loss of a loved one whose presence persists due to the painful prompts of memory. The reflection that this is a 'childish' experience indicates Bryher's realisation of the intensity of her feelings for Berlin: unlike a person, the city has not really died and thus cannot be mourned as a lost object. What has been lost, we might say, is the experience of how the modernist city of Berlin intensified the release of her unconscious; what this chapter of *The Heart to Artemis* perhaps attempts is a process of recovery. In writing about her inner self, Bryher is recalling the exterior space of her 'lost city', a city whose cultural geography in the late 1920s was partly responsible for how she 'found', we might say, her own self.

Heart to Artemis thus offers a fascinating account of modernism, space, and one particular city, demonstrating what it meant to Bryher to 'suffer' from 'geographical emotions'. But in the version of this statement in her earlier article, 'Paris 1900', first published in *Life and Letters Today* in 1937, the second sentence reads differently: 'All my life I have suffered from "geographical emotions". Cities are so much easier to understand than people.'[205] Whereas the version in *Heart to Artemis* ('places are almost as real to me as people') is something of an ontological claim – and a rather puzzling one at that, for why should cities be no less real than people? – the 1937 version ('cities are so much easier to understand than people') is a hermeneutic statement fuelled by Bryher's interest in psychoanalysis. To understand people fully, argues psychoanalysis, requires us to understand them not just as rational actors, but as creatures driven by powerful somatic qualities. It is, of course, debateable if cities are any easier to understand than people, but viewing urban space as exhibiting a similar set of affective qualities to those we normally associate with human beings is an intriguing and provocative idea and indicates how affect flows from spaces to subjects, as well as from subject to subject. Intriguing too, is the notion that to possess 'geographical emotions' is a type of *suffering*, an affect seemingly related to Tomkins' category of Distress-Anguish.[206] However, for Bryher there seems something more ambivalent about the geographical emotions provoked by Berlin: 'suffering' here might be better understood as another example of attunement to the dominant atmosphere of the city, recalling Isherwood's tone at the close of *Goodbye to Berlin*.

Berlin in the Cold

In Bryher and the other writers discussed in this chapter we thus witness many fascinating attempts to understand how cities such as Berlin move us, whether to the raging maelstroms depicted in Expressionism or to somewhat quieter kinds of geographical emotion. The place of Berlin in the history of modernism, therefore, is rightly associated with theorising affective urban geographies and various literary representations of how cities move us. After the Nazi rise to power, however, the geographical emotions of Berlin turned ugly, displacing both the Expressionist angst and the avant-garde utopia of earlier moments in the city's modernist history. Towards the end of *Mr Norris Changes Trains* Isherwood's narrator describes a change in the 'affective atmosphere' of Berlin after the burning of the Reichstag: 'The whole city lay under an epidemic of discreet, infectious fear. I could feel it, like influenza, in my bones.'[207] As Isherwood depicted it at the end of *Goodbye to Berlin*, the city was now replete with negative affects that ached throughout its technological skeleton, the cold of winter a symbol for the mood of fear and suffering brought on by political events. One of the most poignant moments in the final chapter of

Goodbye to Berlin occurs when Christopher visits another of his old haunts, the Café des Westens, the favoured space for the pre-war Expressionist circles around *Die Aktion* and *Der Sturm*:

> Every evening, I sit in the big half-empty artists' café by the Memorial Church, where the Jews and left-wing intellectuals bend their heads together over the marble tables, speaking in low, scared voices. Many of them know that they will certainly be arrested – if not today, then tomorrow or next week. So they are polite and mild with each other, and raise their hats and inquire after their colleagues' families. Notorious literary tiffs or several years standing are forgotten.[208]

Café des Westens had now become Café Melancholy, soon to be part of Bryher's 'lost city', where the 'literary tiffs' of the modernisms that once thrived in this and many other spaces in Berlin were now forgotten. Jews and left-wing intellectuals, once the inside-outsiders who were so prominent in Berlin's modernism, were now profoundly marked as outsiders in their own city. On 6 May 1933 the Hirschfeld Institute was ransacked by a mob, an incident witnessed by Isherwood, at which he quietly uttered the word, 'shame'; a few days later, the library of the Institute was publicly burned on the streets.[209] The restless spaces of Berlin, site of many of modernism's utopian dreams, were now closed, replaced with the dystopian order of Nazi Germany.[210]

Notes

1. Stephen Spender, quoted in Norman Page, *Auden and Isherwood: The Berlin Years* (Basingstoke: Macmillan, 1998), p. 39.
2. Stephen Spender, *World Within World* (London: Readers Union, 1953), p. 110. For one influential cultural history of Weimar Germany see Peter Gay, *Weimar Culture: The Outsider as Insider* (Harmondsworth: Penguin, 1968).
3. Cited in Richard J. Murphy, 'Berlin: Expressionism, Dada, Neue Sachlichkeit' in *The Oxford Handbook of Modernisms*, ed. Peter Brooker, Andrzej Gasiorek, Deborah Longworth and Andrew Thacker (Oxford: Oxford University Press, 2010), pp. 669–86; p. 669.
4. Peter Conrad, *Modern Times, Modern Places: Life and Art in the 20th Century* (London: Thames and Hudson, 1998), p. 319.
5. See Dorothy Rowe, *Representing Berlin: Sexuality and the City in Imperial and Weimar Germany* (Aldershot: Ashgate, 2003).
6. Stefan Zweig, quoted in Otto Friedrich, *Before the Deluge: A Portrait of Berlin in the 1920s* (New York: HarperCollins, 1995), pp. 128–9.
7. Christopher Isherwood, *Christopher and His Kind* (London: Methuen, 1977), p. 17.
8. Erwin Loewenson, a founder of the Expressionist cultural meeting place in Berlin, Der Neue Club, used the term 'vital intensity'; cited in Richard Sheppard, 'German Expressionism' in *Modernism: A Guide to European Literature 1890–1930*, ed. Malcolm Bradbury and James McFarlane (Harmondsworth: Penguin, 1991), pp. 274–91; p. 279; and Ulrich Weisstein, *Expressionism as an International Phenomenon* (1973), cited in Peter Nicholls, *Modernisms: A Literary Guide* (Basingstoke: Macmillan, 1995), p. 142.

9. Heidegger's discussion of *Stimmung* can be found in his *Being and Time*, trans. John Macquarrie and Edward Robinson (Oxford: Blackwell, 1962), pp. 172–9, 388–96. See the account given of this notion in Jonathan Flatley, *Affective Mapping: Melancholia and the Politics of Modernism* (Cambridge, MA: Harvard University Press, 2008), pp. 19–24. See also the discussion in the Introduction to this book.
10. Cited in Brian Ladd, *The Ghosts of Berlin: Confronting German History in the Urban Landscape* (Chicago: University of Chicago Press, 1997), pp. 123–4. It should be noted that Scheffler's comment was intended critically, as he viewed Berlin as 'the capital of all modern ugliness'; see Rowe, *Representing Berlin*, pp. 17–18.
11. Rowe, *Representing Berlin*, p. 10. On the modernity of Berlin see also Iain Boyd Whyte and David Frisby (eds), *Metropolis Berlin: 1880–1940* (Berkeley: University of California Press, 2012); and Andreas Killen, *Berlin Electropolis: Shock, Nerves, and German Modernity* (Berkeley: University of California Press, 2006).
12. Rowe, *Representing Berlin*, p. 31.
13. Eberhard Roters (ed.), *Berlin 1910–1933* (New York: Rizzoli, 1982), p. 17.
14. Killen, *Berlin Electropolis*, p. 22.
15. The term 'metropolitan miniatures' is that of Andreas Huyssen in his *Miniature Metropolis: Literature in an Age of Photography and Film* (Cambridge, MA: Harvard University Press, 2015), pp. 10–17.
16. Robert Walser, *Berlin Stories*, trans. Susan Bernofsky (New York: New York Review Books, 2012), p. 9.
17. Ibid. pp. 74, 62.
18. Cited in Ladd, *Ghosts of Berlin*, pp. 123–4.
19. Mark Twain, 'The Chicago of Europe', *Chicago Daily Tribune*, 3 April 1892, reprinted in Mark Twain, *The Chicago of Europe, and Other Foreign Tales of Travel*, ed. Peter Kaminsky (London: Sterling, 2009), p. 191. The comparison between the cities led to Berlin being described as 'Chicago on the Spree'; see Rowe, *Representing Berlin*, p. 17.
20. See Killen, *Berlin Electropolis*, pp. 8–9.
21. See Anthony Vidler, *Warped Space, Art, Architecture, and Anxiety in Modern Culture* (Cambridge, MA: MIT Press, 2000).
22. For Beard see Tim Armstrong, *Modernism, Technology and the Body: A Cultural Study* (Cambridge: Cambridge University Press, 1998), pp. 17–18.
23. Paul Carter, *Repressed Spaces: The Poetics of Agoraphobia* (London: Reaktion, 2002), p. 32.
24. See the discussion of this text in the Introduction and Chapter 4.
25. Cited in Max Saunders, *Ford Madox Ford: A Dual Life, vol. 1: The World Before the War* (Oxford: Oxford University Press, 1996), p. 176.
26. For an analysis of the link between technological modernisation in Berlin and the development of a discourse of neurasthenia see Killen, *Berlin Electropolis*.
27. For accounts of some of these theorisations see David Frisby, *Fragments of Modernity: Theories of Modernity in the Theories of Simmel, Kracauer, and Benjamin* (Cambridge: Polity, 1986), and Rowe, *Representing Berlin*, pp. 10–30.
28. Georg Simmel, 'The Metropolis and Mental Life' (1903) in *The Blackwell City Reader*, ed. Gary Bridge and Sophie Watson (Oxford: Blackwell, 2002), pp. 11–19; p. 12.
29. Walter Benjamin, 'On Some Motifs in Baudelaire' in *Selected Writings, vol. 4: 1938–1940*, ed. Howard Eiland and Michael W. Jennings (Cambridge, MA: Belknap/Harvard University Press, 2003), p. 327.

30. Douglas Brent McBride, 'A Critical Mass for Modernism in Berlin: *Der Sturm* (1910–32); *Die Aktion* (1911–32); and *Sturm-Bühne* (1918–19)' in *The Oxford Critical and Cultural History of Modernist Magazines, vol. 3: Europe 1880–1940*, ed. Peter Brooker, Sascha Bru, Andrew Thacker and Christian Weikop (Oxford: Oxford University Press, 2013), pp. 773–97; p. 773.
31. Sheppard, 'German Expressionism', pp. 282–5.
32. McBride, 'Critical Mass', p. 777.
33. Cited in Sheppard, 'German Expressionism', p. 281.
34. Rupert Brooke, 'The Old Vicarage, Grantchester' in *Georgian Poetry, 1911–12* (London: Poetry Bookshop, 1912), pp. 33–7; p. 33. For a discussion of this poem's setting see Edward Timms, 'Expressionists and Georgians: Demonic City and Enchanted Village' in *Unreal City: Urban Experience in Modern European Literature and Art*, ed. Edward Timms and David Kelley (Manchester: Manchester University Press, 1985), pp. 111–27. See also Patrick Bridgwater (ed,), *The Poets of the Café des Westens* (Leicester: Leicester University Press, 1984).
35. Christina Lodder, 'Searching for Utopia' in *Modernism: Designing a New World: 1914–1939*, ed. Christopher Wilk (London: V & A, 2006), pp. 23–70; pp. 24–5. Lodder traces this tendency to the influence of William Morris and the Arts and Crafts tradition upon the designers of the Deutscher Werkbund (German Work Association), which was established in 1907 by Hermann Muthesius. It was at the home of Muthesius that Auden first stayed when arriving in Berlin; see Page, *Auden and Isherwood*, pp. 100–1. Muthesius had worked in the 1890s at the German Embassy in London as a cultural attaché, studying the Arts and Crafts movement, which resulted in his book *Das Englische Haus* (*The English House*, 1904). For more on the Werkbund see Roters, *Berlin*, pp. 30–3.
36. Roters, *Berlin*, pp. 55–6.
37. Murphy, 'Berlin', p. 672. For the concept of 'cognitive overload' see Silvio Vietta and Hans-Georg Kemper, *Expressionismus* (Munich: Fink, 1975), pp. 30–40.
38. David Harvey, *The Condition of Postmodernity* (Oxford: Blackwell, 1989), pp. 240–2; Murphy, 'Berlin', p. 671.
39. Kurt Pinthus, cited in Murphy, 'Berlin', p. 672.
40. Nigel Thrift, 'Intensities of Feeling: Towards a Spatial Politics of Affect', *Geografiska Annaler: Series B Human Geography* 86:1 (March 2004), pp. 57–78; p. 57.
41. Christopher Butler, *Early Modernism: Literature, Music and Painting in Europe 1900–1916* (Oxford: Oxford University Press, 1994), p. 179. On this painting see also Rowe, *Representing Berlin*, p. 148.
42. Meidner, '. . . im Nacken das Sternemeer . . .', cited in Butler, *Early Modernism*, p. 180.
43. For a discussion of the historical and cultural significance of Potsdamer Platz see Ladd, *Ghosts of Berlin*, pp. 115–25.
44. Ibid. pp. 116–18.
45. *Berlin für Kenner: Ein Bärenführer bei Tag und Nacht durch die deutsche Reichshauptstadt* (1912), cited in ibid. p. 82.
46. Franz Hessel, *Walking in Berlin*, trans. Amanda de Marco (London: Scribe, 2016), p. 52.
47. For a discussion of these binaries see Andrew Thacker, *Moving Through Modernity: Space and Geography in Modernism* (Manchester: Manchester University Press, 2003), pp. 13–45.
48. For a discussion of Kirchner's depiction of female sexuality in an urban context see Rowe, *Representing Berlin*, pp. 149–54.
49. Cited in Murphy, 'Berlin', p. 671.

50. Ibid. p. 670.
51. Paul Boldt, 'Auf der Terrasse des Café Josty' ['On the Terrace of Café Josty'], *Die Aktion* 2 (13 Nov. 1912), p. 46. German original: 'Der Potsdamer Platz in ewigem Gebrüll / Vergletschert alle hallenden Lawinen / Der Straßentrakte: Trams auf Eisenschienen, / Automobile und den Menschenmüll. / Die Menschen rinnen über den Asphalt, / Ameisenemsig, wie Eidechsen flink. / Stirne und Hände, von Gedanken blink, / Schwimmen wie Sonnenlicht durch dunklen Wald. / Nachtregen hüllt den Platz in eine Höhle, / Wo Fledermäuse, weiß, mit Flügeln schlagen / Und lila Quallen liegen – bunte Öle; / Die mehren sich, zerschnitten von den Wagen. – / Aufspritzt Berlin, des Tages glitzernd Nest, / Vom Rauch der Nacht wie Eiter einer Pest.'
52. Nicholls, *Modernisms*, p. 145.
53. Ibid. p. 144.
54. Murphy, 'Berlin', p. 680.
55. See Huyssen, *Miniature Metropolis*, ch. 5, 'Double Exposure Berlin'.
56. Murphy, 'Berlin', p. 684.
57. Alfred Döblin, *Berlin Alexanderplatz*, trans. Eugene Jolas (London: Continuum, 2004), p. 372.
58. See Eric Bulson, *Novels, Maps, Modernity: The Spatial Imaginary, 1850–2000* (New York: Routledge, 2007), pp. 118–19.
59. Döblin, *Berlin Alexanderplatz*, p. 32.
60. Ibid. p. 33.
61. Huyssen, *Miniature Metropolis*, p. 156.
62. Ibid.
63. Döblin, *Berlin Alexanderplatz*, p. 34.
64. Gregory J. Seigworth and Melissa Gregg, 'An Inventory of Shimmers' in *The Affect Theory Reader*, ed. Gregg and Seigworth (Durham, NC, and London: Duke University Press, 2010), pp. 1–25; pp. 1–2.
65. Döblin, *Berlin Alexanderplatz*, p. 3.
66. Ibid. p. 4.
67. Ibid.
68. Ibid. p. 5.
69. See Roters, *Berlin*, p. 175. The classic contemporary account of film in Germany is that of Siegried Kracauer, *From Caligari to Hitler: A Psychological History of German Film* (1947; Princeton: Princeton University Press, 1970).
70. Ruttmann's film was part of a genre of German 'street films' in the 1920s, along with *Die Strasse* (1923), *Joyless Street* (1928), *Tragedy of the Street* (1927) and *Asphalt* (1929). See Kracauer, *From Caligari to Hitler*, pp. 157–60.
71. For a discussion of the centrality of rhythm to Ruttmann's film, and to other 'city symphony' films see Laura Marcus, '"A Hymn to Movement": The "City Symphony" of the 1920s and 1930s', *Modernist Cultures* 5:1 (2010), pp. 30–46.
72. Marshall Berman, *All that Is Solid Melts into Air: The Experience of Modernity* (London: Verso, 1982), p. 159.
73. Kracauer points to the influence on Ruttmann of another Russian director, Dziga Vertov, who produced his own 'city symphony', *Man with the Movie Camera* (1929). See Kracauer, *From Caligari to Hitler*, p. 185.
74. The British documentary maker and film theorist John Grierson criticised the film for its focus on 'pure form'. See John Grierson, 'First Principles of Documentary' in *The European Cinema Reader*, ed. Catherine Fowler (London: Routledge, 2002), pp. 39–44. A similar criticism was made by Siegfried Kracauer, who noted that Ruttmann 'tends to avoid any critical comment on the reality with which he is faced' and demonstrates a preference for rhythmic montage as a strategy for

depicting the city, rather than political commentary upon the 'inherent anarchy of Berlin life'. See Kracauer, *From Caligari to Hitler*, p. 187.

75. Lodder, 'Searching for Utopia', p. 38.
76. Letter from Lissitzky to Matthew Josephson, 1925, quoted in Josephson, *Life Among the Surrealists: A Memoir* (New York: Holt, Rinehart and Winston, 1962), p. 210.
77. Tobias Boes, 'Germany' in *The Cambridge Companion to European Modernism*, ed. Pericles Lewis (Cambridge: Cambridge University Press, 2011), pp. 33–51; p. 46. And see Malcolm Bradbury (ed.), *The Atlas of Literature* (London: De Agostini, 1996), p. 183.
78. Eberhard Roters, 'Painting' in Roters, *Berlin*, p. 96.
79. Ibid.
80. See Viktor Shklovksy, *Zoo, or Letters Not about Love*, trans. Richard Sheldon (Chicago: Dalkey Archive, 2001), p. xiii.
81. See Robert Williams, *Culture in Exile: Russian Émigrés in Germany, 1881–1941* (Ithaca: Cornell University Press, 1972).
82. See Dieter E. Zimmer, *Nabokov's Berlin* (Berlin: Nicolaische Verlagsbuchhandlung, 2001).
83. See Stephen Bury, '"Not to Adorn Life but to Organize It": *Veshch. Gegenstand. Objet: Revue internationale de l'art moderne* (1922) and *G* (1923–6)' in *Oxford Critical and Cultural History of Modernist Magazines, vol. 3*, pp. 855–67; p. 859.
84. Shklovsky, *Zoo*, p. 4.
85. Ibid. pp. 13, 55, 40.
86. Ibid. p. 29.
87. Ibid. p. 63.
88. Ibid.
89. Ibid. p. 68.
90. Ibid. p. 63.
91. Ibid. pp. 66, 67.
92. Ibid. pp. 63, 67.
93. Ibid. p. 103.
94. See Josephson, *Life Among the Surrealists*, pp. 193, 200.
95. See Friedrich, *Before the Deluge*, pp. 121, 141.
96. A second magazine, *Secession* (1922–4), edited by Gorham Munson, was also published for a brief period in Berlin. For a discussion of this magazine see Chapter 2.
97. Harold Loeb, *The Way It Was* (New York: Criterion Books, 1959), p. 119.
98. Emmy Veronica Sanders, 'America Invades Europe', *Broom* 1:1 (Nov. 1921), pp. 89–93; p. 89.
99. Ibid. pp. 90–1.
100. Ibid. p. 93.
101. Peter Nicholls, 'Destinations: *Broom* (1921–21) and *Secession* (1922–4)' in *The Oxford Critical and Cultural History of Modernist Magazines, vol. 2: North America*, ed. Peter Brooker and Andrew Thacker (Oxford: Oxford University Press, 2012), pp. 636–54; p. 646.
102. Loeb, *Way It Was*, p. 119. And see Josephson, *Life Among the Surrealists*, pp. 208–12, for his encounters with Russian and Central European artists in Berlin.
103. Louis Lozowick [L.L.], 'Russian Berlin', *Broom* 3:1 (Aug. 1922), pp. 78–9; Ilya Ehrenburg, 'Vitrion', *Broom* 3:2 (Sep. 1922), pp. 83–95.
104. See Serge Sabarsky (ed.), *George Grosz: The Berlin Years* (New York: Rizzoli, 1985).

105. George Grosz, *Saturday Night*, *Broom* 4:3 (Feb. 1923), p. 199.
106. Loeb, *Way It Was*, p. 44.
107. Michael North, 'Transatlantic Transfer: Little Magazines and Euro-American Modernism'; available at http://modmags.dmu.ac.uk/file/north_transatlantic_transfer.pdf (last accessed 5 Nov. 2017), p. 4
108. Loeb, cited in North, 'Transatlantic Transfer', p. 7.
109. Ibid.
110. Josephson, *Life Among the Surrealists*, p. 188.
111. Advert, 'The Age of the Machine', *Broom* 5:1 (Aug. 1923), n.p.
112. Loeb, *Way It Was*, p. 128; Josephson, *Life Among the Surrealists*, p. 192.
113. Josephson, *Life Among the Surrealists*, p. 195.
114. See John Sutherland, *Stephen Spender: The Authorized Biography* (London: Penguin, 2004), p. 122.
115. Walter Benjamin, 'A Berlin Chronicle' in *Reflections: Essays, Aphorisms, Autobiographical Writings*, trans. Edmund Jephcott, ed. Peter Demetz (New York: Schocken Books, 1986), pp. 3–60; p. 22.
116. For the concept of heterotopic spaces see Michel Foucault, 'Of Other Spaces', *Diacritics* 16:1 (1986), pp. 22–7; Kevin Hetherington summarises a heterotopia as a space for an 'alternate ordering' of modernity, which 'organize a bit of the social world in a way different to that which surrounds them'; see Kevin Hetherington, *The Badlands of Modernity: Heterotopia and Social Ordering* (London: Routledge, 1997), p. 8.
117. Benjamin, 'Berlin Chronicle', p. 23.
118. See Joachim Schlör, *Nights in the Big City: Paris, Berlin, London 1840–1930* (London: Reaktion, 1998), and Robert Beachy, *Gay Berlin: Birthplace of a Modern Identity* (New York: Vintage, 2015).
119. Robert McAlmon rev. Kay Boyle, *Being Geniuses Together 1920–1930* (London: Michael Joseph, 1970), p. 95.
120. In his autobiography McAlmon comments that 'A deck of "snow", enough cocaine for quite too much excitement, cost the equal of ten cents.' See *Being Geniuses Together*, p. 96.
121. Robert McAlmon, *There Was a Rustle of Black Silk Stockings* (1925; New York: Belmont Books, 1963), p. 19. Contrast this with Isherwood's description of the costume ball for men attended by Conrad Veidt in his *Christopher and His Kind*, pp. 32–3.
122. See the 'Queer Spaces' issue of *English Language Notes* 45:2 (Fall/Winter 2007) for a discussion of this notion.
123. See Schlör, *Nights in the Big City*, p. 278; Page, *Auden and Isherwood*, p. 14.
124. Isherwood, *Christopher and His Kind*, p. 29.
125. Silvan Tomkins, *Shame and its Sisters: A Silvan Tomkins Reader*, ed. Eve Kosofsky Sedgwick and Adam Frank (Durham, NC, and London: Duke University Press, 1995), p. 74.
126. Cited in Humphrey Carpenter, *W. H. Auden: A Biography* (London: Faber, 2010), p. 84.
127. Friedrich, *Before the Deluge*, p. 304.
128. Auden, letter to Patience McAlwee, cited in Carpenter, *Auden*, p. 90.
129. Christopher Isherwood, *Down There on a Visit* (London: Methuen, 1962), p. 38.
130. Isherwood, *Christopher and His Kind*, p. 10. Eveline Kilian argues that the self-referential ambiguities of Isherwood's autobiographical texts rely upon 'his movement through geographical spaces and his construction of specific places as catalysts of displacement'. See Eveline Kilian, '"The Mystery-Magic of Foreignness": Mr Isherwood Changes Places' in *Life Writing and Space*, ed.

Eveline Kilian and Hope Wolf with Kathrin Tordasi (Farnham: Ashgate, 2016), pp. 89–104; p. 89.
131. Foucault, 'Of Other Spaces', p. 25.
132. Christopher Isherwood, *Mr Norris Changes Trains* (1935; Harmondsworth: Penguin, 1969), p. 5.
133. Tomkins, *Shame and its Sisters*, p. 107.
134. Isherwood, *Mr Norris*, p. 5.
135. Ibid.
136. Ibid. p. 6.
137. Ibid. p. 7.
138. Ibid. p. 8.
139. Ibid. p. 11. For Tomkins sweat and facial trembling are examples of the Fear-Terror affect; Tomkins, *Shame and its Sisters*, p. 74.
140. See Page, *Auden and Isherwood*, p. 18 for a list of the various venues in both areas. Isherwood dismissively noted how in the West End there were 'dens of pseudo-vice catering to heterosexual tourists'; see Isherwood, *Christopher and His Kind*, p. 29.
141. This point is made by Page, *Auden and Isherwood*, p. 36. Kilian analyses this idea in terms of Isherwood's Englishness and his maternal heritage; see Kilian, '"Mystery-Magic of Foreignness"', p. 97.
142. Isherwood, *Christopher and His Kind*, pp. 10–11.
143. Ibid. p. 29. Accompanied by Isherwood, John Lehmann's visit to the same bar registered a similar effect: 'This Lokal was a sensational experience for me, a kind of emotional earthquake. . . . Things unimagined by me in all my previous fantasies went on there.' See John Lehmann, *In the Purely Pagan Sense* (1976), cited in Page, *Auden and Isherwood*, p. 17.
144. Foucault, 'Other Spaces', p. 26.
145. W. H. Auden, 'This Loved One' in *Collected Poems*, ed. Edward Mendelson (London: Faber, 1991), p. 36. For reference to other poems composed by Auden while in Berlin see Page, *Auden and Isherwood*, pp. 173–81.
146. Patrick Deer, 'Two Cities: Berlin and New York' in *W. H. Auden in Context*, ed. Tony Sharpe (Cambridge: Cambridge University Press, 2013), pp. 24–34; p. 26.
147. Auden, '1929' in *Collected Poems*, p. 45.
148. Auden, '1929', p. 48.
149. Deer, 'Two Cities', p. 27.
150. Auden, '1929', p. 46.
151. Cited in Richard Davenport-Hines, *Auden* (London: Heinemann), p. 87. It was clearly also an important prompt to his poetry, as it was in Berlin that he revised his first great work, *Paid on Both Sides*, which T. S. Eliot published in *The Criterion* in 1930.
152. Deer, 'Two Cities', p. 25.
153. Tim Armstrong, *Modernism, Technology and the Body: A Cultural Study* (Cambridge: Cambridge University Press, 1998), p. 166. For more on Hirschfeld and the Institute see Beachy, *Gay Berlin*, pp. 160–86.
154. Robert McAlmon and Djuna Barnes had also lived in this road earlier.
155. Page, *Auden and Isherwood*, p. 108.
156. Ibid. p. 109.
157. Isherwood, *Christopher and His Kind*, p. 19.
158. Ibid.
159. Christopher Isherwood, *Goodbye to Berlin* (London: Vintage, 1998), preface.
160. Isherwood, cited in Friedrich, *Before the Deluge*, p. 303.
161. Isherwood, *Goodbye*, pp. 9–10. In his preface the author rejected the notion

that the book was autobiographical, saying that 'Christopher Isherwood' was a 'ventriloquist's dummy'. For more on the text's status as life-writing see Kilian, '"Mystery-Magic of Foreignness"'.

162. Isherwood, *Goodbye*, p. 224.
163. Ibid. p. 228.
164. A point made by Chris Hopkins, *English Fiction in the 1930s: Language, Genre, History* (London: Continuum, 2006), pp. 78–9.
165. Isherwood, *Goodbye*, p. 9.
166. Ibid.
167. Isherwood interview (1970), quoted in Hopkins, *English Fiction in the 1930s*, p. 89.
168. Flatley, *Affective Mapping*, p. 22.
169. Isherwood, *Goodbye*, pp. 252, 253, 254.
170. Ibid. p. 230.
171. Ibid. p. 255.
172. See Isherwood, *Christopher and His Kind*, and Kilian, '"Mystery-Magic of Foreignness"'.
173. Isherwood, *Goodbye*, p. 238
174. Ibid. pp. 255–6.
175. Ibid.
176. Tomkins, *Shame and its Sisters*, pp. 81–3.
177. For Tomkins on shame, see ibid. pp. 133–78.
178. Bryher to H.D., 1 May 1931, cited in Maria Camboni, '"Why, Berlin, Must I Love You So?": Bryher in Berlin, 1927–1932', *HD's Web e-newsletter* (Winter 2008); available at http://www.imagists.org/hd/hdsweb/december2008.pdf (last accessed 5 Nov. 2017).
179. Bryher, *The Heart to Artemis: A Writer's Memoirs* (London: Collins, 1962), p. 26.
180. Interestingly, Bryher also wrote a geography primer, *Picture Geography for Children* (1925).
181. Until relatively recently Bryher's writing has received scant attention and she has mainly been known for her relationship with H.D. and as a patron of various modernist artists, presses and magazines (such as Robert McAlmon and Contact Press, and the magazines *Close-Up* and *Life and Letters Today*). Two of her early novels have been reprinted: see *Development* (1920) and *Two Selves* (1923), published as Bryher, *Two Novels*, ed. Joanne Winning (Madison: University of Wisconsin Press, 2000). Another of her early works was upon the experiments of Soviet Cinema, *Film Problems in Soviet Russia* (1929); see Laura Marcus, *The Tenth Muse: Writing about Cinema in the Modernist Period* (Oxford: Oxford University Press, 2007), pp. 338–41. For two excellent accounts of Bryher in Berlin see Camboni, '"Why, Berlin, Must I Love You So?"', and Susan McCabe, 'Bryher and Berlin: Modernism's Geographical Emotions', *The Berlin Journal* 21 (Fall 2011), pp. 8–13. For a chronology of Bryher's life by Celena Kusch see https://hdis.chass.ncsu.edu/hdcircle/bryher (last accessed 16 Oct. 2017).
182. Bryher, *Heart to Artemis*, p. 206.
183. Ibid. p. 7. Bryher was a friend of Richardson, who also supported her financially.
184. In her later memoir, covering her life in London during World War II, *The Days of Mars: A Memoir* (London: Calder and Boyars, 1972), Bryher commented that her childhood hero had been the Victorian explorer Sir Richard Burton (p. 67).
185. Bryher, *Development* in *Two Novels*, p. 66.
186. See Tim Youngs, 'Travelling Modernists' in *Oxford Handbook of Modernisms*, pp. 267–80. See also Robert Burden, *Travel, Modernism and Modernity* (London: Routledge, 2015).

187. Bryher, *Heart to Artemis*, p. 207. This can also be interpreted as a comment upon her own gender identity, as noted in *Development* where Nancy hopes forlornly that one day she will turn into a boy; Bryher, *Development* in *Two Novels*, p. 24.
188. Bryher, *Heart to Artemis*, p. 217.
189. Ibid. p. 209.
190. Ibid. p. 249.
191. Cited in McCabe, 'Bryher and Berlin', p. 11.
192. Bryher, *Heart to Artemis*, p. 248. She first stayed in the upmarket Hotel Adlon, which contained an international clientele and reminded her very much of New York. She later transferred to the Pension Exquisite on the Ku'damm, much closer to the cultural heart of the city. See Cambioni, '"Why, Berlin, Must I Love You So?"'.
193. See Marcus, *Tenth Muse*, pp. 319–403.
194. See Bryher, 'G.W. Pabst. A Survey', *Close Up*, 1:6 (Dec. 1927); cited in James Donald, Anne Friedberg and Laura Marcus (eds), *Close Up 1927–1933: Cinema and Modernism* (London: Cassell, 1998), p. 19. And see H.D. on Pabst in the same volume; 'An Appreciation', pp. 139–48.
195. For Bryher's links to Freud and other psychoanalytic circles see Susan Stanford Friedman (ed.), *Analyzing Freud: Letters of H.D., Bryher, and their Circle* (New York: New Directions, 2002).
196. See Laura Marcus, 'Cinema and Psychoanalysis: Introduction' in *Close Up 1927–1933*, p. 240.
197. Bryher, *Heart to Artemis*, p. 254.
198. See Marcus, *Tenth Muse*, pp. 323–4, 339–40; and Anne Friedberg, 'Introduction' in *Close Up 1927–1933*, pp. 218–20.
199. For a discussion of the experimental and Expressionist qualities of Toller's play see Raymond Williams, *Drama from Ibsen to Brecht* (Harmondsworth: Penguin, 1973), pp. 298–303.
200. Bryher, *Heart to Artemis*, p. 254.
201. See, for example, Brian Massumi, *Parables for the Virtual: Movement, Affect, Sensation* (Durham, NC, and London: Duke University Press, 2002).
202. Bryher, *Heart to Artemis*, p. 259. While Bryher welcomed modernist architecture, Isherwood disliked the wealthy Grünewald area of the city with its 'expensive ugliness' and its 'cubist flat-roofed steel-and-glass box' villas; see Isherwood, *Goodbye*, p. 25.
203. Bryher, *Heart to Artemis*, p. 254.
204. Ibid. p. 270.
205. Bryher, 'Paris 1900', *Life and Letters Today* 16:8 (Summer 1937), pp. 33–4; p. 33.
206. Tomkins, *Shame and its Sisters*, pp. 109–32.
207. Isherwood, *Mr Norris*, p. 182.
208. Isherwood, *Goodbye*, p. 251. Paul Bowles remembers meeting Isherwood regularly in the Café des Westens: 'We'd have lunch with Stephen Spender, Christopher, and Jean [Ross, the model for Sally Bowles in *Goodbye to Berlin*]. We always had that nucleus. We generally ate at the Café des Westens opposite the Kaiser Gedächtnis Kirche [Memorial Church].' See interview with Paul Bowles, *The Paris Review*, 67 (Fall 1981), p. 41.
209. See Isherwood, *Christopher and His Kind*, p. 101. Hirschfeld himself was abroad at the time, and died in exile in France in 1935.
210. Though for an argument that forms of modernist art persisted in Nazi Germany see Gregory Maertz, 'The Invisible Post-War Museum or the Visibility of Modernist Art in the Third Reich', *Modernism/Modernity* 15:1 (Jan. 2008), pp. 63–86.

4

LONDON

Introduction: A Larger University

In November 1914 the American poet Ezra Pound, who had arrived in London in 1908, drew up a prospectus for a College of Arts that was published in the magazine *The Egoist*. It was designed for American students who wished to learn something of European culture, but without being tied to the formal structures of a university course. Or, as Pound characteristically put it, 'it would be designed to form itself into a centre of intelligent and intellectual activity, rather than a cramming factory where certain data are pushed into the student regardless of his abilities or predilections'.[1] The city of London was, argued Pound, a kind of 'larger university', suggesting that urban experience was itself a form of education. The 'teachers' in the College were thus not to be academics from any 'cramming factory' but would be the modernist writers, artists, and musicians of Pound's acquaintance (many of them also outsiders in London) who were said to be 'the most advanced and brilliant men of our decade': figures such as the French-born sculptor Henri Gaudier-Brzeska, the writer and painter Wyndham Lewis, the artist Edward Wadsworth, the French musician Arnold Dolmetsch, and the American photographer Alvin Langdon Coburn. Several of these figures were involved in the Vorticist movement started by Lewis and Pound, which earlier that year had published the quintessential modernist magazine, *BLAST*. In addition to these figures Pound suggested that London contained important cultural institutions such as the

National Gallery, the British Museum and the museums in South Kensington. Pound set the bar high for incoming students: the College would have 'an intellectual status no lower than that attained by the courts of the Italian Renaissance'.[2]

That the prospectus was never fulfilled was due, amongst other reasons, to the impact of World War I.[3] However, in Pound's plan for the College we can understand something of the importance of the city, in this instance London, for the development of modernism. The prospectus had opened with the following bold claim: 'It has been noted by certain authors that London is the capital of the world, and "Art is a matter of capitals."'[4] In Pound's case the art was that of modernism, the creative work of the individuals he wished, as in the College 'Faculty', to gather together to promote what he termed a 'risorgimento' in the world of culture, a programme that he believed could only take root in major urban centres. Interestingly Pound had first conceived of the College of Arts while staying in another such metropolis, New York, in 1910, imagining the College to be 'a sort of incubator for risorgimenti'.[5] For Pound, then, the symbiosis between modernism and the city that the College of Arts hoped to exemplify was characterised by certain features. There was the presence of other like-minded artists, writers and thinkers who shared a commitment to the experimental and the new in the arts and culture. Many of these individuals were outsiders in London, including Pound himself. The social and cultural experience of the city was also crucial, with the urban imaginary of cities such as London becoming a major prompt to aesthetic innovation. Finally, the city contained major institutions in the cultural field (galleries, bookshops, publishers) that provided the vital infrastructure for modernist production.

This chapter, which is in three broad parts, will thus consider the features identified by Pound, along with other aspects, which were crucial to the development of London as a modernist city. Like previous chapters it will also analyse the affects of modernist space, showing how writers explored the geographical emotions produced by particular locations within London, such as the Metro-Land suburbs; the cultural institutions of Bloomsbury and Fleet Street; the bohemia of Soho and the nightlife of Piccadilly Circus; and the Notting Hill area settled by immigrants to the city. The first part of the chapter opens with a discussion of the material restructuring of the space of London caused by the development of the Tube or underground railway, focusing upon the development of the Metro-Land suburbs and the affective responses to these new spaces by a range of writers, drawing upon texts by Henry James and Virginia Woolf, amongst others. The second part of the chapter then considers the cultural geography of the new modernist institutions in London, Pound's 'larger university', and examines how a series of publishers, bookshops and literary networks helped establish modernism in the city, in the shape of movements such as the Rhymers and the Imagists. The final part of the chapter analyses closely texts by two outsiders to the city, Joseph Conrad and Sam Selvon, whose representations of specific locations in London demonstrate the important role of affect in their responses to the spaces of the city.

By the late nineteenth century there was a growing awareness that London, along with cities such as Paris or Berlin, appeared to manifest a qualitatively different kind of urban experience to previous metropolitan centres: such places warranted the epithet of 'world cities'.[6] For example, the Scottish social theorist Patrick Geddes had used the term in his 1915 book on *Cities in Evolution* to describe cities whose growth meant that they now dominated their neighbouring regions.[7] The hold of London upon the outlying regions was also noted by the eminent geographer Halford Mackinder in his influential book, *Britain and the British Seas* (1902): 'In a manner all south-eastern England is a single urban community. . . . The metropolis in its largest meaning includes all the counties for whose inhabitants London is "Town", whose men do habitual business there, whose women buy there.'[8] For others, London's special qualities as a modern 'world city' were intrinsically linked to its heterogeneous population. Ford Madox Ford had described London in 1905 as 'the world town' not merely due to its size, but because of its 'assimilative powers' over those immigrants that settled within it: 'It assimilates and slowly digests them, converting them, with the most potent of all juices, into the singular and inevitable product that is the Londoner – that is, in fact, the Modern.'[9] Pound also noted that 'all great art is born of the metropolis (or *in* the metropolis)' and that the metropolis was a place 'which accepts all gifts and all heights of excellence, usually the excellence which is *tabu* in its own village. The metropolis is always accused by the peasant of 'being mad after foreign notions".'[10] Being 'mad after foreign notions' was for Pound part of the notion of London as a cosmopolitan 'Vortex', where the flow of ideas and individuals from abroad energised the city and exemplified, in Ford's term, the very idea of the Modern itself. The two writers considered in detail at the end of this chapter, Conrad and Selvon, are brilliant examples that show how the affects experienced by outsiders in the metropolis were central to the forms of modernism produced in London.

The Modernist Underground

Ford's identification of the Londoner with 'the Modern' occurred in his fascinating 1905 book *The Soul of London*, discussed in the Introduction as a text exploring the affective quality of urban life. Ford's technique in this book was broadly that of the literary impressionism he championed along with his friend Joseph Conrad in the early years of the twentieth century and which aimed, as David James summarises, to register 'the world of sensations in ways that could be rich in semantic implication'.[11] One such set of semantically rich impressions occurs in the chapter on 'Roads into London', which concludes with Ford reflecting upon why when he travels into London by train he feels 'a sense of some pathos and of some poetry'.[12] Gazing from a carriage window, Ford notes that one sees 'so many little bits of uncompleted life', and then describes one such incident in Southwark, when in the back yard of a small house he spies a woman being 'hastily' pursued by a man with a stick. The train moves on, and Ford drolly notes that he never found out whether the man was 'going to thrash her, or whether together they were going to beat a carpet'. Ford then reflects on this moment:

> the constant succession of much smaller happenings that one sees, and that one never sees completed, gives to looking out of train windows a touch of pathos and of dissatisfaction. It is akin to the sentiment ingrained in humanity of liking a story to have an end.[13]

Ford's link between narrative conclusions and glimpses from the train window raises the question of how to evaluate the impact of a technological innovation such as the railways upon the space of a city, and how the spatial restructuring of London engineered by the development of the underground railways affected literary representations. The historian David Welsh has comprehensively charted the literary representations of the Underground and argues that one of the attractions of the Tube for writers is because it operates as 'a metaphor of modern urban life'.[14] Developing this idea, the first part of this chapter focuses upon the thematic appearance of the London Underground in modernism and how it altered the forms and styles of modernist writing, where 'uncompleted' endings and 'smaller happenings' are often the norm. If Ford felt 'a sense of some pathos and of some poetry' when travelling by overground train, we might ask, what kinds of affect are registered in poetry or fiction concerning the underground train?

Virginia Woolf, for one, presents a sort of answer in her 1917 short story 'The Mark on the Wall': 'If one wants to compare life to anything one must liken it to being blown through the Tube at fifty miles an hour – landing at the other end without a single hairpin in one's hair!'; it is an experience, continues Woolf, that 'seems to express the rapidity of life, the perpetual waste and repair; all so casual, all so haphazard'.[15] This story, one of Woolf's earliest experiments with the stream of consciousness method, replicates this experience in its narrative flow, with the narrator skipping from subject to subject in a seemingly haphazard fashion. As Julia Briggs notes, here 'the movement of thought is also its subject; like a railway train, it is always carrying the thinker away from a full engagement with passing sights or thoughts, so that knowledge and certainty are never achieved'.[16] Woolf's judgement of the Tube, the name first used for the Central Line of the London Underground from around 1901, is a fine starting point for understanding the cultural meanings of this form of railway transport. For underground systems of transit, which have been with us since the first 'cut and cover' part of the London Metropolitan line was opened in 1863, can be considered to have a number of features distinct from other forms of rail travel.[17] The most important of these unique cultural qualities is the insistently urban nature of underground travel: to adapt Ian Carter's claim that the railway is the central symbol of modernity in the nineteenth century, we might say that the idea of underground rail travel is the central symbol of *urban* modernity in the twentieth century.[18] For Marshall Berman the 'archetypal modern man . . . is a pedestrian thrown into the maelstrom of modern city traffic',[19] and while Berman's focus is upon traffic above ground, we can also burrow below the streets to consider the affective nature of the modern maelstrom lurking there. One must be 'absolutely modern', suggested Arthur Rimbaud, and followed his own advice after staying in London in 1872 with perhaps the first poem set on the London underground railway, 'Métropolitain'.[20]

We can identity two key moments in the early twentieth century when the Underground figures as the central lever of change in the recomposition of the social space of London. The first relates to the development of 'Metro-Land' suburbs from around 1907; the second concerns the design of a number of new underground stations in the late twenties and thirties, such as the reconstruction of Piccadilly station in 1928. This later work, by Frank Pick and Charles Holden, was designed to offer the public a sensory experience of everyday modernism on the Underground.[21] Both projects articulate Woolf's notion of the 'rapidity' of modern life in the sense that they vastly altered quotidian experience for millions of people in a short period of time; yet, contrary to Woolf's conception, there was nothing haphazard or casual about either form of spatial restructuring. There are also two wider themes informing this discussion of the modern Underground: first, the geographical emotions of underground travel, particularly in relation to representations of 'the crowd', the masses and modernity; second, the restructuring of urban social space that accompanied the growth of the Underground, and the cultural understanding of these new geographies.

Metro-Land

In 1904 the Metropolitan line was extended from Harrow-in-the Hill to Uxbridge, and with it 'Metro-Land' was born: 'Metro-Land is a country with elastic borders which each visitor can draw for himself. . . . It lies mostly in Bucks, but choice fragments of Middlesex and Herts may be annexed at pleasure.'[22] A further extension to the Hampstead Railway in 1907 produced another appendage to this new geographical entity. Metro-Land was advertised by the railway companies as a way to escape from the city and its attendant urban problems: the health advantages of living in 'Metro-Land' were often foregrounded in their literature. In 1904 Ruislip was promoted as London's healthiest suburb, an honour later bestowed upon Golders Green ('A Place of Delightful Prospects' according to a 1908 poster). Woolf refers to this extension in a diary entry from July 1907:

> The Twopenny Tube has now burrowed as far as Golders Green; so that sinking into an earth laid with pavement & houses at one end, you rise to soft green fields at the other; the ashen dark & the chill & the cold glitter of electricity is replaced by the more benignant illumination of daylight. Indeed on Sunday there was a sky & a sun; & the exuberant holiday making of the crowd has some excuse.[23]

Golders Green was widely advertised by the Underground companies as a place for Sunday and bank holiday excursions in this period, and an alluring discourse of health and rural retreat was also used by the Underground to promote the restructuring of the city and its suburban northern periphery around Golders Green, Belsize Park, Chalk Farm, and Camden.

The urban historian Lewis Mumford notes how the emergence of faster forms of public transport profoundly altered patterns of work and housing. In major commercial cities in the late nineteenth century traffic jams were common, even though the majority of people, of whatever class, walked to work, sometimes up to two to three miles from their homes. With mass transportation, writes Mumford, 'walking distances no longer set the limits of city growth; and the whole pace of the city extension was hastened'.[24] Another consequence was at the level of the individual experience of commuting: this congruence between land development and transport extension expands our sense of space, but diminishes our grasp on time. As Mumford notes; 'Rapid public transportation, instead of reducing the time required for reaching the place of work, continued to increase the distance and the cost with no gain in time whatever.'[25] In this sense the Underground exemplifies starkly what David Harvey views as the 'time-space compression' of capitalist modernity in the early twentieth century.[26]

Booklets and related advertisements were employed by the Metropolitan Railways to promote the benefits of life in these new areas (see Figs 4.1 and 4.2). There was a heavy reliance, as in these images, upon pictures of 'Country Homes' close to underground stations;[27] the short journey times to the metropolis (20 minutes from Golders Green to Charing Cross); the proximity of golf courses; and walking guides advertising 'Country Walks in Metro-Land'.[28] The advertising was clearly targeted at a particular class and gender, as the claim in the *Country Homes* (1909) booklet indicates: the Metropolitan Railway offers 'City men a quick and frequent service of trains between the City itself and the various residential districts.'[29] Another advert for the Metropolitan line noted that it was 'the short cut to the nearest golf course. From his office he can . . .

Figure 4.1 *Metro-Land* booklet (1920).

Figure 4.2 ‘Houses in Metro-Land’, advert, 1917.

Figure 4.3 'Home by Underground', poster (1933).

be taken in a few minutes by electric train to the links without a change.'[30] One commentator in 1910 noted that 'in this strenuous age business men find it necessary to spend much time in the Metropolis, and yet yearn for the charm, healthfulness and repose of a country residence'[31] (see Fig. 4.3).

The 1920 *Metro-Land* booklet echoed this theme and made an explicit link between modernity and mental health:

> the strain which the London business or professional man has to undergo amidst the turmoil and bustle of Town can only be counteracted by the quiet restfulness and comfort of a residence amidst pure air and surroundings, and whilst *jaded vitality and taxed nerves are the natural penalties of modern conditions*, Nature has, in the delightful districts abounding in Metro-Land, placed a potential remedy at hand.[32]

Of course the contrast between country and city, or the 'strain' versus the 'restfulness' implied by the two geographies, is paradoxically eradicated by the very technology which enables the two to be connected. Golders Green was, as the earlier poster suggests, rural until 1907, but by 1923 the population had doubled and it was part of what E. M. Forster, in *Howards End* (1910), called the 'creeping red rust' of London suburbia.[33] Evelyn Waugh, at the age of four, in 1907, moved to a house that his father had built in the village of North End, Hampstead:

> When we settled there the tube reached no further than Hampstead. Golders Green was a grassy cross-road with a sign pointing to London. . . . All around us lay dairy farms, market gardens and . . . not far off there survived woods where we picked bluebells. . . . Eventually . . . our postal address was altered from Hampstead to Golders Green. My father deplored the change, because Hampstead had historic associations, with Keats and Blake and Constable, while Golders Green meant, to him, merely a tube station.[34]

The escape from the turmoil of the city promised by the extended Tube lines only brought with it increased building and the eradication of bucolic geographies. In the case of Golders Green this was a deliberate strategy by Charles Yerkes, the American financier who developed the Charing Cross, Euston and Hampstead Railway. By extending the line north to the rural setting of Golders Green, Yerkes, who had previously electrified the Chicago tram system, was following an American model whereby traffic aimed to stimulate suburban growth, rather than catering for existing demand.[35]

An example of a more complex mixture of urban and rural geographies is found in the creation of the Hampstead Garden Suburb, started by social reformer Henrietta Barnett in 1906 on garden city principles. Interestingly, Barnett was impelled into action by Yerkes' proposal for extending the Hampstead Tube to include a station on the west of the Heath. Barnett's first response to the Tube extension chimed very much with that of Evelyn Waugh; Barnett wrote of the threatened 'ruin of the sylvan restfulness of that portion of the most beautiful open space near London'. She then organised a group to save some eighty acres of land from the 'rows of ugly villas such as disfigure Willesden and most of the suburbs of London', land which was handed over to London County Council to be preserved as open space.[36] Saving sylvan spaces was one thing, but Barnett was not averse to certain, less ugly in her mind, buildings contiguous to the Tube. In March 1906 the Hampstead Garden Suburb Trust Limited bought 243 acres of land near the Hampstead Heath Extension from the Trustees of Eton College to construct the new garden suburb.

Elizabeth Wilson argues that Barnett's vision for the suburb was one that hoped to reconcile different classes by welcoming all income levels, as well as those with handicaps, and there flourished in the garden cities overall a kind of bohemianism, signalled by bare legs and sandals for both men and women, and a commitment from some to vegetarianism. In the late 1880s, for example, W. B. Yeats lived at Bedford Park, in an area in west London made accessible by the District railway in the 1870s and which attracted several other writers and artists. Bedford Park had the usual garden city mix of a Co-operative store, local drama groups, utopian socialist societies that flourished alongside occult groups, and the character of what Roy Foster dismisses as a 'bargain basement aestheticism'.[37] However, as Wilson notes of garden cities in general, the 'radical bohemianism in these projects for rational living was of the worthy rather than the Parisian dissipated kind', partly since Hampstead, like many other garden cities, and unlike the literary cafés of Paris or the drinking dens of bohemian Soho, was 'dry'.[38] Another distinction needs to be drawn between the socialist and utopian principles behind the Hampstead garden suburb and other garden city projects (guided by Ebenezer Howard's work), and the more expensive, individual homes of other 'metro-land' areas to the north-west of London. Whereas the garden suburbs were sometimes constructed as an ad hoc response to underground expansion, the 'Metro-Land' suburbs of the 1920s were directly constructed by the railway company itself. In 1919 the Metropolitan Railway Country Estates Ltd was established to develop the Metropolitan Railways land holdings, a unique venture that enabled the company to sell more season tickets to those that relocated to the private housing estates of Neasden, Wembley Park, Ruislip and so on.[39]

This drift of the affluent, and proto-bohemian, middle classes out of the city is often perceived as a phenomenon of the 1920s and 1930s, perhaps viewed through the rosy tint of John Betjeman's poetry and his famous television programme from the 1970s on 'Metro-Land', or Julian Barnes' novel of that name from 1980.[40] But the new geography of Metro-Land clearly started prior to World War I, and indicates how the Underground was the impetus for key changes in the restructuring of urban social space; changes, however, that did gather pace after that war. The first property development by the Metropolitan Railway, for example, was the Willesden Park Estate, developed near Willesden Green Tube station in the 1880s and 1890s. As Richard Sennett suggests in *Flesh and Stone*, critics have tended to view the Underground principally as an agent for moving people *into* the city; however, the Underground's developers learnt from Haussmann's rebuilding of Paris: 'they sought to get people *out* of the city, as well as into it'.[41] The main groups to benefit from the Underground's centrifugal movement in this early part of the twentieth century, suggests Sennett, were the clerks of the imperial metropolis and the domestic servants of the wealthy West End areas of Mayfair and Knightsbridge. With affordable mass transportation and new building programmes, the working poor could move from slum conditions in the East End and South Bank to small, but well-constructed terraced houses further north and south of the Thames. It is precisely in this sort of area that Leonard Bast, the doomed clerkly culture-vulture of Forster's *Howards End*, is to be located. The Basts' first home is in south-east London, probably Brixton or Stockwell, and served by the City and South London line which was opened in 1890. It is certainly a far different setting from the home of the Schlegels, one of the central families in the novel, who reside on the north side of the Thames. If we mapped the London locations in *Howards End*, we would notice how Leonard's life is geographically, as well as socially, distinct from that of the Schlegels or Wilcoxes. All of the action involving these two families takes place north of the Thames, whether in the slightly artistic area of Chelsea, where the Schlegels live, or the more aristocratic wealth of the Wilcoxes' Belgravia home. Bast crosses the river to the north; but the two 'respectable' families never cross over to Leonard's side of the river. The Underground was, therefore, instrumental in such forms of spatial separation in the metropolis.

Spatial Phobias

The 'Metro-Land' housing projects in the north of the city, and the high-density homes for clerks in the south, are often taken as a kind of ghostly signifier of modernist disdain for the suburbs and the 'masses' that supposedly inhabited them. Walter Benjamin's comment that the railway is 'the first means of transport . . . to form masses', since it groups together large numbers of passengers, can be refined in the case of the London Underground.[42] The impact of these masses is significant not only in terms of the affective encounters produced between people within a train carriage, but also in the urban geography that resulted from the segregation of the mass once they left the train and drifted to their suburban villas or country homes. Certain locations in London recur as symbols of the negative aspects of the spatial segregation brought by the new Tube lines. The change, for instance, in what was signified by the name 'Golders Green', as already noted in Forster and Waugh, is also evident in other writers of the time. Thus, in T. S. Eliot's 'A Cooking Egg', first published in 1919, the disturbing 'red-eyed scavengers are feeding / In Kentish Town and Golder's [*sic*] Green'.[43] Perhaps the most damning put-down of the working-class character Charles Tansley in Woolf's *To the Lighthouse* (1927) is the following: 'He had married; he lived at Golders Green.'[44]

In Woolf's earlier novel *Jacob's Room* (1922), the Tube journey home by commuters represented a changed relationship between the individual traveller and their environment. Commuters are described as 'little figures, split apart into trousers or moulded into a single thickness' who then move below ground:

> Beneath the pavement, sunk in the earth, hollow drains lined with yellow light for ever conveyed them this way and that, and large letters upon enamel plates represented in the underworld the parks, squares, and circuses of the upper. 'Marble Arch – Shepherd's Bush' – to the majority

> the Arch and the Bush are eternally white letters upon a blue ground. Only at one point – it may be Acton, Holloway, Kensal Rise, Caledonian Road – does the name mean shops where you buy things, and houses.[45]

Woolf here indicates how the individual's sense of space is distorted by the underground environment: names on Underground signs stand in for material spaces, until the dreaded suburbs are reached. Woolf's account emphasises the two key features of the Underground considered here: the changed geography of London and its suburbs; and the psychic experience of being both an individual ('little figures') and a mass ('a single thickness'). This recalls the claim made by Jonathan Crary in *Suspensions of Perception* that modern forms of attentive subjects, such as those before the cinema screen, are placed simultaneously in two positions: 'immersed in a collectivity and simultaneously separated in absorptive solitude'.[46] It seems perfectly accurate as a descriptive of the new techniques, as Crary might put it, that individuals had to learn in order to be good passengers on the Underground: to travel by Tube one must learn to be a 'docile body', in Foucault's phrase, and organise one's perceptions according to certain disciplinary imperatives.[47]

Travel by Tube thus produces the perilous necessity of trying to individualise one's identity and thus distance oneself from the lumpen mass, to echo Crary's dialectic of the modern subject, for traffic in such urban environments forces a mingling in space of social, sexual and class relations: as Benjamin noted, it forms masses. In 1903 the sociologist Simmel argued that the individual's sense of reserve in crowded cities was 'because the bodily closeness and lack of space make intellectual distance really perceivable for the first time'.[48] The experience of the 'narrowness' of the London Underground often appeared to transform 'reserve' into 'antagonism'.

One way to read representations such as that of Eliot and Woolf is in terms of the argument, most clearly articulated by John Carey in *The Intellectuals and the Masses*, that modernism was endemically anti-democratic and that disgust for suburbia was one of the means by which modern intellectuals sharpened their metropolitan critical teeth.[49] I am not at all convinced that this captures what is at stake in these, and other, literary encounters with the Underground and prefer to interpret both the affective disgust of the individual writer for the travelling mass, and the attempt to shape areas of the suburbs as zones for 'healthy' living, as forms of what James Donald and others have described as the 'psychic and spatial diseases of modernity'.[50] As discussed in Chapters 2 and 3, modern urban life in the early twentieth century was often theorised in terms of 'spatial phobias' such as claustrophobia, agoraphobia and neurasthenia. Here we might recall the Metro-Land advertising booklet, which depicted the new suburbs as alleviating the 'taxed nerves' and 'jaded vitality' which are understood to be one of 'the natural penalties of modern conditions'. The geographical emotions engendered while on the Tube are here perceived as negative experiences of the spaces of the modern city.

The anxious rejection of one's travelling companions as a crowd or mass can therefore be read as another spatial phobia, where what produces panic is not an open or closed space but the crowded density of other people.[51] The emphasis in the Metro-Land housing projects exhibits a similarly phobic structure: here the promise is of a flight from the crowded city and the problems of how to live with strangers and anonymous masses, towards suburbs of 'fresh air' and 'health' and, in the case of garden cities, planned forms of social interaction. The fact that many stations on the Metropolitan line (the key line for 'Metro-Land') were overground stations only emphasised the sense of an airy escape from the stygian gloom of what Woolf termed 'hollow drains'.

In a certain sense the spatial environment of the Underground is a perfect example of Benjamin's claim that Baudelaire's poetry reveals how in modern societies 'the expectation roused by the look of the human eye is not fulfilled':[52] in the Tube the expectation is that the gaze will not, might not, should not be returned. An example of the non-returning of the gaze and of a phobic reaction to the other occurs in the third part of T. S. Eliot's 'East Coker', from *Four Quartets*: 'Or as, when an underground train, in the tube, stops too long between stations / And the conversation rises and slowly fades into silence / And you see behind every face the mental emptiness deepen / Leaving only the growing terror of nothing to think about.'[53] These are faces, as Eliot writes in 'Burnt Norton', 'Distracted from distraction by distraction / Filled with fancies and empty of meaning / Tumid apathy with no concentration'.[54]

Passivity, contemplation and the idle gaze seem to characterise the required subject position of the Underground traveller, often producing geographical emotions that veer into phobias. Woolf's *The Years* (1937) is perhaps her fullest treatment both of history and of London life. One interesting passage, which was excised from the galley proofs, concerns a Tube journey set in 1917, between Kew Gardens and Leicester Square. A minor character, Brett Parker, sits next to Mrs Crosby, the faithful servant to the central family in the novel; she then asks if she can read his newspaper:

> He gave it her with a little jerk, and sat staring ahead of him. He had, she noticed, rather fierce blue eyes. Now that she had taken his paper he sat staring at the people in front of him. Since all movement or action was impossible, they were all staring in front of them. There was something in the passive and stolid appearance of the other passengers that seemed to annoy him. He kept crossing and uncrossing his legs. He looked quickly up and down the row of faces. Nobody moved. Nobody spoke. Since there were five more stations to be passed before he reached his station, and since each station took two minutes to reach, he must sit there for

> ten minutes longer. The train rattled and banged. Whenever he found himself shut up somewhere without anything to do, words seemed to come together in his head. His lips moved. What for, what for, what for, the train seemed to be growling as it rattled through South Kensington station. He looked at the respectable ladies in their drab hats and coats; he looked at a young man with a note-book puffing rings of smoke through his nose; he looked at a corpulent red-faced man with a heavy silver chain across his waistcoat. They were all of the respectable classes, save for a flower-woman with a basket at the door. Her naked arms were folded across her breast; a broad gold wedding ring was sunk into the fat of her fingers; and the feather in her bonnet jerked ridiculously as the train shook. Nobody moved or spoke. Everybody seemed to be gloating; to have fed on the garbage in the newspapers; and to be passively chewing the cud. He felt that if this went on he must get up and cry out. Suddenly he caught the reflection of his own face on the glass-lined wall opposite. He saw a red-faced man with a grey moustache staring back at him, quite indistinguishable from the others. . . . It was not his station, but he could sit there no longer looking at his own reflection in the glass. He got up and tried to push his way out between the slowly-moving bodies of his fellow passengers.[55]

The passage crystallises many features of a near-phobic experience of the Underground. Passivity is pronounced, with the body restricted in its seat, and the gaze of the passengers replacing any other physical experience. As if in revolt at this submissive state, Parker obsessively crosses and uncrosses his legs and then calculates how long he must endure this environment. His attitude towards his fellow passengers becomes familiarly antagonistic: the other travellers are 'corpulent', passive and animal-like in their 'feeding' upon the 'garbage' of the newspapers. Parker thus seeks to distinguish himself from this 'mass', but it is a strategy that ultimately fails when he sees his own reflection and realises he too is 'red-faced' and part of that mass. Benjamin's modern gaze at the other is here returned, but the traumatic realisation that nothing distinguishes the self from the other leads to a flight from the train. This is not simply a rejection of the 'mass' – as the passage notes, most of the other travellers are 'of the respectable class' – but a phobic reaction to the geographical emotions produced by the spatial environment of the Tube.

As discussed in Chapter 1, Jean Rhys' fiction in the 1920s and 1930s demonstrated repeatedly how the spaces of Paris produced anxious geographical emotions and spatial phobias in the female protagonists of her novels. Throughout Rhys' work there are also found similar responses to particular spaces within London, the city to which she arrived from the Caribbean island of Dominica in 1907 as a white colonial migrant. Arriving in Southampton after the voyage across the Atlantic, Rhys encountered a train for the first time and boarded it for London along with her aunt: 'Before long we were plunged into black darkness. A railway accident, I thought. We came into the light again. "Was that a railway accident?" – "No, it was a tunnel," my aunt said, laughing.'[56] The difficulty for an outsider like Rhys encountering the spaces of metropolitan modernity is also noted in her novel *Voyage in the Dark* (1934), where one character comments that England is 'a very nice place . . . so long as you don't suffer from claustrophobia'.[57] In *After Leaving Mr Mackenzie* (1930) Rhys represents an anxious encounter on the Underground when a stranger approaches Julia Martin, the novel's heroine, while she travels from the western suburb of Acton to Notting Hill upon the Central line. Julia's mother has just died, but she feels a sense of relief, 'as if she were a child', so that 'everything that she saw was of profound interest and had the power to distract and please her'. She therefore allows herself to gaze rather more freely at the faces of the people she passes, 'not suspiciously or timidly, as was usual with her, but with a gentle and confident expression'.[58] As she waits on the platform a 'short and fat' man engages her in conversation and announces to Julia that he is a stranger who does not know his way about very well. When the train arrives he follows her into a near-empty carriage. Also in the carriage are two men 'with their eyes fixed upon their newspapers' and a woman who, when she sees Julia looking at her, 'drew down her lips with a prim and furtive expression'. Of course, this exchange of gazes recalls the antagonism noticed in the extract from *The Years*, but it also positions Julia as a figure who, by openly looking at other passengers, is flouting the visual regime demanded by the Tube.

The fat man, who has of course sat next to Julia, announces that 'It's a bit lonely here for a stranger.' This is clearly not a comment on the Tube itself, but it does indicate something central to the urban anomie that is exacerbated by the social space of the Underground. The man asks if Julia is a Londoner, and when she says she is not, he comments, 'I thought not. I thought you looked a bit as if you were a stranger too.'[59] The sense that they are both outsiders prompts him into telling Julia that he is from South Africa, along with other details of his travels. Now, 'as if intoxicated by this long monologue about himself' the man invites Julia to dinner, which she refuses. The man then gives her his card and asks that she contact him. Julia, 'smiling mechanically', says yes, lets the card drop into her lap, but then lets it deliberately drop to the floor of the carriage as she departs. The man, after a moment of embarrassment, picks up his card, brushes it, and composes himself once again.

Such an encounter is very familiar in Rhys' fiction, revealing how women alone in cities always appear at risk of unwanted approaches by men. The setting on public transport typifies urban life, where the inside of a Tube carriage is not a retreat from the open street, but a kind of ambivalent public space that enforces encounters, often anxiously, with strangers. The incident indicates how deeply Rhys is aware of the nature of the modernist city, especially for her female characters, where the chance encounter with a stranger appears the norm rather than the exception. When Julia reaches her flat her thoughts are 'confused and blurred' and she experiences a set of powerful affects that are registered by her body: 'her fingertips tingled and the muscles at the back of her neck were tight'.[60] So overwhelmed is she that she imagines that if a stranger were to appear and ask her name, she would not know how to answer. The encounter drains her identity to that of a stranger, acting mechanically in a mechanised environment, where looking at other people produces danger rather than connection. The encounter illustrates Paul Carter's interpretation of agoraphobia as a kind of 'environmental unease or anxiety', where the sufferer feels a sort of disorientation in a space which was meant to be a locus of social engagement. This stems, writes Carter in a telling phrase, 'from the prospect of places being opened up that are not places. . . . The opening they promise is infinitely estranging' for 'the enlarged access they offer produces a concomitant *anomie*'.[61] In many senses this accurately captures one powerful feature of the Underground: a place that is somehow not a place, where the opening to voluminous numbers of other people rarely results in strangers being comforted, but rather in further uneasy geographical emotions.

The counterpoint to these problematic encounters in Rhys and Woolf is provided in the wonderful moment in Henry James' *The Wings of the Dove* (1902) that marks the beginning of the relationship between Kate Croy and Merton Densher.[62] It is also a moment in which a gaze between passengers is emphatically returned. James was another outsider who became an insider and a deeply 'topographical writer' who often utilised the theme of Americans encountering Europe in his works: after first living in London in 1869, he was never again to return to live permanently in the United States.[63] In an essay on 'London' (1886) James noted how the sheer immensity of the metropolis produced idiosyncratic features, such as its atmosphere 'with its magnificent mystifications' which suggest that 'as the great city makes everything, it makes its own system of weather and its own optical laws'.[64] The optical regime of the Underground conditions and enhances the second meeting of Kate and Merton. Previously they have met at a party at which James notes the deeply affective quality of the relationship between the two: 'It wasn't . . . simply that their eyes had met; other conscious organs, faculties, feelers had met as well.'[65] When the two accidentally meet again, after Kate boards a train at Sloane Square, the affective connection of 'faculties' and 'feelers' is immediate. James notes how the environment enables their connection of their geographical emotions: 'It helped them moreover, with strangers on either side, little to talk; though this very restriction perhaps made such a mark for them as nothing else could have done.'[66] In this setting 'they could only exchange the greeting of movements, smiles, abstentions'. Their relationship is governed by its spatial environment and being unable to talk foregrounds their visual connection, while the Tube itself is used as metaphor for the development of their relationship:

> The extraordinary part of the matter was that they were not in the least meeting where they had left off, but ever so much further on, and that these added links added still another between High Street and Notting Hill Gate, and then worked between the latter station and Queen's Road an extension really inordinate.[67]

This is an accidental meeting, but as James notes, it is as 'natural' as anything in London: in an alien environment that stresses looking, to have someone familiar return your gaze establishes a connection that is unusual in this particular space. The interplay of gazes is also emphasised by a man in the carriage with a single eye-glass who Kate realises has noticed how she has been 'strangely affected' by Merton Densher's presence.[68] In contradistinction to Benjamin's idea of modernity being the place where the gaze is not returned, James fashions a redemptive moment from the 'optical laws' operative in the Underground, foregrounding a more positive group of geographical emotions.

Overcoming Modernity

It is difficult, as ever with the shocks of modernism, to recapture today the novelty of the Underground and to understand the kind of reactions described here as phobic. Something of this unease is crystallised, however, in the story of the first escalators, installed at Earls Court in 1911. The public were so wary of the new 'moving staircases' that the Underground allegedly employed a man with a wooden leg, known as 'Bumper Harris', to ride up and down to demonstrate their safety.[69] New technologies, of course, often bring sensations of panic or unease, unnerving our sense of how we affectively relate to a changed environment. What we have seen in the writers discussed here is that such disquiet often fuelled the modernist imaginary, perhaps since modernism itself made strange the familiar forms of writing and representation; as Ford put it, much modernist writing, like the glimpses on a railway journey, consisted of 'uncompleted life'. Equally, the geographical emotions and spatial phobias that accompanied the new social spaces of the Underground provided brilliant material for that impulse within modernism that sought to explore the inner lives of modern subjectivity.

Reaching an accommodation with, or making sense of, these new social spaces and the novel affects they produced is a theme running through many of the depictions of the Underground discussed here. Interesting comparisons can, therefore, be drawn between literary modernism and the work of Frank Pick and Charles Holden in redesigning all aspects of the physical appearance of the London Underground.[70] Pick commissioned both the distinctive

Underground typeface by Edward Johnston (first used in 1916) and posters to advertise the Tube from such artists as E. McKnight Kauffer (see Fig. 4.4). The architect Charles Holden was responsible for many new stations in suburbs to the north and south, stations that were influenced by the styles and materials of high architectural modernism. As Pick noted in 1925: 'we are going to build our stations upon the Morden extension railway to the most modern pattern. We are going to discard entirely all ornament. We are going to build in reinforced concrete.'[71] As Michael Saler argues, in his fascinating account of the London Underground as a form of 'medieval modernism', Pick sought to turn the Underground into a work of art that 'united modern painting, sculpture, and architecture into a glorious *Gesamkunstwerk*, a thing of joy to its makers and its users'[72] (see Fig. 4.5). Such a project can be viewed as an attempt to overcome the phobias of the modern world, alleviating worries about the total environment of the Underground much as Bumper Harris reassured travellers of the safety of escalators.

By presenting the Underground as part of the excitements of modern metropolitan life, Pick sought to advertise the modernist city as a place of pleasurable geographical emotions. The colourful linocuts of the underground by Cyril Power in the 1920s and 1930s represent another attempt to visually depict the Underground with a modernist sensibility. However, Power's 'The Tube Train' (1934) indicates that an ambivalence remains in how the Underground is represented (see Fig. 4.6). Here the presence of human bodies seems to be rather alien, as if they do not quite fit the vortices and moving lines of the Underground, unless their features are moulded into their surroundings, jammed tightly together inside the carriage, perhaps experiencing affects of anger and disgust similar to those of Brett Parker in Woolf's *The Years*. Overcoming the spatial phobias of modernity by means of the aesthetics of modernist style is, one might note, no straightforward manoeuvre.

Thinking of 'Metro-Land' as a peculiar form of social space designed to counter the bad geographical emotions of urban modernity – those 'taxed nerves' of the Metro-Land commuter – leads one to consider the metaphoric role of the Underground. Pick often used organic metaphors to understand the city as a body, with the Underground being imagined as the veins or arteries: 'The arteries and veins may be taken to represent the passenger circulation . . . the arteries must be capable of delivering a full supply of blood to all parts and extremities of the organism.'[73] In distinction from these tropes, one can speculate whether it is more accurate to understand the Underground as the social unconscious of the city: as befits the unconscious it is the site (and sight) of many of our deepest fears and anxieties about urban life – the crowd, the stranger, technology, dehumanisation, confinement – and the sense that somehow our established perceptual grasp upon space is being challenged.[74] As Rosalind Williams notes, the trope of a world underground, from the

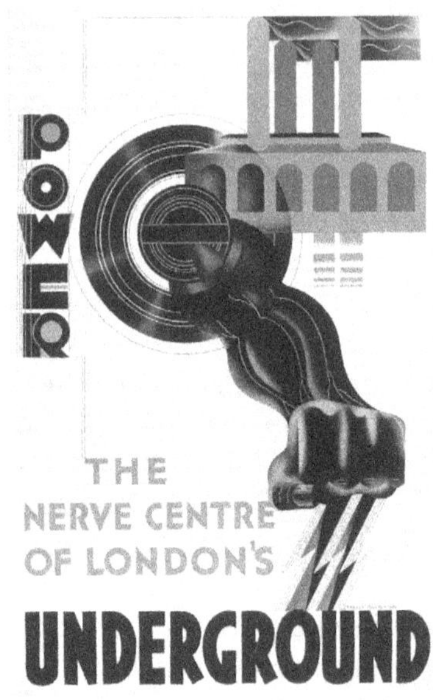

Figure 4.4 'Power' by E. McKnight Kauffer, poster (1931).
© TfL from the London Transport Museum collection.

Figure 4.5 Illuminated tower of Boston Manor Underground station, 1935.
© TfL from the London Transport Museum collection.

Figure 4.6 Cyril Power, 'The Tube Train', linocut (1934). © British Museum.

nineteenth century onwards, has often represented 'the displacement of the natural environment by a technological one',[75] a change that is often felt as a threat to human interactions with social space. But the unconscious is also the locus of desire, and Pick's vision of the Underground as a work of art was an attempt to construct a cityscape which delighted subjects with its positive modernist mood (*Stimmung*), rather than being experienced only as a taxing place to be grimly endured.[76]

Locations of Culture

If the restructuring of the social space of London by the Underground signified the 'rapidity' of modern life to modernist writers, then it was another feature of the cityscape of Pound's 'larger university' that enabled their visions and experiences of the city to emerge. These were what we might call the institutional locations of culture: the independent bookshops and publishers who were to publish low print runs of experimental works and 'little magazines'; and the cafés, salons and literary discussion circles where new ideas were debated and writers and artists networked to advance their careers. Many of these cultural institutions were centrally located in London, but it was the expansion of the Tube that also enabled them to thrive, as it was the workers such as clerks, typists, cooks and waitresses required to service the galleries, cafés and publishing firms that tended to enter the city to work, and then leave for the new suburbs of the city. As Roy Porter notes, in the early twentieth century the Tube aided the relocation of industries from London's burgeoning outer suburbs, moving workers and factories away from the metropolitan centre: this now meant that central London thrived as a place for 'consumption, tourism, leisure and pleasure'.[77] While Porter's examples of this boom are the early department stores, Debenham & Freebody (1909) and Selfridges, opened in the same year, followed by Harrods and Whiteleys, we might note that this was also the period which saw the development of a cultural infrastructure for 'leisure and pleasure' in London, based on publishing firms, the newspaper and periodical press, booksellers, and new networks for literary discussion.

Much recent work on these institutions of modernism, to use Lawrence Rainey's term, has drawn upon Pierre Bourdieu's notion of the field of cultural production, analysing how modernist writers and their works succeeded in developing symbolic value or 'cultural capital', even while their works sold in relatively low numbers in comparison to the mass market in literature which emerged at the end of the nineteenth century.[78] While this work has discussed *how* modernism came to be valued so highly, this chapter now turns to analyse further *where* it occurred: in other words, it is useful to shift Bourdieu's map from the abstract space of the cultural field to locate it materially within the social space of London.[79]

One such location was Harold Monro's Poetry Bookshop, opened in 1912 in Devonshire Street, then a slum area of eighteenth-century houses in Bloomsbury near to the British Library. The bookshop, which moved to Great Russell Street in 1926 and finally closed in 1935, served as a pivotal site for the introduction of modernist poetry in London. The American poet Amy Lowell, visiting London in 1913, was desperate to visit the shop and provided an amusing picture of her visit to a venture she called 'alluringly crazy' in an article in *The Little Review*.[80] Monro suggested that what he called the 'Poetry House' would be a place where ideas would 'meet and concentrate, become expressed, sifted, and circulated' and would operate as nexus for 'an informal Guild'.[81] From here Monro issued many publications that 'circulated' differing ideas of modernism: several very successful *Georgian Anthologies*; Pound's first Imagist anthology, *Des Imagistes* (1914); and three modernist 'little magazines', *The Poetry Review* (1912–15), *Poetry and Drama* (1913–14) and *The Monthly Chapbook* (1919–25).[82] In addition to these productions the bookshop mounted numerous readings and talks by poets such as Eliot, Ford, Robert Graves, Amy Lowell, Harriet Monroe, Pound, Edith Sitwell, Rabindrinath Tagore, Anna Wickham, and Yeats, amongst others. T. E. Hulme lectured on the new poetry in 1912 and a year later the Italian Futurist Marinetti publicised his movement, which was also discussed favourably in *Poetry and Drama*. On the top floor of the building Monro kept two rooms for visiting poets and artists at a low rent: the modernist sculptor Jacob Epstein stayed there for several months in 1913 and 1914, as did Robert Frost. When the bookshop moved to Great Russell Street in the 1920s it served as the meeting place for Eliot's *Criterion* Club dinners, meetings which helped shape editorial policy on this magazine. It is no surprise then to find that Monro's shop was the setting for Mulk Raj Anand's first encounter with the major figures of literary London in his *Conversations in Bloomsbury*.[83]

Monro's vision of a place where ideas would meet, concentrate, and then circulate was thus one of the most successful instances of a location that promoted modernism in London. In the years just prior to World War I there were many other such locations and formations which fostered the emergence of modernism in London, from the art and design work of Roger Fry's Omega Workshops in Bloomsbury to South Lodge, the literary salon of Ford and Violet Hunt in Kensington (where Ford's magazine *The English Review* was founded).[84] Just along from the Poetry Bookshop, alongside the British Museum, was Oakley House, Bloomsbury Street, where one could find the offices of *The New Freewoman/Egoist* magazines edited by Harriet Shaw Weaver and Dora Marsden.[85] Even closer was the Rebel Art Centre in Great Ormond Street, opened in March 1914 by Wyndham Lewis. Originally called the Cubist Art Centre, and funded by Kate Lechmere, it was to be a venue to promote a new 'English' avant-garde. The Centre mounted lectures (including ones by Pound, Marinetti and Ford), offered gallery space and aimed to enrol students in a new Art School, whose prospectus claimed that its teaching would be informed by 'the principles underlying the movements in Painting known as Cubist, Futurist, and Expressionist'.[86] Soon realising, however, that in order to function as avant-garde rebels his group needed a proper name and ism, Lewis launched Vorticism with the publication in June 1914 of the magazine *BLAST*, copies of which could be bought at the Rebel Art Centre.[87]

The Rebel Art Centre soon collapsed, although Pound's putative College of Arts later in 1914 can be interpreted as reviving the educational function of the Rebel Art Centre. *BLAST* itself, as many critics have noted, was the most durable legacy of this project, yet even this most avant-garde of London magazines reveals how something of the cultural infrastructure burgeoning in London from 1910 to 1914 relied upon a set of institutions that were already in place in the capital from the end of the nineteenth century. Writing in *The*

New Age in July 1914 the editor, Alfred Orage, commented upon the publication of *BLAST*:

> Mr Wyndham Lewis' new quarterly magazine, 'Blast' . . . has been announced as the successor of the 'Yellow Book'. It is, I find, not unintelligible . . . but not worth the understanding. . . . What, from this point of view, is its significance? My answer is that it is another sign of the spiritual anarchism of modern society.[88]

At one level Orage comments upon this link because of the reputation of *The Yellow Book* (1894–7) as a controversial Decadent publication, associated forever with the work of Aubrey Beardsley and, erroneously, with Oscar Wilde (although Wilde never published in its pages, the magazine was deeply affected by his trials in the mid-1890s).[89] *BLAST*, with its puce cover, the aggressive rhetoric of its title and contents, and its startling sans-serif typographical experiments, aimed at an aesthetic based upon the affect of *shock*, a feature only emphasised by the censoring in the first issue of Pound's poem 'Fratres Minores', because it mentioned testicles and contained a short description of sexual orgasm.[90] However, both magazines were also published by John Lane, who was in charge of one of the most important institutions of independent publishing in London. Lane, along with Elkin Mathews, started the Bodley Head in 1887, a press associated with publishing aesthetic and Decadent writers and artists such as Oscar Wilde and Aubrey Beardsley, Ernest Dowson, Lionel Johnson and Arthur Symons.[91] Indeed the final four pages of the first *BLAST* were taken up with adverts for Lane's publications, including works by Wilde, Vernon Lee and the painter James Whistler, with the last page displaying a full-page advert for a thirteen-volume reprint set of *The Yellow Book* for £3–5s.

The fact that *BLAST*'s puce cover contained a tint of 1890s yellow is thus more than a coincidence and points to two features crucial for understanding the role played by various London cultural movements in promoting modernism. First, we can note how some of the key institutional features of modernism were already in place in 1914, when both Vorticism and Imagism burst onto the literary scene. The role of a figure like John Lane shows just how important independent cultural institutions such as magazines, presses, bookshops and publishers were for incipient artistic movements, many years prior to the appearance of Monro's Poetry Bookshop. Second, we can note that the structural format of a modernist movement or 'ism' was also highly developed in London by this time. Though Vorticism might have been received as the unintelligible noise of an avant-garde sensibility, as predicted by Orage, he was also correct to note the similarities with earlier isms. Such movements showed embattled artists banding together against a philistine society, aware that without the support of other like-minded individuals their voice would be silenced or ignored. Thus the antipathy to the 'public' shown by many in the 1910s – ('damn the man in the street', said Pound in a 1914 essay in *The Egoist*)[92] – is only a small step from the decadent aesthete in a Wilde play who turns away with a contemptuous shrug from the restrictive morality of the Victorian bourgeoisie. In fact, these two features are linked: the rise of independent institutions of publishing was part of a rejection of Victorian society and the narrow morality of its publishing industry, which had prevented late nineteenth-century authors such as Thomas Hardy and George Moore from expressing themselves freely. Banding together into a coterie, school, movement or ism and taking one's cultural productions to an independent publisher, or starting one's own press or magazine, was by 1914 a well-established feature of literary publishing in London. The shared cultural field of the period between 1880 and 1914 was thus one where the artist tried to retreat from the mainstream institutions of culture, to find new outlets in other independent bodies (such as John Lane the publisher), only to re-engage, once again, with the commercial situation surrounding them. Crucial to this dialectic of engagement and retreat is the form and nature of the *movement* or *ism* itself and the specific geographical locations in which movements met, planned, and advanced projects.

In the case of John Lane, the key location was that of the bookshop, the Bodley Head, that he established with Elkin Mathews in 1887 in Vigo Street, a road just off Regent Street on the borders between bohemian Soho and plush Mayfair.[93] Ernest Rhys noted that the shop became 'a west-end Mecca of poets, young and old'.[94] Shifting from antiquarian bookselling to contemporary authors, the Bodley Head began publishing books by, amongst others, Michael Field, Arthur Symons and Oscar Wilde. These books were marked by their Arts and Crafts commitment to limited edition, high-quality productions, in terms of typography, paper quality and overall design, and thus symbolically opposed the cheap mass market publishing of books and magazines that became established in the late nineteenth century.[95] Employing new designers such as Charles Ricketts[96] and Laurence Housman, the Bodley Head bookshop occupied an important position in Bourdieu's cultural field that marked objects of high symbolic value due, in part, to their low commercial value, a position that modernist texts often came to occupy in the twentieth century.[97] That the bookshop was situated on the edge of the rich shopping streets of Mayfair, but with one eye on the bohemia of Soho, symbolised something of this complex dialectic between the commercial and the aesthetic.

A similar argument concerning the cultural geography of early modernist institutions in London can be made about one of the most important publications of Lane's press, the books of the Rhymers' Club. One of the most famous cultural formations in the prehistory of modernist poetry, the Rhymers' Club is normally linked to a series of Friday evening meetings in Ye Olde Cheshire

Cheese, a pub just off Fleet Street, then London's main location for newspaper production. This location, the centre of the Grub Street of London journalism, perhaps seems surprising for a group conventionally painted as a Decadent band of poets upholding aesthetic values against those of paid journalism. Symbolically, however, the Cheshire Cheese seems perfect, being located between a key Decadent site on the Strand, the Savoy Hotel (later scene of Wilde's downfall) and to the east the heart of London's financial empire, the City. We might, therefore, suggest that the roots of modernist poetry in London can be found midway between aesthetic pleasure and financial knowhow, a geographical position that, as with the Bodley Head bookshop, parallels their location in the wider cultural field.[98]

The relation, however, of the Rhymers' Club to commercial journalism is as complex as is the history of the actual group. W. B. Yeats, perhaps the best-known Rhymer, constructed a myth in his retrospective history of a 'tragic generation' of dissolute poets who by 1900 had either gone insane or drunk themselves to death. Karl Beckson has shown how Yeats misconstrued the history of the Rhymers partly in order to construct his own literary persona: far from being decadent affairs Rhymers' 'meetings were often dull'.[99] Yeats' history also helped shape the idea that a sharper division existed between these 1890s poets and the modernist writers of the 1910s. For Beckson, the Rhymers 'represented a significant attempt to form an organized group . . . to advance their own poetic agenda by attacking the sentimentality and didacticism in Victorian verse'.[100] As a description of a project this could quite easily, for example, be used of the Imagist poets in 1913–14.

The Rhymers' Club numbered many of the leading figures of the 1890s and published two anthologies of their verse in 1892 and 1894; a planned third anthology never appeared. Lionel Johnson described a meeting in 1891 of some eighteen poets including Yeats, Arthur Symons, Oscar Wilde, and the artist Walter Crane, although the latter two never published in the anthologies. The Scottish poet John Davidson was another figure who attended the meetings but was not in the anthologies. Like Davidson, many of the other 'Rhymers' were outsiders from the Celtic 'fringes', such as the Welshman Ernest Rhys and those from Ireland – Yeats, John Todhunter and T. W. Rolleston, who were linked to the Irish Literary Society started in London. The Rhymers also met in members' houses and at the headquarters of the Arts and Crafts organisation, the Century Guild in Fitzroy Street, where Lionel Johnson lived with Guild members Arthur Mackmurdo, Herbert Horne and Selwyn Image. In addition to this Arts and Crafts element, at least two members, Ernest Rhys and Ernest Radford, had close links with London socialist groups such as the Fabians. Radford's poem 'Song in the Labour Movement', published in the second Rhymers' anthology attacks the 'rule of Mammon' and looks forward to the day 'When we have righted what is wrong / Great singing shall your ears entreat; / Meanwhile in movement there is song, / And music in the pulse of feet.'[101]

As a group, then, the Rhymers were not homogenous and the air of Decadence or Symbolism associated with members such as Symons or Yeats was not necessarily the dominant feature of the group. Victor Plarr, for example, noted that though 'they always remained a distinct and independent group' they were 'unidentified with any particular cult or movement, though comprising the exponents of more than one'.[102] Unlike later modernist groups this cultural formation did not enforce a single style upon members: there was, for instance, no Rhymers' manifesto. Yeats noted that the Rhymers were engaged in a search for 'new subject matter, new emotions' and 'new forms', but that they were not 'a school of poets in the French sense', with an agreed agenda for poetic production.[103] This is borne out by the published poetry, which includes diverse elements such as Radford's socialist hymn; the Celtic mysticism of Yeats' 'A Man who dreamed of Fairyland'; symbolist work such as 'Javanese Dancers' by Symons; and a number of poems taking contemporary London as the setting.

One of the most interesting external relationships defining the cultural formation of the Rhymers is that with the world of journalism and publishing, centred on nearby Fleet Street. The 1880s had witnessed a tremendous growth in the power and influence of London journalism, seen in the so-called 'New Journalism' of figures such as W. T. Stead and T. P. O'Connor, increased pay for editors of newspapers, and the rise of mass-circulation weeklies and, soon after, dailies such as the *Daily Mail*. In the 1880s London already had six morning papers and four evening papers; by 1900, according to John Stokes, a London journalist had twenty-four daily papers to submit work to – and even more monthly or quarterly publications to choose between.[104] Other institutions sprung up to support the profession: advice columns in magazines for budding writers, along with schools for journalism such as David Anderson's London School of Journalism, formed in 1887 and located just off Fleet Street; in 1889 a charter was granted to the Institute of Journalists, placing it on a par with law or medicine.[105] Roy Foster notes that Yeats appreciated the Rhymers' Club for its links to a literary establishment that was closely intertwined with Fleet Street journalism. Foster describes the Rhymers as 'a reviewing mafia' with influence on important papers such as the *Star*, *Pall Mall Gazette*, the *Speaker*, *Daily Chronicle* and the *Bookman*.[106] When Davidson submitted his intriguingly named *Fleet Street Eclogues* to the Bodley Head press, the chief reader was Le Gallienne, his fellow Rhymer. When the book appeared Le Gallienne also reviewed it enthusiastically in the *Star* under the name 'Logroller'; another Rhymer, Lionel Johnson, reviewed it in the *Chronicle*. These logrolling practices were bemoaned by critics such as Arthur Waugh, who noted that the Rhymers seemed to have taken over the literary pages of the *Daily Chronicle*.[107] Victor Plarr's later memoir of the Rhymers boldly claimed that 'We were not any of us of Fleet Street', only then to admit, without irony, that he had served an 'apprenticeship there as an assistant sub-editor on a service of news to a paper long since dead in 1887–1888'.[108]

In drawing upon this network of connections to Fleet Street journalism the Rhymers only acknowledged the brute necessities facing a poet in the period, as summed up by Davidson in a newspaper article in 1893:

> The ever-increasing numbers, ambitious of literary distinction, who flock to London yearly, to become hacks and journalists, regard the work by which they gain a livelihood as a mere industry, a stepping-stone to higher things – alas! a stepping-stone on which the majority of them have to maintain a precarious footing all their lives.[109]

One way to understand the operations of a formation such as that of the Rhymers is to see it as a way for an individual poet or writer to keep a foothold, as it were, in both the aesthetic and commercial camps. Drawing upon networks offered by fellow-members of the formation, a writer could gain a livelihood through journalistic industry. Simultaneously the cultural formation presented itself to the world as a purely aesthetic project by appearing as a coterie or 'school', upholding a distance from Fleet Street by being associated with a small independent press, and by publishing a limited edition volume (only 350 copies of the first Rhymers' volume were printed for sale by the Bodley Head). These features thus marked the group as bearers of what Bourdieu terms high symbolic capital, rather than commercial value.[110] In this way, the Rhymers set out a position in the cultural field that was to be adopted by many later modernist groups in London: neither refuting nor totally accepting commercial culture, they moved into, then out of, this commercial zone, in a regular pattern of engagement, retreat, and re-engagement once again.

Such a structure can perhaps also be discerned in Davidson's two volumes of *Fleet Street Eclogues*. These present dialogues between journalists bemoaning their grubby lot in Fleet Street, imagining an escape to a world of pastoral bliss, only to return to their chosen lot. The first poem in the first volume, 'New Year's Day', has 'Brian' spell out his position:

> This trade that we ply with the pen,
> Unworthy of heroes or men,
> Assorts ever less with my humour:
> Mere tongues in the raiment of rumour,
> We review and report and invent:
> In drivel our virtue is spent.[111]

However, Brian's remorseless negativity is countered in the poem by Sandy, who proposes a more glorious view of the journalist:

To us the hour belongs;
Our daily victory is
O'er hydras, giant wrongs,
And dwarf iniquities.
We also may behold,
...
How the future of the world
Was shaped by journalists.[112]

The poem ends, typically, with the journalists toasting themselves with 'ale a-frothing brimmed'.

There is little that is modernist in the style of these poems, other perhaps than a directness of diction (Fleet Street is 'a traffic of lies', announces Brian later), and the choice of the Virgilian eclogue form marks the verse as embedded within traditional forms. However, the contrast between contemporary urban decay and past beauty is not dissimilar to parts of T. S. Eliot's *The Waste Land*, and Eliot himself acknowledged that his early reading of Davidson (especially his poem *Thirty Bob a Week*) had made him aware that English verse could use a more 'colloquial idiom' and present a form in which 'a good many dingy urban images' could be revealed.[113]

Discussing the influence of the Rhymers on Eliot, Yeats and Pound, James Longenbach writes that although the earlier group failed in their opposition to modern commerce 'they alone opposed a suffocating literary climate. Pound and Eliot thought of themselves as the inheritors of that struggle.'[114] Reading Davidson's poems attentively and understanding the Rhymers' close, though often ambiguous, relationship to Fleet Street shows a different picture from that of pure opposition, a picture that has been somewhat occluded in the later depictions by modernist writers of the Rhymers as beaten down by commercial journalism (such as Pound's depiction of Plarr as Monsieur Verog in *Hugh Selwyn Mauberley* or Yeats' account of the group in 'The Grey Rock'). By 1903 Arthur Symons would write that 'The newspaper is the plague, or black death of the modern world. It is an open sewer, running down each side of the street, and displaying the foulness of every day.'[115] That Symons could speak with such bile was, however, probably because he, like his fellow Rhymers, had spent so much time working for, or alongside, this plague, often sharing a drink or three with other 'journalists' in the nearby Cheshire Cheese pub.

One person who attended Rhymers' meetings, although he did not write or recite poetry, was Elkin Mathews. The partnership between Lane and Mathews had ended in 1894, and while Lane moved the Bodley Head press to new premises in the nearby Albany, Mathews continued the Vigo Street bookshop. Mathews became an important publisher for early modernism, producing James Joyce's *Chamber Music*, and early volumes of poetry by Pound such as *Personae* (1909), *Cathay* (1915), and *Lustra* (1916). At one point Mathews lived in the Bedford Park Garden Suburb, next door to the Yeats family, and his friendship with the family led to his publishing many early volumes of W. B. Yeats' early poetry and that of other members of the Irish 'Celtic Movement' centred on Yeats in London.[116] Even when Mathews had to move the shop to nearby Cork Street in 1912 it maintained its fame for visitors: Sylvia Beach, on a brief visit to London prior to opening her own bookshop, Shakespeare and Company, in Paris, collected works by Joyce, Pound and Yeats from the shop; on his first visit to London, Herbert Read, then in the army, was keen to visit as Mathews 'had been publishing the kind of poetry I was interested in'. After meeting Mathews, Read came away with an agreement to publish his first volume of poems, *Songs of Chaos*.[117] As Robert Scholes notes of Mathews, his work in this bookshop meant that he 'had a direct hand in the shaping of new literature'.[118]

It was also through Mathews that Pound joined another cultural formation that was to lead to the emergence of Imagism. This was the Poets' Club, from which a breakaway group emerged, led by T. E. Hulme and F. S. Flint, whom Pound dubbed the 'forgotten school of 1909'; the Imagists he noted, were their 'descendants'.[119] The Poets' Club met in another intriguing location, west from Fleet Street, in St James' Street, a street famous in the eighteenth century for its coffee houses and by the early twentieth century home to many of London's most fashionable gentlemen's clubs, such as Brooks', White's and Boodle's. The Poets' Club met once a month at the United Arts Club, above Rumpelmayer's restaurant, and shared their premises with the Junior Army and Navy Club. The Poets' Club was run by a Scottish banker, Henry Simpson, and Henry Newbolt, later to find fame as a patriotic poet, and they published three anthologies in 1909, 1911 and 1913. The Club seemed to consciously look back to the Rhymers, as members from the earlier group such as Plarr, Rhys, Todhunter, Image and G. A. Greene all attended. Plarr delivered a lecture at the Poets' Club in December 1910 upon 'The Rhymers' Club' drawing attention to those in his audience who were members of the earlier formation.[120] Hulme became honorary secretary of the group and drew up a set of rules that indicate the rather formal nature of the venture: there would be no more than fifty members; officers such as president, honorary secretary and so on; a committee of five; and an annual membership fee of 5 shillings. After dinner had been served the chairman would invite members to read 'original compositions in verse' followed by a 20-minute paper on 'a subject connected with poetry'.[121] Clearly this was a small cultural formation with a well-organised internal structure, its London location adding to the rather masculine flavour of an exclusive club, although women were clearly present and two poets, Lady Margaret Sackville and Marion Cran, were published in the anthologies.

At one such meeting, towards the end of 1908, Hulme delivered 'A Lecture on Modern Poetry', a key document for the theory of Imagist poetry. Hulme described how he could not find models for the poetry he wanted to write until he read French *vers libre* in poets such as Gustave Kahn, and that this discovery aided his thinking that modern poetry must match the times, for each 'age must have its own special form of expression', and that what 'has found expression in painting as Impressionism will soon find expression in poetry in free verse'.[122] This verse will be written without a regular metre, argued Hulme, and will work by the 'juxtaposition of distinct images in different lines'; the poetry will resemble 'sculpture rather than music' as it has to 'mould images, a kind of spiritual clay, into definite shapes'.[123] How Hulme's theory – one he himself described, in an early use of this term, as a 'standpoint of extreme modernism' – was received by the other poets is not recorded. That it did have an impact is demonstrated by the fact that the essence of Pound's first manifesto for Imagism, 'Imagisme' (1913), can be found in the ideas espoused in Hulme's lecture.[124]

After his arrival in London in 1908 Pound attended meetings of the Poets' Club through his friendship with Elkin Mathews.[125] Pound was eager to meet members of the Rhymers' group, particularly Yeats, and probably recognised that the Poets' Club had strong links with them. In 1911 Pound praised the Rhymers as they 'did valuable work in knocking bombast & rhetoric & victorian syrup out of our verse . . . they ring true, as much of Tennyson & parts of Browning do not'.[126] Selwyn Image was described by Pound as 'one of the gang with Dowson, Johnson, Symons, Yeats etc.' and in 1909 Pound wrote to his father that Plarr 'of the old Rhymers' Club' is 'most congenial' and that he was attending meetings of 'a sort of new Rhymers gang on Thursdays'.[127] This new 'gang' was Hulme's breakaway group from the Poets' Club, and Pound's epithet illustrates something of how this cultural formation was structured in a far less formal fashion than that of those who met in St James. Though this group was to form the basis of the Imagists it is significant that Pound views them through the lens of the Rhymers, once again illustrating the continuities in these modernist formations.

Hulme's breakaway from the Poets' Club was stimulated by Flint's review in the *New Age* of the first anthology of the group. Flint, a working-class Londoner with an extensive familiarity with modern French verse, attacked the Poets' Club not for its poetry but rather for what it represented as a cultural formation: unlike the innovations of French poets 'whose discussions in obscure cafés regenerated, remade French poetry' this London group is 'apparently a dining-club and after-dinner discussion association. Evening dress is, I believe, the correct uniform; and correct person – professors, I am told! – lecture portentously to the band of happy and replete rhymesters.' Flint vaguely praises poems by Image, Simpson, Cran and Hulme, but when he thinks 'of this club and its after-dinner ratiocinations, its tea-parties, in "suave South Audley Street"; and then of Verlaine at the Hotel de Ville. . . . I laugh.'[128] Hulme replied decisively the following week, lambasting Flint's obsession with French poets in cafés and 'the illusion that poets must be addicted to circean excess and disordered linen'. Hulme also noted that the meeting place for the poets was in keeping with the London environment: 'We, like Verlaine, are natural. It was natural for a Frenchman to frequent cafés. It would be dangerous as well as affected for us to recite verse in a saloon bar.'[129] It is a fascinating exchange for its focus is not on poetic technique but upon *how* and, crucially, *where* a group of modern poets in London should meet.

Being in a 'gang' rather than a 'club' now seemed the way forward and after this initial spat Flint and Hulme, perhaps surprisingly, became friends and started to meet on Thursdays in a new venue, the Tour d'Eiffel on Percy Street, off Tottenham Court Road, where the food was considerably cheaper than at the Poets' Club.[130] Here gathered ex-Rhymers Radford and Rhys, as well as Edward Storer, Francis Tancred (a Poets' Club member), Florence Farr (a mystic and close friend of Yeats) and three Irish poets, Joseph Campbell, Desmond Fitzgerald and Padraic Colum. This proto-Imagist formation also met in another location, at the London branch of the Irish Literary Society, in Hanover Square in Mayfair, once again demonstrating an overlap with the Irish element in the Rhymers. The Tour d'Eiffel was to become a fabled venue for both the Imagists and Vorticists, with Wyndham Lewis painting a 'Vorticist Room' upstairs and the site becoming memorialised in William Roberts' painting in 1961–2 of 'The Vorticists in the Eiffel Tower Restaurant: Spring 1915'.[131] Geographically, the restaurant was near neither Fleet Street nor St James clubland, but on the eastern edge of the bohemian area of Soho, in an area later to become known as Fitzrovia. As a venue it was thus somewhere between Hulme's dining club and Flint's Frenchified café (as signalled by its title) but, as Brooker points out, another restaurant, Dieudonné's, was probably more closely associated with the later Imagist and Vorticist groups.[132] Dieudonné's was a fairly expensive restaurant and certainly not a place to find the 'disordered linen' Hulme complained about in French cafés. Nevertheless, Dieudonné's hosted a Vorticist dinner to launch *BLAST* in July 1914, and an Imagist dinner just after organised by Amy Lowell, the rich American pretender to the crown of the Imagist group started by Pound. Interestingly, Dieudonné's was located in Ryder Street, a road running off St James' Street, and thus no distance from where the Poets' Club had met. Again this vacillation, between the bohemia of Soho to the north-east and the wealth and status of St James' or Mayfair to the west, demonstrates a cultural geography symbolising how these two important movements positioned themselves in the available field of literary production for modernism in London.

Queer Foreign Fish: Joseph Conrad

When Pound arrived in London in 1908 both the physical fabric of the city and its cultural institutions marked it as a modern world city par excellence.[133] Pound had turned up in London with £3 in his pocket (although further funds from his father were promised) and some copies of his book of poems, *A Lume Spento*. He was thus following the path of so many writers whose migration abroad, whether forced or voluntarily, represents the imagined first step in a journey of aesthetic growth. Many of those in the Rhymers, Imagists and Vorticist were, like Pound, outsiders, even if only from nearby Ireland (Yeats); others came from the English regions (Hulme) or from Scotland (Davidson) or Wales (Rhys). Such figures saw London initially as strangers, but also charted in their works how the affective experience of the modern metropolis – from the bustling modernity of its streets and traffic to the exciting new venues for poetry and the arts – developed their own cultural sensibilities. As Ford had noted, to become a Londoner was in fact to become modern.

One of the earliest modernist texts to explore London as a world city populated with immigrants was Joseph Conrad's *The Secret Agent* (1907).[134] Conrad himself was one of the most deracinated of modern writers, having been born in Russian-controlled Poland, travelled the world as a merchant seaman for fifteen years and finally settled in Britain in 1896. *The Secret Agent* explores groups of anarchists pitted against the bourgeois British state and, as the novel is set in 1886, is described in the dedication to the book as a 'simple tale of the nineteenth century'. In terms of structure and setting, however, it is anything but a 'simple tale'. Temporally, the novel contains several layers: the London it depicts is a strange mixture of muddy Victorian streets where the main mode of transport is by horse-drawn hansom carriage (the novel contains several interesting descriptions of such journeys); the political world of the 1890s (the central plotline, which concerns an attempt to blow up the Greenwich Observatory, was based upon an actual incident from 1894); and a stylistic concern with irony and interior consciousness that we associate with the modernist novel in the early twentieth century. The manner in which the novel handles space and the city is no less complex and shows the problematic nature of the 'assimilative powers' of London as a world city. At one point Verloc, the secret agent of the title, is said to be 'cosmopolitan enough not to be deceived by London's topographical mysteries',[135] a description that points to Conrad's awareness of how the modernist city requires a certain urban consciousness or cognitive map in order to find one's place in this environment.[136] In a preface to the novel composed some years later, Conrad noted that its genesis lay in a revelation of London as a world city:

> the vision of an enormous town presented itself, of a monstrous town more populous than some continents and in its man-made might as if indifferent to heaven's frowns and smiles. ... Irresistibly the town became the background for the ensuing period of deep and tentative meditations.[137]

The central story of Winnie Verloc and her family, writes Conrad, 'had to be disengaged from its obscurity in that immense town', and he had 'to fight to keep at arm's length the memories of my solitary and nocturnal walks all over London in my early days, lest they should rush in and overwhelm each page of the story'.[138] In a sense Conrad, as an exile turned cosmopolitan author, struggles to keep the monster that is London as a 'background' rather than have its 'topographical mysteries' obscure the story of the tragic death of Winnie Verloc's brother Stevie, and of her revenge upon her husband for perpetrating that death.

In this respect Conrad's fears that the city will 'overwhelm' his narrative parallels the way that many characters in the story struggle once they leave the internal space of rooms for the streets of this monstrous town. London streets are represented in an acutely physical and palpable fashion – fog, mud, smells and sounds frequently force their presence upon the characters in the novel, making the city something that, in Ford's words, 'slowly digests them', thus producing a stifling set of geographical emotions. One street is like 'a wet, muddy trench', shops are 'steamy' and 'greasy' and 'smell of fried fish', and when Winnie flees her house after the murder of her husband, 'a slimy dampness enveloped her, entered her nostrils, clung to her hair'.[139] In such instances the city appears alive and exerts a tactile hold upon its citizens. On Adolf Verloc's first journey to the Embassy he walks along a street that is said to possess 'the majesty of inorganic nature, of matter that never dies';[140] later, when at home, Verloc leans against the window and feels that only the glass separates him from 'the enormity of cold, black, wet, muddy, inhospitable accumulation of bricks, slates, and stones' and considers 'the latent unfriendliness of all out of doors with a force approaching to positive bodily anguish'.[141] The city thus possesses a distinctive and threatening materiality and, although there are the familiar tropes of the city crowd as a multitude, as when the Professor thinks of the mass as swarming 'like locusts', this urban matter is entirely separate from its inhabitants. London, Conrad notes drolly, is a town of 'marvels and mud'.[142]

Yet the cosmopolitan citizen must struggle to find a place in this hostile world of matter, and one of the most interesting examples exploring the geographical emotions of the outsider occurs when the Assistant Commissioner visits a Soho restaurant. Leaving his office for the city streets is memorably compared to 'the descent into a slimy aquarium from which the water has been run off' and now a 'murky, gloomy dampness enveloped him'.[143] As he enters the Strand by Charing Cross Station 'the genius of the locality assimilated him' and he is compared to one of the 'queer foreign fish' that frequent this location in the evening.[144] The imagery of the street as an aquarium is a brilliant continuation of the idea of the city as an alien physical environment: humans here are literally like fish out of water, as this aquarium has been drained. The location itself, suggests Conrad, acts upon an individual's identity, transforming the Assistant Commissioner from a 'native' to a 'queer foreign fish', from insider to outsider. 'Assimilation' here is a process which reverses the normal understanding of the term, as used by Ford, for example: here the native inhabitant is assimilated to the uncanny and 'foreign' quality of the *genius loci* itself.

Conrad's meditation upon place, belonging and national identity here is continued when the Assistant Commissioner takes a hansom cab to 'a little Italian restaurant' in Soho, near to the Brett Street location of Verloc's shop. James McLaughlin provides a brilliant analysis of this episode in his account of how Conrad's novel 'constructs the modernist metropolis as a site of social anarchy'.[145] For McLaughlin the restaurant is a 'site where identity is lost by being rendered blank and meaningless', rather than a location that affirms one's own national identity by eating a cuisine that is other to that identity.[146] Since at least the exodus of the French Huguenots in the eighteenth century, Soho had been a destination for immigrants to London, and by the early twentieth century it had become a cosmopolitan area populated by many migrants (including East European Jews, Irish, French, Germans and Italians), leading a newspaper report in 1900 to describe Soho as 'more continental than it is English'.[147] It was also, as McLaughlin and Judith Walkowitz argue, perceived as an area rife with political anarchists and sexual depravity, a reputation that gave this West End area the frisson of the demonised East End of London as depicted in many late nineteenth-century texts.[148] Much is made in the novel of the Soho location in terms of the spatiality of social class in London. Winnie, for example, is acutely aware that she has moved from an upmarket Belgravia address, where her mother kept apartments for rent, to a shop in Soho: towards the novel's end she is described as 'the respectable girl of the Belgravian mansion', an ironic epithet given she has just murdered her husband in the supposedly less respectable location of Soho.

Walkowitz has traced in detail the cultural history of Soho from the later nineteenth century, showing the different stages in its development as a zone of cosmopolitan cultural activity, described in 1887 as 'the foreign quarter of the metropolis'.[149] One key marker of this 'foreignness' was the establishment of French, then Italian restaurants in the area, such as the one visited by the Assistant Commissioner.[150] Walkowitz traces how the rather negative associations of cosmopolitan Soho in the late nineteenth century changed in the first decade of the twentieth century: now Soho became a crucial part of a topography that situated a *Bohemia in London*, as Arthur Ransome's popular book of 1907 would style it.[151] This bohemia self-consciously aped its Parisian parents in the development of a café society, with restaurants whose Frenchified names signalled their cosmopolitan tendencies. Sites such as the Café Royal, the Tour d'Eiffel and the Mont Blanc all attracted writers and artists, and became important locations of emerging modernist formations, as already seen with the Vorticists and the Tour d'Eiffel. The Mont Blanc in Gerrard Street, interestingly, was the venue for another literary network that included Ford, Hilaire Belloc, G. K. Chesterton, John Galsworthy, John Masefield, W. H. Davies, Edward Thomas and, last but not least, Joseph Conrad.[152]

As McLaughlin notes, then, Conrad's negative depiction of the Italian restaurant as a place of 'fraudulent cooking mocking an abject mankind'[153] is linked to the ironic distancing of his narrative voice, a style that Conrad had made his own in his earlier text, *Heart of Darkness*. For Conrad was quite clearly one of the 'queer foreign fish' that inhabited London and its cosmopolitan restaurants, but was equally determined to develop an identity as a 'native' English author. The complexities of this familiar dialectic for the migrant writer between home and abroad, insider and outsider, become crystallised in the scene in the restaurant, for, as McLaughlin writes, 'Conrad is attempting to flee a Soho that powerfully calls him (home).'[154] In the restaurant the Assistant Commissioner 'seemed to lose some more of his identity' and, catching himself in the mirror, is 'struck by his foreign appearance'.[155] As he leaves he reflects upon how patrons of the restaurant lose their national characteristics, just as the dishes of food are also 'denationalized' due to being fraudulent. The Italian restaurant, writes Conrad, with delicious irony, 'is such a peculiarly British institution'.[156] The social space of this Soho is, therefore, seen not as a site of cosmopolitan freedom, but as a location for becoming, in Conrad's revealing term, 'unplaced'.[157] Or as Walkowitz concludes of this incident, here 'everyone is both foreign and native'.[158]

London Unplaced: Sam Selvon

Feeling 'unplaced' is a common perception in the work of the many migrant and postcolonial writers after Conrad who tried to locate themselves within London. As Anna Snaith notes, successful generations of colonial outsiders in the inter-war years engaged closely with cultural and political institutions within London to overcome the geographical emotion of being 'unplaced'.[159] London in the 1920s and 1930s was thus home to the International Students' Club, the Drury Lane Club (for non-white colonials), the West African Students' Union, the India League and the League of Coloured Peoples, organisations and institutions often founded by colonial outsiders visiting the centre of empire. For other figures, existing cultural institutions like bookshops became important locations for their development: in addition to Mulk Raj Anand in Monro's Poetry Bookshop, we can also note how the major West Indian intellectual C. L. R. James claimed that his own 'intellectual formation' in London in the 1930s owed much to the time he spent in Charles Lahr's Progressive Bookshop in Holborn.[160] However, as Bill Schwarz notes, this 'black metropolis' was more than just a city where these outsiders felt 'unplaced'; it also 'generated the resources for the creation of a rich array of subaltern networks of the colonised' that resulted in a political culture central to anti-colonial struggles.[161] Overcoming the feeling of being 'unplaced' often came from a cultural politics which recognised the complex geographical ties between London and its colonies, or, as Snaith suggests, such colonial writers 'produce' London 'in ways that reflect their outsiderness, and always with an eye to the relational nature of national spaces within the empire'.[162] In a sense many of the texts written by colonial outsiders aimed to 'unplace' London itself from its position at the centre of empire.

The 'queer foreign fish' of Conrad's Soho can thus be linked to a later moment in the history of modernist London, showing once again how important it is to pay attention to the particular spatial histories of the city. John McLeod has written persuasively in *Postcolonial London* of the 'spatial creolization' of London by immigrant writers from the Caribbean after World War II, focusing upon an area 'stretching east–west from Soho to Notting Hill'. As McLeod notes, the 'arrival in West London of newcomers from once-colonized countries after the Second World War had a significant impact on an area of the city already distinguished by a long history of transcultural settlement'.[163] However, even earlier, by the 1930s, Soho contained clubs and cafés (for example, the Big Apple Club in Gerrard Street) designed explicitly for black migrants to London. Also in Soho in the 1930s and 1940s were many black music clubs that emulated New York's Cotton Club, places where black musicians mingled with Jewish political activists in a new reworking of the cosmopolitan experience.[164] Such locations added a new layer of 'spatial creolization', to use McLeod's useful term, to the streets of Soho once frequented by the 'queer foreign fish' of European outsiders.

Sam Selvon's *The Lonely Londoners* (1956) offers a particularly interesting version of the encounter between the colonial outsider and the modernist metropolis. For Selvon's narrative of encounter relates directly to London's history as an imperial city after World War II, exploring 'those who had come to the metropolis from colonized or capitalized regions'.[165] The 1948 Nationality Act had welcomed immigrants from Britain's former and existing colonies as 'citizens of the United Kingdom and its Colonies', and those that migrated from the West Indies, as represented in Selvon's novel, are often referred to as the 'Windrush Generation' after the ship that brought several hundred passengers from Jamaica to London in 1948. Selvon's novel, which mainly concerns immigrants arriving in London from Trinidad, his own birthplace, engages with London's complex status as an imperial metropolis and as a city of modernity. The very opening sentence of the novel presents a textual space in which the experience of the outsider in the city mingles with various discourses of modernism and modernity:

> One grim winter evening, when it had a kind of unrealness about London, with a fog sleeping restlessly over the city and the lights showing in the blur as if is not London at all but some strange place on another planet, Moses Aloetta hop on a number 46 bus at the corner of Chepstow Road and Westbourne Grove to go to Waterloo to meet a fellar who was coming from Trinidad on the boat-train.[166]

The obvious intertextual reference here is to T. S. Eliot's *The Waste Land*, with its famous portrayal of London as an 'unreal city'.[167] The reference here to London fog echoes Eliot's 'Under the brown fog of a winter dawn, / A crowd flowed over London bridge', while also picking up a tradition of modernist writers such as Conrad who used fog or mist as a metaphor for confused perception or narrative obscurity: in London, the image suggests, the outsider cannot quite see things clearly.[168] Selvon's 'unrealness' is a quite different term, however, and demonstrates a reworking of Eliot's high modernism through the grammar of the Trinidadian dialect employed in the novel. Readers expecting a novel written in Standard English might trip up not only over 'unrealness', perhaps expecting to see 'unreality' here, but also over the phrase 'as if is not London', thinking that there is an 'it' missing between 'if' and 'is'. What we see here, as throughout *The Lonely Londoners*, is that the textual space of the novel captures a London overlayered with different social spaces. By 1956 the city was familiar with the modernist innovations of Eliot and other pre-war writers, but the dialectal uses of English from West Indian immigrants had also started to be heard more strongly throughout its streets. Selvon's novel thus demonstrates Raymond Williams' point that immigrant writers to a modernist city such as London brought with them linguistic practices that might be 'marginalized or suppressed', but which could also interact with the 'dominant language' of Eliotic modernism to produce 'new language effects'.[169] The 'strangeness and distance' noted by Williams as features of modernist style derive, in Selvon's text, from the encounter of the immigrant with a new environment. Selvon's stress on the 'unrealness' of London emphasises the perception of the outsider, viewing London as 'some strange place on another planet', yet wresting the experience of this strange urban space into the very aesthetic form of his sentences, as Selvon hybridizes a West Indian colloquial style with an Anglo-American high modernism.

Selvon's encounter with modernist style will be discussed shortly, but another key feature of his depiction of the city in the novel's opening pages is that of the mundane reality of urban transport. As discussed earlier in this chapter, new forms of urban transport transformed the spaces of London, and in *The Lonely Londoners* the wider journey from the colony to the metropolis by the boat train is paralleled by the many references to urban travel in the text, starting with Moses' journey on the 46 bus. Moses' journey starts in the Notting Hill/Westbourne Green/Bayswater area of west London, an area that grew to be well known in the 1950s for becoming the home of many of the West Indian immigrants to London. Many of Colin MacInnes' novels of the period, for example, such as *City of Spades* (1957) and *Absolute Beginners* (1959), are set in this location and concern the mixing of the immigrants with the local white communities.[170] Interestingly, it is the same area that another colonial outsider, Julia Martin in Jean Rhys' *After Leaving Mr Mackenzie*, inhabits. Julia at one point lives in a boarding-house in Notting Hill, in a 'labyrinth of streets, all exactly alike', near to the Chepstow Road of *The Lonely Londoners*.[171] Selvon's novel traces the geography of this part of London in detail throughout the novel, but the first key scene in the text refers to another social space of significance for the migrant to the city, the station at Waterloo, where boat trains would arrive from ports such as Southampton. When Moses arrives at Waterloo he experiences 'a feeling of homesickness that he never felt in the nine-ten years he in this country'. This is because the station is 'a place of arrival and departure'.[172] Waterloo is a space of transit, one that encourages a sense of being 'unplaced', a site which produces a melancholy affect in Moses: 'the station is that sort of place where you have a soft feeling'.[173] It also produces a yearning for home: 'perhaps he was thinking is time to go back to the tropics, that's why he feeling sort of lonely and miserable'.[174]

The same geographical emotion of dislocation is experienced by Galahad, the person Moses has met off the boat train and whom, in the course of the novel, Moses befriends and helps to become orientated in the city. On his first day in London Galahad, in search of a job, refuses help from Moses to find the labour exchange and finds himself standing outside Queensway Tube station when 'a feeling of loneliness and fright come on him all of a sudden'.[175] The foggy environment of London in winter affects Galahad deeply: 'When he look up, the colour of the sky so desolate it make him more frighten. It have a kind of melancholy aspect about the morning that making him shiver.'[176] This affect intensifies when he thinks he might be unable to find his way back to the room he is sharing with Moses, and becomes similar to the symptoms of spatial phobias discussed earlier in the chapter: 'A feeling come over him as if he lost everything he have – clothes, shoes, hat – and he start to touch himself here and there as if he in a daze.'[177] In many ways this is the classic experience of alienation or anomie in the modern city, as diagnosed by sociologists such as Georg Simmel and Max Weber.[178] Such works have frequently been used as a context for the earlier modernism of Eliot or Döblin but are also clearly relevant for understanding Selvon's depiction of the city in the 1950s; however, now the urban alienation is overlaid with the experience of the Caribbean colonial migrant.[179] When Galahad feels the hand of a policeman on his shoulder, his panic increases: 'is as if the hand paralyse him and he can't move'.[180] What is intriguing is that the reason the policeman has approached him is because Galahad does not act properly in the urban environment. 'Move along now, don't block the pavement',[181] says the policeman, aware that to dwell in a modern city such as London entails *movement* on its streets. Moses comes to Galahad's rescue at this point (he feels 'dead with joy' to see Moses[182]), and educates him in another aspect of moving through modernity: how to catch a bus appropriately by queuing in the correct British fashion and by paying with coins, not large notes.

A similar encounter with the technology of urban transport occurs when Tanty, an elderly Jamaican immigrant, tries to overcome her fear of travelling by bus or Tube. Tanty lives in a working-class part of the Harrow Road, but treats the area like a 'small village and never go to the city'.[183] One day she decides to 'travel out of the district' and 'she decide to brave London'.[184] Tanty is initially concerned about travel by bus as 'They too tall, I feel as if they would capsize',[185] and so takes the Tube, with some trepidation, into central London. She feels pleased with herself for successfully negotiating an urban space outside of the 'village' of the Harrow Road, and so decides to brave travelling home by bus. This proves somewhat traumatic as she has to go onto the top deck of the bus, which exacerbates her fear that it might topple over: 'She was so frighten that she didn't bother to look out of the window and see anything, and when she get off at the Prince of Wales she feel relieved.'[186] This, seemingly mundane, episode recapitulates the affective and phobic representations of new modes of transport in the city discussed earlier in this chapter, and also recalls similar accounts in the chapters on Vienna and Berlin. Now, however, the anxiety of the new is experienced somewhat differently and signifies a rite of passage for the colonial migrant to the city. Tanty's episode ends with the proud assertion that her successful journey means that, in some way, she is becoming a Londoner: 'Now nobody could tell she that she ain't travel by bus and tube in London.'[187] To negotiate the Tube and bus is thus another stage in overcoming the sensation of being 'unplaced'.

Much like Tanty's journey, Selvon's depiction of the city swings between positive and negative affects. The more experienced London-dweller Moses articulates the familiar problems of becoming part of a country when one is an immigrant. He complains that this 'is a lonely miserable city' that is 'not like home' and is a place where nobody 'does really accept you. They tolerate you.'[188] In other places Selvon depicts characters who demonstrate an affective joy at the modernity of the city. Galahad, for example, eulogises central London sites such as Piccadilly Circus, for 'that circus represent life, that circus is the beginning and the ending of the world', and the Tube station is where he meets his lover, Daisy, for it is 'a place everybody know, everybody does have dates there, is a meeting place'.[189] Piccadilly Circus Tube station is a fascinating location for this meeting, as it was one of the stations rebuilt by Charles Pick and Charles Holden in the 1920s to demonstrate the modernity of London. Opened in 1928, after three years of rebuilding, the new circular station concourse used expensive Travertine marble, along with improved ventilation and artificial lights, and aimed to make 'the station level beneath Piccadilly Circus as bright and attractive as the circus itself'.[190] In Woolf's *The Waves* (1931) Jinny stands in the redesigned space and feels that above is where 'great avenues of civilization meet . . . and strike this way and that. I am in the heart of life.'[191] In a novel where the theme of empire is quite prominent, David Bradshaw rightly notes that Jinny's sense of being at the 'heart of life' is another example of how Woolf locates her fiction in 'London's most highly charged and significant socio-political spaces.'[192] The redesigned station concourse contained five murals, one of which, by Stephen Bone, depicted a map of the world, with Piccadilly Circus at the centre of the British Empire, and lines radiating outwards to all parts of the earth (see Fig. 4.7). Pick had worked earlier for the Empire Marketing Board and this cartographic display of British

Figure 4.7 Mural by Stephen Bone, Piccadilly Circus, c. 1928. © TfL from the London Transport Museum collection.

imperialism was intended, in Michael Saler's words, 'to remind travellers of the larger family to which many of them belonged'.[193]

A little later a world clock was installed which, as Galahad notes in *The Lonely Londoners*, 'does tell the time of places all over the world'.[194] This London location, then, with its 'avenues of civilization' in Woolf's words, or as Selvon puts it 'the beginning and the ending of the world', was thus a pointed official representation of space, in Lefebvre's terms, demonstrating the intertwined spaces of the metropolis and empire.[195]

However, for Galahad it is the myriad sights and sounds of urban life, including the advertisements, that delight him about Piccadilly Circus, and his account bursts with positive affects, illustrating Lefebvre's notion that representational space (in contrast to the official representation of space in the empire map) is 'alive' with an 'affective kernel' embracing the 'loci of passion':[196]

> Always, from the first time he went there to see Eros and the lights, that circus have a magnet for him. . . . Every time he go there, he have the same feeling like when he see it the first night, drink coca-cola, any time is guinness time, Bovril and the fireworks, the million flashing lights, gay laughter, the wide doors of theatres, the huge posters, everready batteries, rich people going into tall hotels, people going to the theatre, people sitting and standing and walking and talking and laughing and buses and cars and Galahad Esquire, in all this, standing there in the big city, in London. Oh Lord.[197]

The use of stream of consciousness here echoes a writer such as Virginia Woolf who, in *Mrs Dalloway*, used the technique to capture the flow and sensory overload of modernist London. Selvon here shows himself to be, in Peter Kalliney's words, an inheritor and transformer of modernism, demonstrating how postcolonial writing 'seized the aesthetic territories and material spaces charted by metropolitan modernism'.[198] However, while Clarissa Dalloway is a native Londoner, Galahad's attachment to this particular location is as an outsider, signalled in the repeated word 'in' ('in all this', 'in the big city', 'in London'). The emphasis is thus upon the process of becoming located *in* London, replacing the geographical emotion of being 'unplaced' with a feeling of belonging. Another way to apprehend this moment is by seeing is as an example of Michel de Certeau's distinction between understanding a geographical location as a place, which implies a sense of fixity and official discourse, and understanding it as part of what he calls a 'spatial practice', determined by the 'ways of operating' of individual subjects walking through the location: Galahad here is 'actualising space', in de Certeau's terms, transforming Piccadilly Circus as a place identified with empire in the map in the Tube station into a spatial story of lights, laughter and other sensations.[199]

If Galahad cannot necessarily afford these consumer products, trips to the theatre or hotels, he can take still take affective pleasure in the fact of being 'in' this 'big city', experiencing its sights and sounds. It is a common experience for many poor and working-class people in large cities to simply take pleasure in being part of the sensorium of the urban experience by walking the streets or travelling cheaply by public transport. Another character in the novel is directly identified with the positive affects of metropolitan life by being named Big City. Originally from an orphanage in Trinidad, he has dreams of the cities of the world that result in his nickname:

> 'Big City for me,' he would say. 'None of this smalltime village life for me. Is New York and London and Paris, that is big life. You think I going to stay in Trinidad when the war over? This small place? No, not this old man.'[200]

One of the sections of the novel most informed by earlier forms of modernist style is the ten pages of unpunctuated stream of consciousness which acts as a paean to sexual encounters during summer in the city:

> all these things happen in the blazing summer under the trees in the park on the grass with the daffodils and tulips in full bloom and a sky of blue oh it does really be beautiful then to hear the birds whistling and see the green leaves come back on the trees and in the night the world turn upside down and everybody hustling that is life that is London.[201]

The passage reworks Molly Bloom's monologue at the close of *Ulysses*, translating Molly's sexual imaginings into an account of the relations between the West Indian emigrants and the white women of the city. The passage explores sexual stereotypes between black and white, but also depicts the city and its spaces, such as parks and gardens, as sites for unlicensed sexual pleasure. Winter in London has an 'atmosphere like a sullen twilight hanging over the big city',[202] but when the 'sweetness of summer' appears Galahad says 'he would never leave the old Brit'n as long as he live'.[203]

Towards the end of the novel Selvon pauses to puzzle over what urban life amounts to for an outsider in the city, in a passage which appears to blur the thoughts of Moses and those of the author:

> The changing of the seasons, the cold slicing winds, the falling leaves, sunlight on green grass, snow on the land, London particular. Oh what it is and where it is and why it is, no one knows, but to have said: 'I walked on Waterloo Bridge,' 'I rendezvoused at Charing Cross,' 'Piccadilly Circus is my playground,' to say these things, to have lived these things, to have lived in the great city of London, centre of the world. To one day lean against the wind walking up the Bayswater Road (destination

> unknown), to see the leaves swirl and dance and spin on the pavement (sight unseeing), to write a casual letter home beginning: 'Last night, in Trafalgar Square. . . .'[204]

In this recitation of the names of places in 'London particular' Selvon recalls Walter Benjamin's theory of the affective power of street names: 'street names are like intoxicating substances that make our perceptions more stratified and richer in spaces. One could call the energy by which they transport us into such a state their *vertu évocatrice*, their evocative power.'[205] The 'evocative power' of London place names (Trafalgar Square, Piccadilly Circus, Waterloo Bridge), and the tangled spatial affects they produce, also preoccupy Selvon as Moses ponders:

> What is it that a city have, that any place in the world have, that you get so much to live it you wouldn't leave it for anywhere else? . . . why is it, that in the end, everyone cagey about saying outright that if the chance come they will go back to them green islands in the sun?[206]

Selvon's questioning of urban life recalls Leopold Bloom in James Joyce's *Ulysses*, musing on the 'stream of life' in the city and regarding the city as in a constant state of renewal: 'Cityful passing away, another cityful coming, passing away too: other coming on, passing on.'[207] *The Lonely Londoners* centrally concerns the renewal of the city by the arrival and movement of immigrants from the colonies. Bloom and Moses, as narrators of modern urban existence, thus share the status of outsiders, as Bloom's Jewish identity is constantly emphasized by the other Dubliners throughout *Ulysses*. But Bloom is still a native of the city and proclaims his Irish identity against the taunts of the xenophobic Citizen in the 'Cyclops' episode by saying: 'I was born here. Ireland.'[208] It is a claim that Moses cannot make and as much as he enjoys 'London particular' and is 'cagey' about returning to the Caribbean, the geographical emotions associated with his origins in 'them green islands in the sun' echo throughout the narrative.[209] Thus the novel navigates a struggle to overcome feeling 'unplaced' in 'the great city of London, centre of the world', a city where the map of empire in Piccadilly Circus Tube station acts as a reminder of how 'green islands in the sun' are connected with the imperial metropolis. The spatial practice of Galahad is thus one strategy for negotiating the complex geographical emotions surrounding London and the Caribbean, viewing Piccadilly Circus as a 'playground' of affect.

A different spatial practice appears at the end of the novel as Moses, his identity blurring once again with that of Selvon the author, has something of an epiphany while 'liming on the Embankment near to Chelsea' and wondering about saving up his money to go home next year 'before he change his mind again.'[210] Moses thinks 'he see some sort of profound realisation in his life' and understands that underneath the laughter and summer pleasures of the migrants in the city there is 'a great aimlessness, a great restless, swaying movement that leaving you standing in the same spot'.[211] Pursuing these ideas, he detects that while on the surface things do not look too bad, underneath,

> you bounce up a kind of misery and pathos and a frightening – what? He don't know the right word, but he have the right feeling in his heart. As if the boys laughing, but they only laughing because they fraid to cry, they only laughing because to think so much about everything would be a big calamity – like how he here now, the thoughts so heavy like he unable to move his body.[212]

The geographical emotions Moses experiences here make him 'restless' yet root him to the spot, his body petrified, a spatial image of affect that beautifully captures how the migrant outsider somehow feels in geographical limbo between a past life in the colony and a present existence in the imperial metropolis, unable yet to move into a future time and place. The initial affects Moses experiences are thus classically non-representational – he cannot articulate the 'right word' but has 'the right feeling in his heart'. However, he then reflects on this experience again:

> Still, it had a greatness and a vastness in the way he was feeling tonight, like it was something solid after feeling everything else give way, and though he ain't getting no happiness out of the cogitations he still pondering, for is the first time that he ever find himself thinking like that.[213]

These feelings of 'greatness' and 'vastness' lead to a further 'profound realisation', as Moses/Selvon now wonders if he might become a 'new literary giant' by writing a book detailing the experiences of the black newcomers to the modernist metropolis of London. Representing the geographical emotions of these outsiders in the city is thus another spatial practice for overcoming the feeling of being 'unplaced', producing new 'spatial stories'.[214] If Moses/Selvon was not, unlike Bloom in Dublin, born in the city, he can at least remake it and reimagine London from the point of view of the outsider, and in true modernist fashion make the city new all over again. In so doing Selvon's text also demonstrates a revising of modernism to take account of this moment in the spatial history of the British Empire. Outsiders in the cities of modernism can thus become insiders too.

Notes

1. Ezra Pound, 'Preliminary Announcement of the College of Arts', *The Egoist*, 21:1 (2 Nov. 1914), pp. 413–14.
2. Ibid.
3. See A. David Moody, *Ezra Pound: Poet. A Portrait of the Man and His Work,*

vol. 1: The Young Genius 1885–1920 (Oxford: Oxford University Press, 2007), p. 264.

4. Pound, 'College of Arts', p. 413.
5. Pound, Letter to Margaret Cravens, quoted in Moody, *Ezra Pound*, p. 130.
6. This is, however, to ignore the claims of locations from the ancient world to be 'world cities', such as Babylon, Ninevah or Rome, as well as the medieval Muslim cities of Al Andaluz, such as Cordoba or Granada. On the general history of cities see Lewis Mumford, *The City in History: Its Origins, its Transformations, and its Prospects* (Harmondsworth: Penguin, 1961). For the history of London see Roy Porter, *London: A Social History* (London: Penguin, 2000).
7. Patrick Geddes, *Cities in Evolution: An Introduction to the Town Planning Movement and to the Study of Civics* (London: Williams and Norgate, 1915), pp. 46–59.
8. H. J. Mackinder, *Britain and the British Seas*, 2nd edn (Oxford: Clarendon Press, 1907), p. 258.
9. Ford Madox Ford, *The Soul of London*, ed. Alan G. Hill (London: Everyman, 1995), p. 13.
10. Pound, letter to Harriet Monroe, Nov. 1913 in *The Selected Letters of Ezra Pound 1907–1941*, ed. D. D. Paige (London: Faber, 1950), p. 25.
11. David James, 'Modernist Narratives' in *The Oxford Handbook of Modernisms*, ed. Peter Brooker, Andrzej Gasiorek, Deborah Longworth and Andrew Thacker (Oxford: Oxford University Press, 2010), pp. 85–107; p. 92. See also Ford's two-part essay, 'On Impressionism', *Poetry and Drama* 6 (June 1914), pp. 167–75, and *Poetry and Drama* 8 (Dec. 1914), pp. 323–34. For a detailed analysis of this movement see Jesse Matz, *Literary Impressionism and Modernist Aesthetics* (Cambridge: Cambridge University Press, 2001), and Tamar Katz, *Impressionist Subjects: Gender, Interiority and Modernist Fiction in England* (Urbana and Chicago: University of Illinois Press, 2000).
12. Ford, *Soul of London*, p. 42.
13. Ibid.
14. David Welsh, *Underground Writing: The London Tube from George Gissing to Virginia Woolf* (Liverpool: Liverpool University Press, 2010), p. 268. For other discussions of the cultural history of the Underground see David Ashford, *London Underground: A Cultural Geography* (Liverpool: Liverpool University Press, 2013); David L. Pike, *Subterranean Cities: The World Beneath Paris and London, 1800–1945* (Ithaca: Cornell University Press, 2005); and Michael T. Saler, *The Avant-Garde in Interwar England: Medieval Modernism and the London Underground* (Oxford: Oxford University Press, 1999).
15. Virginia Woolf, 'The Mark on the Wall' in *A Haunted House* (Harmondsworth: Penguin 1973), pp. 43–52; pp. 44–5.
16. Julia Briggs, *Virginia Woolf: An Inner Life* (London: Penguin, 2006), p. 61.
17. For the history of the development of the Underground see Christian Wolmar, *The Subterranean Railway: How the London Underground Was Built and How It Changed the City Forever* (London: Atlantic Books, 2004).
18. Ian Carter, *Railways and Culture in Britain: The Epitome of Modernity* (Manchester: Manchester University Press, 2001), p. 4.
19. Marshall Berman, *All that Is Solid Melts into Air: The Experience of Modernity* (London: Verso, 1982), p. 159. Berman is here commenting upon Baudelaire's depiction of the city.
20. Arthur Rimbaud, 'Métropolitain' in *Oeuvres poétiques* (Paris: Garnier-Flammarion, 1964), p. 167. In 1911 Jules Romains composed a prose poem, 'L'Equipe du Métropolitain', about workers on the Paris Metro.

21. The best account of the work of Pick and Holden can be found in Saler, *Avant-Garde in Interwar England.*
22. [Anon.], *Metro-Land: A Comprehensive Description of the Country Districts Served By the Metropolitan Railway* (London: Metropolitan Railways, 1924), p. 27. The first Metro-Land booklet was published in 1915. For a discussion of Metro-Land see Ashford, *London Underground*, pp. 93–114.
23. Virginia Woolf, *A Passionate Apprentice: The Early Journals of Virginia Woolf*, ed. Mitchell A. Leaska (London: Hogarth Press, 1990), p. 365.
24. Mumford, *City in History*, p. 489.
25. Ibid. p. 490.
26. See David Harvey, *The Condition of Postmodernity* (Oxford: Blackwell, 1989), ch. 16.
27. See [Anon.], *Country Homes: The Official Guide of the Metropolitan Railway Comprising Residential Districts of Buck, Herts. and Middlesex* (London: Metropolitan Railways, 1909).
28. [Anon.], *A Selection of Country Walks in Middlesex, Hertfordshire and Buckinghamshire* (London: Metropolitan Railways, 1910).
29. [Anon.], *Country Homes*, p. 1.
30. Quoted in Wolmar, *Subterranean Railway*, p. 245.
31. G. A. Selcon, 'Pullman Cars on the Metropolitan Railway', *The Railway and Travel Monthly* 1:3 (July 1910), p. 228.
32. Cited in [Anon.], *Metro-Land: British Empire Exhibition Number* (1924; London: Southbank, 2004), p. xv. Emphasis added.
33. J. P. Thomas, *Handling London's Underground Traffic* (London: London's Underground, 1928), p. 216; E. M. Forster, *Howards End* (1910; Harmondsworth: Penguin, 1983), p. 329.
34. Evelyn Waugh, *A Little Learning* (1964); cited in Sheila Taylor (ed.), *The Moving Metropolis: A History of London's Transport since 1800* (London: Laurence King, 2001), p. 181.
35. Taylor, *Moving Metropolis*, p. 141. For more on the impact of Yerkes see Wolmar, *Subterranean Railway*, ch. 8. Yerkes' development of the Underground formed the basis for the final novel in Theodore Dreiser's Cowperwood Trilogy, *The Stoic*, published posthumously in 1947. See Ashford, *London Underground*, pp. 45–62.
36. See the Hampstead Garden Suburb Trust, http://www.hgs.org.uk/history/index.html (last accessed 5 Nov. 2017).
37. Roy Foster, *W. B. Yeats: A Life, vol. 1: The Apprentice Mage* (Oxford: Oxford University Press, 1998), p. 60.
38. Elizabeth Wilson, *The Sphinx in the City: Urban Life, the Control of Disorder, and Women* (London: Virago, 1991), p. 103.
39. [Anon.], *Metro-Land* (1924), pp. xii–xiii.
40. Betjeman's film was first broadcast in 1973 by the BBC; Julian Barnes, *Metroland* (London: Jonathan Cape, 1980).
41. Richard Sennett, *Flesh and Stone: The Body and the City in Western Civilization* (London: Faber, 1994), p. 332.
42. Walter Benjamin, *The Arcades Project*, trans. Howard Eiland and Kevin McLaughlin (Cambridge, MA: Belknap/Harvard University Press, 1999), p. 602.
43. First published in the little magazine *Coterie* 1 (May–Dec. 1919), p. 45
44. Virginia Woolf, *To the Lighthouse*, ed. Stella McNichol (London: Penguin, 1992), p. 213.
45. Virginia Woolf, *Jacob's Room*, ed. Sue Roe (London: Penguin, 1992), pp. 55–6.

46. Jonathan Crary, *Suspensions of Perception: Attention, Spectacle and Modern Culture* (Boston, MA: MIT Press, 2000), p. 370.
47. Michel Foucault, *Discipline and Punish: The Birth of the Prison*, trans. Alan Sheridan (Harmondsworth: Penguin, 1977), pp. 135–69.
48. Georg Simmel, 'The Metropolis and Mental Life' (1903) in *The Blackwell City Reader*, ed. Gary Bridge and Sophie Watson (Oxford: Blackwell, 2002), pp. 11–19; p.16.
49. John Carey, *The Intellectuals and the Masses: Pride and Prejudice among the Literary Intelligentsia, 1880–1939* (London: Faber, 1992).
50. James Donald, 'This, Here, Now: Imagining the Modern City' in *Imagining Cities: Scripts, Signs, Memories*, ed. Sallie Westwood and John Williams (London: Routledge, 1997), pp. 181–201; p. 193–4.
51. Paul Carter, *Repressed Spaces: The Poetics of Agoraphobia* (London: Reaktion, 2002), p. 31.
52. Walter Benjamin, 'On Some Motifs in Baudelaire' in *Selected Writings, vol. 4: 1938–1940*, ed. Howard Eiland and Michael W. Jennings (Cambridge, MA: Belknap/Harvard University Press, 2003), pp. 313–54; p. 339.
53. T. S. Eliot, *Collected Poems 1909–1962* (London: Faber, 1974), p. 200.
54. Ibid. pp. 192–3.
55. Virginia Woolf, *The Years*, ed. Jeri Johnson (Harmondsworth: Penguin, 1998), pp. 364–5.
56. Jean Rhys, *Smile Please: An Unfinished Autobiography* (London: Penguin, 1981), p. 98.
57. Jean Rhys, *Voyage in the Dark* (1934; Harmondsworth: Penguin, 1969), pp. 26, 151, 70. For a discussion of the spatial and geographical dimensions to Rhys' encounter with London see Andrew Thacker, *Moving Through Modernity: Space and Geography in Modernism* (Manchester: Manchester University Press, 2003), pp. 192–219, and Anna Snaith, *Modernist Voyages: Colonial Woman Writers in London, 1890–1945* (Cambridge: Cambridge University Press, 2014), pp. 133–51.
58. Jean Rhys, *After Leaving Mr Mackenzie* (Harmondsworth: Penguin, 1971), p. 101.
59. Ibid. p. 102.
60. Ibid. p. 103.
61. Carter, *Repressed Spaces*, p. 210. See also Marc Augé for the idea of non-places: 'The traveller's space may thus be the archetype of *non-place*'; Augé, *Non-Places: Introduction to an Anthropology of Supermodernity*, trans. John Howe (London: Verso, 1995), p. 86.
62. For an interesting analysis of the 1997 film adaptation of this novel, focusing upon this incident, see Charlotte Brunsdon, '"A Fine and Private Place": The Cinematic Spaces of the London Underground', *Screen* 47:1 (Spring 2006), pp. 1–7.
63. For a discussion of James as a 'topographical writer' see Robert Burden, *Travel, Modernism and Modernity* (London: Routledge, 2015), pp. 155–95.
64. Henry James, *English Hours* (London: Heinemann, 1905), p. 16.
65. Henry James, *The Wings of the Dove* (Harmondsworth: Penguin, 1986), p. 89.
66. Ibid. p. 90.
67. Ibid.
68. Ibid.
69. See Lawrence Menear, *London's Underground Stations: A Social and Architectural Study* (London: Midas, 1983), p. 21. The wooden leg, according to legend, came from being crushed between two Tube carriages. Wolmar, however, suggests that the story was apocryphal; see *Subterranean Railway*, p. 182.

70. See Ashford, *London Underground*, pp. 63–92, and Saler, *Avant-Garde in Interwar England*, pp. 92–147.
71. Quoted in Christian Barman, *The Man Who Built London Transport: A Biography of Frank Pick* (Newton Abbot: David and Charles, 1979), p. 118.
72. Saler, *Avant-Garde in Interwar England,* p. 28.
73. From Pick's 1927 lecture on the 'Growth and Form in Cities', cited in Barman, *Man Who Built London Transport*, p. 248. The image is also used by Sennett, *Flesh and Stone*, p. 334.
74. Lefebvre suggests that the city has an 'underground and repressed life, and hence an "unconscious" of its own'; see Henri Lefebvre, *The Production of Space*, trans. D. Nicholson-Smith (Oxford: Blackwell, 1991), p. 36
75. Rosalind Williams, *Notes on the Underground: An Essay on Technology, Society, and the Imagination* (Cambridge, MA: MIT Press, 1990), p. 4. And see Pike, *Subterranean Cities.*
76. For the idea of *Stimmung* (mood) see Jonathan Flatley, *Affective Mapping: Melancholia and the Politics of Modernism* (Cambridge, MA: Harvard University Press, 2008), pp. 19–24.
77. Porter, *London: A Social History*, p. 404, and see pp. 397–405.
78. See, inter alia, Lawrence Rainey, *Institutions of Modernism: Literary Elites and Public Culture* (New Haven: Yale University Press, 1998); John Xiros Cooper, *Modernism and the Culture of Market Society* (Cambridge: Cambridge University Press, 2004); Kevin J. H. Dettmar and Stephen Watt (eds), *Marketing Modernism: Self-Promotion, Canonization, and Rereading* (Ann Arbor: University of Michigan Press, 1996); and Joyce P. Wexler, *Who Paid for Modernism? Art, Money, and the Fiction of Conrad, Joyce, and Lawrence* (Fayetteville: University of Arkansas Press, 1997). For Bourdieu see Pierre Bourdieu, *The Field of Cultural Production: Essays on Art and Literature*, ed. Randal Johnson (Cambridge: Polity, 1993).
79. For one such attempt see Peter Brooker, *Bohemia in London: The Social Scene of Early Modernism* (Basingstoke: Palgrave Macmillan, 2004).
80. Amy Lowell, 'The Poetry Bookshop', *The Little Review* 2:3 (May 1915), pp. 19–22; p. 19.
81. Harold Monro, 'The Bookshop', *Poetry Review*,1:3 (Nov. 1912), pp. 498–500; pp. 500, 499.
82. For discussion of the Monro magazines see Dominic Hibberd, 'The New Poetry, Georgians and Others: *The Open Window* (1910–11), *The Poetry Review* (1912–15), *Poetry and Drama* (1913–14), and *New Numbers* (1914)', and Mark Morrisson, 'The Cause of Poetry: Thomas Moult and *Voices* (1919–21), Harold Monro and *The Monthly Chapbook* (1919–25)', both in *The Oxford Critical and Cultural History of Modernist Magazines, vol. 1: Britain and Ireland, 1880–1955*, ed. Peter Brooker and Andrew Thacker (Oxford: Oxford University Press, 2009), pp. 176–98 and 405–27; for Monro's bookshop see Joy Grant, *Harold Monro and the Poetry Bookshop* (London: Routledge and Kegan Paul, 1967), and Bartholomew Brinkman, '"A Place Known to the World as Devonshire Street": Modernism, Commercialism, and the Poetry Bookshop' in *The Rise of the Modernist Bookshop: Books and the Commerce of Culture in the Twentieth Century*, ed. Huw Osborne (Farnham: Ashgate, 2015), pp. 113–30.
83. Mulk Raj Anand, *Conversations in Bloomsbury* (Oxford: Oxford University Press, 1995), pp. 10–24; this book is discussed in the Introduction.
84. See Brooker, *Bohemia in London*, for an account of many of these groups.
85. On these magazines see Jean-Michel Rabaté, 'Gender and Modernism: *The Freewoman* (1912), *The New Freewoman* (1913), and *The Egoist* (1914–19)' in *Modernist Magazines, vol. 1*, pp. 269–89; for the wider context in which they

worked see Lucy Delap, *The Feminist Avant-Garde: Transatlantic Encounters of the Early Twentieth Century* (Cambridge: Cambridge University Press, 2007). Oakley House was also the site of the Blavatsky Institute, home of theosophy; see Helen Carr, *The Verse Revolutionaries: Ezra Pound, H.D., and the Imagists* (London: Jonathan Cape, 2009), p. 618.

86. Cited in Mark Antliff and Vivien Greene (eds), *The Vorticists: Manifesto for a Modern World* (London: Tate, 2010), pp. 21–2.
87. For a detailed reassessment of the Vorticists see Mark Antliff and Scott W. Klein (eds), *Vorticism: New Perspectives* (New York: Oxford University Press, 2013).
88. R.H.C [Alfred Orage], 'Readers and Writers', *New Age* 15:10 (9 July 1914), p. 229.
89. For an account see Laurel Brake, 'Aestheticism and Decadence: *The Yellow Book* (1894–7), *The Chameleon* (1894), and *The Savoy* (1896)' in *Modernist Magazines, vol. 1*, pp. 76–100.
90. See Paul O' Keefe, *Some Sort of Genius: A Life of Wyndham Lewis* (London: Pimlico, 2001), pp. 155–6.
91. See James G. Nelson, *The Early Nineties: A View from the Bodley Head* (Cambridge, MA: Harvard University Press, 1971).
92. Ezra Pound, 'Wyndham Lewis', *The Egoist* 1 (15 June 1914), p. 233.
93. They were later assisted by the poet Richard Le Galliene. For Mathews see James G. Nelson, *Elkin Mathews: Publisher to Yeats, Joyce, Pound* (Madison: University of Wisconsin Press, 1989).
94. Rhys cited in Nelson, *Early Nineties*, p. 12.
95. For an overview of how this affected periodical publication in the period see Andrew Thacker, 'Introduction: Fin de Siècle Ventures (1884–1905)' in *Modernist Magazines, vol. 1*, pp. 69–75.
96. Ricketts was at the centre of another London coterie of artists, associated with his residence in the Vale, Chelsea, which resulted in another 'little magazine', *The Dial* (1889–97). See J. G. P. Delaney, *Charles Ricketts: A Biography* (Oxford: Clarendon Press, 1990).
97. See Bourdieu, *Field of Cultural Production*, p. 75.
98. For more on Fleet Street and modernism see Patrick Collier, *Modernism on Fleet Street* (London: Ashgate, 2006).
99. See Karl Beckson, *London in the 1890s: A Cultural History* (New York: Norton, 1992), pp. 71–2; the description of the meetings as 'dull' is found in George Mills Harper and Karl Beckson, 'Victor Plarr on "The Rhymers' Club": An Unpublished Lecture', *English Literature in Transition, 1880–1920* 4 (2002), pp. 379–85; p. 380.
100. Beckson, *London in the 1890s*, p. 73.
101. Ernest Radford, 'Song in the Labour Movement' in *The Second Book of The Rhymers' Club* (London: Elkin Mathews and John Lane, 1894), p. 72.
102. Victor Plarr, 'The Rhymers' Club', *English Literature in Transition, 1880–1920* 45:4 (2002), pp. 379–85; p. 387. This is the text of a lecture given to the Poets' Club in 1910.
103. W. B. Yeats, 'The Rhymers' Club' (1892), cited in Nelson, *Early Nineties*, pp. 156–7.
104. John Stokes, *In the Nineties* (London: Harvester Wheatsheaf, 1989), p. 17 and ch.1 *passim*.
105. For details see Peter Keating, *The Haunted Study: A Social History of the English Novel 1875–1914* (London: Secker and Warburg, 1989), pp. 293–303; Philip Waller, *Writers, Readers, and Reputations: Literary Life in Britain 1870–1918* (Oxford: Oxford University Press, 2006), ch. 10.

106. Foster, *W. B. Yeats*, p. 108.
107. See Beckson, *London in the 1890s*, p. 78.
108. Plarr, 'Rhymers Club', p. 389.
109. Cited in Beckson, *London in the 1890s*, p. 78.
110. Bourdieu, *Field of Cultural Production*, p. 75.
111. John Davidson, 'New Year's Day' in *Fleet Street Eclogues* (London: John Lane, 1893), pp. 3–16; p. 3.
112. Ibid. p. 13.
113. From T. S. Eliot, preface to *John Davidson: A Selection of His Poems* (1961); cited in Eliot, *Inventions of the March Hare: Poems 1909–1917*, ed. Christopher Ricks (London: Faber, 1996), p. 398. The many other Rhymers' poems that took London as a subject matter may also have influenced Eliot.
114. James Longenbach, *Stone Cottage: Pound, Yeats, and Modernism* (New York: Oxford University Press, 1998), p. 170.
115. Arthur Symons, *Studies in Prose and Verse* (New York: E. P. Dutton, 1904), p. 3.
116. See Nelson, *Elkin Mathews*, pp. 72–111.
117. Ibid. pp. 25–7.
118. Scholes cited in ibid. p. 29.
119. Pound, prefatory note to 'The Complete Poetical Works of T. E. Hulme' in Pound, *Collected Shorter Poems* (London: Faber, 1984), p. 251. For more on the early history of Imagism see Carr, *Verse Revolutionaries*, pp. 134–51.
120. Plarr, 'Lecture', p. 386.
121. See Robert Ferguson, *The Short Sharp Life of T. E. Hulme* (London: Penguin/Allen Lane, 2002), p. 44.
122. Hulme, 'A Lecture on Modern Poetry' in his *Selected Writings*, ed. Patrick McGuinness (Manchester: Carcanet, 1998), pp. 61, 64.
123. Ibid. pp. 64, 66.
124. For a wider assessment of Hulme's influence on modernism see Andrzej Gasiorek and Edward P. Comentale (eds), *T. E. Hulme and the Question of Modernism* (Aldershot: Ashgate, 2006).
125. See Robert M. Crunden, *American Salons: Encounters with European Modernism 1885–1917* (New York: Oxford University Press, 1993), p. 208.
126. Cited in ibid. p. 201.
127. See Longenbach, *Stone Cottage*, pp. 11–13.
128. F. S. Flint, 'Book of the Week', *New Age* 4:16 (11 Feb. 1909), p. 327.
129. Hulme, 'Belated Romanticism', *New Age* 4:17 (18 Feb. 1909), p. 350.
130. See Carr, *Verse Revolutionaries*, p. 134.
131. See Brooker, *Bohemia in London*, pp. 123–31 for the role of the restaurant in these groups.
132. Ibid. pp. 114–23.
133. See Moody, *Ezra Pound*, pp. 68–73, for an account of Pound's difficult early months in London.
134. Joseph Conrad, *The Secret Agent* (Harmondsworth: Penguin, 1986). *The Secret Agent* was first published in book form in 1907, a year after serial publication in the American magazine *Ridgeways: A Militant Weekly for God and Country*; see http://www.conradfirst.net/conrad/home (last accessed 5 Nov. 2017).
135. Conrad, *Secret Agent,* p. 53.
136. For discussion of the urban topography of the novel see Robert Hampson, 'Spatial Stories' in *Geographies of Modernism: Literatures, Cultures, Spaces,* ed. Peter Brooker and Andrew Thacker (London: Routledge, 2005), pp. 54–64. The concept of cognitive mapping, popularised by Fredric Jameson, is originally

found in Kevin Lynch, *The Image of the City* (Cambridge, MA: MIT Press, 1960).
137. Conrad, *Secret Agent*, p. 41.
138. Ibid.
139. Ibid. pp. 141, 162, 239.
140. Ibid. p. 53.
141. Ibid. p. 84.
142. Ibid. pp. 103, 240.
143. Ibid. p. 150.
144. Ibid. p. 151.
145. James McLaughlin, *Writing the Urban Jungle: Reading Empire in London from Doyle to Eliot* (Charlottesville: University Press of Virginia, 2000), p. 23. My discussion of this incident owes much to McLaughlin's account.
146. Ibid. p. 24.
147. Cited in ibid. p. 136. And see John Eade, *Placing London: From Imperial Capital to Global City* (New York: Berghahn Books, 2000), pp. 49–64.
148. See Judith Walkowitz, *Nights Out: Life in Cosmopolitan London* (New Haven: Yale University Press, 2012). Much of the demonisation of London's East End in the late nineteenth century stemmed from the fact of its large immigrant populace, particularly Jews from Central Europe; see Porter, *London: A Social History*, p. 367.
149. Walkowitz, *Nights Out*, p. 22.
150. The establishment of an Italian community, for example, linked to the food industry had led to the formation in 1886, in Gerrard Street in Soho, of the Società Italiana Cuochi-Camerieri ('Italian Hotel and Restaurant Employees Benefit Society'), an organisation designed to support those working in the food trade and which by 1897 had some 450 members.
151. See Brooker, *Bohemia in London*, pp. 6–7.
152. See McLaughlin, *Writing the Urban Jungle*, p. 146.
153. Conrad, *Secret Agent*, p. 151.
154. McLaughlin, *Writing the Urban Jungle*, p. 148.
155. Conrad, *Secret Agent*, p. 151.
156. Ibid. p. 152.
157. Ibid.
158. Walkowitz, *Nights Out*, p. 40.
159. Snaith, *Modernist Voyages*, pp. 3–5. See also Peter J. Kalliney, *Commonwealth of Letters: British Literary Culture and Emergence of Postcolonial Aesthetics* (Oxford: Oxford University Press, 2013).
160. See Huw Osborne, 'Counter-Space in Charles Lahr's Progressive Bookshop' in *Rise of the Modernist Bookshop*, pp. 131–61; p. 135.
161. Bill Schwarz, 'Black Metropolis, White England' in *Modern Times*, ed. Mica Nava and Alan O'Shea (London: Routledge, 1996), pp. 176–207; p. 178.
162. Snaith, *Modernist Voyages*, p. 4.
163. John McLeod, *Postcolonial London: Rewriting the Metropolis* (London: Routledge, 2004), p. 27.
164. See Walkowitz, *Nights Out*, ch. 7.
165. Raymond Williams, *The Politics of Modernism: Against the New Conformists*, ed. Tony Pinkney (London: Verso, 1989), p. 78. For an overview of Black British writing and geography see James Proctor, *Dwelling Places: Postwar Black British Writing* (Manchester: Manchester University Press, 2003). On other West Indian intellectuals in Britain see Bill Schwartz (ed.), *West Indian Intellectuals in Britain* (Manchester: Manchester University Press, 2003). For a discussion of Selvon in

the context of modernism see J. Dillon Brown, *Migrant Modernism: Postwar London and the West Indian Novel* (Charlottesville: University of Virginia Press, 2013), pp. 103–32.
166. Sam Selvon, *The Lonely Londoners* (London: Penguin, 2006), p. 1.
167. A point made by Susheila Nasta in her introduction to the novel, ibid. p. vii.
168. See Peter Brooker, 'Early Modernism' in *The Cambridge Companion to The Modernist Novel*, ed. Morag Shiach (Cambridge: Cambridge University Press, 2007), pp. 32–47; pp. 37–8.
169. Williams, *Politics of Modernism*, p. 78.
170. At the centre of *Absolute Beginners* is a representation of a 'race riot' in Notting Hill in 1958.
171. Rhys, *After Leaving Mr Mackenzie*, p. 84.
172. Selvon, *Lonely Londoners*, p. 4.
173. Ibid. p. 5.
174. Ibid.
175. Ibid. p. 23.
176. Ibid.
177. Ibid. p. 24.
178. See Simmel, 'Metropolis and Mental Life'; Max Weber, 'The Nature of the City' in *Classic Essays on the Culture of Cities*, ed. Richard Sennett (Englewood Cliffs: Prentice Hall, 1969), pp. 23–46.
179. For an analysis of this sort in relation to Joyce see Desmond Harding, *Writing the City: Urban Visions and Literary Modernism* (London: Routledge, 2003), ch. 4.
180. Selvon, *Lonely Londoners*, p. 24.
181. Ibid.
182. Ibid. p. 25.
183. Ibid. p. 68.
184. Ibid. p. 69.
185. Ibid.
186. Ibid. p. 71.
187. Ibid. p. 71. In the 1960s many West Indians were recruited explicitly to work for London Transport, particularly from Barbados; see Wolmar, *Subterranean Railway*, p. 296. This is the background to a short story by Selvon, 'Working the Transport' in his *Ways of Sunlight* (Harlow: Longman, 1987), pp. 120–35; see the discussion in Ashford, *London Underground*, pp. 138–43.
188. Selvon, *Lonely Londoners*, p. 126.
189. Ibid. p. 79.
190. Charles Pick, quoted in Saler, *Avant-Garde in Interwar London*, p. 109.
191. Virginia Woolf, *The Waves* (London: Granada, 1977), p. 131.
192. David Bradshaw, '"Great Avenues of Civilization": The Victoria Embankment and Piccadilly Circus Underground Station in the Novels of Virginia Woolf and Chelsea Embankment in *Howards End*' in *Transits: The Nomadic Geographies of Anglo-American Modernism*, ed. Giovanni Cianci, Caroline Patey and Sara Sullam (Bern: Peter Lang, 2010), pp. 190–210; p. 203. And see Welsh, *Underground Writing*, pp. 178–87, for more on Woolf and the Tube.
193. Saler, *Avant-Garde in Interwar London*, p. 111.
194. Selvon, *Lonely Londoners*, p. 72.
195. Lefebvre, *Production of Space*, pp. 38–9.
196. Ibid. p. 42.
197. Selvon, *Lonely Londoners*, p. 79.
198. Peter Kalliney, *Cities of Affluence and Anger: A Literary Geography of Modern Englishness* (Charlottesville: University of Virginia Press, 2007), p. 107. For

Kalliney's comparative reading of *Lonely Londoners* and *Mrs Dalloway* see pp. 106–11.
199. See Michel de Certeau, *The Practice of Everyday Life*, trans. Steven Randall (Berkeley: University of California Press, 1984), pp. 117–18. For an explication of de Certeau's ideas here see Thacker, *Moving Through Modernity*, pp. 29–36.
200. Selvon, *Lonely Londoners*, p. 83.
201. Ibid. p. 101.
202. Ibid. p. 93.
203. Ibid. p. 101.
204. Ibid. pp. 133–4.
205. Benjamin, *Arcades Project*, p. 518.
206. Selvon, *Lonely Londoners*, p. 134.
207. James Joyce, *Ulysses*, ed. Jeri Johnson (Oxford: Oxford University Press, 1993), p. 156.
208. Ibid. p. 317.
209. Selvon, *Lonely Londoners*, p. 134.
210. Ibid. p. 138.
211. Ibid. p. 139.
212. Ibid.
213. Ibid.
214. De Certeau, *Practice of Everyday Life*, p. 115.

AFTERWORD: OTHER CITIES, OTHER MODERNISMS

The reader of this volume has moved from Paris, Vienna and Berlin to arrive finally in London. As noted in the Introduction, this has been partly to defamiliarise London for Anglophone readers, forcing them to see it firmly as a place in Europe and as a city connected to these other European capitals through networks of exchange, travel and influence. The book thus aims to demonstrate how these four cities can be considered as nodal points within a particular transnational region of the globalised world of modernism.[1] The stories of these cities demonstrate the importance of the physical restructuring of urban space and the creation of new cultural institutions for the formation of the particular modernisms found in this small region of the world. Hopefully the book indicates the reasons why these four cities exerted such an affective pull upon writers and artists from elsewhere, demonstrating the geographical emotions that attracted so many outsiders to Paris, Vienna, Berlin and London.

This book thus highlights the regional transnationalism informing modernism in these four major capitals. A different project might be to explore the cultural geography of uneven relations between what could be characterised as the major and minor cities of modernism, between, for instance, the first and second cities in a particular nation-state (London and Birmingham, Paris and Marseilles).[2] Another approach would be to explore the transnational relationships between what some characterise as the peripheral cities of European modernism, some of which are national capitals and some of which are not, such as the links between Futurism in Milan and Futurism in Lisbon, for example.[3] The explanations for the uneven relationships between cities are complex yet fascinating avenues to explore in the future.

This book argues that at the forefront of such projects would be the primacy of affect as experienced by outsiders in these multiple cities, expanding our understanding of what I call here a study of the geographical emotions of modernism. Another way in which work on spatial affect in modernism could be extended would be temporally. How outsiders are affected by cities, and how they represent these experiences in styles that we can label modernist, is, arguably, a feature of much writing after 1945. As Chapter 4 demonstrates in the discussion of Sam Selvon's *Lonely Londoners*, many texts of postcolonial urban writing bear the markings of earlier forms of modernism. This is also true, to take one example, of a much more contemporary postcolonial text, Teju Cole's novel of 2011, *Open City*.[4] Cole's novel traces the travels of Julius, a young Nigerian doctor, in two cities, New York and Brussels, and at the forefront of his experiences as an outsider in these places are familiar, yet also new, kinds of geographical emotion and explorations into the transnational spaces of modernism. Julius is another version of the Parisian *flâneur*, whose 'aimless wandering' through New York City takes him into areas where he ruminates upon both the spatial history of particular locations and his own affects and emotions in these places.[5] He starts to understand the different neighbourhoods of the city as 'made of a different substance, each seemed to have a different air pressure, a different psychic weight', and, to take one small example, his depiction of the subway recalls many earlier literary representations of this crucial modern experience:

> The sight of large masses of people hurrying down into underground chambers was perpetually strange to me, and I felt that all of the human race were rushing, pushed by a counterinstinctive death drive, into movable catacombs. Above-ground I was with thousands of others in their solitude, but in the subway, standing close to strangers, jostling them and being jostled by them for space and breathing room, all of us re-enacting unacknowledged traumas, the solitude intensified.[6]

The intense geographical emotions here, of restless movement, the feelings of solitude, trauma and strangeness, allied to the trope of the subway as a place of death, recall many of the early phobic representations of the Tube in London discussed in Chapter 4.

Cole's text might be viewed, therefore, as a modernism of the now. Many of the issues raised in this book about how outsiders view cities, and about how central aspects of modernism were shaped by affective encounters with urban space, also point forwards to our present age. Indeed, ongoing work in modernist studies that extends and expands our understanding of the where and when of modernism suggests that this topic of modernism, space and the city remains of enduring interest and continuing relevance.[7] If we look at one of the most influential of critics writing on urban modernism in the 1980s, Marshall Berman, we see that his vision of an urban culture shaped by modernism and modernity is one that he projects very much into the future:

> It may turn out, then, that going back can be a way to go forward: that remembering the modernisms of the nineteenth century can give us the vision and courage to create the modernisms of the twenty-first. This act of remembering can help us bring modernism back to its roots, so that it can flourish and renew itself, to confront the adventures and dangers that lie ahead. To appropriate the modernities of yesterday can be at once a critique of the modernities of today and an act of faith in the modernities – and in the modern men and women – of tomorrow and the day after tomorrow.[8]

It should be clear by now that Berman's ideas permeate much of my own thinking on what he called 'modernism in the streets',[9] from reflecting upon my own upbringing in that second city of British modernity, Birmingham, to the four metropolitan cities discussed in this volume, and onto new forms of modernisms. Perhaps the key message I take from Berman, and what I hope this book demonstrates, is that the complex feelings that attend being in modern cities, whether as an insider or outsider, are fundamental to the geographical emotions that inform and shape the multiple productions of modernism, whether of yesterday, today or tomorrow.

Notes

1. On modernism as a global phenomenon see, inter alia, Mark Wollaeger and Matthew Eatough (eds), *The Oxford Handbook of Global Modernisms* (New York: Oxford University Press, 2012), and Susan Stanford Friedman, *Planetary Modernisms: Provocations on Modernity Across Time* (New York: Columbia University Press, 2015).
2. See Jason Finch, Lieven Ameel and Markku Salmela (eds), *Literary Second Cities* (Basingstoke: Palgrave, 2017).
3. For the concept of a 'peripheral modernism' see Benita Parry, 'Aspects of Peripheral Modernism', *Ariel* 40:1 (2009), pp. 27–55.
4. Teju Cole, *Open City* (New York: Random House, 2011).
5. Ibid. p. 3.
6. Ibid. p. 7.
7. See, for example, David James, *Modernist Futures: Innovation and Inheritance in the Contemporary Novel* (Cambridge: Cambridge University Press, 2012).
8. Marshall Berman, *All that is Solid Melts into Air: The Experience of Modernity* (London: Verso, 1982), p. 36.
9. The title of Berman's final book, *Modernism in the Streets: A Life and Times in Essays* (London: Verso, 2017).

BIBLIOGRAPHY

Allen, Sharon Lubkemann, *EccentriCities: Writing in the Margins of Modernism, St. Petersburg to Rio de Janeiro* (Manchester: Manchester University Press, 2013).

Anand, Mulk Raj, *Conversations in Bloomsbury* (Oxford: Oxford University Press, 1995).

Angier, Carole, *Jean Rhys: Life and Work* (Harmondsworth: Penguin, 1992).

[Anon.], *Country Homes: The Official Guide of the Metropolitan Railway Comprising Residential Districts of Buck, Herts. and Middlesex* (London: Metropolitan Railways, 1909).

——, *Metro-Land: A Comprehensive Description of the Country Districts Served By the Metropolitan Railway* (London: Metropolitan Railways, 1924).

——, *Metro-Land: British Empire Exhibition Number* (1924; London: Southbank, 2004).

——, *A Selection of Country Walks in Middlesex, Hertfordshire and Buckinghamshire* (London: Metropolitan Railways, 1910).

Antliff, Mark and Vivien Greene (eds), *The Vorticists: Manifesto for a Modern World* (London: Tate, 2010).

Antliff, Mark and Scott W. Klein (eds), *Vorticism: New Perspectives* (New York: Oxford University Press, 2013).

Apollinaire, Guillaume, *Apollinaire on Art: Essays and Reviews, 1902–1918*, ed. Leroy C. Brenig, trans. Susan Suleiman (New York: Viking Press, 1972).

——, *Calligrammes* (Paris: Gallimard, 1966).
——, *Selected Poems*, trans. Martin Sorrell (Oxford: Oxford University Press, 2015).
Ardoin, Paul, S. E. Gontarski and Laci Mattison (eds), *Understanding Bergson, Understanding Modernism* (London: Bloomsbury, 2013).
Armstrong, David, 'Reclaiming the Left Bank: Jean Rhys's "Topography" in *The Left Bank* and *Quartet*' in *Rhys Matters: New Critical Perspectives*, ed. Mary Wilson and Kerry L. Johnson (New York: Palgrave Macmillan, 2013), pp. 169–85.
Armstrong, Tim, *Modernism, Technology and the Body: A Cultural Study* (Cambridge: Cambridge University Press, 1998).
Ashford, David, *London Underground: A Cultural Geography* (Liverpool: Liverpool University Press, 2013).
Attridge, Derek, 'Once More with Feeling: Art, Affect and Performance', *Textual Practice* 25:2 (2011), pp. 329–43.
Auden, W. H., *Collected Poems*, ed. Edward Mendelson (London: Faber, 1991).
Auden, W. H. and Christopher Isherwood, *The Ascent of F6: A Tragedy in Two Acts* (London: Faber, 1936).
Augé, Marc, *Non-Places: Introduction to an Anthropology of Supermodernity*, trans. John Howe (London: Verso, 1995).
Bachelard, Gaston, *The Poetics of Space*, trans. Maria Jolas (Boston, MA: Beacon Press, 1969).
Baedeker, Karl, *Paris et ses environs: Manuel du voyageur* (Leipzig: Baedeker, 1924).
Barman, Christian, *The Man Who Built London Transport: A Biography of Frank Pick* (Newton Abbot: David and Charles, 1979).
Barnes, Julian, *Metroland* (London: Jonathan Cape, 1980).
Beach, Sylvia: Papers, Firestone Library, Princeton University, Princeton.
Beachy, Robert, *Gay Berlin: Birthplace of a Modern Identity* (New York: Vintage, 2015).
Beasley, Rebecca, *Theorists of Modernist Poetry: T. S. Eliot, T. E. Hulme, Ezra Pound* (London: Routledge, 2007).
Beaumont, Matthew and Michael Freeman (eds), *Railways and Modernity: Time, Space, and the Machine Ensemble* (Bern: Peter Lang, 2007).
Beckson, Karl, *London in the 1890s: A Cultural History* (New York: Norton, 1992).
Beller, Steven, *Vienna and the Jews 1867–1938: A Cultural History* (Cambridge: Cambridge University Press, 1989).
Bely, Andrei, *Petersburg: A Novel in Eight Chapters*, trans. David McDuff (London: Penguin, 2011).
Benjamin, Walter, *The Arcades Project*, trans. Howard Eiland and Kevin

McLaughlin (Cambridge, MA: Belknap/Harvard University Press, 1999).
——, 'A Berlin Chronicle' in *Reflections: Essays, Aphorisms, Autobiographical Writings*, trans. Edmund Jephcott, ed. Peter Demetz (New York: Schocken Books, 1986), pp. 3–60.
——, *Illuminations*, ed. Hannah Arendt (London: Fontana, 1973).
——, 'On Some Motifs in Baudelaire' in *Selected Writings, vol. 4: 1938–1940*, ed. Howard Eiland and Michael W. Jennings (Cambridge, MA: Belknap/Harvard University Press, 2003), pp. 313–54.
Bennett, Gwendolyn, 'Tokens' in *Ebony and Topaz: A Collectanea*, ed. Charles S. Johnson (Manchester, NH: Ayer, 1927), pp. 149–50.
——, 'Wedding Day, A Story', *Fire!!* 1 (1926), pp. 25–8.
Benstock, Shari, *Women of the Left Bank: Paris, 1900–1940* (London: Virago, 1987).
Berkley, George E., *Vienna and Its Jews: The Tragedy of Success 1880s–1980s* (Cambridge, MA: Madison Books, 1988).
Berman, Jessica, *Modernist Commitments: Ethics, Politics, and Transnational Modernism* (New York: Columbia University Press, 2011).
Berman, Marshall, *All that Is Solid Melts into Air: The Experience of Modernity* (London: Verso, 1982).
——, *Modernism in the Streets: A Life and Times in Essays* (London: Verso, 2017).
Binckes, Faith, *Modernism, Magazines, and the British Avant-Garde: Reading Rhythm* (Oxford: Oxford University Press, 2010).
Blau, Eve, *The Architecture of Red Vienna 1919–1934* (Cambridge, MA: MIT Press, 1999).
Bluemel, Kristin (ed.), *Intermodernism: Literary Culture in Mid-Twentieth Century Britain* (Edinburgh: Edinburgh University Press, 2009).
Boes, Tobias, 'Germany' in *The Cambridge Companion to European Modernism*, ed. Pericles Lewis (Cambridge: Cambridge University Press, 2011), pp. 33–51.
Bohn, Willard, *Apollinaire and the International Avant-Garde* (Albany, NY: SUNY Press, 1997).
——, 'Apollinaire and "the New Spirit": *Le festin d'Esope* (1903); *Les Soirées de Paris* (1912–14); and *L'élan* (1915–16)' in *The Oxford Critical and Cultural History of Modernist Magazines, vol. 3: Europe 1880–1940*, ed. Peter Brooker, Sascha Bru, Andrew Thacker and Christian Weikop (Oxford: Oxford University Press, 2013), pp. 120–42.
Boldt, Paul, 'Auf der Terrasse des Café Josty' ['On the Terrace of Café Josty'], *Die Aktion* 2 (13 Nov. 1912), p. 46.
Bondi, Liz, Joyce Davidson and Mick Smith, 'Introduction: Geography's "Emotional Turn"' in *Emotional Geographies*, ed. Joyce Davidson,

Liz Bondi and Mick Smith (Farnham: Ashgate, 2005), pp. 1–18.

Bourdieu, Pierre, *The Field of Cultural Production: Essays on Art and Literature*, ed. Randal Johnson (Cambridge: Polity, 1993).

Bowlby, Rachel, '"The Impasse": Jean Rhys's *Good Morning, Midnight*' in *Still Crazy After All These Years: Women, Writing and Psychoanalysis* (London: Routledge, 1992), pp. 34–58.

Bowles, Paul, 'Interview', *The Paris Review*, 67 (Fall 1981), pp. 39–66.

Bradbury, Malcolm (ed.), *The Atlas of Literature* (London: De Agostini, 1996).

Bradbury, Malcolm and Alan McFarlane (eds), *Modernism 1890–1930* (Harmondsworth: Penguin, 1976).

Bradshaw, David, '"Great Avenues of Civilization": The Victoria Embankment and Piccadilly Circus Underground Station in the Novels of Virginia Woolf and Chelsea Embankment in *Howards End*' in *Transits: The Nomadic Geographies of Anglo-American Modernism*, ed. Giovanni Cianci, Caroline Patey and Sara Sullam (Bern: Peter Lang, 2010), pp. 190–210.

Brake, Laurel, 'Aestheticism and Decadence: *The Yellow Book* (1894–7), *The Chameleon* (1894), and *The Savoy* (1896)' in *The Oxford Critical and Cultural History of Modernist Magazines, vol. 1: Britain and Ireland, 1880–1955*, ed. Peter Brooker and Andrew Thacker (Oxford: Oxford University Press, 2009), pp. 76–100.

Brandstätter, Christian (ed.), *Vienna 1900 and the Heroes of Modernism* (London: Thames and Hudson, 2005).

Breton, André, *Nadja*, trans. Richard Howard (London: Penguin, 1999).

Bridgwater, Patrick (ed.), *The Poets of the Café des Westens* (Leicester: Leicester University Press, 1984).

Briggs, Julia, 'Hope Mirrlees and Continental Modernism' in *Gender in Modernism: New Geographies, Complex Intersections*, ed. Bonnie Kime Scott (Urbana and Chicago: University of Illinois Press, 2007), pp. 261–303.

——, '"Modernism's Lost Hope": Virginia Woolf, Hope Mirrlees and the Printing of Paris' in *Reading Virginia Woolf* (Edinburgh: Edinburgh University Press, 2006), pp. 80–95.

——, *Virginia Woolf: An Inner Life* (London: Penguin, 2006).

Brinkman, Bartholomew, '"A Place Known to the World as Devonshire Street": Modernism, Commercialism, and the Poetry Bookshop' in *The Rise of the Modernist Bookshop: Books and the Commerce of Culture in the Twentieth Century*, ed. Huw Osborne (Farnham: Ashgate, 2015), pp. 113–30.

Britzolakis, Christina, '"This Way to the Exhibition": Genealogies of Urban

Spectacle in Jean Rhys's Interwar Fiction', *Textual Practice* 21:3 (2007), pp. 457–82.

Brooke, Rupert, 'The Old Vicarage, Grantchester' in *Georgian Poetry, 1911–12* (London: Poetry Bookshop, 1912), pp. 33–7.

Brooker, Peter, *Bohemia in London: The Social Scene of Early Modernism* (Basingstoke: Palgrave Macmillan, 2004).

——, 'Early Modernism' in *The Cambridge Companion to The Modernist Novel*, ed. Morag Shiach (Cambridge: Cambridge University Press, 2007), pp. 32–47.

——, *New York Fictions: Modernity, Postmodernism, The New Modern* (London: Longman, 1996).

Brooker, Peter, Sascha Bru, Andrew Thacker, and Christian Weikop (eds), *The Oxford Critical and Cultural History of Modernist Magazines, vol. 3: Europe 1880–1940* (Oxford: Oxford University Press, 2013).

Brooker, Peter, Andrzej Gasiorek, Deborah Longworth, and Andrew Thacker (eds), *The Oxford Handbook of Modernisms* (Oxford: Oxford University Press, 2010).

Brooker, Peter and Andrew Thacker (eds), *Geographies of Modernism: Literatures, Cultures, Spaces* (London: Routledge, 2005).

—— (eds), *The Oxford Critical and Cultural History of Modernist Magazines, vol. 1: Britain and Ireland, 1880–1955* (Oxford: Oxford University Press, 2009).

—— (eds), *The Oxford Critical and Cultural History of Modernist Magazines, vol. 2: North America, 1894–1960* (Oxford: Oxford University Press, 2012).

Broom: An International Magazine of the Arts Published by Americans in Italy, vols 1–6, Nov. 1921–Jan. 1924.

Brown, J. Dillon, *Migrant Modernism: Postwar London and the West Indian Novel* (Charlottesville: University of Virginia Press, 2013).

Brown III, Ralph W., 'Making the Third Man Look Pale: American–Soviet Conflict in Vienna during the Early Cold War in Austria, 1945–1950', *The Journal of Slavic Military Studies* 14:4 (2001), pp. 81–109.

Brunsdon, Charlotte, '"A Fine and Private Place": The Cinematic Spaces of the London Underground', *Screen* 47:1 (Spring 2006), pp. 1–7.

Bryher, *The Days of Mars: A Memoir* (London: Calder and Boyars, 1972).

——, *The Heart to Artemis: A Writer's Memoirs* (London: Collins, 1962).

——, 'Paris 1900', *Life and Letters Today* 16:8 (Summer 1937), pp. 33–4.

——, *Two Novels*, ed. Joanne Winning (Madison: University of Wisconsin Press, 2000).

Bulson, Eric, 'Milan, the "Rivista", and the Deprovincialization of Italy: *Le Papyrus* (1894–6); *Poesia* (1905–9); *Il Convegno* (1920–40); *Pan* (1933–5); and *Corrente di vita giornale* (1938–40)' in *The Oxford Critical and*

Cultural History of Modernist Magazines, vol. 3: Europe 1880–1940, ed. Peter Brooker, Sascha Bru, Andrew Thacker and Christian Weikop (Oxford: Oxford University Press, 2013), pp. 511–35.

——, *Novels, Maps, Modernity: The Spatial Imaginary, 1850–2000* (New York: Routledge, 2007).

Burden, Robert, *Travel, Modernism and Modernity* (London: Routledge, 2015).

Bury, Stephen, '"Not to Adorn Life but to Organize It": *Veshch. Gegenstand. Objet: Revue internationale de l'art moderne* (1922) and *G* (1923–6)' in *The Oxford Critical and Cultural History of Modernist Magazines, vol. 3: Europe 1880–1940*, ed. Peter Brooker, Sascha Bru, Andrew Thacker and Christian Weikop (Oxford: Oxford University Press, 2013), pp. 855–67.

Butler, Christopher, *Early Modernism: Literature, Music, and Painting in Europe 1900–1916* (Oxford: Oxford University Press, 1994).

Callard, Felicity and Constantina Papoulias, 'Affect and Embodiment' in *Memory: Histories, Theories, Debates*, ed. Susannah Radstone and Bill Schwarz (New York: Fordham University Press, 2010), pp. 246–62.

Camboni, Maria, '"Why, Berlin, Must I Love You So?": Bryher in Berlin, 1927–1932', *HD's Web e-newsletter* (Winter 2008); available at http://www.imagists.org/hd/hdsweb/december2008.pdf (last accessed 5 Nov. 2017).

Carey, John, *The Intellectuals and the Masses: Pride and Prejudice among the Literary Intelligentsia, 1880–1939* (London: Faber, 1992).

Carpenter, Humphrey, *W. H. Auden: A Biography* (London: Faber, 2010).

Carr, Helen, *The Verse Revolutionaries: Ezra Pound, H.D., and the Imagists* (London: Jonathan Cape, 2009).

Carter, Ian, *Railways and Culture in Britain: The Epitome of Modernity* (Manchester: Manchester University Press, 2001).

Carter, Paul, *Repressed Spaces: The Poetics of Agoraphobia* (London: Reaktion, 2002).

Casanova, Pascale, *The World Republic of Letters*, trans. M. B. DeBevoise (Cambridge, MA: Harvard University Press, 2004).

Casey, Edward S., *The Fate of Place: A Philosophical History* (Berkeley: University of California Press, 1997).

Cendrars, Blaise, *Selected Writings*, ed. Walter Albert (New York: New Directions, 1966).

Childs, Donald J., *From Philosophy to Poetry: T. S. Eliot's Study of Knowledge and Experience* (London: Athlone Press, 2001).

Clough, Patricia Ticineto with Jean Halley (eds), *The Affective Turn: Theorizing the Social* (Durham, NC: Duke University Press, 2007).

Cole, Teju, *Open City* (New York: Random House, 2011).

Collier, Patrick, *Modernism on Fleet Street* (London: Ashgate, 2006).

Conrad, Joseph, *The Secret Agent* (1907; Harmondsworth: Penguin, 1986).
Conrad, Peter, *Modern Times, Modern Places: Life and Art in the 20th Century* (London: Thames and Hudson, 1998).
Cooper, John Xiros, *Modernism and the Culture of Market Society* (Cambridge: Cambridge University Press, 2004).
Cowley, Malcolm, *Exile's Return: A Literary Odyssey of the 1920s*, ed. Donald W. Faulkner (London: Penguin, 1994).
Crary, Jonathan, *Suspensions of Perception: Attention, Spectacle and Modern Culture* (Boston, MA: MIT Press, 2000).
Crunden, Robert M., *American Salons: Encounters with European Modernism 1885–1917* (New York: Oxford University Press, 1993).
Davenport-Hines, Richard, *Auden* (London: Heinemann, 1995).
David-Fox, Katherine, 'Prague-Vienna, Prague-Berlin: The Hidden Geography of Czech Modernism', *Slavic Review* 59 (2000), pp. 735–60.
Davidson, John, 'New Year's Day' in *Fleet Street Eclogues* (London: John Lane, 1893), pp. 3–16.
De Certeau, Michel, *The Practice of Everyday Life*, trans. Steven Randall (Berkeley: University of California Press, 1984).
Deer, Patrick, 'Two Cities: Berlin and New York' in *W. H. Auden in Context*, ed. Tony Sharpe (Cambridge: Cambridge University Press, 2013), pp. 24–34.
Delaney, J. G. P., *Charles Ricketts: A Biography* (Oxford: Clarendon Press, 1990).
Delap, Lucy, *The Feminist Avant-Garde: Transatlantic Encounters of the Early Twentieth Century* (Cambridge: Cambridge University Press, 2007).
Deleuze, Gilles and Félix Guattari, *What is Philosophy?*, trans. Graham Burchell and Hugh Tomlinson (London: Verso, 1994).
Dell, Simon, 'After Apollinaire: *SIC* (1916–19); *Nord-Sud* (1917–18); and *L'Esprit Nouveau* (1920–5)' in *The Oxford Critical and Cultural History of Modernist Magazines, vol. 3: Europe 1880–1940*, ed. Peter Brooker, Sascha Bru, Andrew Thacker and Christian Weikop (Oxford: Oxford University Press, 2013), pp. 143–59.
Dettmar, Kevin J. H. and Stephen Watt (eds), *Marketing Modernism: Self-Promotion, Canonization, and Rereading* (Ann Arbor: University of Michigan Press, 1996).
Döblin, Alfred, *Berlin Alexanderplatz*, trans. Eugene Jolas (London: Continuum, 2004).
Donald, James, 'This, Here, Now: Imagining the Modern City' in *Imagining Cities: Scripts, Signs, Memories*, ed. Sallie Westwood and John Williams (London: Routledge, 1997), pp. 181–201.
Donald, James, Anne Friedberg and Laura Marcus (eds), *Close Up 1927–1933: Cinema and Modernism* (London: Cassell, 1998).

Douglas, Ann, *Terrible Honesty: Mongrel Manhattan in the 1920s* (New York: Farrar, Straus, and Giroux, 1995).
Downie, David, *Paris, Paris: Journey into the City of Light* (New York: Broadway, 2011).
Doyle, Laura, 'Toward a Philosophy of Transnationalism', *Journal of Transnational American Studies* 1:1 (2009); available at http://escholarship.org/uc/item/9vr1k8hk (last accessed 30 Oct. 2017).
Doyle, Laura and Laura Winkiel (eds), *Geomodernisms: Race, Modernism, Modernity* (Bloomington: Indiana University Press, 2005).
Drazin, Charles, *In Search of The Third Man* (London: Methuen, 2000).
Duffy, Enda, *The Speed Handbook: Velocity, Pleasure, Modernism* (Durham, NC: Duke University Press, 2009).
Eade, John, *Placing London: From Imperial Capital to Global City* (New York: Berghahn Books, 2000).
Eagleton, Terry, *Exiles and Émigrés: Studies in Modern Literature* (London: Chatto and Windus, 1970).
Edwards, Brent Hayes, *The Practice of Diaspora: Literature, Translation, and the Rise of Black Internationalism* (Cambridge, MA: Harvard University Press, 2003).
Ehrenburg, Ilya, 'Vitrion', *Broom* 3:2 (Sep. 1922), pp. 83–95.
Eliot, T. S., *Collected Poems 1909–1962* (London: Faber, 1974).
——, 'A Cooking Egg', *Coterie* 1 (May-Dec. 1919), p. 45.
——, *To Criticize the Critic and Other Writings* (London: Faber, 1965).
——, *Inventions of the March Hare: Poems 1909–1917*, ed. Christopher Ricks (London: Faber, 1996).
——, *The Sacred Wood: Essays on Poetry and Criticism* (London: Methuen, 1960).
——, *Selected Prose*, ed. Frank Kermode (London: Faber, 1975).
Elkin, Lauren, *Flâneuse: Women Walk the City in Paris, New York, Tokyo, Venice and London* (London: Vintage, 2017).
Ellis, Markman, *The Coffee House: A Cultural History* (London: Weidenfeld and Nicolson, 2004).
Fabre, Michel, *Black American Writers in France, 1840–1980* (Urbana: University of Illinois Press, 1991).
Feigel, Lara, 'Buggery and Montage: Birmingham and Bloomsbury in the 1930s' in *Woolfian Boundaries*, ed. Anna Burrells, Steve Ellis, Deborah Parsons and Kathryn Simpson (Clemson, SC: Clemson University Digital Press, 2007), pp. 51–7.
——, *The Love-Charm of Bombs: Restless Lives in the Second World War* (London: Bloomsbury, 2013).
Felski, Rita, *The Limits of Critique* (Chicago: Chicago University Press, 2015).
Felski, Rita and Susan Fraiman, 'Introduction' to Special Issue of *New Literary*

History on Mood, *New Literary History* 43:3 (Summer 2012), pp. v–xii.
Ferguson, Robert, *The Short Sharp Life of T. E. Hulme* (London: Penguin/ Allen Lane, 2002).
Finch, Jason, Lieven Ameel, and Markku Salmela (eds), *Literary Second Cities* (Basingstoke: Palgrave, 2017).
Fitch, Noel Riley, *Sylvia Beach and the Lost Generation: A History of Literary Paris in the Twenties and Thirties* (London: Norton, 1985).
Fitzgerald, F. Scott, *The Collected Short Stories* (London: Penguin, 1986).
Flanner, Janet, *Paris was Yesterday, 1925–1939* (London: Virago, 2003).
Flatley, Jonathan, *Affective Mapping: Melancholia and the Politics of Modernism* (Cambridge, MA: Harvard University Press, 2008).
Flint, F. S., 'Book of the Week', *New Age* 4:16 (11 Feb. 1909), p. 327.
Ford, Madox Ford, 'On Impressionism', *Poetry and Drama* 6 (June 1914), pp. 167–75, and *Poetry and Drama* 8 (Dec. 1914), pp. 323–34.
——, *The Soul of London*, ed. Alan G. Hill (London: Everyman, 1995).
Forgacs, Eva and Tyrus Miller, 'The Avant-Garde in Budapest and in Exile in Vienna: *A Tett* (1915–16); *Ma* (Budapest 1916–19, Vienna 1920–5); *Egység* (1922–4); *Akaszott Ember* (1922); *2×2* (1922); *Ék* (1923–4); *Is* (1924); *365* (1925); *Dokumentum* (1926–7); and *Munka* (1928–39)' in *The Oxford Critical and Cultural History of Modernist Magazines, vol. 3: Europe 1880–1940*, ed. Peter Brooker, Sascha Bru, Andrew Thacker and Christian Weikop (Oxford: Oxford University Press, 2013), pp. 1136–41.
Forster, E. M., *Howards End* (1910; Harmondsworth: Penguin, 1983).
Foster, Roy, *W. B. Yeats: A Life, vol. 1: The Apprentice Mage* (Oxford: Oxford University Press, 1998).
Foucault, Michel, *Discipline and Punish: The Birth of the Prison*, trans. Alan Sheridan (Harmondsworth: Penguin, 1977).
——, 'Of Other Spaces', *Diacritics* 16:1 (1986), pp. 22–7.
Freud, Sigmund, 'Analysis of a Phobia in a Five-Year-Old Boy ("Little Hans")' in *Case Histories I*, Penguin Freud Library, vol. 8 (Harmondsworth: Penguin, 1990), pp. 167–305.
Friedman, Susan Stanford (ed.), *Analyzing Freud: Letters of H.D., Bryher, and their Circle* (New York: New Directions, 2002).
——, *Mappings: Feminism and the Cultural Geographies of Encounter* (Princeton: Princeton University Press, 1998).
——, *Planetary Modernisms: Provocations on Modernity Across Time* (New York: Columbia University Press, 2015).
Friedrich, Otto, *Before the Deluge: A Portrait of Berlin in the 1920s* (New York: HarperCollins, 1995).
Frisby, David, *Fragments of Modernity: Theories of Modernity in the*

Theories of Simmel, Kracauer, and Benjamin (Cambridge: Polity, 1986).

Gasiorek, Andrzej and Edward P. Comentale (eds), *T. E. Hulme and the Question of Modernism* (Aldershot: Ashgate, 2006).

Gay, Peter, *Freud: A Life for Our Time* (London: Papermac, 1995).

——, *Weimar Culture: The Outsider as Insider* (Harmondsworth: Penguin, 1968).

Geddes, Patrick, *Cities in Evolution: An Introduction to the Town Planning Movement and to the Study of Civics* (London: Williams and Norgate, 1915).

Gillies, Mary Ann, 'Bergsonism' in *A Concise Companion to Modernism*, ed. David Bradshaw (Oxford: Blackwell, 2003), pp. 95–115.

——, *British Modernism and Bergson* (Montreal and Kingston: McGill-Queen's University Press, 1996).

GoGwilt, Christopher, *The Fiction of Geopolitics: Afterimages of Culture from Wilkie Collins to Alfred Hitchcock* (Stanford: Stanford University Press, 2000).

——, 'The Interior: Benjaminian Arcades, Conradian Passages, and the "Impasse" of Jean Rhys' in *Geographies of Modernism: Literatures, Cultures, Spaces*, ed. Peter Brooker and Andrew Thacker (London: Routledge, 2005), pp. 65–75.

——, *The Passage of Literature: Genealogies of Modernism in Conrad, Rhys, and Pramoedya* (Oxford: Oxford University Press, 2010).

Gordon, Lyndall, 'Eliot and Women' in *T. S. Eliot: The Modernist in History*, ed. Ron Bush (Cambridge: Cambridge University Press, 1991), pp. 9–22.

Grant, Joy, *Harold Monro and the Poetry Bookshop* (London: Routledge and Kegan Paul, 1967).

Greene, Graham, *The Third Man and The Fallen Idol* (1950; London: Vintage, 2001).

Gregg, Melissa and Gregory J. Seigworth (eds), *The Affect Theory Reader* (Durham, NC: Duke University Press, 2010).

Grierson, John, 'First Principles of Documentary' in *The European Cinema Reader*, ed. Catherine Fowler (London: Routledge, 2002), pp. 39–44.

Gronberg, Tag, *Designs on Modernity: Exhibiting the City in 1920s Paris* (Manchester: Manchester University Press, 1998).

Grossberg, Lawrence, 'Affect's Future: Rediscovering the Virtual in the Actual' in *The Affect Theory Reader*, ed. Melissa Gregg and Gregory J. Seigworth (Durham, NC: Duke University Press, 2010), pp. 309–38.

Gruber, Helmut, *Red Vienna: Experiments in Working-Class Culture 1919–1934* (New York: Oxford University Press, 1991).

Guignon, Charles, 'Moods in Heidegger's *Being and Time*' in *What is an Emotion? Classic Readings in Philosophical Psychology*, ed. Cheshire

Calhoun and Robert C. Solomon (New York: Oxford University Press, 1984), pp. 230–43.

Hall, Peter, *Cities in Civilization: Culture, Innovation, and Urban Order* (London: Weidenfeld and Nicolson, 1998).

Hampson, Robert, 'Spatial Stories' in *Geographies of Modernism: Literatures, Cultures, Spaces*, ed. Peter Brooker and Andrew Thacker (London: Routledge, 2005), pp. 54–64.

Hansen, Arlen J., *Expatriate Paris: A Cultural and Literary Guide to Paris of the 1920s* (New York: Arcade, 1990).

Harding, Desmond, *Writing the City: Urban Visions and Literary Modernism* (London: Routledge, 2003).

Hargrove, Nancy Duvall, *T. S. Eliot's Parisian Year* (Gainesville: University Press of Florida, 2009).

Harper, George Mills and Karl Beckson, 'Victor Plarr on "The Rhymers' Club": An Unpublished Lecture', *English Literature in Transition, 1880–1920* 4 (2002), pp. 379–85.

Harvey, David, *The Condition of Postmodernity* (Oxford: Blackwell, 1989).

——, *Paris, Capital of Modernity* (London: Routledge, 2003).

——, *The Urban Experience* (Oxford: Blackwell, 1989).

Heaney, Seamus, *North* (London: Faber, 1975).

Hegglund, Jon, *World Views: Metageographies of Modernist Fiction* (New York: Oxford University Press, 2012).

Heidegger, Martin, *Being and Time*, trans. John Macquarrie and Edward Robinson (Oxford: Blackwell, 1962).

——, 'Building, Dwelling, Thinking' in *Poetry, Language, Thought*, trans. Albert Hofstadter (New York: New Directions, 1971), pp. 143–62.

Hemingway, Ernest, *Fiesta: The Sun Also Rises* (London: Arrow Books, 2004).

——, *A Moveable Feast* (London: Arrow Books, 2004).

Hessel, Franz, *Walking in Berlin*, trans. Amanda de Marco (London: Scribe, 2016).

Hetherington, Kevin, *The Badlands of Modernity: Heterotopia and Social Ordering* (London: Routledge, 1997).

Hewitt, Nicholas, 'Shifting Cultural Centres in Twentieth-Century Paris' in *Parisian Fields*, ed. Michael Sheringham (London: Reaktion, 1996), pp. 30–45.

Hibberd, Dominic, 'The New Poetry, Georgians and Others: *The Open Window* (1910–11), *The Poetry Review* (1912–15), *Poetry and Drama* (1913–14), and *New Numbers* (1914)' in *The Oxford Critical and Cultural History of Modernist Magazines, vol. 1: Britain and Ireland, 1880–1955*, ed. Peter Brooker and Andrew Thacker (Oxford: Oxford University Press, 2009), pp. 176–98.

Highmore, Ben, *Cultural Feelings: Mood, Mediation and Cultural Politics* (London: Routledge, 2017).

Hiles, Timothy, 'Reality and Utopia in Munich's Premier Magazines: *Simplicissimus* (1896–1944) and *Jugend* (1896–1940)' in *The Oxford Critical and Cultural History of Modernist Magazines, vol. 3: Europe 1880–1940*, ed. Peter Brooker, Sascha Bru, Andrew Thacker and Christian Weikop (Oxford: Oxford University Press, 2013), pp. 709–26.

Holmes, Deborah and Lisa Silverman (eds), *Interwar Vienna: Culture between Tradition and Modernity* (New York: Camden House, 2009).

Hones, Sheila, 'Text as It Happens: Literary Geography', *Geography Compass* 2:5 (2008), pp. 1301–17.

Hopkins, Chris, *English Fiction in the 1930s: Language, Genre, History* (London: Continuum, 2006).

Horsley, Jessica, '"There You Have Munich": *Der Blaue Reiter* (1912); *Revolution* (1913); and *Der Weg* (1919)' in *The Oxford Critical and Cultural History of Modernist Magazines, vol. 3: Europe 1880–1940*, ed. Peter Brooker, Sascha Bru, Andrew Thacker and Christian Weikop (Oxford: Oxford University Press, 2013), pp. 727–49.

Houen, Alex, 'Introduction: Affecting Words', *Textual Practice* 25:2 (2011), pp. 215–32.

Howells, Coral Ann, 'Introduction: Jean Rhys' in *The Gender of Modernism: A Critical Anthology*, ed. Bonnie Kime Scott (Bloomington: Indiana University Press, 1990), pp. 372–7.

Hughes, Langston: Papers, Beinecke Library, Yale, New Haven.

Huidobro, Vicente, 'Tour Eiffel', *Nord-Sud* 6–7 (Aug.–Sep. 1917), pp. 24–5.

Hulme, Peter, *Remnants of Conquest: The Island Caribs and their Visitors, 1877–1998* (Oxford: Oxford University Press, 2000).

Hulme, T. E., 'Belated Romanticism', *New Age* 4:17 (18 Feb. 1909), p. 350.

——, *Selected Writings*, ed. Patrick McGuinness (Manchester: Carcanet, 1998).

Hurston, Zora Neale, *Color Struck*, *Fire!!* (1926), pp. 7–14.

Hussey, Andrew, *Paris: The Secret History* (London: Bloomsbury, 2006).

Huyssen, Andreas, 'The Disturbance of Vision in Vienna Modernism', *Modernism/Modernity* 5:3 (Sep. 1998), pp. 33–47.

——, *Miniature Metropolis: Literature in an Age of Photography and Film* (Cambridge, MA: Harvard University Press, 2015).

Hynes, Samuel, *The Auden Generation: Literature and Politics in England in the 1930s* (London: Bodley Head, 1976).

Isherwood, Christopher, *Christopher and His Kind* (London: Methuen, 1977).

——, *Down There on a Visit* (London: Methuen, 1962).

——, *Goodbye to Berlin* (London: Vintage, 1998).

——, *Mr Norris Changes Trains* (1935; Harmondsworth: Penguin, 1969).

James, David, *Modernist Futures: Innovation and Inheritance in the Contemporary Novel* (Cambridge: Cambridge University Press, 2012).

——, 'Modernist Narratives' in *The Oxford Handbook of Modernisms*, ed. Peter Brooker, Andrzej Gasiorek, Deborah Longworth and Andrew Thacker (Oxford: Oxford University Press, 2010), pp. 85–107.

James, Henry, *English Hours* (London: Heinemann, 1905).

——, *The Wings of the Dove* (Harmondsworth: Penguin, 1986).

Janik, Allan and Stephen Toulmin, *Wittgenstein's Vienna* (New York: Simon and Schuster, 1973).

Joannou, Maroula, '"All Right, I'll Do Anything for Good Clothes": Jean Rhys and Fashion', *Women: A Cultural Review* 23:4 (2012), pp. 463–89.

Johnson, Erica L., 'Haunted: Affective Memory in Jean Rhys's *Good Morning, Midnight*', *Affirmations: of the Modern* 1:2 (Spring 2014), pp. 15–38; available at http://tinyurl.com/gpyoky6 (last accessed 30 Oct. 2017).

Johnson, Erica L. and Patricia Moran (eds), *Jean Rhys: Twenty-First-Century Approaches* (Edinburgh: Edinburgh University Press, 2015).

Johnstone, J. K., 'John Lehmann and Bloomsbury' in *John Lehmann: A Tribute*, ed. A. T. Tolley (Ottawa: Carleton University Press, 1987), pp. 78–98.

Jones, Colin, *Paris: The Biography of a City* (London: Viking Penguin, 2005).

Jones, Donna V., *The Racial Discourses of Life Philosophy: Négritude, Vitalism, and Modernity* (New York: Columbia University Press, 2010).

Josephson, Matthew, *Life among the Surrealists: A Memoir* (New York: Holt, Rinehart, and Winston, 1962).

Joyce, James, *Ulysses*, ed. Jeri Johnson (Oxford: Oxford University Press, 1993).

Kalliney, Peter, *Cities of Affluence and Anger: A Literary Geography of Modern Englishness* (Charlottesville: University of Virginia Press, 2007).

___, *Commonwealth of Letters: British Literary Culture and Emergence of Postcolonial Aesthetics* (Oxford: Oxford University Press, 2013).

Kant, Immanuel, *The Critique of Judgement*, trans. James Creed Meredith (Oxford: Clarendon Press, 1952).

Kaplan, Caren, *Questions of Travel: Postmodern Discourses of Displacement* (Durham, NC: Duke University Press, 1996).

Kaspi, André and Antoine Marès (eds), *Le Paris des étrangers: Depuis un siècle* (Paris: Imprimerie Nationale, 1989).

Katz, Daniel, *American Modernism's Expatriate Scene: The Labour of Translation* (Edinburgh: Edinburgh University Press, 2007).

Katz, Tamar, *Impressionist Subjects: Gender, Interiority and Modernist Fiction in England* (Urbana and Chicago: University of Illinois Press, 2000).

Keating, Peter, *The Haunted Study: A Social History of the English Novel 1875–1914* (London: Secker and Warburg, 1989).

Kern, Stephen, *The Culture of Time and Space: 1880–1918* (Cambridge, MA: Harvard University Press, 1983).

Kilian, Eveline, '"The Mystery-Magic of Foreignness": Mr Isherwood Changes Places' in *Life Writing and Space*, ed. Eveline Kilian and Hope Wolf with Kathrin Tordasi (Farnham: Ashgate, 2016), pp. 89–104.

Killen, Andreas, *Berlin Electropolis: Shock, Nerves, and German Modernity* (Berkeley: University of California Press, 2006).

Kitchen, Rob, *The Third Man* (London: BFI, 2003).

Knowlson, James, *Damned to Fame: The Life of Samuel Beckett* (London: Bloomsbury, 1996).

Kracauer, Siegfried, *From Caligari to Hitler: A Psychological History of German Film* (1947; Princeton: Princeton University Press, 1970).

Kristeva, Julia, *Strangers to Ourselves*, trans. Leon S. Roudiez (London: Harvester Wheatsheaf, 1991).

Kynaston, David, *The City of London, vol. II: Golden Years 1890–1914* (London: Pimlico, 1995).

Ladd, Brian, *The Ghosts of Berlin: Confronting German History in the Urban Landscape* (Chicago: University of Chicago Press, 1997).

Le Corbusier, *The City of Tomorrow and its Planning*, trans. Frederick Etchells (New York: Dover, 1987).

Leeming, David, *Stephen Spender: A Life in Modernism* (New York: Henry Holt, 1999).

Lefebvre, Henri, *The Production of Space*, trans. D. Nicholson-Smith (Oxford: Blackwell, 1991).

Lehan, Richard, *The City in Literature: An Intellectual and Cultural History* (Berkeley: University of California Press, 1998).

Lehmann, John, *The Noise of History* (London: Hogarth Press, 1934).

——, *The Whispering Gallery: Autobiography I* (London: Longmans, 1955).

Lewis, Pericles (ed.), *The Cambridge Companion to European Modernism* (Cambridge: Cambridge University Press, 2011).

Lippit, Seiji M., *Topographies of Japanese Modernism* (New York: Columbia University Press, 2002).

Lodder, Christina, 'Searching for Utopia' in *Modernism: Designing a New World: 1914–1939*, ed. Christopher Wilk (London: V & A, 2006), pp. 23–70.

Loeb, Harold, *The Way It Was* (New York: Criterion Books, 1959).

Longenbach, James, *Stone Cottage: Pound, Yeats, and Modernism* (New York: Oxford University Press, 1998).

Lowell, Amy, 'The Poetry Bookshop', *The Little Review* 2:3 (May 1915), pp. 19–22.

Lozowick, Louis [L.L.], 'Russian Berlin', *Broom* 3:1 (Aug. 1922), pp. 78–9.

Lukács, Georg, *The Historical Novel*, trans. H. and S. Mitchell (London: Merlin, 1962).

Lynch, Kevin, *The Image of the City* (Cambridge, MA: MIT Press, 1960).

Mackinder, H. J., *Britain and the British Seas*, 2nd edn (Oxford: Clarendon Press, 1907).

Maderthaner, Wolfgang and Lisa Silverman, '"Wiener Kreise": Jewishness, Politics, and Culture in Interwar Vienna' in *Interwar Vienna: Culture between Tradition and Modernity*, ed. Deborah Holmes and Lisa Silverman (New York: Camden House, 2009), pp. 59–80.

Maertz, Gregory, 'The Invisible Post-War Museum or the Visibility of Modernist Art in the Third Reich', *Modernism/Modernity* 15:1 (Jan. 2008), pp. 63–86.

Marcus, Laura, '"A Hymn to Movement": The "City Symphony" of the 1920s and 1930s', *Modernist Cultures* 5:1 (2010), pp. 30–46.

——, *The Tenth Muse: Writing about Cinema in the Modernist Period* (Oxford: Oxford University Press, 2007).

Massumi, Brian, 'The Autonomy of Affect', *Cultural Critique* 31 (Autumn 1995), pp. 83–109.

——, *Parables for the Virtual: Movement, Affect, Sensation* (Durham, NC, and London: Duke University Press, 2002).

Matz, Jesse, *Literary Impressionism and Modernist Aesthetics* (Cambridge: Cambridge University Press, 2001).

Mayakovsky, Vladimir, *Mayakovsky: Poems*, trans. Herbert Marshall (New York: Hill and Wang, 1965).

McAlmon, Robert, *There Was a Rustle of Black Silk Stockings* (1925; New York: Belmont Books, 1963).

McAlmon, Robert rev. Kay Boyle, *Being Geniuses Together 1920–1930* (London: Michael Joseph, 1970).

McBride, Douglas Brent, 'A Critical Mass for Modernism in Berlin: *Der Sturm* (1910–32); *Die Aktion* (1911–32); and *Sturm-Bühne* (1918–19)' in *The Oxford Critical and Cultural History of Modernist Magazines, vol. 3: Europe 1880–1940*, ed. Peter Brooker, Sascha Bru, Andrew Thacker and Christian Weikop (Oxford: Oxford University Press, 2013), pp. 773–97.

McCabe, Susan, 'Bryher and Berlin: Modernism's Geographical Emotions', *The Berlin Journal* 21 (Fall 2011), pp. 8–13.

McCourt, John, *The Years of Bloom: James Joyce in Trieste 1904–20* (Madison: University of Wisconsin Press, 2000).

McCracken, Scott, 'Imagining the Modernist City' in *The Oxford Handbook of Modernisms*, ed. Peter Brooker, Andrzej Gasiorek, Deborah Longworth and Andrew Thacker (Oxford: Oxford University Press, 2010), pp. 637–54.

McKay, Claude, *A Long Way from Home* (1937; London: Pluto Press, 1985).

McLaughlin, James, *Writing the Urban Jungle: Reading Empire in London from Doyle to Eliot* (Charlottesville: University Press of Virginia, 2000).

McLeod, John, *Postcolonial London: Rewriting the Metropolis* (London: Routledge, 2004).

Menear, Lawrence, *London's Underground Stations: A Social and Architectural Study* (London: Midas, 1983).

Mirrlees, Hope, *Collected Poems*, ed. Sandeep Parmar (Manchester: Carcanet Press, 2011).

Mitchell, Jennifer, 'The Trouble with "Victim": Triangulated Masochism in Jean Rhys's *Quartet*' in *Rhys Matters: New Critical Perspectives*, ed. Mary Wilson and Kerry L. Johnson (New York: Palgrave Macmillan, 2013), pp. 189–212.

Mitchison, Naomi, *Vienna Diary 1934* (Glasgow: Kennedy and Boyd, 2009).

Mitter, Partha, *The Triumph of Modernism: India's Artists and the Avant-Garde 1922–1947* (London: Reaktion, 2007).

Monnier, Adrienne, *The Very Rich Hours of Adrienne Monnier*, trans. Richard McDougall (Lincoln: University of Nebraska Press, 1996).

Monro, Harold, 'The Bookshop', *Poetry Review* 1:3 (Nov. 1912), pp. 498–500.

Moody, A. David, *Ezra Pound: Poet. A Portrait of the Man and His Work, vol. 1: The Young Genius 1885–1920* (Oxford: Oxford University Press, 2007).

Moretti, Franco, *Atlas of the European Novel, 1800–1900* (London: Verso, 1998).

——, *Graphs, Maps, Trees: Abstract Models for a Literary History* (London: Verso, 2005).

Morrisson, Mark, 'The Cause of Poetry: Thomas Moult and *Voices* (1919–21), Harold Monro and *The Monthly Chapbook* (1919–25)' in *The Oxford Critical and Cultural History of Modernist Magazines, vol. 1: Britain and Ireland, 1880–1955*, ed. Peter Brooker and Andrew Thacker (Oxford: Oxford University Press, 2009), pp. 405–27.

Mulholland, Terri, 'Between Illusion and Reality, "Who's to Know": Threshold Spaces in the Interwar Novels of Jean Rhys', *Women: A Cultural Review* 23:4 (2012), pp. 445–62.

——, *British Boarding Houses in Interwar Women's Literature: Alternative Domestic Spaces* (Abingdon: Routledge, 2017).

Mumford, Lewis, *The City in History: Its Origins, its Transformations, and its Prospects* (Harmondsworth: Penguin, 1961).

Munson, Gorham , *The Awakening Twenties: A Memoir-History of a Literary Period* (Baton Rouge: Louisiana State University Press, 1985).

——, 'An Old Song to New Music', *Secession* 1 (Spring 1922), p. 25.

Murphy, Richard J., 'Berlin: Expressionism, Dada, Neue Sachlichkeit' in *The Oxford Handbook of Modernisms*, ed. Peter Brooker, Andrzej Gasiorek,

Deborah Longworth and Andrew Thacker (Oxford: Oxford University Press, 2010), pp. 669–86.
Murry, John Middleton, 'Art and Philosophy', *Rhythm* 1:1 (Summer 1911), pp. 9–12.
——, 'Bergson in Paris', *The New Age* 9:5 (1 June 1911), pp. 115–16.
Musil, Robert, *The Man Without Qualities*, 3 vols, trans. Eithne Wilkins and Ernst Kaiser (London: Picador, 1979).
Nadell, Martha, '"Devoted to Younger Negro Artists": *Fire!!* (1926) and *Harlem* (1928)' in *The Oxford Critical and Cultural History of Modernist Magazines, vol. 2: North America, 1894–1960*, ed. Peter Brooker and Andrew Thacker (Oxford: Oxford University Press, 2012), pp. 801–24.
Nelson, James G., *The Early Nineties: A View from the Bodley Head* (Cambridge, MA: Harvard University Press, 1971).
——, *Elkin Mathews: Publisher to Yeats, Joyce, Pound* (Madison: University of Wisconsin Press, 1989).
Ngai, Sianne, *Ugly Feelings* (Cambridge, MA: Harvard University Press, 2005).
Nicholls, Peter, 'Destinations: *Broom* (1921–4) and *Secession* (1922–4)' in *The Oxford Critical and Cultural History of Modernist Magazines, vol. 2: North America, 1894–1960*, ed. Peter Brooker and Andrew Thacker (Oxford: Oxford University Press, 2012), pp. 636–54.
——, *Modernisms: A Literary Guide* (Basingstoke: Macmillan, 1995).
North, Michael, *Reading 1922: A Return to the Scene of the Modern* (New York: Oxford University Press, 1999).
——, 'Transatlantic Transfer: Little Magazines and Euro-American Modernism'; available at http://modmags.dmu.ac.uk/file/north_transatlantic_transfer.pdf (last accessed 5 Nov. 2017).
O'Connell, Shaun, *Remarkable, Unspeakable New York: A Literary History* (Boston, MA: Beacon Press, 1995).
O' Keefe, Paul, *Some Sort of Genius: A Life of Wyndham Lewis* (London: Pimlico, 2001).
Olsen, Donald J., *The City as a Work of Art: London, Paris, Vienna* (New Haven: Yale University Press, 1986).
Osborne, Huw, 'Counter-Space in Charles Lahr's Progressive Bookshop' in *The Rise of the Modernist Bookshop: Books and the Commerce of Culture in the Twentieth Century* (Farnham: Ashgate, 2015), pp. 131–61.
—— (ed.), *The Rise of the Modernist Bookshop: Books and the Commerce of Culture in the Twentieth Century* (Farnham: Ashgate, 2015).
Outka, Elizabeth, *Consuming Traditions: Modernity, Modernism, and the Commodified Authentic* (Oxford: Oxford University Press, 2009).
Page, Norman, *Auden and Isherwood: The Berlin Years* (Basingstoke: Macmillan, 1998).

Parmar, Sandeep, 'Introduction' to Hope Mirrlees, *Collected Poems* (Manchester: Carcanet Press, 2011), pp. ix–xlviii.

Parry, Benita, 'Aspects of Peripheral Modernism', *Ariel* 40:1 (2009), pp. 27–55.

Parsons, Deborah L., *Streetwalking the City: Women, the City and Modernity* (Oxford: Oxford University Press, 2000).

Patell, Cyrus and Bryan Waterman (eds), *The Cambridge Companion to the Literature of New York* (Cambridge: Cambridge University Press, 2010).

Peat, Alexandra, *Travel and Modernist Literature: Sacred and Ethical Journeys* (New York: Routledge, 2011).

Perloff, Marjorie, *Edge of Irony: Modernism in the Shadow of the Habsburg Empire* (Chicago: University of Chicago Press, 2016).

——, *The Futurist Moment: Avant-Garde, Avant Guerre, and the Language of Rupture* (Chicago: University of Chicago Press, 2003).

Pichon, Birgitte and Karl Riha (eds), *Dada Zurich: A Clown's Game from Nothing* (New York: G. K. Hall, 1996).

Pike, David L., *Subterranean Cities: The World Beneath Paris and London, 1800–1945* (Ithaca: Cornell University Press, 2005).

Pinsker, Shachar, 'The Urban Literary Café and the Geography of Hebrew and Jewish Modernism in Europe' in *The Oxford Handbook of Global Modernisms*, ed. Mark Wolleger with Matt Eatough (New York: Oxford University Press, 2012), pp. 433–60.

Plarr, Victor, 'The Rhymers' Club', *English Literature in Transition, 1880–1920* 45:4 (2002), pp. 379–85.

Polgar, Alfred, 'Theorie des "Café Central"' in *And den Rand geschrieben* (Berlin: Ernst Rowohlt, 1926), pp. 85–91.

Poli, Bernard J., *Ford Madox Ford and the Transatlantic Review* (Syracuse, NY: Syracuse University Press, 1967).

Porter, Roy, *London: A Social History* (London: Penguin, 2000).

Pound, Ezra, *Collected Shorter Poems* (London: Faber, 1984).

——, *Gaudier-Brzeska: A Memoir* (1916; New York: New Directions, 1970).

——, 'Patria Mia VIII', *The New Age* 11:26 (24 Oct. 1912), pp. 611–12.

——, 'Preliminary Announcement of the College of Arts', *The Egoist* 21:1 (2 Nov. 1914), pp. 413–14.

——, *The Selected Letters of Ezra Pound 1907–1941*, ed. D. D. Paige (London: Faber, 1950).

——, *Selected Prose 1909–1956*, ed. William Cookson (London: Faber, 1973).

——, 'Wyndham Lewis', *The Egoist* 1 (15 June 1914), p. 233.

Probyn, Elspeth, *Blush: Faces of Shame* (Minneapolis: University of Minnesota Press, 2005).

Proctor, James, *Dwelling Places: Postwar Black British Writing* (Manchester: Manchester University Press, 2003).

'Queer Spaces', special issue of *English Language Notes* 45:2 (Fall/Winter 2007).

Rabaté, Jean-Michel, 'Gender and Modernism: *The Freewoman* (1912), *The New Freewoman* (1913), and *The Egoist* (1914–19)' in *The Oxford Critical and Cultural History of Modernist Magazines, vol. 1: Britain and Ireland, 1880–1955*, ed. Peter Brooker and Andrew Thacker (Oxford: Oxford University Press, 2009), pp. 269–89.

——, *1913: The Cradle of Modernism* (Oxford: Blackwell, 2007).

Radford, Ernest, 'Song in the Labour Movement' in *The Second Book of The Rhymers' Club* (London: Elkin Mathews and John Lane, 1894), p. 72.

Rainey, Lawrence, *Institutions of Modernism: Literary Elites and Public Culture* (New Haven: Yale University Press, 1998).

Rainey, Lawrence, Christine Poggi and Laura Witman (eds), *Futurism: An Anthology* (New Haven: Yale University Press, 2009).

Remy, Michael, *Surrealism in Britain* (Aldershot: Ashgate, 1999).

R.H.C [Alfred Orage], 'Readers and Writers', *New Age* 15:10 (9 July 1914), p. 229.

Rhys, Jean, *After Leaving Mr Mackenzie* (1930; Harmondsworth: Penguin, 1971).

——, *The Collected Short Stories* (New York: Norton, 1987).

——, *Good Morning, Midnight* (1939; Harmondsworth: Penguin, 1969).

——, *Letters 1931–1966*, ed. Francis Wyndham and Diana Melly (London: Penguin, 1985).

——, *Quartet* (1928; Harmondsworth: Penguin, 1973).

——, *Smile Please: An Unfinished Autobiography* (London: Penguin, 1981).

——, 'Vienne' in *Modernism: An Anthology*, ed. Lawrence Rainey (Oxford: Blackwell, 2005), pp. 946–9.

——, *Voyage in the Dark* (1934; Harmondsworth: Penguin, 1969).

Rimbaud, Arthur, *Oeuvres poétiques* (Paris: Garnier-Flammarion, 1964).

Roters, Eberhard (ed.), *Berlin 1910–1933* (New York: Rizzoli, 1982).

Rowe, Dorothy, *Representing Berlin: Sexuality and the City in Imperial and Weimar Germany* (Aldershot: Ashgate, 2003).

Sabarsky, Serge (ed.), *George Grosz: The Berlin Years* (New York: Rizzoli, 1985).

Sadler, Michael T. H., 'Fauvism and a Fauve', *Rhythm* 1:1 (Summer 1911), pp. 14–18.

Said, Edward, *Culture and Imperialism* (London: Vintage, 1993).

Saillet, Maurice: Collection, Harry Ransom Center, Austin, Texas.

Saler, Michael T., *The Avant-Garde in Interwar England: Medieval Modernism and the London Underground* (Oxford: Oxford University Press, 1999).

Sanders, Emmy Veronica, 'America Invades Europe', *Broom* 1:1 (Nov. 1921), pp. 89–93.

Sauer, Walter, 'Habsburg Colonial: Austria-Hungary's Role in European Overseas Expansion Reconsidered', *Austrian Studies* 20 (2012), pp. 5–23.

Saunders, Max, *Ford Madox Ford: A Dual Life*, 2 vols (Oxford: Oxford University Press, 1996, 2012).

Savory, Elaine, *The Cambridge Introduction to Jean Rhys* (Cambridge: Cambridge University Press, 2009).

Sawicki, Nicholas, 'The View from Prague: *Moderní revue* (1894–1925); *Volné směry* (1896–1949); *Umělecký měsíčník* (1911–14); *Revoluční sborník Devětsil* (1922); *Život* (1922); *Disk* (1923–5); *Pásmo* (1924–6); and *ReD* (1927–31)' in *The Oxford Critical and Cultural History of Modernist Magazines, vol. 3: Europe 1880–1940*, ed. Peter Brooker, Sascha Bru, Andrew Thacker and Christian Weikop (Oxford: Oxford University Press, 2013), pp. 1074–98.

Schlör, Joachim, *Nights in the Big City: Paris, Berlin, London 1840–1930* (London: Reaktion, 1998).

Schorske, Carl, *Fin-de-Siècle Vienna: Politics and Culture* (Cambridge: Cambridge University Press, 1981).

Schwarz, Bill, 'Black Metropolis, White England' in *Modern Times*, ed. Mica Nava and Alan O'Shea (London: Routledge, 1996), pp. 176–207.

—— (ed.), *West Indian Intellectuals in Britain* (Manchester: Manchester University Press, 2003).

Sedgwick, Eve Kosofsky, *Touching Feeling: Affect, Pedagogy, Performativity* (Durham, NC: Duke University Press, 2003).

Segal, Harold B., *The Vienna Coffeehouse Wits 1890–1938* (West Lafayette: Purdue University Press, 1993).

Seigworth, Gregory J. and Melissa Gregg, 'An Inventory of Shimmers' in *The Affect Theory Reader*, ed. Gregg and Seigworth (Durham, NC, and London: Duke University Press, 2010), pp. 1–25.

Selcon, G. A., 'Pullman Cars on the Metropolitan Railway', *The Railway and Travel Monthly* 1:3 (July 1910), p. 228.

Selvon, Sam, *The Lonely Londoners* (1956; London: Penguin, 2006).

——, 'Working the Transport' in *Ways of Sunlight* (Harlow: Longman, 1987),pp. 120–35.

Senghor, Léopold Sédar, 'Negritude: A Humanism of the Twentieth Century' in *Colonial Discourse and Post-Colonial Theory: A Reader*, ed. Patrick Williams and Laura Chrisman (New York: Harvester Wheatsheaf, 1993), pp. 27–35.

Sennett, Richard , *The Fall of Public Man* (London: Faber, 1986).

——, *Flesh and Stone: The Body and the City in Western Civilization* (London: Faber, 1994).

Sharpley-Whiting, T. Denean, *Bricktop's Paris: African American Women in Paris between the Two World Wars* (Albany, NY: SUNY Press, 2015).

Sheppard, Richard, 'German Expressionism' in *Modernism: A Guide to European Literature 1890–1930*, ed. Malcolm Bradbury and James McFarlane (Harmondsworth: Penguin, 1991), pp. 274–91.

Shklovksy, Viktor, *Zoo, or Letters Not about Love*, trans. Richard Sheldon (Chicago: Dalkey Archive, 2001).

Silverman, Lisa, *Becoming Austrian: Jews and Culture between the World Wars* (Oxford: Oxford University Press, 2012).

Simmel, Georg, 'The Metropolis and Mental Life' (1903) in *The Blackwell City Reader*, ed. Gary Bridge and Sophie Watson (Oxford: Blackwell, 2002), pp. 11–19.

——, 'The Stranger' (1908) in *The Sociology of Georg Simmel*, trans. Kurt Wolff (New York: Free Press, 1950), pp. 402–8.

Smith, Neil, 'Contours of a Spatialized Politics: Homeless Vehicles and the Production of Geographical Scale', *Social Text* 33 (1992), pp. 54–81.

Snaith, Anna, *Modernist Voyages: Colonial Woman Writers in London, 1890–1945* (Cambridge: Cambridge University Press, 2014).

Soja, Edward W., *Thirdspace: Journeys to Los Angeles and Other Real-and-Imagined Places* (Oxford: Blackwell, 1996).

Spector, Scott, 'The Habsburg Empire' in *The Cambridge Companion to European Modernism*, ed. Pericles Lewis (Cambridge: Cambridge University Press, 2011), pp. 52–74.

——, 'Modernism Without Jews: A Counter-Historical Argument', *Modernism/Modernity* 13:4 (Nov. 2006), pp. 615–33.

Spender, Stephen, *Returning to Vienna* (New York: Banyan Press, 1947).

——, *Vienna* (London: Faber, 1934).

——, *World Within World* (London: Readers Union, 1953).

Stansell, Christine, *American Moderns: Bohemian New York and the Creation of a New Century* (New York: Henry Holt, 2000).

Stein, Gertrude, *The Autobiography of Alice B. Toklas* (Harmondsworth: Penguin, 1966).

Stewart, Kathleen, *Ordinary Affects* (Durham, NC: Duke University Press, 2007).

Stokes, John, *In the Nineties* (London: Harvester Wheatsheaf, 1989).

Stovall, Tyler, *Paris Noir: African Americans in the City of Light* (New York: Houghton Mifflin, 1996).

Sutherland, John, *Stephen Spender: The Authorized Biography* (London: Penguin, 2004).

Sweeney, Fionnghuala and Kate Marsh (eds), *Afromodernisms: Paris, Harlem and the Avant-Garde* (Edinburgh: Edinburgh University Press, 2013).

Symons, Arthur, *Studies in Prose and Verse* (New York: E. P. Dutton, 1904).

Tally Jr., Robert T. (ed.), *Geocritical Explorations: Space, Place, and Mapping in Literary and Cultural Studies* (New York: Palgrave Macmillan, 2014).

—— (ed.), *The Routledge Handbook of Literature and Space* (London: Routledge, 2017).

——, *Spatiality* (London: Routledge, 2013).

Tambling, Jeremy, 'Judaism and Heterogeneity in the Modernist Long Novel', *Modernist Cultures* 10:3 (2015), pp. 357–79.

Taylor, Julie (ed.), *Djuna Barnes and Affective Modernism* (Edinburgh: Edinburgh University Press, 2012).

——, *Modernism and Affect* (Edinburgh: Edinburgh University Press, 2015).

Taylor, Sheila (ed.), *The Moving Metropolis: A History of London's Transport since 1800* (London: Laurence King, 2001).

Tester, Keith (ed.), *The Flâneur* (London: Routledge, 1994).

Thacker, Andrew, *Moving Through Modernity: Space and Geography in Modernism* (Manchester: Manchester University Press, 2003).

——, 'Placing Modernism' in *Moving Modernisms: Motion, Technology, and Modernity*, ed. David Bradshaw, Laura Marcus and Rebecca Roach (Oxford: Oxford University Press, 2016), pp. 11–26.

——, '"A True Magic Chamber": The Public Face of the Modernist Bookshop', *Modernist Cultures* 11:3 (Autumn 2016), pp. 429–51.

Thomas, J. P., *Handling London's Underground Traffic* (London: London's Underground, 1928).

Thrift, Nigel, 'Intensities of Feeling: Towards a Spatial Politics of Affect', *Geografiska Annaler: Series B Human Geography* 86:1 (March 2004), pp. 57–78.

——, *Non-Representational Theory: Space, Politics, Affect* (London: Routledge, 2008).

Timms, Edward, 'Cultural Parameters between the Wars: A Reassessment of the Vienna Circles' in *Interwar Vienna: Culture between Tradition and Modernity*, ed. Deborah Holmes and Lisa Silverman (New York: Camden House, 2009), pp. 21–31.

——, 'Expressionists and Georgians: Demonic City and Enchanted Village' in *Unreal City: Urban Experience in Modern European Literature and Art*, ed. Edward Timms and David Kelley (Manchester: Manchester University Press, 1985), pp. 111–27.

——, *Karl Kraus, Apocalyptic Satirist: The Post-War Crisis and the Rise of the Swastika* (New Haven: Yale University Press, 2005).

——, 'Musil's Vienna and Kafka's Prague: The Quest for a Spiritual City' in *Unreal City: Urban Experience in Modern European Literature and Art*, ed. Edward Timms and David Kelley (Manchester: Manchester University Press, 1985), pp. 247–63.

Timms, Edward and David Kelley (eds), *Unreal City: Urban Experience in Modern European Literature and Art* (Manchester: Manchester University Press, 1985).

Tomkins, Silvan, *Shame and its Sisters: A Silvan Tomkins Reader*, ed. Eve Kosofsky Sedgwick and Adam Frank (Durham, NC: Duke University Press, 1995).

Twain, Mark, *The Chicago of Europe, and Other Foreign Tales of Travel*, ed. Peter Kaminsky (London: Sterling, 2009).

Van Dijk, Maite, 'Vive la France! Munch, Van Gogh and French Modern Art' in *Munch: Van Gogh*, ed. Maite van Dijk, Magne Bruteig and Leo Jansen (Brussels: Mercatorfonds, 2015), pp. 100–23.

Vidler, Anthony, *Warped Space: Art, Architecture, and Anxiety in Modern Culture* (Boston, MA: MIT Press, 2000).

Vietta, Silvio and Hans-Georg Kemper, *Expressionismus* (Munich: Fink, 1975).

Von Hofmannsthal, Hugo, 'A Letter' in *The Lord Chandos Letter, and Other Writings*, trans. Joel Rotenberg (New York: New York Review Books, 2005), pp. 117–28.

Walkowitz, Judith, *Nights Out: Life in Cosmopolitan London* (New Haven: Yale University Press, 2012).

Walkowitz, Rebecca, *Cosmopolitan Style: Modernism Beyond the Nation* (New York: Columbia University Press, 2006).

Waller, Philip, *Writers, Readers, and Reputations: Literary Life in Britain 1870–1918* (Oxford: Oxford University Press, 2006).

Walser, Robert, *Berlin Stories*, trans. Susan Bernofsky (New York: New York Review Books, 2012).

Walsh, Rebecca, *The Geopoetics of Modernism* (Gainesville: University Press of Florida, 2015).

Ward, Ivan, *Phobia* (London: Icon Books, 2001).

Weber, Max, 'The Nature of the City' in *Classic Essays on the Culture of Cities*, ed. Richard Sennett (Englewood Cliffs: Prentice Hall, 1969), pp. 23–46.

Welsh, David, *Underground Writing: The London Tube from George Gissing to Virginia Woolf* (Liverpool: Liverpool University Press, 2010).

Westphal, Bertrand, *Geocriticism: Real and Fictional Spaces* (New York: Palgrave Macmillan, 2011).

Wexler, Joyce P., *Who Paid for Modernism? Art, Money, and the Fiction of Conrad, Joyce, and Lawrence* (Fayetteville: University of Arkansas Press, 1997).

White, Edmund, *The Flâneur: A Stroll through the Paradoxes of Paris* (London: Bloomsbury, 2001).

Whyte, Iain Boyd and David Frisby (eds), *Metropolis Berlin: 1880–1940* (Berkeley: University of California Press, 2012).

Wilder, Gary, *The French Imperial Nation-State: Négritude and Colonial Humanism between the Two World Wars* (Chicago: Chicago University Press, 2005).

Williams, Raymond, *Drama from Ibsen to Brecht* (Harmondsworth: Penguin, 1973).
——, *Marxism and Literature* (Oxford: Oxford University Press, 1977).
——, *The Politics of Modernism: Against the New Conformists*, ed. Tony Pinkney (London: Verso, 1989).
Williams, Robert, *Culture in Exile: Russian Émigrés in Germany, 1881–1941* (Ithaca, NY: Cornell University Press, 1972).
Williams, Rosalind, *Notes on the Underground: An Essay on Technology, Society, and the Imagination* (Cambridge, MA: MIT Press, 1990).
Wilson, Elizabeth, *The Sphinx in the City: Urban Life, the Control of Disorder, and Women* (London: Virago, 1991).
Wilson, Mary and Kerry L. Johnson (eds), *Rhys Matters: New Critical Perspectives* (New York: Palgrave Macmillan, 2013).
Winning, Joanne, '"Ezra through the Open Door": The Parties of Natalie Barney, Adrienne Monnier and Sylvia Beach as Lesbian Modernist Cultural Production' in *The Modernist Party*, ed. Kate McLoughlin (Edinburgh: Edinburgh University Press, 2013), pp. 127–46.
Wiser, William, *The Crazy Years: Paris in the Twenties* (London: Thames and Hudson, 1983).
Wittgenstein, Ludwig, *Tractatus Logico-Philosophicus* (1922), trans. D. F. Pears and B. F. McGuinness (London: Routledge and Kegan Paul, 1961).
Wollaeger, Mark and Matthew Eatough (eds), *The Oxford Handbook of Global Modernisms* (New York: Oxford University Press, 2012).
Wolmar, Christian, *The Subterranean Railway: How the London Underground Was Built and How It Changed the City Forever* (London: Atlantic Books, 2004).
Woolf, Virginia, *Jacob's Room*, ed. Sue Roe (1922; London: Penguin, 1992).
——, 'The Mark on the Wall' in *A Haunted House* (Harmondsworth: Penguin 1973) , pp. 43–52.
——, *A Passionate Apprentice: The Early Journals of Virginia Woolf*, ed. Mitchell A. Leaska (London: Hogarth Press, 1990).
——, *To the Lighthouse*, ed. Stella McNichol (1927; London: Penguin, 1992).
——, *The Waves* (1931; London: Granada, 1977).
——, *The Years*, ed. Jeri Johnson (1937; Harmondsworth: Penguin, 1998).
Youngs, Tim, 'Travelling Modernists' in *The Oxford Handbook of Modernisms*, ed. Peter Brooker, Andrzej Gasiorek, Deborah Longworth and Andrew Thacker (Oxford: Oxford University Press, 2010), pp. 267–80.
Zemgulys, Andrea, 'Menu, Memento, Souvenir: Suffering and the Social Imagination in *Good Morning, Midnight*' in *Rhys Matters: New Critical Perspectives*, ed. Mary Wilson and Kerry L. Johnson (New York: Palgrave Macmillan, 2013), pp. 21–40.

Zimmer, Dieter E., *Nabokov's Berlin* (Berlin: Nicolaische Verlagsbuchhandlung, 2001).

Ziolkowski, Saskia Elizabeth, 'Svevo's *Uomo Senza Qualità*: Musil and Modernism in Italy' in *Gender and Modernity in Central Europe: The Austro-Hungarian Monarchy and its Legacy*, ed. Agatha Schwartz (Ottawa: University of Ottawa Press, 2010), pp. 83–102.

INDEX

CPSIA information can be obtained
at www.ICGtesting.com
Printed in the USA
JSHW041356021220
9945JS00003B/56

9 780748 633487